1989

S0-AHN-114

MUSIC FOR PIANO
AND
ORCHESTRA

MUSIC FOR PIANO AND ORCHESTRA

AN ANNOTATED GUIDE

Maurice Hinson

INDIANA UNIVERSITY PRESS
Bloomington

To My Daughters
Jane and Susan

Manufactured in the United States of America

Library of Congress Cataloging in Publication Data

Hinson, Maurice.
Music for piano and orchestra.

Includes indexes.
1. Piano with orchestra—Bibliography.   2. Concerto
(Piano)—Bibliography.   I. Title.
ML128.P3H53   016.7856'61   80–8380
ISBN 0–253–12435–2   1 2 3 4 5 85 84 83 82 81

Contents

Preface

The medium of piano and orchestra has fascinated composers ever since the piano was invented. Even before then, the use of harpsichord or organ and orchestra appealed to many composers. The basic concept is expressed well by Donald Francis Tovey: "Nothing in human life and history is much more thrilling or of more ancient and universal experience than the antithesis of the individual and the crowd; an antithesis which is familiar in every degree, from flat opposition to harmonious reconciliation, and with every contrast and blending of emotion, and which has been of no less universal prominence in works of art than in life. Now the concerto forms express this antithesis with all possible force and delicacy . . ." (*Essays in Musical Analysis,* Vol. III, 99.7–8).

The concerto forms and/or concepts are present (more or less successfully) in most of the works in this book. Like my earlier books—*Guide to the Pianist's Repertoire* (Indiana University Press, 1973, and *Supplement,* 1978), which described solo piano literature, and *The Piano in Chamber Ensemble* (Indiana University Press, 1978)—the present volume aims at answering the key questions: What is there? What is it like? Where can I get it?

Selection. The following criteria were followed to make this volume manageable. 1. All compositions listed are written for more than eight instruments (including piano). Ensembles this size and larger would probably require a conductor, and this consideration suggested a logical and reasonable division between chamber and orchestral music. 2. The time span covered is mainly from 1700 to the present, but a few works written before 1700 are included because of their special musical interest. The listing contains some music composed before the invention of the piano, but each work has been tried on the piano and felt to be effective on this instrument. 3. In selecting composers an attempt was made to cover all standard composers and to introduce contemporary composers of merit. 4. Most of the works feature the piano and are usually known as solo concertos or solo works with orchestra, but some compositions listed use the piano in a more chamberlike manner. Indeed, many of them contain the term "chamber" in their titles, i.e., Alban Berg's *Chamber Concerto (Kammerkonzert).* Also included are works scored for piano and strings or band; for various combinations of piano(s), other solo instruments, voices(s), or tape; for piano one-hand, three-hands, and four-hands; and for prepared piano. (The reader should consult the indexes for specific ensembles.) 5. I have made a point of including many works on interest and quality in the Intermediate to Moderately Difficult grades (see the special index for this category). 6. A few outstanding transcriptions, by such composers as Bach, Beethoven, Busoni, and Liszt, have been included. 7. Information on works listed but not described has been obtained from publishers' catalogues.

Special effort has been made to examine as many contemporary works as possible, both published and unpublished. Recent avant-garde pieces are difficult to judge since most of them have not yet met the test of time, although many avant-garde techniques of the 1950s, 60s, and 70s are becoming more refined and are being accepted into the compositional style of the 1980s. A number of contemporary composers use the piano strictly as a sonorous sound source rather than identify the instrument with its past history. Larry Austin, in an article entitled "Is the Concerto Dead? Yes" (*Source* IV/2 [1970]: 55–56), contends that the answer for many avant-garde composers is indeed yes. But even avant-garde composers continue to add their own special contributions to the concerto literature, as can be seen by examining works of Cage, Carter, Maderna, and Van Baaren. And so it appears that music for piano and orchestra is still being written by almost all our prominent and many less well-known composers. If any trend can be noticed it is a decline in the number of concertos composed and performed by the composers, and since the 1940s most important concertos have been commissioned works, such as those by Barber, Carter, and Ginastera.

A certain amount of subjectivity is unavoidable in a book of this nature, but I have attempted to be as fair and objective as possible. Composers who wish to submit compositions for possible inclusion in future editions are encouraged to do so.

Because of constant change in the publishing world it is impossible to list only music currently in print. Some works known to be out of print were listed because of their merit, and many of them can be located at second-hand music stores, in the larger university or municipal libraries, or, more especially, in the Library of Congress.

Acknowledgments. Many people in many places have generously given me their help. I gratefully acknowledge the assistance of Martha Powell, Music Librarian of the Southern Baptist Theological Seminary; Elmer Booze and Rodney Mill of the Library of Congress; David Fenske, Music Librarian at Indiana University; Marion Korda, Music Librarian at the University of Louisville; Fernando Laires of the Peabody Conservatory of Music; Lee Luvisi of the University of Louisville; Luiz Moura de Castro, University of Hartford; my graduate assistant, Wesley Roberts; and the Southern Baptist Theological Seminary for making possible the typing of the manuscript and the aid of graduate assistants through the years. The American Composers Alliance Library, the Finnish Music Information Center, and the Canadian Music Centre have been most helpful, as have the many composers who have graciously supplied me with scores and tapes.

Without the generous assistance of numerous publishers this volume would not be possible. Special appreciation goes to William Giannone of Boosey & Hawkes, Inc.; Norman Auerbach of European American Music; Don Malin and Gerald Siani of Belwin–Mills Publishing Corp.; Donald Gillespie of C. F. Peters Corp.; Susan Brailove of Oxford University Press; Ernst Herttrich of G. Henle Verlag; Barry O'Neal of G. Schirmer, Inc.; W. Ray Stephens of Frederick Harris Music Co., Ltd.; Mike Warren of Alphonse Leduc; Judy Carnoske and Terry

Rothermich of Magnamusic–Baton, Inc.; and George Hotton of Theodore Presser Co.

I hope that my analyses will shed light on *how* something has been accomplished by the composer but they are too short, in a volume such as this, to explain clearly the compositional *why*. They can give only the "bare bones" of a composition but cannot express the complete spirit of the music. In the last resort I must rely on what Mr. Neville Cardus has called his "sensitized palate": the physical impact of the music can result in boredom, in interest, or in enthralment.

My wish is that this volume will continue to help lead the reader through the magnificent repertoire of the piano.

Louisville, Kentucky   Maurice Hinson
January 1980

Using the Guide

Arrangement of entries. All composers are listed alphabetically. Sometimes biographical or stylistic comments follow the composer's name and dates. Under each composer's name, individual works are listed by year of composition, opus number, or title, or by a combination of the three. If nothing is indicated after the title, e.g., *Concerto, Dialogue, Variazioni Sinfoniche,* etc., the reader may assume that the work is for piano and orchestra. Works for piano and orchestra are listed first; works for two or more instruments are usually listed near the end of the composer entry. Careful effort has been made to list many of the cadenzas written for the Beethoven and Mozart concertos. The composer's cadenza should be used if it exists. When the composer did not leave a cadenza, one is left with the choice of using another composer's cadenza or writing one's own. Cadenzas have been written by many "hacks" whose style and taste have no resemblance to the original composer's. Some cadenza writers have even forgotten that Mozart's keyboard had only about five octaves!

Descriptions. Descriptions have been limited to general style characteristics, form, particular and unusual qualities, interpretative suggestions, and pianistic problems inherent in the music. Editorial procedures found in a particular edition are mentioned. The term "large span" is used when spans larger than an octave are required. "Expanded tonality" refers to techniques commonly found in contemporary writing up to ca. 1950. "Octotonic" refers to lines moving in the same direction one or more octaves apart. "Shifting" or "flexible meters" indicates that varied time signatures are used with the space mentioned (a few bars, a movement, the entire work). "Proportional rhythmic relationships," e.g., ⌐ 5″ 4 ⌐, indicates five notes are to be played in the space for four. The designation "3 with 2" means three notes in one voice are played with (against) two notes in another. "Chance music" (aleatory) is described or mentioned, not analyzed, since it has no definitely ordered sequence of events. "Stochastic techniques" refers to "a probabilistic compositional method," introduced by Iannis Xenakis, in which the overall contours of sound are specified but the inner details are left to random or chance selection" (DCM, p. 708). The term "avant-garde" is used to connote something bold, progressive, and risky. It is not meant as a derogatory term. Perhaps the avant-garde movement is ending!

Grading. An effort has been made to grade the piano part in representative works of each composer. Five categories of grading are used: Intermediate (Int.), for the above-average high school pianist; Intermediate to Moderately Difficult (Int. to M-D); Moderately Difficult (M-D), for the above-average college pianist; Moderately Difficult to Difficult (M-D to D); and Difficult (D), for advanced pianists. To provide a better understanding of this grading, the following standard works will serve as guides for the basic levels:

Int.: C. H. Graun, *Concerto* F, Op. 2/4
　　　J. Haydn, *Concerto* C, Hob. XIV/4
　　　F. Kuhlau, *Concerto* C, Op. 7
　　　D. Kabalevsky, *Concerto* III "Youth"
M-D.: J. S. Bach, *Concerto* d, S. 1052
　　　W. A. Mozart, *Concerto* C, K. 415
　　　E. MacDowell, *Concerto* d, Op. 23
　　　R. Starer, *Concerto* I
D.: J. S. Bach, Brandenburg *Concerto* V, S. 1050
　　　L. Beethoven, *Concerto* IV G, Op. 58
　　　S. Rachmaninoff, *Rhapsody on a theme of Paganini*
　　　E. Carter, *Concerto*

These categories must not be taken too strictly but are only listed for general indications of technical and interpretative difficulties.

Details of entries. When known, the date of composition is given after the title of the work. Then, in parentheses, are as many of the following as apply to the particular work: the editor, the publisher, the publisher's number, and the copyright date. When more than one edition is available, the editions are listed in order of preference, the most desirable first. The number of pages and the performance time are frequently listed. Timings in all cases are approximate. If the number of pages is listed, it is understood to be for the two-piano arrangement unless otherwise indicated (full, miniature, octavo score). The spellings of the composer's names and of the titles of the compositions appear as they do on the music being described. Specifically related books, dissertations or theses, and periodical articles are listed following individual compositions or at the conclusion of the discussion of a composer's work, and a more extended bibliography appears at the end of the book. Scores with the orchestral part arranged for a second piano exist for the great majority of the listed works. Some early works (before about 1750) and a few recent ones (after 1920), may not have such two-piano scores. Check with the individual publishers. Sometimes it is impossible to tell from a publisher's catalogue if a work listed for piano, percussion, and strings is for the piano and percussion solo with string orchestra, or if it is for piano solo with percussion and string orchestra; nor is it always possible to tell whether the work is available in a two-piano arrangement.

The Edwin A. Fleisher Collection of Orchestral Music (Free Library of Philadelphia, Philadelphia, PA 19103) is one of the largest lending collections of orchestral music in the United States. It is not intended to supplant commercial sources from which orchestras may buy or rent orchestrations, but it can lend those in the public domain. Music protected by copyright or under contract to a publisher can be lent only upon clearance from the publisher or, in the case of unpublished music, the composers or their accredited representatives. Music may be lent to recognized orchestras, universities, colleges, conservatories, and other organizations interested in the furtherance of music. *In no case is music lent to individuals.* Written request should be forwarded to the address above.

Sample Entries and Explanations

Robert Schumann. *Introduction and Allegro* d Op. 134 1853 (GS; Busoni—Br&H; Pauer—Schott; Augener) 15 min. The piece is in the key of d minor; the opus number is 134; the date of composition is 1853; the publishers are G. Schirmer, Breitkopf and Härtel (Busoni edition), Schott (Pauer edition), and Augener; and the work takes approximately 15 minutes to perform.

Karl Friedrich Abel. *Concerto* E Op. 11/3 (H. Höckner—CFP 4409a 1935) 34pp. E-flat major is the key; Höckner is the editor, C. F. Peters the publisher, and the publisher's number is 4409a; this edition was copyrighted in 1935; the two-piano score is 34 pages long.

Other assistance. See "Abbreviations" (pp. xii–xiv) for terms, publishers, books, and periodicals referred to in the text, and the directories, "American or Parent Companies of Music Publishers" and "Addresses of Music Publishers" (pp. xv–xxiii), to locate publishers. Eleven special indexes direct the user to entries in the test for music in special categories.

Abbreviations

AA	Authors Agency of the Polish Music Publishers	CPE	Composer/Performer Edition
ACA	American Composers Alliance	D	Difficult
AMC	American Music Center	DCM	*Dictionary of Contemporary Music,* ed. John Vinton (New York: E. P. Dutton, 1974).
AME	American Music Editions		
AMP	Associated Music Publishers		
AMT	*American Music Teacher*	DDT	Denkmäler deutscher Tonkunst
APRA	Australasian Performing Right Association Ltd.	DM	Diletto Musicale (Doblinger)
BB	Broude Brothers	Dob	Doblinger
BBD	*A Bio-Biographical Dictionary of Twelve-Tone and Serial Composers,* by Effie B. Carlson (Metuchen, NJ: Scarecrow Press, 1970).	DSS	Drustva Slovenskih Skladateljev
		DTOe	Denkmäler der Tonkunst in Oesterreich
		DVFM	Deutscher Verlag für Musik
BMC	Boston Music Co.	EAM	Editorial Argentina de Música
BMI	Broadcast Music, Inc.		
Bo&Bo	Bote & Bock	EBM	Edward B. Marks
Bo&H	Boosey & Hawkes	EC	Edizioni Curci
BPL	Boston Public Library	ECS	E. C. Schirmer
Br	Bärenreiter	EMB	Editio Musica Budapest
Br&VP	Broeckmans & Van Poppel	EMM	Editiones Mexicanas de Música
ca.	circa	EMT	Editions Musicales Transatlantiques
CeBeDeM	CeBeDeM Foundation		
CF	Carl Fischer	ES	Edition Suecia
CFE	Composers Facsimile Edition	ESC	Max Eschig
		EV	Elkan-Vogel
CFP	C. F. Peters	Fl	Fleisher, Edwin A.
CHF	Ceský Hudebni Fond	FSF	Fast, Slow, Fast
CM	*Current Musicology*	GD	Groves Dictionary (see Bibliography)
CMC	Canadian Music Centre		
CMP	Contemporary Music Project	Gen	General Music Publishing Co.

GM	Gehrmans Musikförlag	MT	*Musical Times*
GS	G. Schirmer	MTP	Music Treasure
H&G	Hüllenhagen & Griehl		Publications
Hin	Hinrichsen	MWV	Musikwissenschaftlicher
HM	Hortus Musicus		Verlag
	(Bärenreiter)	Nag	Nagel's Music-Archive
IEM	Instituto de extension	NK	Norsk
	Musicale		Komponistfoernung
	Calle Compañia	NME	New Music Edition
	Universidad de Chile	NMO	Norsk Musikförlag
	Compañia 1264	NMS	Nordiska Musikförlaget
	Santiago, Chile	NYPL	New York Public
IMC	International Music Co.		Library
IMI	Israel Music Institute	OUP	Oxford University Press
IMP	Israel Music Publication	Ph	Philharmusica Edition
	(see IMI)	PIC	Peer International
Int.	Intermediate		Corporation
IU	Indiana University	PNM	*Perspectives of New*
	School of Music Library		*Music*
JAMS	*Journal of the American*	PQ	*Piano Quarterly*
	Musicological Society	PRS	Performing Right
JF	J. Fischer		Society
JWC	J. W. Chester	PWM	Polskie Wydawnictwo
K	Kalmus		Muzyczne
K&S	Kistner & Siegel	R&E	Ries & Erler
LC	Library of Congress	Ric	Ricordi
M&M	*Music and Musicians*	Ric Amer	Ricordi Americana,
MAB	Musica Antiqua		S.A.
	Bohemica (Artia)	SA	Sonata-Allegro
MC	Mildly Contemporary	SACEM	Société des Auteurs,
MCA	M.C.A. Music (Music		Compositeurs et Editeurs
	Corporation of America)		de Musique
M-D	Moderately Difficult	Sal	Salabert
MH	Musikk-Huset	SAZU	Slovenska Akademija
MJQ	MJQ Music	S&B	Stainer & Bell
M&L	*Music and Letters*	SDM	Servico de
MO	*Musical Opinion*		Documentacao Musical
MQ	*Musical Quarterly*		da Ordem dos Musicos
MR	Music Review		do Brazil
MSNH	*Music since Nineteen*		Av. Almte. Barroso,
	Hundred (see		72–7⁰ Andar
	Bibliography)		Rio de Janeiro, Brazil
MS, MSS	manuscript(s)	SP	Shawnee Press

STIM	Swedish Performing Right Society	TP	Theodore Presser Co.
SUISA	Société Suisse des Auteurs et Editeurs	UE	Universal Edition
		UME	Unión Musical Española
		WH	Wilhelm Hansen
SZ	Suvini Zerboni	WIM	Western International Music
TONO	Norsk Komponistforenings Internasjonale Musikkbyrå		

American Agents or
Parent Companies of Music Publishers

1. Associated Music Publishers, Inc., 866 Third Avenue, New York, NY 10022.
2. Belwin-Mills Publishing Corp., 25 Deshon Drive, Melville, NY 11746.
3. Boosey & Hawkes, Inc., P. O. Box 130, Oceanside, NY 11572.
4. Brodt Music Co., P. O. Box 9345, Charlotte, NC 28299.
5. Alexander Broude, Inc., 225 West 57th Street, New York, NY 10019.
6. Broude Bros., Ltd., 56 West 45th Street, New York, NY 10036.
7. Concordia Publishing House, 3558 South Jefferson Avenue, St. Louis, MO 63118.
8. Henri Elkan Music Publisher, 1316 Walnut Street, Philadelphia, PA 19107.
9. Elkan-Vogel Inc. (see Theodore Presser), Presser Place, Bryn Mawr, PA 19010.
10. European American Music Corp., 195 Allwood Road, Clifton, NJ 07012.
11. Carl Fischer, Inc., 56–62 Cooper Square, New York, NY 10003.
12. Edwin Fleisher Music Collection, Free Library, Philadelphia, PA 19103.
13. Sam Fox Publishing Co., 73–942 Highway 111, Suite 11, Palm Desert, CA 92260.
14. M C A Music, 25 Deshon Drive, Melville, NY 11746.
15. Magnamusic-Baton, 10370 Page Industrial Boulevard, St. Louis, MO 63132.
16. Edward B. Marks Music Corp., 1790 Broadway, New York, NY 10019.
17. Oxford University Press, Inc., 200 Madison Avenue, New York, NY 10016.
18. C. F. Peters Corp., 373 Park Avenue South, New York, NY 10016.
19. Theodore Presser Co., Presser Place, Bryn Mawr, PA 19010.
20. E. C. Schirmer Music Co., 112 South Street, Boston, MA 02111.
21. G. Schirmer, Inc., 866 Third Avenue, New York, NY 10022.
22. Shawnee Press, Inc., Delaware Water Gap, PA 18327.
23. Southern Music Publishing Co., 1740 Broadway, New York, NY 10019.
24. Summy-Birchard Co., 1834 Ridge Avenue, Evanston, IL 60204.
25. Location or American agent unverified.

Publishers No Longer in Business

André	Haslinger	Pond
Broderip & Wilkinson	Hofmeister	Probst
Clementi	Hummel	Raabe & Plothow
Corri, Pearce & Co.	Janet	Senff
Coventry & Hollier	Hunwald	Sieber
Diabelli	Longman & Broderip	Siegel
Erard	Mechetti	Steiner
Fritsch	Nadermann	Welcher
Hainauer	Ozi	

Addresses of Music Publishers

A number following the name of a publisher corresponds to that of its American agent or parent company (see previous directory).

Academie Serbe des Sciences et des Arts
Belgrade, Yugoslavia

Accura Music
Box 887
Athens, OH 45701

Ahn & Simrock
Meinekestrasse 10
1 Berlin 15, West Germany

J. Albert
139 King St.
Sydney, Australia

Alkor (see Bärenreiter)

American Composers Alliance—
Composers Facsimile Editions
170 West 74th Street
New York, NY 10023

American Music Editions   11
263 East 7th Street
New York, NY 10009

Amphion Editions Musicales (see
E. C. Kerby, Ltd.)

A-R Editions
315 West Gorham Street
Madison, WI 53703

Ars Polona (see Polskie
Wydawnictwo Muzyczne)

Ars Viva Verlag   2, 10
Mainz, Germany

Artia   3
Smeckach 30
Prague I, Czechoslovakia

Edwin Ashdown, Ltd.   3, 4

Augener   25

Authors Agency of the Polish Music
Publishers

ul. Hipoteczna 2, 00–950
Warsaw, Poland

Australasian Performing Right
Association, Ltd.
P. O. Box 291
Crow's Nest, NSW
Australia 2065

Averbadjian State Music Publishers
Baku, USSR

Bärenreiter Verlag   10,15
Heinrich Schütz Allee 35
35 Kassel-Wilhelmshöhe, Germany

Barger & Barclay
P. O. Box 22673
Ft. Lauderdale, FL

M. Baron Co.
Box 149
Oyster Bay, NY 11771

Barry & Cia. (Argentina)   3

Bela Bartok Archive
22 Tulip Street
Cedarhurst, NY 11516

M. P. Belaieff   18

Berandol Music Ltd. (Canada)   1

Biedermann   25

Gerald Billaudot, Editeur
14, rue de l'Echiquier
Paris 10, France

Birchard (see Summy-Birchard)

Richard Birnbach
Dürevstrasse 281
1 Berlin 45, Lichterfelde-W
West Germany

Boelke-Bomart Music Publications   1
Hillsdale, NY 12529

Boethius Press Ltd., Clarabricken,

Clifden Co., Kilkenny, Ireland
F. Bongiovanni
  Bologna, Italy
Boston Music Co.
  116 Boylston Street
  Boston, MA 02116
Boston Public Library
  Boston, MA
Bote & Bock 1
Breitkopf & Härtel 1
  Postschliessfach 74
  Walkmühlstrasse 52
  6200 Wiesbaden 1, West Germany
Breitkopf & Härtel
  Postschliessfach 107
  Karlstrasse 10
  701 Leipzig C1, East Germany
Broadcast Music, Inc. 1
Broadcast Music Canada 1
Max Brockhaus
  Leipzig, West Germany
Canadian Music Centre
  1263 Bay Street
  Toronto, Ontario M5R 2Ca,
    Canada
Cantabilé Enterprises
  P. O. Box 27027, Sunnyside
  Pretoria 0132, South Africa
Carisch, S. P. A. 3
  Via General Fara 39
  20134 Milan, Italy
Casa Musicale Sonzogno di Piero
    Ostali
  Milan, Italy
CeBeDeM (Centre Belge de
    Documentation Musicale) 8
  4, boulevard de l'Empereur
  B-1000 Brussels, Belgium
Chant du Monde 14
Chappell & Co. 19
Cheský Hudebni Fond (a rental
    library)
  Prague, Czechoslovakia
J. W. Chester

Eagle Court
  London EC1M 5QD, England
Chopin Institute Edition 16
Choudens 18
Franco Colombo, Inc. 2
Congress Music Publications
  New World Tower
  100 N. Biscayne Blvd.
  Miami, Fl 33132
Contemporary Music Project
  Library Editions
  University Microfilms
  300 N. Zeeb Road
  Ann Arbor, MI 48106
Cora
  Milan, Italy
Costallat 19
G. Cotta'sche
  Stuttgart and Berlin, Germany
J. B. Cramer & Co., Ltd. 4
Cranz 23
Cuadernos de Musica
  Havana, Cuba
Cunningham Music Corp.
  4 North Pine Street
  Nyack, NY 10960
Curlew Music Publishers, Inc.
  Att: Herman Langinger
  1311 N. Highland Avenue
  Hollywood, CA 90028
J. Curwen & Son (England) 23
A. Cuypstr
  Amsterdam, Holland
Czech Music Information Center
  Besedni 3
  Prague, Czechoslovakia
Dan Fog Musikförlag
  Graabrødretorv 1
  DK 1154 Copenhagen K, Denmark
Dantalian, Inc.
  11 Pembroke Street
  Newton, MA 02158
Francis Day
  30 rue de l'Echiquier

Helsinki 10, Finland
Fema Music Publications
  P. O. Box 395
  Naperville, IL 60540
Fermata do Brasil S.A.
  Avenida Ipiranga, 1123
  01039 São Paulo (SP) Brasil
Finnish Music Information Centre
  Runeberginkatu 15 A
  SF-00100 Helsinki 10, Finland
J. Fischer & Bro.   2
  Harristown Road
  Glen Rock, NJ 07452
Dan Fog Musikförlag
  Graabrødretorv 1
  DK 1154 Copenhagen K, Denmark
A. Forlivesi & Co.   2
  Via Roma 4
  Florence, Italy
Forsyth Brothers, Ltd.   2
  190 Grays Inn Road
  London WC1X 8EW, England
Fredonia Press
  3947 Fredonia Drive
  Hollywood, CA 90068
Theodore Front
  155 N. San Vicente Blvd.
  Beverly Hills, CA 90211
Galaxy Music Corp.   20
Gate Music Co.
  c/o Sam Fox
  P.O. Box 850
  Valley Forge, PA 19482
Carl Gehrmans Musikförlag
  Post Box 505
  S-101 26 Stockholm, Sweden
General Music Publishing Co.,
  Inc.   23
  P. O. Box 267
  Hastings-on-Hudson, NY 10706
Musikverlag Hans Gerig   2, 15
  Cologne, Germany
Goodwin & Tabb
  London, England

Guild Publications of California
  2784 La Cuesta Drive
  Hollywood, CA 90046
Gulbenkian Foundation
  Parque de Sta. Gertrudes à Avda.
  de Berna
  Lisbon, Portugal
Hamelle & Co. (France)   9
Wilhelm Hansen   15
T. B. Harms Co.
  100 Wilshire Blvd., Suite 700
  Santa Monica, CA 90401
Otto Harrassowitz
  P. O. Box 2929
  6200 Wiesbaden, Germany
Frederick Harris Music Co., Ltd.
  P. O. Box 670
  Oakville, Ontario,
  Canada L6J SC2
Heinrichshofens Verlag (Germany) 18
G. Henle Verlag   4, 15
Henmar Press (USA)   18
Henn Editions
  8 rue de Hesse
  Geneva, Switzerland
Heugel & Cie.   19
Editions Heuwekemeijer   8, 9, 18
Highgate Press   20
Hinrichsen Edition (England)   18
Friedrich Hofmeister (Germany)   18
Horn of Gabriel Music Publishers
  107 W. Monument St., Suite G A
  Baltimore, MD 21201
Hudební Matice
  Ve Smečkach 30
  Prague 1, Czechoslovakia
Hug (Switzerland)   18
Hüllenhagen & Griehl
  Loogestr. 28
  2 Hamburg 20, West Germany
Iceland Music Information Centre
  Laufasvegi 40
  Reykjavik, Iceland
Imudico

c/o John Dowd
Milligan College
Milligan, TN 37682
Musica Ukraina
Kiev, USSR
Musichna Ukraina
Kiev, Ukraina USSR
(see Harrassowitz)
Musika
Leningrad, USSR
Editions Musikk-Huset   18
Musikverlag Hans Gerig   2, 15
Musikwissenschaftlicher Verlag
G.m.b.H.
Leipzig, Germany
Muzicală (see Editura Muzicală a
Uniunii Compozitorilor din
R.P.R.)
Muzička Naklada
Zagreb, Yugoslavia
Muzyka
Moscow and Leningrad, USSR
Nagel's Musik-Archive   1
Naklada Saveza Kompozitora
Jugoslovije
Zagreb, Yugoslavia
Naouka i Izkustvo
Sophia, Rumania
Nauchno Delo
Belgrade, Yugoslavia
New Music Edition   19
New York Public Library
Library of the Performing Arts
Lincoln Center
New York, NY 10023
Nippon Hōsō Kyokai
Japan Broadcasting Corp.
Tokyo, Japan
Pierre Noel   19
Otto Heinrich Noetzel Verlag   18
Nordiska Musikförlaget   15
Norsk Komponistforening
Society of Norwegian Composers
Klingenberggaten 5

Oslo 1, Norway
Norsk Musikförlag   15
North & Son
666 Fifth Avenue
New York, NY 10019
Norton Critical Scores
W. W. Norton
500 Fifth Avenue
New York, NY 10036
Novello & Co., Ltd.
145 Palisade Street
Dobbs Ferry, NY 10522
Oliver Ditson   19
Ongaku No Toma Sha (Japan)   19
Orbis
Stalinova 46
Prague 12, Czechoslovakia
Ostara Press, Inc.
1092 Skyline Drive
Daly City, CA 94015
Panton   3
Paragon Music Publishers
57 Third Avenue
New York, NY 10003
Paterson's Publications, Ltd.   11
Peer International Corp.   23
People's Republic of China   25
The Performing Right Society, Ltd.
29–33 Berners Street
London W1P 4AA, England
Philharmusica Edition
P. O. Box 180
West Nyack, NY 10994
Polish Music Publications   16
Polskie Wydawnictwo Muzyczne (see
Polish Music Publications)
Promotoro Hispano Americana de
Musica (see Peer International
Corporation.)
Rahter   1
Regaldi Music Co.
279 Warwick Avenue
Teaneck, NJ 07666
Reuter & Reuter Forlags AB

Portland, OR 97219
Süddeutscher Musikverlag (Willy
  Müller)   18
Supraphon   3
Edizioni Suvini Zerboni   3
Swedish Performing Right Society   12
  Eriks Musikhandel och Förlag AB
  Karlävagen 40
  Stockholm, Sweden
Technisonor
  Paris, France
Tetra (see Alexander Broude)
Til Udgivelse af Dansk Musik
  Copenhagen, Denmark
Tischler & Jangenberg
  Nibelungenstrasse 48
  D-8000 Munich 19, West Germany
Tonos Verlag (see Seesaw Music
  Corp.)
Transcontinental Music
  1674 Broadway
  New York, NY 10019
Udruženje Kompozitora Hrvatske
  9 Berislaviceva
  Zagreb, Yugoslavia
Uitgave Artur Meulemansfonds
  Antwerp, Belgium
Unión Musical Española   1
Universal Edition (Vienna, London,
  Zurich)   10
University of California Press
  2223 Fulton Street
  Berkeley, CA 94720
Valstybine Grozines
  Riga, USSR
Verlag Neue Musik
  East Berlin, Germany
Musikverlag C. F. Vieweg   18

Verlag von Holm Pälz
  Würzburg, West Germany
Arno Volk Verlag   14
Warner Brothers
  75 Rockefeller Plaza
  New York, NY 10019
Wa Wan Press
  Reprint by Arno Press
  330 Madison Avenue
  New York, NY 10017
Josef Weinberger, Ltd.   3
Weintraub Music Co.   18
Western International Music
  2859 Holt Avenue
  Los Angeles, CA 90034
Western Music Library
  c/o H. T. Fitzsimons Co., Inc.
  615 N. LaSalle Street
  Chicago, IL 60610
Joseph Williams Editions   20
M. Witmark and Sons
  c/o Seven Arts Music
  75 Rockefeller Plaza
  New York, NY 10019
Lawrence Wright Music Co.
  Wright House
  Denmark St. (Charing Cross Road)
  London WC2, England
Editore Gugliemo Zanibon   2, 18
Zenemükiado Vallalat (Editio Musica
  Budapest—EMB)   3
Zen-On Music Co., Ltd.   23
Edizioni Suvini Zerboni   3
Wilhelm Zimmermann,
  Musikverlag   18
Zurfluh
  73 Boulevard Raspail
  Paris 6, France

A

Erkii Aaltonen (1910–   ) Finland
Concerto I 1948 (Finnish Music Information Centre) 27 min.
Concerto II 1954 (Finnish Music Information Centre) 32 min. Both of these
    M-D works display skilful instrumentation and programmatic effects.

Marcello Abbado (1926–   ) Italy
Double Concerto for Violin, Piano and Double Orchestra (Ric 1965) 15 min. Re-
    produced from holograph. Full score, 90pp. One large movement. Expres-
    sionistic, pointillistic, chromatic. Cadenza for piano and violin together. D.

Louis Abbiate (1866–1933) Monaco
Concerto Italien A Op.96 (F. Durdilly, Ch. Hayet 1925) 124pp. Three large move-
    ments. Finale is a set of variations on a Tema di Saltarello. Big, dramatic,
    virtuoso writing in late nineteenth-century style. M-D.

Karl Friedrich Abel (1725–1787) Germany
Abel was the last distinguished performer on the bass viol. He composed numerous popular instrumental works—symphonies, concertos, and chamber music.
He was a pupil of J.S. Bach at the Thomaskirche and after having spent some
time in the orchestra at the Dresden Court Chapel, he was co-director with Bach's
youngest son, Johann Christian, of the important subscription concerts in London,
the "Bach-Abel Concerts." His style of writing has some similarity to that of the
Mannheim School, and his work exercised a certain influence on the early compositions of W. A. Mozart.
Concerto Eb Op.11/3 (H. Höckner—CFP 4409a 1935) 34pp. For piano, 2 violins,
    viola, cello, double bass, 2 flutes. Preface in German and English. Allegro
    maestoso; Tempo di Menuetto. The soloist may provide light harmonic filler
    in the tutti passages depending on the quantity and quality of orchestral
    performers present. Could be performed with seven instrumentalists, one on
    each part. Int. to M-D.

Eduard A. Abramian (1923–   ) USSR
Concerto I Bb 1950 (USSR 1965) 87pp. Three movements (FSF). Late Romantic-
    Impressionistic idiom. Virtuoso elements. D.

Robert Abramson (1928–   ) USA
Dance Variations 1965 (Gen 902) 28½ min. In one movement consisting of seven
    variations, double fugue, chorale, and finale.

1

Jean Absil (1893–1974) Belgium
Many of Absil's earlier works were written in a conventional idiom, but in later years he turned to a more personal, austere style. Unconventional rhythmic procedure was the norm in his writing.
Concerto I Op.30 1937 (CeBeDeM; Fl) 35pp. 14 min. Competition piece at the 1938 Concours Ysaÿe (later called the Queen Elisabeth Competition) in Brussels. Allegro moderato ma enerigo; Andante; Finale—Molto vivo. MC, rhythmically intricate and harmonically opulent, some atonal sections. D.
Concerto II Op.131 1967 (H. Elkan) 19 min. Maestoso—Allegro moderato: based on meters of $4 + 3 + 2$ with an underlying waltz tempo. Andante: expressive, fantasy element present, half-step usage important. Allegro: rhythmic combinations in 2- and 3-bar phrases; virtuosic; dynamics gradually increase to help develop this colorful finale. M-D.
Concerto III Op.162 1973 (H. Elkan) 35pp. 20 min. Andante moderato; Andante; Allegro moderato. Neoclassic, MC. M-D.

Isidor Achron (1892–1948) USA
Concerto b♭ Op.2 1937 (CF) 41pp. 17 min. In one movement. Expanded tonality, contrasting sections. M-D.

Murray Adaskin (1906–   ) Canada
Adaskin blends contrapuntal ingenuities with syncopated quips in an idiom always accessible and pleasant to the ear. His works discard conventional formulas and develop their own logic.
Capriccio 1961 (CMC) 19 min. Neoclassic; superbly fashioned and finished; sculptured chasteness. Neat use of thirds and sixths is a delight. M-D.

Richard Addinsell (1904–   ) Great Britain
Warsaw Concerto (Chappell 1942) 30pp. 8½ min. From the motion picture *Dangerous Moonlight*. Also available in a piano-band version (Erik Leidzen—Chappell). Dramatic, sectional, showy, tuneful. M-D.
The Smoky Mountains 1950 (Chappell) 42pp., 13½ min. Andante molto moderato; Valley Song; Old Joe Clark. Large pianistic gestures à la Rachmaninoff, MC, pleasant and effective. M-D.

John Addison (1920–   ) Great Britain
Addison was educated at Wellington College and the Royal College of Music. His music is mainly cheerful and light, and his technical craft is outstanding, somewhat in the style of Poulenc or Jean Françaix.
Concertino (OUP) 15 min. Allegro: syncopated rhythms cleverly integrated with orchestral forces, thin textures, quiet closing. Andante grazioso: changing chords, filigree figuration, some changing meters, chromaticism exploited in mid-section. Vivace: punctuated chords in syncopation move over keyboard, trills in upper register, freely tonal. A gifted teen-ager would enjoy this work. Int. to M-D.

Conversation Piece (OUP) 12 min.

Variations 1949 (Galaxy) 12 min. Variations flow into one another naturally. Eclectic style with strong Impressionistic tendencies. M-D.

Wellington Suite (OUP).

Vasif Adigezalov (1935–   ) USSR

Concerto (Averbadjian State Music Publishers 1962; LC) 72pp. Allegretto; Andante sostenuto; Allegro giocoso. Freely tonal around C. Colorful, dramatic. Cadenza at end of first movement. Virtuoso pianism required. D.

Ilya S. Aisberg (1872–   ) USSR

Concerto e Op.15 1928 (USSR) 69pp. Three large contrasting sections in one movement. Modal; late nineteenth-century pianistic idiom. M-D.

Capriccio Hébraïque Op.20 (UE 10138 1931) 41pp. One movement, sectional. Same techniques as described for Op.15. M-D.

Isaac Albéniz (1860–1909) Spain

Albéniz was a prolific composer for the piano and one of Spain's finest pianists. His works are a composite of Lisztian pianistic techniques and the idioms and rhythms of Spanish popular music.

Spanish Rhapsody Op.70 (C. Halffter—UME 1962; IMC) 12 min. Originally composed for two pianos in 1886. The Halffter transcription provides an effective complement and adds strength and a pedestal that shows off the work beautifully. Lisztian; concert-popularistic in tone. M-D.

Concerto Fantastico a Op.78 1887 (UME 1975) 66pp., 24 min. Allegro ma non troppo; Reverie et Scherzo; Allegro. Chopin, Schumann, and Liszt influences are present, but this early work also forecasts the colorful *evocación* of popular Spanish music that is characteristic of Albéniz's later writing. Fairly free treatment of the classic concerto form (hence the title!). Each movement is a kind of freely improvised fantasy. Forceful gestures, rhythmic outbursts, elegant harmony, and warm instrumental color are the most interesting elements of the work. Beautifully fashioned for a virtuoso. M-D to D.

Eugen d'Albert (1864–1932) Germany, born Scotland

D'Albert was a Liszt student and composer firmly in the progressive mold of his day.

Concerto I b Op.2 1883–84 (Bo&Bo 1884; Fl) 46 min. In one movement. This attractive but oversized work is full of virtuosic opportunities and exuberant display for the soloist. Its form and pianism were greatly admired by Liszt. M-D to D.

Concerto II E Op.12 1892 (Bo&Bo; Fl) 20 min. A single movement in which four contrasting sections flow into each other seamlessly. There is a brief glittering episode for piano alone, approximating a cadenza, shortly before the end. Sprawling themes. One of the finest concertos in the Liszt tradition. M-D.

Dante Alderighi (1898–1968) Italy
Concerto II (SZ 1940) 33 min. Moderato; Intermezzo; Allegro marcato. Freely
   tonal around e; MC. Virtuosity required. D.
Divertimento 1952 (SZ) for piano and string orchestra.

Anatolii N. Aleksandrov (1888–   ) USSR
Concerto Op.101 (USSR 1976) 112pp. Lugubre; Alla marcia; Andante semplice;
   Allegro energico. Freely tonal around b♭-B♭. Dramatic, with broad gestures
   and virtuosic skips. Enormous octave technique required. D.

Boris Aleksandrovich Aleksandrow (1905–   ) USSR
Concerto-Fantasia (USSR 1972). One large tonal, colorful movement M-D.

Raffaele d'Alessandro (1911–1959) Switzerland
Concerto II Op. 54 (Foetisch 1954) 91pp. Allegro moderato; Andantino—
   Scherzo—Andantino; Cadenza e Finale (Rondo). Somewhat Impressionis-
   tic, strong melodies, some flexible meters, MC. M-D.

Josef Alexander (1910–   ) USA
Concerto c 1936 (Fl) 23 min. Allegro moderato, maestoso; Andante con moto;
   Presto.

Franco Alfano (1876–1954) Italy
Divertimento 1934 (Ric) 14 min. Introduzione e Aria; Recitativo e rondo. Freely
   tonal, neoclassic. The piano is treated as an obbligato. M-D.

Joseph Alfidi (1949–   ) USA
Alfidi studied at the Juilliard School, the Conservatoire in Brussels, and the
Chapelle Musicale Reine Elisabeth.
Concerto II g (Gate Music Co.) 20 min. Allegro moderato; Andante sostenuto;
   Vivace. Reveals depth for a nine-year-old composer. Vigorous, inventive.
   Has remarkable emotional impact, touched here and there by moments of
   explosive humor and brilliant effects. Int. to M-D.

René Alix (1907–1966) France
Concerto Op.16 (Choudens 1969) 30 min. Post-Romantic idiom, some modal
   usage. M-D to D.

Charles Henri Valentin Alkan (1813–1888) France
Much interest has been generated recently in this unknown contemporary of
Chopin, Liszt, Anton Rubinstein, and César Franck. Busoni placed him among
"the greatest of the post-Beethoven piano composers."
First Concerto da Camera a Op.10 1828 (Musica Obscura; Billaudot). Allegro
   moderato; Adagio (available separately from Musica Obscura); Rondo. Similar pianistically in some ways to the Liszt E♭ Concerto. Runs and fioritura
   are enriched by massive chords, sonorous effects, and virtuoso scope. The
   light orchestral accompaniment is somewhat like that of the Chopin *Concerts,* and it is even marked *ad libitum.* M-D.

Carlos Vianna de Almeida (1906–   ) Brazil
Introduçao e Dança Brasileira (Fermata do Brasil 1956; IU) 14pp. Andante opening leads to faster dance section. Tonal. Nineteenth-century pianistic gestures. M-D.

Eyvind Alnaes (1872–1932) Denmark
Concerto D Op.27 1919 (WH) 71pp. 33 min. Allegro moderato; Lento; Allegro
(Tempo di Valse). Written in a post-Brahmsian idiom. M-D.

Carlos Roqué Alsina (1941–   ) Argentina
Approach Op.30 1972–73 (SZ). For piano, percussion, and orchestra with tape
and speaker. 15 min. The pianist also performs on various other instruments.
Directions in Italian and German. Avant-garde techniques displayed with
versatility; *ppp* ending. M-D.
Señales 1977 (SZ) 14 min. Abrupt shifts between layers of sound; solid craft;
sustained excitement. M-D.

Alearco Ambrosi (1931–   ) Italy
Dialoghi Notturni (Ric) 58 pp. One movement. Meditative writing in outer sections surrounds big climaxes in middle section. Changing meters, expressionistic, clusters. Large span required. D.

Hermann Ambrosius (1897–   ) Germany
Concerto E♭ Op.51 1927 (Max Brockhaus) 89pp. Virtuoso writing, MC, post-
Brahms idiom. Large cadenza at end of second movement leads to finale. D.
Concerto g 1946 (Fl) 23pp. Allegro; Largo e con espressivo; Allegro giocoso.

Ugo Amendola (–   ) Italy
Concerto (EC 1975) 91pp. Prima menzione al Concorso Internazionale "Prince
Pierre de Monaco 1972." Liberamente; Adagio; Rondo—Allegro con brio.
Expanded tonality around d, many octaves, neoclassic. M-D.

René Amengual (1911–1954) Chile
Amengual's compositions were influenced by French Impressionism and to some
extent by jazz.
Concerto 1941 (IEM; IU) full score, 116pp. Allegro; Lento; Scherzo; Rondo.
Freely tonal, traditional forms, strong Ravel influence. M-D.

William Ames (1901–   ) USA
Concerto (ACA) full score, 104pp., 25 min. One movement, neoclassic, cadenza,
varied and contrasting sections, *ppp* closing. M-D to D.
Nocturne and Scherzo 1942 (ACA). For two pianos and string orchestra. Full
score, 18pp. Adagio: chords in strings while pianos have legato octotonic
lines with some melodic interest. Scherzo: vivace 6/8; short; scampers to a
dimenuendo conclusion. M-D.

Fikret Amirov (1922–   ) USSR, **Nazirova E.M. Rza-Kyzy** (1928–   )
USSR.   Joint composers.

Concerto on Arabian Themes 1957 (USSR 1959) 76pp. Three movements (FSF). Modal, theatrical, based on Azerbaijanian folk music. M-D.

Pierre Ancelin (1934–   ) France

Concerto Op.14 1962 (Choudens 20165). For piano, oboe, and chamber orchestra. Full score, 81pp., 14 min. One large movement with contrasting sections. Expanded tonal idiom, octotonic, flexible meters, *ppp* ending. Both piano and oboe are used more in a chamber ensemble style than in solo capacities. Large span required. M-D.

Concerto Gioioso Op.33 1971 (Billaudot). For piano, flute, and strings. Allegro giocoso; Larghetto Sereno; Vivace, con spirito. Neoclassic, flexible meters, mildly dissonant. Piano is treated both soloistically and as an ensemble partner. M-D.

Garland Anderson (1933–   ) USA

Concertino (AME 1969) 16pp. Allegro; Andante; Allegro. An excellent work for younger students, well developed, tuneful, MC. Int. to M-D.

Jurriaan Andriessen (1925–   ) The Netherlands

Concertino 1943 (Donemus) 15 min.

Concerto 1948 (Donemus) 26 min.

Willem Andriessen (1887–1964) The Netherlands

Concerto 1908 (Donemus) 30 min.

Paul Angerer (1927–   ) Austria

Konzert 1956 (Dob 1960). For piano, strings, and brass. 10 min. One movement, neoclassic, MC. M-D.

Konzert (Dob 1968). For piano and strings. 22 min. Freely tonal; writing not totally convincing throughout. M-D.

Hugo Anson (1894–1958) Great Britain

Concerto (Novello 1941). For two pianos and orchestra. 59pp. One movement, contrasting sections, freely tonal, MC. M-D.

George Antheil (1900–1959) USA

Concerto 1926 (MS available from Mrs. Antheil, 8450 De Longpre Ave., Los Angeles, CA 90069) 25 min. Moderato; Largo; Allegro.

Theodore Antoniou (1935–   ) USA, born Greece

Antoniou's "works combine conventional and electronic media to explore 'extremely abstract relationships, such as the movements of sounds, the possible combinations of dialogue, the several ways of playing an instrument . . . problems of space, sound, movement, and event' " (DCM, 14).

Concertino Op.16B 1962 (Br 4378). For piano, strings, and percussion. 24pp., 13 min. Freely tonal, changing meters, octotonic, wide leaps, expressive chromatic chords, shifting rhythms, dramatic arpeggi gestures. Good octave technique required. M-D.

Concertino Op.21 1963 (Br 4377 1973). For piano and band. 49pp., 13 min.

Allegro; Adagio; Presto. Minor seconds and major sevenths are prevalent, widely spread arpeggiated chords, repeated chords and insistent rhythms, octotonic, clusters, pointillistic, piano cadenza, extreme ranges, exciting. Improvisation required. M-D to D.

Events I 1968 (Br 6018 1974). For piano, violin, and orchestra. 18 min. Performance instructions in German and English. Symphonia; Antithesis; Stichomythie; Epilogos. Experimental notation, avant-garde. M-D.

Fluxus II (Br 6739 1975). For piano and chamber orchestra. 22pp. Photostat. Explanations in English.

Hans Eric Apostel (1901–1972) Austria

Apostel studied with Schoenberg and Berg.

Konzert Op. 30 (UE 13174 1960) 51pp., 22 min. The composer provides an analysis in the score. Allegro marziale: ABA; B section is a theme and variations. Grave: in five parts; central section is a scherzo. Allegro: ABA; cadenza using all five main themes of the work appears before the return of A. Twelve-tone, much octotonic writing for the piano, block chords, mainly linear, skillful orchestral usage. M-D.

Violet Archer (1913–   ) Canada

Archer has a vocabulary that is strictly contemporary, but she is not an extremist. Her idiom is governed by what she has to say in terms of music. Her works shows a loftiness of purpose, an economy of means, and a mastery of musical media.

Concerto I 1956 (BMI Canada; Fl) 17 min. Allegro energico; lively, dissonant counterpoint. Adagio molto, expressivo e cantabile: Romantic in character. Allegro ma non troppo: bright, scherzo-like. Strong melodic lines, contrapuntal mastery, based on functions of the twelve-tone scale. Piano part is thoroughly integrated with the orchestra; brilliant passages are featured in the outer movements. A Canadian critic has called this work "possibly the best concerto by a Canadian." M-D.

José Ardeval (1911–   ) Cuba, born Spain

The nationalist and neoclassic orientation in Ardeval's music of the 1930s and 40s gave way in the early 50s to the influence of Webern. In 1967 Ardeval began using aleatory procedures as well.

Concerto 1944 (PIC). For piano, winds, and percussion. 24 min. Lento—Allegro moderato: canonic treatment of themes between piano and orchestra, between both hands, and between trumpets. Rondeletto: folk-like theme; dialogue between piano and orchestra. Passacaglia—Fuga: somber, deeply expressive. Fine craftsmanship throughout, with strong linear and polytonal influences. M-D to D.

Anton Arensky (1861–1906) Russia

Arensky wrote in a most effective salon style.

Concerto F Op.2 1883 (USSR 1975; Paul Pabst—Rahter; Fl) 25 min. Allegro maestoso; Andante con moto; Allegro molto. Superficially attractive; piano part is well displayed; much repetition, undistinguished material. An effective hodgepodge of Chopin, Liszt, and Tchaikowsky. M-D.

Fantasy on Russian Folksongs Op.48 1900 (USSR; Jurgenson; Fl) 9 min. Allegro maestoso; Andante con moto; Scherzo—finale. This is a concerto in all but name. Melodic freshness, distinctive expressive lines, catchy tunes. M-D.

Fantasy on Themes by Riabinin (USSR 1979) 30pp. A concise and engaging rhapsody, loose in design, based on tunes collected by the pioneer Russian folklorist Trophim Riabinin. There is no attempt at forming the material into a symphonic structure, as Arensky simply writes a fantasia around his tunes in the manner of his teacher Tchaikowsky. Makes a strong impression. M-D.

Dominick Argento (1927–   ) USA

Argento has taught at the University of Minnesota since 1958.

Divertimento 1955 (Bo&H 1967; Fl). For piano and string orchestra. 15 min. Veloce e giocoso: rhythmically oriented, dramatic gestures. Moderato cantabile: melodic, chromatic, Quasi allegretto mid-section. Allegro energico: strong syncopations, octotonic, martellato chords, brilliant conclusion. M-D.

Albert Arlen (1905–   ) Great Britain, born Australia

The "Alamein" Concerto (Chappell) 7½ min. Photo of MS.

Thomas A. Arne (1710–1778) Great Britain

Concerto IV B♭ (A. Carse—Augener 1954) 11 min. Con spirito; Minuetto; Giga. Concertos IV and V were originally intended as interludes during productions of Arne's oratorios so that he might entertain the audience with some virtuosic and improvisational display. Int. to M-D.

Concerto V g 1750s (Nag 210; A. Carse—Augener 1952; S&B) 12 min. Arne gives the soloist plenty to work with. Largo: noble; in sharp, dotted rhythms. Allegro con spirito: Handelian; in normal concerto form, with solo episodes between the orchestral statements of the main theme. Adagio: short; in free style for soloist alone; provides a good opportunity for improvisation. Vivace: in minuet rhythm and concerto form. A gifted teen-ager would enjoy this work. M-D.

See: Robin Langley, "Arne's Keyboard Concertos," MT 1621 (March 1978): 233–36.

Richard Arnell (1917–   ) Great Britain

Arnell writes in an eclectic style and has composed in almost all forms.

Divertimento I Op. 5 1939 (Hin; Fl). For piano and chamber orchestra. 17 min. Moderato; Andante con moto; Allegro.

Concerto Op.44 (Schott 10135 1951) 26 min. Allegro; Andante, con moto; Poco presto. Many octaves and full chords, octotonic, syncopated, bitonal. Cadenza at end of second movement. Four-octave right-hand crossing over left hand; MC. M-D.

Sections (Hin) 25 min.

Malcolm Arnold (1921–   ) Great Britain

Arnold writes within the diatonic system and believes it affords the best opportunity for creating musical ideas. Atonal music leads, he says, to a state of musical meandering.

Concerto for Phyllis and Cyril Op.104 (GS). For two pianos, three-hands, and orchestra. 13 min. An irresistible work, full of *joie de vivre*. The finale has a feeling of spectacle infused with great exuberance. M-D.

Concerto for Piano Duet and Strings (Lengnick 1951) 21 min.

Claude Arrieu (1903–   ) France

Concerto C 1938 (Billaudot). For two pianos and orchestra. 14 min. Allegro; Andante; Vivo. Octotonic, mildly Impressionistic, MC, lovely sonorities, bitonal, glissandi. M-D.

Johannes Aschenbrenner (1903–   ) Germany

Divertimento (H&G). For piano and chamber orchestra. 25 min.

Kurt Atterberg (1887–1974) Sweden

Atterberg's music uses traditional forms and borrows extensively from Swedish folk materials.

Rapsodi Op.1 1909 (STIM) 11 min.

Concerto b♭ Op.37 1927–35 (Br&H 5669 1937) 35 min. Pesante allegro; Andante; Furioso. Written in a grand, post–nineteenth-century style reminiscent of Brahms and Reger. A short cadenza at the end of the Andante leads to the Furioso. M-D.

Louis Aubert (1877–1968) France

Fantaisie b Op.8 1899 (Durand 1908) 16 min. Impressionistic, florid style, "tangential modalities and tonalities serve as asymptotes for a series of thematic fragments" (MSNH, 22).

Pierre Auclert (1905–   ) France

Concerto (Amphion 1951) 16 min. Adagio: chromatic, broad gestures. Allegretto: dancelike, sprightly, octotonic, changing meters, glissandi, large skips in left hand, melody intertwined in inner voices, dramatic conclusion, MC. D.

Concerto (Leduc 1954) 30pp. One-movement form written in a sophisticated Ravel idiom with touches of mild polytonality. Contains a profusion of double notes. M-D.

Lydia Martinova Auster (1912–   ) USSR

Concerto Op.18 (USSR 1966) 112pp. Three movements (FSF). Post-Romantic style, complete range of instrument exploited. M-D.

Larry Austin (1930–   ) USA

Austin's "later works have used open form processes combined with modern technological and theatrical resources" (DCM, 30).

Open Style for Orchestra with Piano Soloist 1965 (CPE). "In this work a specified latitude of choice is available to the performers, who rely on a system of analog notation, using coordinates one centimeter apart, to control and coordinate the flow of the music. The rhythm is nonmetrical" (DCM, 30).

Charles Avison (1709–1770) Great Britain

Avison was one of Georgian England's great originals.

Concerto A Op.9/2 (OUP). For keyboard and strings. Melodically graceful; with rhythmic vigor and strong Geminiani influence. Requires swift, zestful, and bouncy performance, especially in the outer movements. Int. to M-D.

Aaron Avshalomov (1894–1965) USA, born Russia

Avshalomov lived in China from 1928 to 1946. He was especially interested in integrating Chinese melodic and rhythmic characteristics with Western forms and instrumentation.

Concerto upon Chinese Themes and Rhythms G 1935 (Ric; ACA; Fl) 35 min. Allegro moderato; Adagio; Allegro non troppo. Despite its title, the concerto uses borrowed thematic material only in the nocturnelike slow movement, whose principal theme is an ancient Chinese melody. The outer movements follow the virtuoso Romantic concerto tradition: a big SA with elaborate cadenza and a lively rondo. M-D.

B

Kees van Baaren (1906–1970) The Netherlands
During the 1960s van Baaren "grew closer to Webern's style, as manifest in his fondness then for brevity, asymmetrical melodic and rhythmic units, pointillistic sound textures, and sophisticated handling of serial techniques" (DCM, 43).
Concertino 1934 (Donemus) 13 min. Neoclassic. M-D.
Concerto 1964 (Donemus) 13 min. A one-movement work in eight sections. Piano and orchestra are treated equally. Structure of the piano part is frequently based on principles of continuity that differ from those of the orchestral element. Pointillistic; everything notated precisely. Mood varies from angry brilliance to romantic warmth. D.

Arno Babadzhanjan (1921–   ) USSR
Heroic Ballad "Symphonic Variations for Piano and Orchestra" (USSR) 21 min. Dramatic, sectional colorful, freely tonal around e-E, MC. M-D.

Stanley Babin (1932–   ) USA, born Latvia
Babin received his musical training in Israel and at the Curtis Institute of Music.
Concerto 1967 (MCA) 20 min. Allegro con brio; Andante sostenuto; Vivace.

Victor Babin (1908–1972) USA, born Russia
Babin studied with Artur Schnabel and performed as a duo team with his wife, Vitya Vronsky.
Concerto I (Augener 1937). For two pianos and orchestra. 29 min. Allegro con fuoco; Passacaglia; Intermezzo; Rondo—Presto. A brilliant virtuoso work. The finale has a tarantella flavor. M-D to D.
Concerto II 1956 (Belaieff 1961). For two pianos and orchestra. 23 min. Moderato; Molto vivo e ben ritmico; Molto sostenuto, intimo e calmo; Finale alla fuga—Allegro con spirito. A well-written concert piece with a brilliant conclusion. D.

Grazyna Bacewicz (1913–1969) Poland
Bacewicz, a fine violinist, was Poland's outstanding woman composer in her generation.
Koncert 1949 (PWM) 21 min. Allegro moderato; Andante; Molto allegro. Pandiatonic idiom; not much variety in the piano texture. M-D.
Concerto for Two Pianos and Orchestra 1966 (PWM 139) 17 min. Tempo mutabile; Larghetto; Vivace. Large chromatic gestures, strong structural unity, glis-

sandi, clusters, flexible meters, Bartók and Shostakovitch influence. Large
span required. M-D.

Carl Philipp Emanuel Bach (1714–1788) Germany

Bach wrote 56 concertos for one or two keyboard instruments and orchestra and
hardly a fifth of them are available in modern editions. Some of these concertos
were arranged from works for other solo instruments, but by far the largest number
were conceived for the harpsichord and intended for the composer's own use. The
keyboard concertos form the largest single group of orchestral music in C. P. E.
Bach's output; they span his entire career, from his nineteenth year (1733) to the
end of his life. They contain development sections, and sometimes such formal
experiments as a minuet fourth movement or the running together of the second
and third movements.

Under C. P. E. Bach's leadership the north-German keyboard concerto became a well-defined musical genre. In its regular alternation of tuttis and solos it
perpetuated the Baroque tradition, although the solos gained in prominence and
the orchestral accompaniments in delicacy. Its chief merit, however, was not in
any of its formal aspects but in its spirit: Emanuel's concertos, in particular, never
dropped to the level of entertainment music. Perhaps that is why they continued
to be performed in northern Germany well into the nineteenth century. And it is
significant that the master whose works eventually supplanted them was
Beethoven.

Numbers preceded by W. refer to Wotquenne's *Thematisches Verzeichnis der
Werke von C. P. E. Bach* (Br&H 1905). A new thematic catalogue by Eugene Helm
is forthcoming from Yale University Press.

Concerto g W.6 1740 (Oberdörffer—Br 2005).

Concerto D W.18 1745 (H. Riemann—Steingräber).

Concerto d W.23 1748 (G. Wertheim—Br&H 3771). Strong empfindsam ("sensitive") writing as contrasted with Bach's later *galant* style. This work,
intense and dark-hued, is closely connected to J. S. Bach's legacy. Allegro:
large movement containing four ritornellos and dialogue orchestral writing.
Poco andante: orchestral unisons suggestive of the Andante of Beethoven's
Fourth Concerto. Allegro assai: unison orchestral subject, lengthy sequential
mid-section, dramatic tension. M-D.

Concerto a W.26 1750 (G. Amft—Kahnt 1905; Fl) 23 min. Allegro assai; Andante; Allegro assai. Contains some charming thematic work. The closing
of the first movement conveys an impression of Bach's power of expression,
with a climax reminiscent of Beethoven's Coriolanus Overture. M-D.

Concerto D W.27 1750 (E. Kulukundis—A-R Editions 1969). Allegro; Siciliano;
Allegro. May be performed with strings only or in its final version with
winds. Of all Bach's concertos, the final version of this work is the only one
to call upon the resources of the full Classical orchestra. M-D.

Concerto A W.29 1753 (H. M. Kneihs—Eulenburg).

Concerto c W.31 1753 (G. Balla—EMB/Br Nag 253 1976) 23 min. Allegro di molto; Adagio–Allegretto. This previously unpublished concerto is one of the grandest; Bach himself referred to it as one of his "showpieces." The dialogue slow movement ranks with the finest of such dialogues in the entire repertory. Ornaments are realized in small notes throughout the score. M-D.

Concerto F W.33 1755 (F. Oberdörffer—Br 2004 1952) 31pp. With realized figured bass.

Concerto G W.34 1755 (H. Winter—Sikorski 1964) 55pp. First edition. Haydn is anticipated in the third movement.

Concerto Eb W.35 1759 (H. Winter—Sikorski 1964) 36pp. First edition.

Concerto D W.43/2 1772 (L. Landshoff—Heinrichshofen 1967). Adagio di molto; Andante; Allegretto. Not difficult but brilliant sounding. Int. to M-D.

Concerto Eb W.43/3 1771 (H. Riemann—Steingräber). Allegro; Larghetto; Presto. Generally light-hearted; emotional depths achieved by dramatic and poetic surprises; mosaic of contrasting ideas and textures. M-D.

Concerto c W.43/4 1771 (H. Riemann—Steingräber). One large movement that includes a recapitulation of the opening section and a four-bar reminiscence of the minuet. An excellent example of Bach's formal unorthodoxy; testifies to the adventurousness of his mind. M-D.

Concerto G W.43/5 1771 (H. Riemann—Steingräber).

W.43/1-6 (all published in 1772) were written with an eye to their market potential.

Concerto F. W.46 1740 (H. Swartz—Steingräber; Fl). Double concerto for harpsichord, piano, and orchestra. 25 min. Allegro; Largo; Allegro assai. Displays the two keyboard instruments against the orchestra rather than against each other. The crown of the work is the extended minor-mode Largo, which is permeated with a pathetic and profound expression. The closing Allegro ends in a dazzling display of virtuosity. M-D.

Concerto Eb W.47 1788 (Jacobi—Br 2043; G. Davis—Eulenburg 1279; H. Swartz—Steingräber; Fl). Double concerto for piano, harpsichord, and orchestra. 18 min. Allegro molto; Larghetto; Presto. Written at the end of Bach's last creative period; contains characteristics of the Viennese school. The technical aspects of the two instruments are handled identically. The charm of their contrast lies in their different timbres. Strong dramatic contrasts, mellow lyricism, quixotic humor. One of the most dazzling virtuoso pieces of the Classical era. M-D.

Concertos W.96–110 are patterned after the Austrian divertimentos for keyboard and orchestra, of which Wagenseil left many examples.

Sonatina d W.107 1764 (Br 2006) 15 min. Adagio; Allegro ma non troppo; Allegretto. Twelve *sonatinas* (Bach's term) for piano (two of them for two pianos) accompanied by various combinations for instruments, were written in Berlin between 1762 and 1764. As opposed to concertos, they have a greater variety of musical form, which in W.107 approaches that of the divertimento, suite, or sonata. The first movement is in d, the second and third in F. All are in SA design with the two principal sections repeated. M-D.

See: Charles H. Buck III, "Revisions in Early Clavier Concertos of C. P. E. Bach: Revelations from a New Source," JAMS 29/1 (Spring 1976):127–32.

Leon Crickmore, "C. P. E. Bach's Harpsichord Concertos," M&L 39 (July 1958):227–41.

———. "The Keyboard Concertos of C. P. E. Bach," thesis, Birmingham University (England), 1956.

C. R. Haag, "The Keyboard Concertos of Karl Philipp Emanuel Bach," Ph.D. diss., University of California, Los Angeles, 1956.

Jane R. Stevens, "The Keyboard Concertos of Carl Philipp Emanuel Bach," Ph.D. diss., Yale University, 1965.

Muriel M. Waterman, "The Double Keyboard Concertos of Carl Philipp Emanuel Bach," thesis, University of Arizona, 1970.

Johann Christian Bach (1735–1782) Germany

J. C. Bach's 37 keyboard concertos display many characteristics typical of the *galant* concerto, including a strong first subject and a cantabile ritornello theme in the first movement. Solo piano writing is generally rather simple, with Alberti bass figures in the left hand while the right hand displays conventional runs and arpeggio figuration. The solo instrument normally plays the figured or thorough bass part during the tuttis. Many of these concertos are still unpublished. They had a strong influence on Mozart and provide excellent preparation for the Mozart piano concertos. ("Terry" refers to Charles S. Terry, *John Christian Bach* [London: Oxford University Press, 1929]).

Six Concertos Op.1 1763 (Hummel; Welcker; NYPL has a complete set). In Bb, A, F, G, C, D. These concertos are the smallest in scale; doubtless they were designed as much for domestic performance as for concert use. Most of them have purring Alberti basses in the left hand supporting lightly singing tunes in the right hand. Thirds and arpeggios make the greatest demands on the performer. Int. to M-D.

Concerto G Op.1/4 (Rutgers University Press 1953, Documents of the Musical Past I). For keyboard and strings. Allegro; Andante; Allegro.

Six Concertos Op.7 1770–75 (Hummel). For harpsichord or piano and strings. In C, F, D, Bb, Eb, G. These works are more characteristic in their invention and include a couple of miniature masterpieces (No. 5 in Eb, most notably). This set, in particular, had a strong influence on Mozart.

Concerto F Op.7/2 (T. Johnson, D. McCorkle—Fl) 26pp. Allegro con spirito; Tempo di minuetto; Allegretto. M-D.

Concerto D Op.7/3 (K. Reckzeh—SB 1947).

Concerto Eb Op.7/5 (Döbereiner—CFP; Illy—De Santis; Eulenburg; Wais—Steingräber) 15 min. Allegro di molto; Andante; Allegro. Three distinct, self-contained movements. Int. to M-D.

Concerto G Op.7/6 (Kastner—Schott; Riemann—Steingräber).

Six Concertos Op.13 1777? (Welcker; NYPL has a complete set). In C, D, F, B♭, G, E♭. This set more than hints at the Classical style not only in the cut of the themes and the scale of the developments but also in the nature of the contrasts. It is true concert music.

Concerto D Op.13/2 (Landshoff—CFP; Carse—Augener) 14 min. Allegro con spirito; Andante; Allegro non tanto. A gifted teen-ager would enjoy this work; very Mozartian in sound. Int. to M-D.

Concerto B♭ Op.13/4 (Landshoff—CFP 4329; Fl) 15 min. Allegro; Andante; Andante con moto. One of Bach's finest concertos. It was very special to Joseph Haydn, who set it in a solo piano version ten years after Bach's death; this version is still extant in a London edition. The finale is a set of variations based on a Scottish folk tune. Int. to M-D.

Concerto G Op.13/5 (Schott).

Concerto f (Martini—Nag 170). Composed in Berlin between 1750 and 1754. Allegretto: highly melodic. Andante e grazioso: strong Italian operatic influence although this work was probably written before J. C. Bach left for his sojourn in Italy. Allegro: vigorous unisons in dotted rhythms; C. P. E. Bach influence. Int. to M-D.
See: Terry, 298.

Concerto A 1771? (Schott 2320). Cadenzas by Li Stadelmann.
See: Terry, 297.

Concerto A (Hoffmann—Möseler 1963) 40pp. No.12 of the concertos in MS. Includes realized figured bass.
See: Terry, 300.

Concerto E (Riemann—Steingräber 106) 36pp. No.13 of the Ms concertos. Un poco Allegro; Adagio; Allegro. More advanced than the Berlin concertos. Shows Bach under the influence of Martini and Italian models. M-D.

See: Jane Bolen, "The Five Berlin Cembalo Concertos, P.390, of John Christian Bach: A Critical Edition," diss., Florida State University, 1974.

Johann Christoph Friedrich Bach (1732–1795) Germany
J. C. F. Bach was a famous performer of J. S. Bach's music, but his own reputation as a composer was over shadowed by that of his brother C. P. E. Bach. J. C. F. Bach was primarily a lyrical composer and was at his best in simple, sincere melodies.

Concerto E (Möseler 1966). For keyboard and strings. 36pp. Fluent, expressive but not flamboyant, touched lightly with *empfindsamkeit,* that peculiarly introspective touchstone of German Romanticism. More interpretative than technical problems. Int. to M-D.

Concerto E♭ (E. Seiler—Bo&Bo 1966). For piano, viola obbligato, and orchestra. 25 min. Arranged for two pianos and viola. A long first movement (14 min.) leaves behind Baroque mannerisms and uses a large amount of Alberti bass.

Ideas not always well developed; style somewhat similar to that of younger brother Johann Christian Bach. M-D.

Johann Sebastian Bach (1685–1750) Germany

In Bach's keyboard concertos the relationship between soloist and orchestra is not clearly defined. In some movements the solo part is in close union with the orchestra as part of the contrapuntal texture; in other movements the orchestra is silent throughout. The concerto-grosso idea is still very much a part of Bach. In some movements there are places that might be embellished and filled out, but the inexperienced player must not get carried away, but should always try to add ornaments in *bon goût* ("good taste").

Bach did not compose any original keyboard concertos, unless we designate the *Brandenburg* No.5 as a harpsichord concerto. All his solo keyboard concertos are transcriptions for harpsichord of his own or other composers' violin concertos. He used them for convivial music making at the Collegium Musicum, which he directed for a while (in Leipzig) in his spare time. Bach exercised considerable freedom with the originals, quite often changing the parts around, altering the basses, and even recomposing some of the melodies. They offer a unique opportunity to study Bach's incomparable art as a transcriber and arranger.

Concerto d S.1052 (CFP; Br&H; Schott; GS; Eulenburg; WH; Lea; CF) 23 min. Composed between 1730 and 1731. Allegro; Adagio; Allegro. The outside movements present challenges with respect to balance. The noble Adagio is similar in expressive content to the middle movement of the *Italian Concerto*. M-D.

Concerto E S.1053 (Sikorski; Br&H; CFP; WH; Lea; Fl; USSR) 18 min. Composed before 1731. Allegro; Sicilano; Allegro.

Concerto D S.1054 (CFP; Br&H; Lea; CF: Fl) 27 min. Composed between 1729 and 1736. [No tempo or character indication]; Adagio e sempre piano; Allegro.

Concerto A S.1055 (CFP; Br&H; K; Lea; CF; WH) 16 min. Composed between 1729 and 1736. Allegro: strong first movement with musical interest tossed between strings and keyboard. Larghetto: has beautiful flowing keyboard solo. Allegro ma non tanto: florid figuration demands a moderate tempo, so less-brilliant effects than usual are obtained. M-D.

Concerto f S.1056 (CFP; Br&H; K; Schott; Lea; CF; IMC; Heugel; Eulenburg; SZ; Schott Frères; WH) 12 min. Composed ca.1730. On a smaller scale than S.1052. [No tempo indication]: echo effects. Largo: expressive; more familiar in its simpler version. Presto: a lively finale. M-D.

Concerto F S.1057 (Br&H; Möseler; Fl) 15 min. Transcribed after 1729. A transcription of the *Brandenburg Concerto* No.4, composed between 1717 and 1721. [No tempo indication]; Andante; Allegro assai.

Concerto g S.1058 (Br&H; IMC; CF) 12 min. [No tempo indication]; Andante; Allegro assai. A transcription of *Concerto* a, S.1041, for violin, composed between 1717 and 1723. Transcribed between 1729 and 1736.

Concerto d S.1059 (Möseler). For keyboard, oboe, and strings. Composed around 1730. Reconstructed from S.35.

Concerto c S.1060 (CFP; Br&H; K; Eulenburg; IMC; CF; GS; Fl) for two keyboard instruments and orchestra. Composed between 1729 and 1736. Allegro; Adagio; Allegro. The strings have more importance here than in S.1061. M-D.

Concerto C S.1061 (CFP; Br&H; IMC; Augener; CF; GS; Fl). For two keyboard instruments and orchestra. 20 min. Composed between 1727 and 1730. [No tempo indication]; Adagio ovvero largo; Fuga. The strings are relegated to a minor role and are not used in the middle movement. The Finale is an exhilarating fugue. M-D.

Concerto c S.1062 (Br&H; CFP). For two keyboard instruments and orchestra. Composed between 1729 and 1736. 14 min. [No tempo indication]; Andante; Allegro assai.

Concerto d S.1063 (Br&H; CFP; Eulenburg; K; Fl). For three keyboard instruments and orchestra. Composed between 1730 and 1733. 15 min. Allegro: ritornello, rondo; first piano is more brilliant and prominent than the others. Alla siciliano: opens with the three pianos in unison; then the first piano continues with a flowing figuration, dominated by its main theme. Allegro: light-hearted. M-D.

Concerto C S.1064 (Br&H: CFP; Eulenburg; K; Lea; CF; Fl). For three keyboard instruments and orchestra. Composed between 1730 and 1733 for performance by J. S., W. F., and C. P. E. Bach. Bach apparently adapted this work from a concerto for three violins, now lost, which may not have been his own. It is weightier than S.1063 and has a more elaborate slow movement. Both require much rehearsal to resolve the ensemble problems. M-D.

Concerto a S.1065 (Br&H; Eulenburg; K; Fl). For four keyboard instruments and orchestra. 11 min. After *Concerto* b for four violins by Vivaldi, published ca.1712. This is the grandest and most exciting of all J. S. Bach's Vivaldi transcriptions. Allegro: main theme is heard several times interspersed with episodes for the soloist. Largo: Bach wrote out in full what Vivaldi had only suggested in Baroque musical shorthand, especially in the arpeggio passages in the middle section. Allegro: gigue rhythm; Bach filled in Vivaldi's harmonies and achieved the richest possible effect. M-D.

All the multiple keyboard concertos require ensemble experience, careful balance of sonority, and strict performance discipline.

Concerto a S.1044 (Br&H; CFP; Eulenburg; CF). For keyboard, violin, and flute, accompanied by strings and flute. This is not a true triple concerto but a sort of companion piece to the *Brandenburg Concerto* No. 5. Its origin goes back to a keyboard Prelude and Fugue a S.894 (a 1725 Ms.). It is an austere work filled with intricate writing and a monolithic webb of triplets. The middle movement was taken from the *Sonata* No.3 d S.527, for organ. Allegro: highly pianistic; continuous brilliant passagework and arpeggi. Adagio ma non tanto e dolce: allotted entirely to the three soloists; equal treatment of the three melodic parts, at times in strict canon, question and answer. Alla breve: fugal relationship in the strong rhythmic motion of thematic material; broad melodic outlines; piano explores lower register (bar 85 onward); free cadenza introduced near the end of the movement is left to the imagination of the pianist, with only the transition to the final tutti written out. The technical difficulties of the outer movements make us marvel at the extraordinary command of the keyboard Bach must have possessed. M-D.

Brandenburg Concerto No. 5 D S.1050 (Br; Eulenburg; CFP; Ph; Lea). For keyboard, flute, violin, and orchestra. Allegro; Affettuoso; Allegro. Could be considered Bach's first original harpsichord concerto. The three concertino instruments, keyboard, solo violin, and transverse flute, do not function as a group, and generally the keyboard predominates. Bravura writing including chain trills and a 65-bar cadenza in the first movement. A unique work. M-D to D.

Works for Three and Four Harpsichords (R. Eller, K. Heller—Br 5045). New complete edition, Series VII, vol.6. Includes S.1063, 1064, 1065.

Seven Concerti for One to Four Pianos (Eulenburg M224).

Sixteen Concerti for Harpsichord (after Vivaldi and others) (Lea 69). This is the old Bach-Gesellschaft edition.

P. D. Q. Bach (1807–1742)? Germany

Concerto for Piano versus Orchestra (TP) 25 min. This work sets music back several hundred years. It is very funny, even for people who like music but don't know why. Requires an outgoing sense of humor. Int. to M-D.

Wilhelm Friedemann Bach (1710–1784) Germany

W. F. Bach's keyboard concertos were of great importance for the further development of this form. Friedemann continued the line laid down by his father, J. S. Bach, in his solo concertos: he gradually changed the traditional merging of solo and tutti into a separation of the two groups but without leaving the keyboard part unaccompanied for long stretches. The orchestral part is longer, is worked out more in detail, and has more separately developed sections of its own than was usual in the old concerto style. The F. numbers refer to the thematic index by Martin Falck, *W. F. Bach* (Leipzig: Kahnt, 1913).

Concerto D. F.41 (Riemann-Steingräber 1893; NYPL) 27pp. Allegro: effective even if a little fussy at times. Andante: b; strikingly beautiful. Presto: in 3/8; cheerful. Int. to M-D.

Concerto e F.43 (Upmeyer—Vieweg; Riemann—Steingräber; K). Composed between 1733 and 1747. Allegretto; Adagio; Allegro.

Concerto F F.44 (Riemann—Steingräber 148 1893). Allegro ma non troppo; Adagio molto; Presto. Combines tutti and solo parts, especially from the third solo entrance on (in the first movement). The breathlessly urging sequences in the middle movement (in f) betray the sentiment of this pre-Classic period. M-D.

Concerto a F.45 (K; Riemann—Steingräber). Three movements (FSF). Contains many tensions and a strong emotional quality, enhanced by chromaticism and the sharp give and take between soloist and orchestra. First movement contains hand-crossings. A lovely pastoral middle movement is followed by an excited Allegro with phrases of nagging despondency. M-D.

Concerto E♭ F.46 (Schwartz—Steingräber). For two pianos and orchestra. Splendid writing throughout. The solo theme of the first movement, with its suspensions, already has an early Classical sound. The second movement is a lovely Andante cantabile duet during which the orchestra is silent. Influence from Mannheim and the opera buffa show the latest advance in style. Int. to M-D.

Concerto f (Smigelski—Sikorski 486) 17 min. Allegro di molto; Andante; Prestissimo. Has been erroneously attributed to C. P. E. Bach.

Concerto c (Eickemeyer—Schott 2165). Probably by Kirnberger.

Henk Badings (1907–   ) The Netherlands
Badings's style has been referred to as Romantic modernism. It is oriented toward the Brahms–Reger–Hindemith tradition.

Atlantische Dansen 1955 (Donemus) 12 min. Ragtime; Blues; Tango. Clever; character of each dance is effectively captured. M-D.

Concertino (Triple Concerto) 1942 (Henmar). For piano, violin, cello, and chamber orchestra. 20 min.

Concerto I 1939 (Donemus) 30 min. Heavy; dark instrumentation; broadly contoured melodic lines. M-D.

Concerto for Two Pianos and Orchestra 1964 (Donemus) 24 min.

Zakir Bagirov (1916–   ) USSR
Concerto (USSR).

Edgar Leslie Bainton (1880–1956) England, born Australia
Concerto-Fantasia (S&B 1922; Fl) 45pp. Quasi cadenza, lento poi accel.; Scherzo; Improvisation. Romantic gestures throughout. M-D.

Tadeusz Baird (1928–   ) Poland
"Until the late 1950's Baird's music followed in the late-Romantic tradition, and the penchant for lyricism then evident has continued to be present. He began using 12-tone procedures about 1956" (DCM, 50).

Koncert 1949 (PWM) 18 min. Poco allegro; Adagio non troppo ma molto tranquillo, cantabile e espressive (In modo d'una canzona rustica); Allegro (Alla danza). Freely tonal; tertian sonorities; lacking in pianistic expertise at places. M-D.

Leonardo Balada (1933–   ) Spain, living in USA
Concerto I 1964 (Gen) 21 min. Moderato; Lento: cadenza; Brillante e con fuoco. Twelve-tone influence, pointillistic, expressionistic. Thin textures, much imitation (especially in the Moderato), flexible meters. Colorful subtle sonor-

ities in Lento sections. Percussive quality of piano exploited in finale until
Lento section returns. *Pp* conclusion. M-D.
Concerto for Piano and Band (GS 1980).

Mili Balakirev (1837–1910) Russia
Balakirev was the guiding spirit behind the Russian group known as "The Five."
He was a competent pianist but could never perform his own *Islamey.*
Concerto F♯ Op. 1 "Youth" 1855 (USSR) 41pp. An extended movement (only
    this movement was ever finished) that owes much to Mozart, Beethoven,
    Chopin, Hummel, and Schumann. Not great music but well worth sampling.
    M-D.
Concerto E♭ (Zimmermann—USSR) 31½ min. In vol. 3, book 2 of Complete
    Piano Works. Begun in 1861 but set aside until 1909, when two move-
    ments were completed. The finale was put together after Balakirev's death
    by Liapunov and published in 1911. A large, assertive work in the
    Romantic–nationalist tradition. Masterful piano writing. The first movement
    is excellently scored for the orchestra. Three giant symphonic movements:
    Allegro non troppo; Adagio; Allegro risoluto. D.
    See: Edward Garden, "Three Russian Piano Concertos," *M&L* 60 (April
    1979); 166–79.

Andrei M. Balanchivadze (1906–   ) USSR
Concerto I c (Soviet Composer 1977) 88pp. Tonal, overly dramatic. M-D.
Concerto II C (USSR 1955) 84pp. Allegro moderato; Adagio; Allegro ma non
    troppo. Materials overextended. M-D.
Concerto III a (USSR 1959) 58pp. Allegro; Andante; Allegro vivo. Similar to
    Kabalevsky's style in the 1950s. Thinner textures than in *Concertos* I and II.
    M-D.
Concerto IV (Soviet Composer 1974). Lento; Andante mosso; Andante; Toccata;
    Lento; Theme and Variations. Broadly conceived, freely tonal. D.

Esther Ballou (1915–1973) USA
Concerto 1964 (ACA) 32 min. Maestoso—Allegro moderato: octotonic, cadenza.
    Scherzo: staccatissimo figuration divided between the hands; waltz serves as
    trio. Molto lento: short cadenzas, expressive lines. Allegro ritmico: broad
    dramatic gestures, fast octaves, cadenza; dashing coda concludes with a
    black key glissando. M-D to D.
Prelude and Allegro 1951 (ACA) 7 min. Diatonic style with touches of dissonance.
    Piano enters at mid-point in the Prelude with a chordal melody. Brief ca-
    denza-like passage leads to the Allegro, which is more angular and in a
    spirited, light-hearted mood. Material from the opening movement is re-
    stated at the end of the Allegro, with the piano ornamenting the texture with
    trills and octaves. M-D.

Aleksandr A. Baltin (1931–   ) USSR
Concerto-Ballade 1959 (USSR 1965) 51pp. One movement with contrasting

sections. Freely tonal; uses key signatures. Post-Brahmsian pianistic idiom, highly expressive and emotional style. Piano and orchestra treated equally. M-D.

Gennadii Ivanovich Banchchikov (1943–   ) USSR
Banchchikov's development has been influenced by German music, mainly that of Richard Strauss and Arnold Schoenberg. He has written many scores for radio and television.
Concerto 1963 (USSR).

Alain Bancquart (1934–   ) France
La Naissance du Geste (Jobert 1964). For piano and strings. 15½ min. Tres doux, hesitant; Vite et fluide. Cadenza passages; fughetto in first movement. Expressionistic; coloristic writing throughout. Requires careful attention to subtle pianissimos. M-D.

Jacques Bank (1943–   ) The Netherlands
Alexandre's Concerto 1978 (Donemus). For piano, winds, and percussion. 25 min. Photostat of composer's Ms.

George Barati (1913–   ) USA, born Hungary
Barati's music has been influenced by his contacts with Bartók and Kodály at the Liszt Conservatory in Budapest, and by performing in many orchestras under many distinguished conductors.
Concerto 1973 (ACA) 23 min. Andante; Vivace e vigoroso. Freely tonal; good balance, proportion, and design. Emotion coupled with intellect and excitement with precision. M-D.

Samuel Barber (1910–1981) USA
Barber is in what is regarded as the mainstream of musical tradition. He is a superb craftsman with a fine sense of musical form and logic combined with highly developed lyricism. His expressive, highly emotional, and accessible writing has made him a great favorite with audiences.
Concerto Op.38 1962 (GS) 26 min. Harold Schonberg said of this work, "It may be that Mr. Barber has supplied a repertory piece" (*New York Times,* September 25, 1962). It has held up well with performances since it was introduced. Allegro appassionato: opens with a recitative section for solo piano, followed by an exposition section and extensive development; brilliant cadenza preceeds the recapitulation. Canzona: melodic material presented first by the flute, then by the solo piano, and finally by muted strings. Allegro molto: brilliant toccata-like finale in 5/8; uses an ostinato figure in the piano as a background for various themes; also has two interspersed contrasting sections. The work is difficult but extremely effective for the pianist. Barber continues the pianistic tradition of Liszt, Rachmaninoff, and Prokofiev while adding his own sophisticated insights. A twentieth-century masterpiece displaying a highly idiomatic, virtuoso, flamboyant style and some of the most elaborate keyboard textures of the century. D.

René Barbier (1890–   ) Belgium
Barbier's Romantic style is based on Classical tradition. His works display solid construction and dramatic development, and his orchestral pallette is sumptuous.
Concertino I Op.28 1922 (Elkan) 30 min.
Concerto II Op.43 1934 (Elkan) 40 min.

Milton Barnes (1931–   ) Canada
Classical Concerto 1973 (CMC) 23½ min. Introduction—Fantasy: cadenza-like, arpeggi figures, repeated chords. Andante cantabile, molto sostenuto: melodic; cadenza passage leads attacca to Rondo: much imitation, freely tonal. Built on extension of nineteenth-century pianism. M-D.

Henri Barraud (1900–   ) France
Barraud's "musical style has been influenced by wide-ranging interests including Gregorian chant, Notre Dame organa, Josquin des Prez, Monteverdi, and such contemporary composers as Debussy, Stravinsky, Schoenberg, and Webern" (DCM, 55).
Concerto 1939 (Bo&H).
Concerto 1947 (Costallat) 20½ min. Allegro; Andante; Finale. Expanded tonal idiom around d, octotonic. Well constructed if a little short on inspiration. MC. M-D.
Concertino 1956 (EMT). For piano and winds. 58pp.

Hans Barth (1897–1956) USA
In 1928 Barth built a portable quarter-tone piano for which he composed a number of works, including the two concertos listed below.
Concerto Op.11 1928 (Fl) 19 min.
Concerto 1930 (Fl) 9 min.

Béla Bartók (1881–1945) Hungary
Bartók is one of the half-dozen major composers of this century. He was a marvelous pianist, gave first performances of many of his works, and wrote several pieces for piano and orchestra expressly for his own use. His early works are derivative of both Debussy and Richard Strauss, but in late 1904 Bartók began to explore Hungarian folk music with his friend Zoltán Kodály. This music with its austerity of line, cruder and harder texture, exotic modal character, and irregular rhythms altered his whole compositional approach. Through assimilation with this material his melodies became declamatory; his tonalities were free, with extensive use of modal harmonies; and his rhythms turned complex and often savage. His concertos are a summation of the Classical concerto inherited from Mozart, Schumann, and Brahms.
Rhapsody Op.1 1904 (EMB 1955) 17 min. This work was first written for solo piano, but Bartók rewrote it for piano and orchestra to use during his Paris visit of 1905, when he competed (unsuccessfully) for the Rubinstein Prize. It is a virtuoso work in the Liszt tradition and abounds with complex exploitations of the keyboard. Structurally it is related to Liszt's *Rhapsodies*,

with an opening lassú followed by the friss. The themes are based on gypsy modifications of Hungarian tunes, and the two sections share organically related thematic material. While the harmonic treatment is still traditional and traceable to Liszt and Strauss, abrupt harmonic changes and unexpected modulations give the piece a fresh sound. The piano carries the musical burden throughout, while the orchestra acts primarily as a foil and accompanist. The work should be heard more frequently. It is about as difficult as the more demanding Liszt *Rhapsodies.* M-D to D.

Scherzo Op.2 1904–1905 (EMB) 29 min. First called *Burlesque,* this work was probably written under the influence of Strauss's composition of the same name. After a long introductory Adagio ma non troppo, the main Allegro begins, followed by a development and a recapitulation. A lyrical Andante forms the trio, followed by a transformation of the opening material. The whole work is in a distinct burlesque spirit, contains unusual rhythmic configurations, and is roughly equivalent in difficulty to the *Rhapsody* Op.1. The role of the piano is virtuosic, but it does not dominate in the manner of a concerto. M-D to D.

Concerto I e 1926 (Bo&H; Ph) 23 min. The first of Bartók's works for piano and orchestra that was written with full creative maturity. It is the least accessible of the concertos, having an idiom similar to that of the *Piano Sonata* of the same year. Tone clusters; percussive treatment of the piano; fragmentary treatment of thematic material; frequent use of minor seconds, minor ninths, and major sevenths; and relatively few contrapuntal intricacies are characteristic of the writing. Allegro moderato: linear texture; strong rhythmic propulsion; corresponds to the Classical SA; has unusually awkward leaps and clusters of notes over wide stretches. Andante: long duet for piano and percussion seems to be a forerunner of the *Sonata for Two Pianos and Percussion.* Allegro: the theme is more easily recognized by its rhythmic pattern than by its melody. This work is by no means accessible or "pleasant" but has enormous vitality and sharpness coupled with formidable performance problems. D.

Concerto II 1931 (Bo&H; Ph) 25 min. Like other keyboard works of the period, this concerto displays the characteristic percussive treatment of the piano and barbaric rhythmic tension. It exhibits an arching, variation-like structure, as is found in *String Quartets* Nos.4 and 5, with material from the first movement recurring in the finale. In the outer movements the piano is constantly active in an almost Bach-like way. Allegro: in SA design with a traditional cadenza near the end; great thematic economy; much more use of contrapuntal textures than is employed in *Concerto* I. Adagio–Presto–Adagio: ternary in structure, having slow chorale-like sections framing a breathlessly driven Presto of more than 200 bars; its mood is another of Bartók's evocations of "night music." Allegro molto: a seven-part rondo with most of the thematic material related to the first movement, but in a new rhythmic transformation. This work is enormously demanding, both musically and physically; yet it has grown rapidly in popularity over the last 25 years, especially among younger pianists. D.

Concerto III 1945 (Bo&H) 23 min. This essentially serene work is one of Bartók's most expressive compositions. It shows a marked trend toward both structural lucidity and tonal clarity. The strong martellato texture of *Concerto* I and the savage rhythmic vitality of *Concerto* II are entirely absent. Allegretto: in SA design; centers around E. Adagio religioso: contains the first use by Bartók of the word *religioso,* to indicate the character of the opening theme; in ternary form, with a "night music" trio based on birdcalls Bartók had taken down in Asheville, N.C., in 1944; begins in C, but shifts to an E tonal level immediately before the finale. Allegro vivace: a lively scherzo with a fugato section serving as a trio. Although this concerto was written shortly before the end of Bartók's life (some of it literally on the composer's deathbed—the final 17 bars remaining to be fully scored), there is no lessening of the composer's contrapuntal skill, as evidenced by the inversions, strettos, canons, and other devices. If the concerto seems weaker than its predecessors, it is only because of its great refinement of idiom. M-D.

Concerto for Two Pianos, Percussion and Orchestra 1940 (Bo&H) 25 min. Soon after arriving in the United States in 1940, Bartók arranged the *Sonata for Two Pianos and Percussion* into a concerto with orchestra, for use in concerts with his wife. The piano and percussion parts are practically unchanged from the earlier version; the orchestra adds color rather than new thematic material. The work is enhanced considerably by the orchestral arrangement. A conventional instrumentation of woodwinds, brass, and strings is used.

See: Maurice Hinson, *The Piano in Chamber Ensemble* (Bloomington: Indiana University Press, 1979), p. 451, for a fuller discussion of this work.

See: Jack Edwin Guerry, "Bartók's Concertos for Solo Piano: A Stylistic and Formal Analysis," Ph.D. diss., Michigan State University, 1964, 216pp.

Colin Mason, "Bartók and the Piano Concerto," *The Listener,* 65 (September 10, 1959): 412.

John Alfred Meyer, "The Piano Concerto of Bartók," MA thesis, University of Western Australia, 1968.

―――. "Beethoven and Bartók, a Structural Parallel," *MR,* 31 (1970): 315–21.

Leslie Bassett (1923–   ) USA

Bassett's style is based on textural sounds and colors that help to convey a specific mood. The composer uses various kinds of tones and groupings of instruments to achieve his methods of counterpoint.

Forces 1972 (CF). For solo piano, cello, violin, and orchestra. 12 min. Uses some unmetered measures with approximate duration indicated in seconds or by contents. Freely tonal figuration in piano; harmonics; clusters. First movement: quarter note = 138. Second movement: quarter note = 66. M-D.

Concerto for Two Pianos and Orchestra 1976 (CFP) 15 min. Three movements. "The pianos should be placed to the left and right of the conductor, separated by at least ten feet, with the lids removed for balance of sound" (from the score). Strings and percussion are used to take full advantage of the stereophonic, coloristic, and dialogistic possibilities of the ensemble. The opening ing runs in the upper register of the pianos, which are taken up later by the strings, have a particularly haunting quality. Marcato chords in one piano, figurative decoration in the other, harmonics, stopped strings, flexible meters, tremolo chords in alternating hands. Brooding and intense dialogue at one point, then very lyrical; nervous syncopations. M-D.

Stanley Bate (1911–1959) Great Britain
Bate's works reveal the direct influence of his teacher Hindemith and of Vaughan Williams.
Concerto II Op.28 (Lengnick 3734 1952) 80pp. Allegro di bravura; Andante affettuoso; Rapide–Andante maestoso–Allegro vivace. Expanded tonality around C, octotonic, pianistic, glissandi, dramatic gestures with full chords moving over keyboard. M-D.
Concerto III Op.61 1952 (TP).

Marion Bauer (1887–1955) USA
American Youth Concerto Op. 36 (GS 1946; USSR 1969) 14 min. Majestic; Dignified, yet lyric; Humorous. Freely tonal, clever, thin textures, not easy, MC. Int. to M-D.

Jürg Baur (1918–   ) Germany
Baur's early compositional development was influenced by Reger, Hindemith, and Bartók. "Subsequently he was drawn to Schönberg's 12-tone technique and around 1960 to serialism" (DCM, 60). Since 1956 he has headed the Schumann Conservatory in Düsseldorf.
Konzertante Musik 1958 (Br&H 6317) 22 min. Improvisation: atmospheric, fragmented, prelude-like; atonal and sonorous piano writing. Scherzo: arch form, scalar percussive activity, cross-accents. Variationen: 24-bar theme and 8 variations; piano part stands out in each variation. Rhapsodie: sectional, dramatic octaves, contrasting 5/8 section, cadenza, opening material from the Improvisation returns, ostinato figures, impressive coda. M-D to D.

Arnold Bax (1883–1953) Great Britain
Influences from Celtic folklore and the great Irish poets, with this literature's love of mystery, symbolism, and fantasy, are to be found in much of the music of Bax. He has a highly individual feeling for melody combined with elements of Impressionism and an unusual chromatic harmony. Bax's output for piano is large and exhibits great facility in the writing.
Symphonic Variations 1916 (Chappell) 33 min. The theme is initially given in the orchestra, then following a piano cadenza accompanied by strings, five var-

iations are heard. Each variation has a title, to give the listener a clue as to its emotional content: Nocturne, Strife, The Temple, Play, and Triumph. The work closes with a restatement of the opening theme given in the full orchestra. M-D.

Morning Song ("Maytime in Sussex") (Chappell 1946) 7½ min. Modal, colorful, Impressionistic. M-D.

Concertante 1950 (Chappell). For piano, left-hand and orchestra. 24 min. Three movements, Classical idiom, economically designed in its harmonic and contrapuntal techniques. Initially the work was called a *Concerto,* but in view of the slenderness of the piano part limited to the left hand, its designation was changed to *Concertante.* M-D.

See: B. James, "Arnold Bax and the Concerto," *Arnold Bax Society Bulletin* 2 (1970): 4–6.

Friedrich Bayer (1902–   ) Germany
Concerto b 1935 (Lienau) 51pp. Allegro moderato; Andantino; Presto; Finale—Schnell. Late-Romantic style, pianistic. M-D.

Mrs. H. H. A. Beach (1867–1944) USA
Amy Beach is finally being recognized as one of the finest American composers.
Concerto c♯ Op.45 1899 (Schmidt 1900; Fl) 35 min. This large-scale, impressive virtuoso vehicle in the Romantic idiom contains some compelling moments. Liszt and Brahms influences. Allegro moderato: SA, by far the largest movement; works over a broad, melodic theme, somewhat reminiscent of the finale of Dvořák's *New World* Symphony; big cadenza. Scherzo: ABA, perpetual motion, subtle syncopation in piano over muted strings, continual 16ths in piano part. Largo: monothematic, tripartite, broad, melodic, introduction to the Finale: five-part rondo, dancelike, 6/8 and bolero rhythms, big cadenza, interrupted before the close by a recurrence of the Largo. Demands virtuoso technique and great endurance. D.

See: Dean Elder, "Where Was Amy Beach All These Years?" *Clavier* 15 (December 1976):14–17.

Gustavo Becerra Schmidt (1925–   ) Chile
Becerra Schmidt is Cultural Attaché of the Embassy of Chile in Bonn, West Germany.
Concerto 1958 (IEM; IU) full score, 156 pp. Allegro: chromatic clusters in alternating hands, fast-moving figuration between hands, syncopated chords, complete range exploited, many mirror inversions. Second movement [untitled], quarter note = 80: flowing chromatic thin lines evolve into moving chromatic chords; lyrical. Presto furioso: 5/8, two large sections, chromatic gestures with syncopated octaves, rhythmic patterns divided between piano and orchestra; builds to exciting climax. The sonorities and techniques of the piano are well integrated with the orchestra. M-D to D.

Conrad Beck (1901–   ) Switzerland

Concertino in Three Movements 1927 (Schott 2068) 18 min. Allegro vivace; Lento; Allegro energico. Excellent craft displayed in the tonal and dissonant linear voice leading. Anti-virtuosic, in the spirit of Hindemith. Requires fine imagination, good musicianship, and excellent finger velocity. M-D.

Concerto 1933 (Schott 3276) 33 min. Largo; Andante sostenuto; Allegro scherzando. Highly chromatic, constant movement, turgid harmonies. Large span required. M-D to D.

John J. Becker (1886–1961) USA

Becker developed a personal harmonic style and was quite adventurous as a composer for his time.

Concerto Arabesque 1930 (New Music; AMC) 15 min. A one-movement work divided into sections by tempo changes and cadenza passages. Rich harmonic pallette with a preferance for major sevenths and nineths. Imitative techniques used considerably. M-D.

Satirico (Second Concerto) 1938 (ACA) 20 min. Utilizes material from *Mockery* for piano and band.

Soundpiece I 1935 (ACA) 12 min. Identical with *Soundpiece* IA, for piano and string quintet, but uses multiple strings.

Dance Masque (ACA) 15 min.

Concerto (ACA). For piano, violin, and orchestra. 15 min.

See: Don Chance Gillespie, "John Becker: Midwestern Musical Crusader," Ph.D. diss., University of North Carolina, 1977.

John Beckwith (1927–   ) Canada

Beckwith leans toward the French neoclassic school with strong influences from Virgil Thomson and Aaron Copland.

Concerto–Fantasy 1958 (BMI) 23 min. Slow to Allegro: rhythmical. Fairly slow: expressive; in variation form; includes a fugue; cleverly merges piano and celesta. Fast: animated style with rondo dimensions; exciting and effective; contains serial passages based on free, nonchromatic rows. Contains some unusual sonorities. M-D.

Thomas Beecham (1879–1961) Great Britain

Concerto A (Belwin-Mills 1947). 22 min. Based on themes by Handel. Four movements.

Ludwig van Beethoven (1770–1827) Germany

The piano concertos of Beethoven are landmarks in the literature. The Neue Beethoven Ausgabe ("New Beethoven Edition") (Henle) has not yet issued these works. Until this series completes this section or some other publisher provides an outstanding edition, we have usable scores, but are sadly lacking in scholarly perspective. Only the *"Triple" Concerto* Op.56 (Br 4072) and the piano cadenzas (Br 4291) are presently (1979) in the New Beethoven Edition.

CADENZAS:

Beethoven's cadenzas were composed around 1808 in the more mature style of his "middle period."

Original Cadenzas to Concertos I–V (Br 4291; Br&H; K3195; F. Busoni—Heinrichshofen N4005). For Concertos I—IV (Dob).

"New Cadenzas" for Concertos I–IV (Kempff—Bo&Bo; A. Rubinstein—Schott).

Concerto I C Op.15 (Moscheles—Durand; Ganz—CF; Casadesus—EV; Gould—Banger & Barclay). The Gould cadenza to the first movement was reprinted in *Contemporary Keyboard* 6 (August 1980):30–32.

Concerto II B♭ Op. 19 (Moscheles—Durand; Tagliapietra—Hin).

Concerto III c Op.37 (Dreyschock—Musica Obscura; Liszt—Musica Obscura; Stojowski—Heugel; Moscheles—Durand; R. Slenczynska—GS; Tovey—OUP; C. Schumann—CFP; Backhaus—Heinrichshofen; Medtner—USSR; Alkan—Costallat: Alkan transcribed the entire first movement for solo piano and wrote a cadenza that is almost as long as the entire first movement).

Concerto IV G Op.58 (Bülow—Musica Obscura; C. Schumann—CFP; Moscheles—Durand; Godowsky—Schlesinger).

Concerto V E♭ Op.73 (Brahms, in complete edition, Br&H; Backhaus—Heinrichshofen; d'Albert—Br&H; Moscheles—Durand).

CONCERTOS:

Concerto I C Op.15 1798 (Ruthardt—CFP; F. Kullak—GS; d'Albert—Br&H; Pauer—CFP; Philipp—Durand; Tagliapietra—Ric; K; Dunhill, Carse—Augener; Eulenburg; Lebert—Cotta'sche; CF; Zen-On). Allegro con brio; Largo; Rondo—Allegro. Requires a reading full of fire and pomp. Although an early work, it is characteristically robust, rambunctious, and wonderfully original—an impressive achievement, longer and more positive than its predecessor, Op.19. The first of the three cadenzas to the first movement is surely the finest. M-D.

Concerto II B♭ Op.19 1795 (Kullak—GS; Thern—UE; Ruthardt—CFP; d'Albert—Br&H; K; Philipp—Durand; Eulenburg; Lebert—Cotta'sche; Dunhill, Carse—Augener). Allegro con brio; Adagio; Rondo—Molto allegro. Because this work was not published until 1801, it acquired a misleading number and opus number. This is the earliest and shortest of Beethoven's standard five but it is far from the weakest in its motivic workmanship. It is the most Haydnesque of the five. The orchestral exposition in the opening movement is one of the finest Beethoven ever composed. This concerto is amazingly zippy and unpretentious. Int. to M-D.

Concerto III c Op.37 1800 (F. Kullak—GS; Liszt—Cotta'sche; d'Albert—Br&H; Levitzki—GS 1929; Eulenburg; Pauer—CFP; Billaudot; Tagliapietra—Ric; Panseron—Jobert; Ruthardt—CFP; Philipp—Durand; CF; Zen-On; K). Allegro con brio; Largo; Rondo—Allegro. Displays a richer tonal texture and has more commanding gestures than do Nos.I and II. Beethoven's cadenza for the first movement is dry and perfunctory. See the long list of composers who have composed a cadenza for this movement. Technical demands are greater here than in Concertos I and II. The slow movement, in the surprising key of E, is one of the most beautiful Beethoven ever composed. The rondo finale is commanding and vivacious in the grand manner. M-D.

Concerto IV G Op.58 1805–6 (Kullak—GS; Br&H; Liszt—Cotta'sche; Eulenburg; Ph; Pauer—CFP; Philipp—Durand; Tagliapietra—Ric; Ruthardt—CFP; K; Thern—UE; d'Albert—Br&H; Zen-On). Allegro moderato: of symphonic proportions; in a break with tradition, the piano opens the work. Andante con moto: one of the high points in all of Beethoven's music. Rondo—Vivace: lively first subject and dreamy second. The most inward and subtle of the "five" and also the most demanding technically. In essence, the tender, spacious, subtle detail here is often more difficult to realize than the more outspoken magisterial generalities of No. V. A gentle feeling dominates the entire work. D.

See: Paul Rutman, "An Examination of Cadenzas to Beethoven's *Piano Concerto No. 4 in G Major,* Op.58, with an Original Cadenza (original composition)," DMA diss., The Juilliard School, 1974.

Concerto V E♭ Op.73 1809 (Kullak—GS; Liszt—Cotta'sche; Pauer—CFP; d'Albert—Br&H; K; Ruthardt—CFP; Durand; Thern—UE; Tagliapietra—Ric; CF; Dunhill, Carse—Augener; Eulenburg; Zen-On). This work sounds more difficult to the layman than any of the concertos. The frequent juxtaposition of such remote tonalities as E♭ and B make it distant, magisterial, and aloof. No one had composed a concerto on such a grand scale before, and few have approached, let alone surpassed, these dimensions since. Allegro: bravura passages for orchestra and solo immediately establish a mood of sweeping and imperious grandeur; the orchestra sets forth the two principal themes, following which the piano assumes the leading role in the imposing drama of this movement; at the point where it is customary for the soloist to introduce a cadenza of his own writing, Beethoven directs that no cadenza be inserted and that the soloist continue with the material that follows. Adagio un poco mosso: in quasi-variation form; much of the material grows out of the theme first heard in the muted violins; at the close of the movement the solo piano whispers a new theme, a suggestion of the main theme of the third movement, and then it plunges without pause into Rondo—Allegro: a brilliant finale; uses Beethoven's cadenza as it is written into the score. M-D.

Concerto E♭ 1784 (Br; Eulenburg 1281) 28 min. Allegro moderato; Larghetto; Rondo. This work gives an unusual insight into the pianistic ability of Beethoven at age 14. He played it at the Bonn court, and it was intended to provide a vehicle for his virtuosity. Consists of many runs with figurations, broken chords, scale passages in thirds and sixths, flowing and sweeping passages. The Rondo displays a true interplay between solo and tutti. Shows influence of C. G. Neefe (Beethoven's teacher in Bonn) and J. C. Bach, for the work abounds in joyous melodies reminiscent of folk song and folk music. Because of the small orchestral requirements it can be performed in the intimate atmosphere of chamber music. M-D.

Tempo di Concerto D (Br&H 1890; CF). Composed between 1788 and 1793. The first movement of an unfinished piano concerto. Imbued with Mozartian elements (the principal theme is almost a quotation of the Finale of Sonata C K.330 of Mozart). Orchestration seems more Beethoven-like. Int. to M-D.

Rondo B♭ Op.posth.Wo06 ca. 1794–95 (Br&H, Supplemente zur Gesamtausgabe, edited by Willy Hess). Beethoven composed *Concerto* II in B♭ in 1795 and revised it three years later. That this attractive and unpretentious Rondo was the original last movement of the *Concerto* can be determined from the many thematic similarities it bears to the finale he wrote later. It contains a graceful and beautifully contrasting Andante section. Int. to M-D.

Concerto D Op.61A 1806 (W. Hess—Br&H 6565 1970) 43 min. Allegro ma non troppo; Larghetto; Rondo—Allegro. Beethoven's own piano and orchestral version of his famous *Concerto* D Op.61 for violin and orchestra, made after the suggestion of Muzio Clementi. The essential character of the work is not changed even though the left-hand parts are not equal in invention to the original violin edition. The violin part, with slight modifications, is given to the right hand. Piano cadenzas were composed specifically for this version. The cadenza for the first movement is over 130 bars, with repeats, and calls for a kettledrum obbligato. All three Beethoven cadenzas are rather wild and fully pianistic. M-D.

Concerto C Op.56 "Triple" 1804–1805 (CFP; Br; Eulenburg; CF). For piano, violin, cello, and orchestra. 36 min. A difficult work to present convincingly: it seemingly lacks much of the usual Beethoven intensity and assertiveness, and even as astute a critic as Donald Francis Tovey has suggested that it may be more important for its treatment of textures than for the kind of drama and tension thay typify most of Beethoven's music. The orchestra plays a subservient role, perhaps to a greater degree than in many of the other Beethoven concertos. Nevertheless, when it is stylishly performed, its kinship to Beethoven's other late concertos becomes evident and its nature is revealed—a distinguished example of middle-period sun-drenched Beethoveniana! M-D.

Fantasia Op.80 1808 (Br&H; CFP; Novello). For piano, chorus, and orchestra. 21 min. This work is perhaps an unconscious study for the finale of the Ninth Symphony and is a mixture of concerto and cantata. It stands as a unique record of Beethoven as an improviser, for the first part of the work is a kind of impromptu fantasia. The piano opens with an Adagio introduction and also takes up the main theme; here the influence of the "Joy" theme of the Ninth Symphony is strongly felt. There is a section with variations, by the winds, the whole orchestra, and the soloist, on an early song by Beethoven, "Gegenliebe" (Requited Love). At times the piano races up and down in tandem with soloists, choir, and orchestra. It is not an entirely successful experiment but it is full of beauties and unmistakably bears the giant's imprint. M-D.

See: Roger Fiske, *Beethoven Concertos and Overtures* (London: British Broadcasting Corp., 1970).

Ezra G. Rust, "The First Movements of Beethoven's Piano Concertos," diss., University of California, Berkeley, 1970.

O'sai Belaka (1933–   ) USA?

Concerto a (IU). For piano, drums, and orchestra. Full score, 62pp. Orchestra begins. Pianist is told to create theme; rock and chordal bass suggested. Free piano solo, right hand is to play "big" chords with indicated bass figure. Free piano cadenza to be improvised. Only four bars are notated for the piano throughout the entire work. The pianist should be a very good improviser before taking this on. Can be any difficulty the pianist wants and is able to make it.

Louis Noël Belaubre (1932–   ) France

Concerto I (Billaudot).

Concerto II (Billaudot 1972) 68pp. Proposition: five expansive and complex variations. Interrogations: rhapsodic, flexible recitatives. Dithyramb: percussive, covers complete range of keyboard, neoclassic, rondo form. Form is more inventive than the material. Virtuoso technique required. D.

Georg Antonin Benda (1722–1795) Bohemia

The historical importance of Benda lies in the fact that his compositions created a link between the late Baroque and the Viennese Classical music. He was a close friend of C. P. E. Bach, whose influence can be seen in many of Benda's keyboard works. Mozart greatly appreciated Benda.

Concerto F ca.1780 (Racek—Suprahon 1976 MAB 77). Full score 84pp. For keyboard and strings. Preface and critical note in Czech, German, and English. Allegro; Andantino quasi allegretto; Allegro assai. In its cyclical construction this work approaches the three-movement concertante symphonies, without minuet. The middle movement, with its unusually deep melodic inspiration, is one of the most important of Benda's musical expressions. M–D.

Concerto g (Kapral MAB 10; Orbis). For keyboard and strings. 48pp. Allegro non troppo; Andante; Presto. Introductory material in Czech and French.

Concerto G (Bethan—Nag 144 1939). For keyboard and strings. More archaic than the other listed concertos as regards the form of the ritornellos and the succession and distribution of themes. M–D.

Three Concerti G, f, b. ca.1770 (MAB 45). Introductory material in Czech, French, and English. All three works contain numerous examples of Mozartisms, although Benda did not know Mozart's music at the time he wrote them. *Concerto* G: Allegro moderato; Andante con moto; Allegretto scherzando. Cheerful and captivating; pianoforte is the unquestioned instrument; bears strong harmonic resemblance to some of Boccherini's cello quintets; outstanding finale. M–D. *Concerto* f: Allegro; Larghetto con sordini; Allegro di molto. Int. to M–D. *Concerto* b: Allegro; Arioso; Allegro. Int. to M-D.

Concertos f and b have affinities with C. P. E. Bach. Their sensuous slow movements combine the older idiom nicely with the new style of the 1760s and 1770s. The keyboardist must supply the cadenzas.

Paul Ben Haim (1897–   ) Israel, born Germany
Ben Haim is one of the most important composers to emerge from Israel. His interest in the folklore of Bokhara, Yemen, Persia, and other regions in the Near East have colored his writing, although his early roots reach back to the 1930s in Germany. Ben Haim is a pianist, and this affinity for the instrument is reflected in his idiomatic writing.

Concerto Op. 41 1949 (IMP) 32 min. An introductory section leads into the main Allegro con brio (Vision): SA design; rhapsodic cadenza; soft coda unexpectedly has a brilliant conclusion. Andante (Voices in the Night): evocative, poetic nocturne with a Mediterranean landscape atmosphere; joined without break to Rondo (Dance): Oriental festival finale. Effective and brilliant. M-D.

Capriccio 1960 (IMP) 12 min. The main mood of the work is indicated by the quotation from a Sephardic love song, which heads the score. The slow opening, given to the piano, contains the main thematic material expressed in a free, rhapsodic manner. The theme is given to the orchestra, and eventually both soloist and orchestra have it before a set of variations begins. The final variation is a rondo, and the theme receives a toccata-like working out. New episodes are introduced, the pace slows, and the opening mood returns before the short, fast coda. M-D.

Rhapsody 1971 (IMP) 17pp. For piano and strings.

Arthur Benjamin (1893–1960) Australia
Concertino (Schott 1304 1928) 14 min. One large movement. Contrasting sections, neoclassic. Requires large span. M-D.

Concerto Quasi una Fantasia 1949 (Bo&H 1952) 25 pp. One large movement that includes cadenzas, slow sections, a scherzo, a Passacaglia, and a coda, which returns to the opening material. The Passacaglia has nine variations with No.9 an extravagant cadenza. A powerful climax concludes the work. Displays a high degree of virtuosity with over-use of octaves. M-D to D.

Thomas Edward Benjamin (1940–   ) USA
Concert Music 1968 (AMC) "Concerto for Piano and Orchestra." 20 min.

Richard Rodney Bennett (1936–   ) Great Britain
Bennett worked with Pierre Boulez for two years and composed a number of student works in total serial style. This influence, plus the English characteristics of flowing lines and airy sophistication, are found in his piano concerto.

Piano Concerto 1968 (UE 14655) 25 min. Outstanding workmanship creates highly sensitive pianistic sonorities blended with a colorful orchestral pallette. Orchestra requires large percussion section. All four movements are derived from a tone row heard at the beginning of the work in the left-hand triads of the piano part. Moderato: ABA with suggestion of development in mid-section. Scherzo—Presto: seven-part arch plan. Lento: ABA, common materials throughout. Vivo: rondo-like; follows the Lento without a break. M-D.

Party Piece "for Young Players" (UE 15425 1971) 8½ min. For piano and chamber orchestra. Jazz-inspired rhapsody in one movement. Outer giocoso sections surround an Andante, blues-style mid-section. Suggestions for simplifying a few tricky spots are given. The whole piece is highly rhythmic, not too difficult, and effective when given an "above average" performance. M-D.

Robert Russell Bennett (1894–   ) USA
Bennett's works reveal a comprehensive grasp of musical styles, both past and present.
Concerto 1963 (Chappell). For piano, violin, and orchestra.

William Sterndale Bennett (1816–1875) Great Britain
Bennett was one of the most prominent musical figures of his age. He was praised for his compositions by both Mendelssohn and Schumann. His concertos have moments of dazzling pianism. Bennett had an unusually precocious and sophisticated musical mind.
Concerto III c Op.9 1833 (Kistner; LC) 36pp. Allegro con maesta; Romanza; Allegro agitato. Polished writing, lovely tunes, worth investigating, Schumann was very fond of the Romanza. M-D.
Concerto IV f OP.19 (Augener; Kistner) 20 min. Allegro con maesta; Barcarolle; Presto. Reveals a solid craft in the blending of tutti and solist. The Barcarolle makes a particularly favorable impression. M-D.
Capriccio E Op.22 1840–41 (Kistner) 8 min. Allegro giojoso: filagree figuration à la Mendelssohn, scherzo-like passages, long trills. Charming if a little dated. M-D.
See: Geoffrey Bush, "William Sterndale Bennett (1816–75)," M&M 23 (February 1975): 32–34 for a discussion of the piano concertos.

Peter Benoit (1834–1901) Belgium
Concerto c Op.43 "Symfonisch Gedicht" 1864 (Metropolis 1969) 39pp. Moderato–Allegretto–Allegro; Andante; Allegro molto. Symphonic poem written in a Romantic idiom with thick chromatic sonorities and lovely lyric lines. Numerous ideas; shows traces of Wagner. Pianistic and effective. M-D.

Pascal Bentoiu (1927–   ) Rumania
Bentoiu's music is a synthesis of modal, tonal, and serial idioms. It also includes jazz and tape works.
Concert Op.5 1954 (Editura Muzicală a Uniunii Compozitorilor 1960) 25 min.

Allegro moderato; Adagio; Rondo. Expanded tonal idiom around C, MC, glissandi, tremolo chords in alternating hands. Large cadenza at end of first movement. M-D to D.

Niels Viggo Bentzon (1919–   ) Denmark
The major influences in Bentzon's music have been jazz and the work of Hindemith, Schoenberg, and Bartók. Bentzon's works are distinguished by compact contrapuntalism and harmonic clarity.
The following are all published by Wilhelm Hansen.
Concerto Op.49 1948 29 min. Allegro moderato; Andante in modo di variazione; Quasi toccata—Allegro. A large, imposing work based on nineteenth-century traditions but clothed in a twentieth-century idiom with strong bitonal implications. D.
Concerto IV Op.96 1954. 34 min.
Brilliantes Concertino on Mozart's "Ein Mädchen oder Weibchen" Op.108 1956.
Symphonic Fantasy Op.119. 12 min. For two pianos and orchestra.
Rhapsody Op.131 1961. 31 min.
Concerto V Op.149 1963. 25 min.
Concerto VI Op.195. 25 min.
Concerto VII Op.243 (WH) 23 min.
Chamber Concert for Three Pianos and Eight Instruments Op.52 1948. 18 min. Instruments: clarinet, bassoon, two trumpets, double bass, and percussion. An arsenal of pianistic ensemble techniques, with the pianos occupying the central core of the work. M-D.

Nicolai Berezowsky (1900–1953) USA, born Russia
Fantasy Op.9 (AMP 1944). For two pianos and orchestra. 12 min. Freely tonal around b; contrasted sections; MC. M-D.

Alban Berg (1885–1935) Austria
Even though Berg embraced the dodecaphonic style as a pupil of Schoenberg, his art in part issues from the world of German Romanticism. This Romantic trend in his temperament makes his music the most accessible of the twelve-tone school.
Chamber Concerto (Kammerkonzert) 1923–25 (UE 8439) For piano, violin, and 13 wind instruments. 35 min. Epigraphe; Thema con variazioni; Adagio; Rondo ritmico con introduzione. Berg wrote this work as a birthday gift for his teacher, Arnold Schoenberg. It is the first of his works in a strict twelve-tone system, and it contains elements of his musical style ranging from post-Romantic lyricism to Schoenbergian expressionism. This numerological work is written with the number 3 in mind, after the trinity of the twelve-tone school, Schoenberg, Webern, and Berg. This pattern is followed in the rhythmic and harmonic constructions, the use of three groups of instruments (keyboard, strings, and winds), and the three movements. In the Epigraphe, which precedes the work, there is a musical anagram using the letters in the names of Schoenberg, Webern, and Berg, which can be translated into musical notes and from which three principal themes are derived. The first

movement is for piano solo and winds, the second is scored for violin solo and winds, and the third combines all the instruments, as well as themes from the first two movements. Difficult, with extreme ensemble and musical problems.

See: John Paul Tardif, "Historical and Performance Aspects of Alban Berg's Chamber Concerto for Piano, Violin, and Thirteen Winds" DMA diss., Peabody Conservatory of Music, 1976.

Gunnar Berg (1909–   ) Denmark
Pour Piano et Orchestre 1959 (Fog) 16 min. Rapid meter shifts, many dynamic indications, pointillistic pirouettes, klangfarbenclichés. M-D.

Natanael Berg (1879–1957) Sweden
Konsert c♯(STIM) 28 min.

Hans Willy Bergen (1920–   ) Germany
Three Sketches (Edition Modern 1956) 8½ min. Burleske; Romanze; Rondo Perpetuo. Neoclassic, freely tonal, clever. M-D.

Jean Berger (1909–   ) USA, born Germany
Concertino (Mannheimer) 13 min. In three movements.

Theodor Berger (1905–   ) Austria
Concerto Manuale 1950 (Sikorski) For two pianos, strings, marimba, metalophone, timpani, and tambourine. 12½ min. Shows off the individual characteristics of keyboard, percussion instruments, and strings. The thematic material is allocated in strict accordance with the potentials of each group of instruments, e.g., pianos and percussion are not given cantilena passages. "The work is in three eight-note keys, and apart from one or two brief passages in the coda there is no change of key within each structural or periodic section. The instruments actually engender the thematic material" (from record jacket, Musical Heritage Society MHS 3202). M-D.

Luciano Berio (1925–   ) Italy
Berio, one of Italy's leading composers, is director of the Studio di Fonologia di Musicale of the Italian Radiotelevision in Milan. His interest in electronic music has broadened tremendously in the last few years, and he has incorporated serial principles in composing electronic music.
Points on a Curve to Find—Piano Concerto 1973–74 (GS). For piano and 22 instruments. Kind of a neoclassic concerto, as the pianist has a continuous Scarlatti-like toccata in the style of unstable patterning. Makes a virtue out of the piano's limitation, namely, the extremely rapid decay of its tones. Berio describes the work as follows: "The part of the piano (almost always monophonic) should be understood as a curve, as a continuous line, almost constantly recurring, on which the other instruments are set in order to interpret and clarify the characteristic harmonies" (from record jacket, RCA ARL1–2291).
Concerto for Two Pianos and Orchestra 1973 (UE 15783 1978) 48 leaves, 24½

min. Explanations in German, English, and Italian. In this highly dramatic work the solo piano parts are well integrated with the orchestral components, in spite of the directions in the score: "As much as possible, the pianists must create the impression that two different pieces of music are going on, and that the 'occurrences' do not break the continuous articulation of the tone-groups." A strong tritonal element suggests Scriabin influence. On the occasion of its premiere, March 15, 1973, Berio commented: "The relationship between soloist and orchestra is a problem that must ever be solved anew, and the word 'concerto' can be taken only as a metaphor" (from record jacket, RCA Victor ARL 1–1674). "The work suggests a highly mobile relationship between soloists and orchestra in that the soloists often assume the role of accompanists to individual players from the orchestra. But, despite the 'new' relationship between soloists and orchestra, the rhythmic and tonal organization is more traditional. Not only are there rhythmic ostinati reminiscent of the early Stravinsky, there are also strong indications of a G-centered tonality" (Joshua Berrett, from same record jacket). M-D.

Lennox Berkeley (1903–   ) Great Britain
Berkeley is a composer who always pays equal attention to the mind and the ear. His works display inherent drama, are unforced, and are underscored by solid construction.
Concerto B♭ Op.29 1947 (JWC) 25 min. Allegro moderato; Andante; Vivace. Freely tonal, brilliant piano writing. At a few places the music sounds Romantic without apology. Clever and effective theme introduces the finale. M-D.
Sinfonia Concertante (JWC 1973) full score, 95pp.
Concerto for Two Pianos and Orchestra Op.30 1948 (JWC) 30 min. Molto moderato: ABA introduction leads to the Theme and (11) Variations. Magical in integrating the instruments with the orchestra. Expert piano writing; influences of Mozart, Chopin, Ravel, and Stravinsky are turned to advantage, MC. M-D.

Isak I. Berkovich (1902–   ) USSR
Concerto C Op.44 (GS 7704) 26pp. For student and teacher. Int.
Concerto III Op.48 (Musichna Ukraina 1968) 35pp. Late-Romantic idiom, no movement division, weak motivic development. Int. to M-D.

Leonard Berkowitz (1919–   ) USA
Berkowitz studied with Paul Hindemith. He teaches at California State University, Northridge.
Concerto for Piano and Winds 1967 (MCA) 22 min. MS copy easy to read. Three untitled movements (FSF). Neoclassic, bimodal, octotonic, carefully notated articulation, effective use of trills, solid writing throughout, MC. A few sections feature the piano alone. M-D.

Herman Berlinsky (1910–   ) USA, born Germany
For the Peace of Mind 1952 (TP). For piano, oboe, and string orchestra. 23 min.
Complicated patterns, mystical flights, strong emotional intensity, modal,
MC. M-D.

Seymour Bernstein (1927–   ) USA
Concerto "For Our Time" 1972 (Schroeder & Gunther) 11 min. Tries to express
our times musically, with many extremes represented. Gathering: exciting;
clever; concludes with the *South Bristol Rag*. Lament for Vietnam: freely
expressive in cantabile style. Jubilation: introduces parts of familiar tunes
from Bach to Sousa. Light, frivolous. M-D.

Leonard Bernstein (1918–   ) USA
Bernstein is one of our most versatile and talented musicians. Stravinsky, jazz,
and Latin-American idioms have all influenced his musical style.
The Age of Anxiety (Symphony II for Piano and Orchestra) 1947–49 (GS) 30 min.
Inspired by W. H. Auden's poem "The Age of Anxiety: A Baroque Eclogue."
Part one—The Prologue: a merry scene in a New York bar. The Seven Ages:
in seven athematic variations. The Seven Stages: with seven variations making "an inner and highly symbolic journey." Part Two—The Dirge: a do-
decophonic lamentation of three men and a girl in a taxicab, voicing their
need of a protective father figure, the "colossal Dad." The Masque: "a
fantastic piano-jazz' in the form of a scherzo. The Epilogue: wherein the
entire ensemble makes "a positive statement of the newly-recognized faith."
This is one of the most notable revivals of the jazz style in a piano concerto.
M-D to D.

Wallace Berry (1928–   ) USA
Concerto 1963 (CF) 22 min. In five uninterrupted sections.

Gerard Bertouille (1898–   ) Belgium
Bertouille integrates the modern extensions of consonance or tonality into a language that is well ordered and natural. He uses dissonance naturally but the tonal
pole always remains perceptible.
Concerto 1953 (H. Elkan).

Franz Berwald (1796–1868) Sweden
Berwald developed a style uniquely his own although he was strongly influenced
by Mendelssohn and Berlioz. In addition to composing and conducting, Berwald
founded an orthopedic institute in Berlin, managed a glass works in northern
Sweden, and established a sawmill!
Concerto D 1855 (Hammar—Br 4906) vol.6 of Complete Works. 19½ min.
Critical commentary in English. Preface in German and English. Allegro
con brio; Andantino; Allegro. Displays many formulas of nineteenth-century
salon music in a full-blown early Romantic style. It is Schumannesque in its
contours and general feeling. Berwald was not a pianist, but he gives the

soloist plenty of opportunity for display while the orchestra mainly provides the accompaniment. He even suggests on the title page that the piano part could be performed without an orchestra. In reality, it is a rather long sonata with orchestra ad libitum. Constantly mellifluous; high spirited; a large amount of decorative writing. M.-D.

Bruno Bettinelli (1913–   ) Italy
Concerto II (Ric 1969). Holograph difficult to read. 25 min. Tempo Improvvisazione; Intermezzo; Toccata. Borders on the atonal most of the time. M-D to D.
Concerto for Two Pianos and Orchestra 1962 (Ric). Holograph. 17 min. Allegro moderato; Lento; Deciso. Ideas passed between pianists and orchestra in a highly satisfactory manner, MC. M-D.
Concerto per Piano ed Orchestra con Timpano Obbligato (Ric 1956) 24 min. Mosso; Tranquillo; Mosso. Ideas are cleverly and carefully worked out. Octotonic, neoclassic. M-D.

Lorne M. Betts (1918–   ) Canada
Concerto I 1955 (CMC 1972) 20 min. Fast–light; Slow; Fast. Neoclassic, freely tonal, Romantic middle movement, strong repeated figurations in finale. M-D.
Concerto II (CMC) 15 min.

Jean-Pierre Beugniot (1935–   ) France
Concerto (Editions Françaises de Musique/Technisonor). For piano, trumpet, and strings. 23 min.

Thomas S. Beversdorf (1924–   ) USA
Concerto Op.14A 1951 (IU). For two pianos and orchestra. 18 min. Allegro moderato; freely tonal, flexible meters, dramatic rubato gestures in piano parts, octotonic, cadenza passages for both pianos. Andante sostenuto: full chords, filagree *ppp* arpeggios. Allegro vivace: toccata-like, blistering sonorities, strong rhythms, fast octaves, exciting throughout, superb conclusion. "The concerto was written in such a manner as to be a show piece for the two pianos and playable by a very average, small orchestra" (composer, in a letter to the author, January 3, 1980). M-D.

Philip Bezanson (1916–1975) USA
Concerto 1952 (ACA) 22 min. Allegro con moto; Andante; Allegro assai.

Vanraj Bhatia (1927–   ) India
Concerto 1955 (Novello). For piano and strings. 15 min. In one movement.

Günter Bialas (1907–   ) Germany
From 1959 to 1973 Bialas taught at the Hochschule in Munich, Germany.
Jazz-Promenade 1956 (Edition Modern 918) 10 min.
Concerto Lirico 1967 (Br TP124) 18 min. Preludio; Andantino grazioso; Allegro.

Expressionistic, twelve-tone influence, some use of pointillistic technique, advanced Hindemithian idiom. M-D to D.

Antonio Bibalo (1922–   ) Norway, born Italy

Concerto I 1955 (WH) 40 min. Toccata; Elegia; Finale. Piano and orchestra are well integrated. Neoclassic, strong Bartók influence in the rhythms, MC. M-D.

Concerto II 1971 (WH) 25 min. Lento—Allegro giusto; Largo; Allegro molto. Free twelve-tone usage, cadenza passages, octotonic. Well constructed. D.

Henk Bijvanck (1909–   ) The Netherlands

Concerto 1943 (Donemus) 24 min.

Abraham Wolfe Binder (1895–1966) USA

Rhapsody "King David" (Belwin-Mills) 20 min.

Zinovii Iurevich Binkin (1913–   ) USSR

Concertino (USSR 1974). For piano and sympho—jazz. One large movement. Jazz elements rather effective. M-D.

Keith W. Bissell (1912–   ) Canada

Concertino 1961–2 (CMC). For piano and strings. 9½ min. Allegro: fugal textures, octotonic. Andante: tuneful. Allegro: flexible meters, freely tonal. M-D.

Marcel Bitsch (1921–   ) France

Concerto 1950 (Leduc 20730). For piano and 13 instruments. 19 min. Maestoso; Allegro; Adagio; Allegro vivo. Genuine Gallic neoclassicism, splendid pianism. The music is very much alive. M-D.

Concerto II 1953 (Leduc 21319) 18 min. Freely tonal, no movement division, quasi-cadenza sections. Contains some effective moments. M-D to D.

Concertino 1953 (Leduc 21333). For piano and chamber orchestra. 15 min. Allegro; Andante; Presto. Many patterns; rhythms spring naturally from the mobile contexts. M-D.

Jean Bizet (1924–   ) France

Concerto II "Da Camera" (EMT).

Bruno Bjelinski (1909–   ) Yugoslavia

Concertino (Udruzenje Kompozitora Hrvatske 1957) 57pp. For piano and chamber orchestra.

Serenade (UE 1967). For piano, trumpet, strings, and percussion.

Boris Blacher (1903–1975) Germany

The major influences on the music of Blacher were Schoenberg and the rhythmic innovations of Stravinsky. Jazz also found its way into some of his works. His use of serial techniques was very personal, and his usage differed considerably from Boulez's and Stockhausen's. He also developed a system of variable meters, a technique that governed most of his compositions composed during the 1950s and 1960s.

Concerto I Op.28 1948 (Bo&Bo 1962) 20 min. Three movements. Diatonic materials in tertial, quartal, and quintal sonorities; linear texture; piano writing mainly unison or two-voiced. Finale is the most interesting movement pianistically. M-D.

Concerto II (in variablen Metren) Op.42 1952 (Bo&Bo) 18 min. The variable-meter concept applies to the varying number of eighth notes in each measure. Andante: opens with a slow introduction; the Andante returns after the cadenza to close the movement. Moderato: uninteresting thematic material made duller by thin textures. Molto vivace: fast octaves, challenging pianistic figurations. Transparent orchestral scoring. M-D.

Variationen über ein Thema von Muzio Clementi Op.61 (Concerto III) 1961 (Bo&Bo) 20 min. The ascending notes C–D–E–F–G and descending F–E♭–D in sixteenth notes inspire sixteen variations, the final one serving as a coda. Colorful neoclassic treatment. M-D.

Maurice Blackburn (1914–   ) Canada
Blackburn's symphonic works have been influenced by Stravinsky, Honegger, and Poulenc.

Concertino C 1948 (CMC). For piano, woodwinds, and brass. 19½ min. Classical in form and style. First movement is based on two contrasting themes, developed in SA design. Second movement is a slow theme and variations. Finale is a rondo with a touch of folk dance. M-D.

Easley Blackwood (1933–   ) USA
Concerto 1970 (AMC) 23 min. Based on nineteenth-century rhetoric in twentieth-century musical language. Relatively straightforward rhythmically; harmonically elusive but convincing. The slow middle movement, with the asymmetric linear piano part juxtaposed against the orchestra, is the most interesting. M-D to D.

Dmitrii D. Blagoi (1930–   ) USSR
Capriccio 1960 (Soviet Composer). One movement. Brilliant gestures and figurations. M-D.

Emile R. Blanchet (1877–1943) Switzerland
Koncertstück A♭ Op.14 (Rozsavölgyi 1912) 63pp. Contains some piquant harmony and unusual sound of rhythm effects. M.-D.

Arthur Bliss (1891–1975) Great Britain
Bliss was a facile, prolific composer, one of the group of post-Elgar composers. His somewhat neoclassic style shows a definite leaning toward English Romanticism, and his idiom is essentially traditional. He was Musical Director of the BBC from 1941 to 1944, knighted in 1950, and made Master of the Queen's Music in 1953.

Concerto B♭ 1939 (Novello) 35 min. Allegro con brio; Adagio; Andante maestoso–Molto vivo. Bliss was commissioned by the British Council to write a concerto for the 1939 New York World's Fair, which is dedicated to "the people of the United States." It is a difficult virtuoso work with much display for the piano. The outer movements are virile and strong, while the middle movement contains lyricism of great sensitivity and poignancy. Chromatically opulent but firmly anchored in tonality. Deserves to be heard. D.

Baraza 1946 (Novello). From the film *Men of Two Worlds*. Concert piece for piano and orchestra with men's voices ad lib. 8 min. In the two-piano arrangement the vocal parts are deleted. "Baraza is a Swahili word meaning a discussion in council between an African chief and his headman" (from the score). In three short uninterrupted movements. Maestoso ma non troppo lento: cadenza leads directly to Larghetto; Vivace. Freely tonal, strong rhythms, full sonorities, octotonic in the Larghetto, dramatic conclusion. M-D.

Concerto for Two Pianos and Orchestra 1933 (OUP) 12 min. A revised version of *Concerto for Tenor, Piano, Strings and Percussion* of 1920. In one movement, with a form similar to that of a fantasia. A number of contrasting motives are used, with a dissonant harmonic treatment. The writing is effective and brilliant with some biting dissonance. Difficult ensemble problems. M-D to D.

Marc Blitzstein (1905–1964) USA

Concerto 1931 (Fl) 24 min. Moderato molto–Allegro; Largo assai; Allegro non troppo (alla passacaglia). Written in a "white-note" diatonic style sprinkled with dissonance and a touch of jazz. M-D.

Ernest Bloch (1880–1959) USA, born Switzerland

Bloch's music was influenced by synagogue cantillation and combined this ornate style with nineteenth-century Romanticism. It has a rhapsodic, intense quality, with poetry and mysticism, plus an unmistakably Semitic quality.

Concerto Grosso I 1925 (A. Broude). For piano and string orchestra. 22 min. Written during Bloch's final year as director of the Cleveland Institute of Music. The composer here proves that a modern thinking and compositional approach can be incorporated within the framework of an older form. Neoclassic and neobaroque characteristics permeate the entire work. Prelude: tremendously strong with bold rhythmic motion. Dirge: a song of lamentation. Pastoral and Rustic Dances. Fugue: full of robust motion and modern harmonies. Piano has little solo function. M-D.

Concerto Symphonique 1948 (Bo&H) 38 minutes. A huge, intense, powerful work that makes great demands on the soloist. Pesante: almost monothematic in construction; large piano cadenza. Allegro vivace: scherzo-like, with rapid figurations in the piano. Allegro deciso: episodic, brilliant, and effective. Musically challenging; one of Bloch's most important compositions. The thick orchestral texture at times threatens to overpower the solo instrument. Solo part very difficult; requires strength and endurance. D.

Scherzo Fantasque 1949 (GS) 9 min. Highly effective for the pianist, although not of excessive difficulty. Written in a rather dissonant idiom. The work is made up of a number of brief, contrasting motives that are often used in striking rhythmic patterns. A short central section supplies contrast by using ideas from the more rapid opening section in a modified form. A recapitulation of the opening material and coda end the work. The writing for both piano and orchestra is colorful and imaginative. M-D.

Waldemar Bloch (1906–   ) Austria
Klavierkonzert II 1963 (Dob) 23 min. Allegro molto: cadenza; Adagio; Presto. Freely tonal; neoclassic; effective piano writing. M-D.

Sven Blohm (1907–1956) Sweden
Konsertstycke a (STIM) 15 min.

Erik Blomberg (1922–   ) Sweden
Dialogue between Piano and Orchestra (ES) 8 min.

Karl Birger Blomdahl (1916–1968) Sweden
Blomdahl's music is marked by clear architectonic form, in which the course of movements often builds to a great climax, and rhythmic vitality.
Chamber Concerto 1953 (Schott 10278). For piano, woodwind, and percussion. 16 min. One large movement with various tempi and mood contrasts: Lento; Allegro; Adagio; Presto. Twelve-tone influence present, although the tonal and rhythmic organization is reminiscent of Bartók. Energetic and driving rhythmic pulse. M-D.

Robert Blume (1900–   ) Switzerland
Konzert (Möseler). For piano and chamber orchestra.

Felix M. Blumenfeld (1863–1931) Russia
Allegro de Concert Op.7A 1887 (Belaieff; Fl). Virtuosic and tuneful. Dated, but has some effective places. M-D.

François-Adrien Boieldieu (1775–1834) France
Concerto F (Drescher—F. Colombo) 22 min. Allegro; Pastorale con variazioni. A pleasant, lighthearted two-movement work. Theme-and-variations finale has great charm and contains some highly colored and original effects. M-D.

Rob du Bois (1934–   ) The Netherlands
Du Bois's music explores chance techniques and utilizes unusual instrumental playing devices.
Concerto 1960 rev. 1968 (Donemus) 13 min.
Cerle (Donemus 1963). For piano, nine winds, and percussion. 14 min.
Le Concerto pour Hrisanide 1971 (Donemus) 23 min.

Otis Bardwell Boise (1845–1912) USA
Boise studied under Hauptmann, Richter, Moscheles, and Kullak. He was professor of theory and composition at the Peabody Institute.
Concerto g Op.36 1874 (Hofmeister 1889). Allegro; Andante con moto; Finale. Perhaps the earliest titled American concerto. Contains many bombastic moments. Sidney Lanier said of this work: "it was the fulfillment of the best

promise, well worth any encouragement of native talent, taste and advancement of American art" (quoted in Lubor Keefer, *Baltimore's Music* [Baltimore, 1962], p. 208).

Paul Boisselet (–   ) France
Jazz-Concerto 1946 (Sal) 6 min.

Maurice Boivin (1918–   ) Canada
Boivin is a member of the teaching staff at the Conservatoire de la Province de Québec.
Lac Champlain Poem pour piano et orchestra 1962 (CMC) 17 min. Impressionistic; parallel syncopated chords; freely tonal, MC. M-D.

Laci Boldemann (1921–1969) Sweden, born Finland
Konsert Op.13 1956 (STIM) 21 min. Rhythmically vital throughout; written in a moderate modernistic style related to Bartók and Hindemith; strong and attractive melodies. M-D.

Willem Frederik Bon (1940–   ) The Netherlands
Dialogues and Monologues Op.17 1967 (Donemus) 20 min.

Bernard van den Boogaard (1952–   ) The Netherlands
Concerto D 1976 (Donemus) 20 min. Piano is to be amplified. Large orchestration. Highly chromatic, complex figuration, flexible meters, clusters, many tempo changes, pointillistic, expanded tonality. Ensemble problems. M-D.

Edmund von Borch (1906–1944) Germany
Concerto Op.20 (Schott) 25 min.

David Borden (1938–   ) USA
Trudymusic 1967 (CMP; LC) 4 min. "Settings for piano and orchestra of segments of piano music by other composers. The piano part remains unchanged from the originals while the orchestral accompaniment employs pointillistic and other textural non-tonal techniques. The works quoted are from Chopin, Haydn, Beethoven and Gregory Biss. The pieces may be played separately or collectively and in any order desired. From time to time, new sections will be added to *Trudymusic*" (from the score). M-D.

Charles Bordes (1863–1909) France
Rapsodie Basque Op.9 (Sal 1921; Fl) 15 min. Contains interesting uneven elastic phrases. Sectional, based on Basque tunes. M-D.

Johanna Bordewijk-Roepman (1892–1971) The Netherlands
Concerto 1940 (Donemus) 20 min.

Pavel Bořkovec (1894–1972) Czechoslovakia
"In the late 1920's Bořkovec was a leading figure in moving Czech music from late romanticism into a neoclassic expression" (DCM, 92).
Concerto I 1931 (Hudebni Matice) 20 min. Largo–Allegro; Adagio–Andante; Allegro vivace. Notable for its definitely formed stylization. Written in a virtuoso MC idiom with strong Prokofiev influence. D.

Concerto II 1949–50 (Artia 1964) 23 min. Agitato; Poco lento; Vivace. Displays variety and order. Brilliant writing for the pianist excellently combined with the orchestral part. MC. One of the finest contemporary Czech piano concertos. M-D to D.

Concerto Grosso 1941–42 (Artia). For two violins, cello, orchestra, and piano obbligato.

Enrico Bormioli (1895–   ) Italy

Allegro da Concerto (Concert Allegro) (SZ) 9 min.

Variazioni Sinfoniche (On a Theme of Paganini) (SZ) 14 min. Uses the Paganini *Caprice* No.24, which was used by Liszt, Rachmaninoff, Dallapiccola, and others. Theme, twelve contrasting variations, and finale. MC. M-D.

Felix Borowski (1872–1956) USA, born Great Britain

Concerto d 1921 (CF) 20 min. Moderato maestoso; Andante; Allegro con fuoco. In a post-Brahms highly Romantic idiom. M-D.

Siegfried Borris (1906–   ) Germany

Concerto Op.58 (Sirius). For piano and chamber orchestra. 25 min.

Serge Bortkiewicz (1877–1952) USSR

Concerto B♭ Op.16 (K&S 1913; Fl) 24 min. Lento: many tempo and mood changes, large dramatic coda. Andante sostenuto: lyric opening, grandiose mid-section, returns to opening lyric idea. Molto vivace e con brio (Tema russo): effective bravura writing throughout. Strong Liszt influence; brilliant and grateful but unoriginal. M-D.

Concerto III c "Per Aspera ad Astra" Op.32 (Sikorski 1927; Rahter 314) 86pp. One large contrasted movement. Kind of a pastiche of the pianistic devices that Anton Rubinstein, Tchaikowsky, and Rachmaninoff used to better advantage. Brilliantly and idiomatically laid out for the keyboard. M-D to D.

Dmitrii S. Bortnianskii (1751–1825) Russia

Sinfonie Concertante 1790 (USSR 1953) facsimile, full score, 88pp. Orchestration is for strings, bassoon, and harp. Allegro maestoso; Larghetto; Allegretto. Cadenza required in middle movement. Classic style, tuneful. Int. to M-D.

Arthur Bosman (1908–   ) Brazil, born Belgium

Cymbalum (Rhapsody for Piano and Orchestra) (PIC) 12 min. In one movement. Brilliant nineteenth-century gestures recalling Liszt, plus a few MC effects. M-D.

Henriëtte Bosmans (1895–1952) The Netherlands

Concertino 1928 (Donemus) 14 min.

Will Gay Bottje (1925–   ) USA

Concerto 1960 (ACA) 20 min. First movement: quarter note = c.68–70, expanded tonal concept, virtuoso figuration. Scherzo: to be played with "a spirit of lightness and tongue in cheek throughout" (from the score). Variations: dramatic punctuated octave opening, big chords, alternating figuration between hands, quasi cadenza, somewhat freer declamatory closing. M-D to D.

Facets (ACA). For piano and band. 19½ min.

Rhapsodic Variations (ACA). For piano, viola, and strings.

André Boucourechliev (1925–   ) France, born Bulgaria
Concerto (Sal) 21 min.

Pierre Boulez (1925–   ) France
The style of Boulez stems from Schoenberg, Webern, Messiaen, and Debussy. He has also worked in electronic media and with indeterminancy. Since the late 1950s he has been rewriting earlier works and has adhered to the concept of a work in progress. "The idea is that a composition is never finished in a definitive form but always remains open to further creation and elaboration" (DCM, 96).

Symphonie Concertante 1950 (MS available from composer: c/o Georges Pompidou Arts Center, Paris, France).

Francis de Bourguignon (1890–1961) Belgium
Concertino Op.99 1952 (CeBeDeM) 11 min. Allegro; Lento; Allegro. Freely tonal, Impressionistic. M-D.

Roger Boutry (1932–   ) France
Berceuse and Rondo (Zurfluh 1968) 7 min. Thin textures, quasi-cadenza. Charming. Int.

Concerto (Sal) 18 min.

Concerto Fantasy 1965 (Sal). For two pianos and strings. 27 min. Allegramente; Scherzo; Andante quasi adagio; Theme and (5) variations; Allegro moderato. Orchestra carries much of the line, with both pianos adding color and mood. Neoclassic, exciting writing that would have much audience appeal. M-D to D.

Paul Bowles (1910–   ) USA
Concerto for Two Pianos and Percussion or Orchestra 1946 (AME) 20 min. In four movements. First version: two pianos, winds, and percussion. Second version: two pianos and full orchestra.

George Frederick Boyle (1886–1948) USA, born Australia
Concertino 1935 (Fl) 15 min. Carnival; Pastorale; March.

Concerto d (GS 1912; Fl) 25 min. Moderato; Tranquillo ma non troppo lento. Highly influenced by Brahms; strongly oriented toward the nineteenth century. Excellent craft throughout. M-D.

Darijan Božič (1933–   ) Yugoslavia
Audiostructurae 1976 (Gerig) 14 min.

Elongations (Gerig). For piano and 12 instruments. 7 min.

Edward Fliflet Braein (1924–   ) Norway
Capriccio Op.9 (NK) 12 min.

Antonio Braga (1929–   ) Italy
Concerto Exotique 1959 (Choudens 1967) 24 min. Three movements (FSF). Expanded tonality, weak thematic material. M-D.

Mario Braggiotti (1909–   ) USA, born Italy
Pianorama (Fantasy on a Given Theme for Piano and Orchestra) (Belwin-Mills) 20 min.

Johannes Brahms (1833–1897) Germany
Brahms is considered a Classicist in a Romantic world, but he gradually honed the Classical conciseness, balance, and control of his mature works out of very Romantic beginnings. His three piano sonatas of the early 1850s (Opp. 1, 2, and 5) show an almost Lisztian bravura and intensity. The first concerto also shows this grand expressiveness, but in the last movement we find a tendency toward greater conciseness. Both concertos display exceedingly pianistic writing that demands virtuosity of heroic proportions.
Concerto I d Op.15 (Br&H; CFP; GS; Eulenburg; IMC; CF) 50 min.
    Maestoso–Poco piu moderato; Adagio; Rondo—Allegro non troppo. This work was complete in the spring of 1858 but the music of the first two movements goes back some four years to an early attempt at a symphony (Brahms's actual *First Symphony* appeared over twenty years later), which in turn became an aborted sonata for two pianos. The seriousness, even passion, of the music, especially in the first movement, may reflect events of the early and middle 1850s. The first movement is remarkably expansive, presenting broad dramatic and melodic ideas in enormous, arching phrases. The unsettling opening motive is powerful and angular. A long, poignant, lyrical theme, almost a lament, follows and slowly leads back to the dramatic opening gesture, now in canon. A syncopated motive, like a fanfare, in D (the tonic major) closes the first section. Now the solo piano enters with a new, undulating theme back in d. After the piano and orchestra expand it and the first two ideas from the opening of the movement, the soloist alone presents a beautiful new soaring melody in the relative major (Poco più moderato). The fanfare-like motive returns, but now totally transformed into a peaceful, pastoral melody. The soloist and the orchestra together broadly expand these two lyrical ideas and come to a restful cadence. A sudden outburst of double octaves from the piano introduces the energetic development section. The return of the opening motive for the recapitulation is especially powerful and commanding, with the soloist at the heights of virtuosity. The Adagio and Rondo are less broadly rhapsodic than the large opening movement. However, the enormous phrases of the Adagio tend to disguise its simple ABA form. It presents a quality of transcendent calm in the key of D, and after a middle section in b, the home key of D returns only *after* the opening theme gets under way. The soloist brings a great chromatic enrichment to this return of the first theme. An extensive coda, in which

there is a short, fluttering cadenza for the piano, closes the movement. The finale is a Beethovenian rondo (ABACABA), and its main theme, a vigorous, ascending idea, is a transformation of the piano's soaring melody from the first movement. The central theme (C) is also based on this ascending gesture, and it in turn is treated to a brief fugato. For its final return, the A theme is transformed into a stately, distant march in the tonic major. Near the end of the movement the soloist has two brief cadenzas. D.

See: Tedd Joselson, "Master Class—Brahms' First Piano Concerto," CK 5 (February 1979): 65.

Concerto II B♭ Op.83 1881 (Br&H; CFP; GS; Durand: Eulenburg; IMC; CF; Simrock). This concerto is the work of a serene senior master. It was not until this late date in his career, that Brahms was sufficiently satisfied with a work to deem it worthy of dedication to the "dear friend and teacher Eduard Marxen," with whom he had studied more than three decades earlier. It was first performed at Budapest on Nov. 9, 1881, with Brahms at the piano. It has four instead of the customary three movements. Allegro non troppo: complex and involved SA design with a coda of great importance based on the opening material. Allegro appassionato: vigorous and impassioned movement occupying the position of a scherzo; built on two basic melodies, the first dynamic and powerful, the second tranquil and sweet. Andante: slow and expressive; opening cello solo dominates the entire movement; concludes with a short coda. Allegretto grazioso: built on a rather unorthodox rondo form; piano part more conspicuous than in the previous movements; with lightning octaves, swift arpeggios, and exhausting display passages against the sonorous orchestral background; enormous, brilliant climax; great power and heroic sweep essential for the fullest effect. D.

See: Dayton Daryl, "The Piano Concertos of Brahms," *Symphony Magazine,* Los Angeles Philharmonic Orchestra, 34th season (1952–53): 22.

Linda Faye Ferguson, "The Concertos of Johannes Brahms: An Historical and Analytical Approach to the Compositional Process," thesis, Texas Christian University, 1973.

Jan Brandts-Buys (1868–1933) The Netherlands

Concerto F Op.15 1897 (Schlesinger). Displays well-bred eclecticism of the late-Romantic period in Germany. The first and last movements are symphonic, containing much thematic work in the orchestra. M-D.

Rudolf Braun (1869–1925) Austria

Concerto (UE). For piano left-hand and orchestra.

Walter Braunfels (1882–1954) Germany

Concerto A Op.21 (Leuckart 1912; Fl) 30 min. Allegro, ma mon troppo; Adagio; Allegro. Post-Romantic tendencies, virtuoso spots. M-D to D.

Divertimento 1950 (Noetzel 1960) 15½ min. Contrasting sections, neoclassic. Exploits the piano intelligently. M-D.

Algis Bronius Brazinskas (1937–   ) USSR
Concerto Op.2 (Musika 1964) 60pp. Allegro con brio; Andante; Vivo. MC, flashy
    writing in the outer movements. Has some affinity with the Khachaturian
    Piano Concerto. M-D.

Hans Brehme (1904–1957) Germany
Concerto Op.32 (Schott) 27 min.

Therese Brenet (1935–   ) France
Concerto pour un Poeme Inconnu (Rideau Rouge 1968). For piano, string orches-
    tra, and ondes martenot. 16½ min. Trés sonore, grand, trés majestueux et
    scandé; Trés lent; Sombre, un peu saccade. Dramatic gestures, expanded
    tonality, flexible meters, cadenza passages for the piano, dynamic extremes,
    clusters, coloristic. Piano mainly provides atmosphere. M-D.

Gaston Brenta (1902–1969) Belgium
Brenta is a melodist who had a liking for long and well-articulated phrases,
broadly developed and full of expression.
Concerto 1949 (Leduc 1960) 17 min. Three movements (FSF). Expanded tonality,
    long cantabile phrases, expressive, expansive in developmental concept.
    M-D.
Concerto 1953 (CeBeDeM) 20 min.
Concerto II 1968 (H. Elkan) 19 min. Required work at the 1968 Queen Elisabeth
    Competition. Three movements (FSF). Outer movements have a well-de-
    fined rhythmical layout and reveal solid technical and instrumental qualities.
    The middle movement is a short passacaglia. Colorful orchestration. The
    work conveys an animated impression, mainly on account of the captivating
    thematic statement with its jazz and marching rhythms. M-D.

Cesar Bresgen (1913–   ) Austria
Mayenkonzert 1937 (Schott) 16 min. Kume, kume, gselle min; Guckguck hat
    sich z'tot gefalln; Loba (nach einem alten Schweizer Mairuf). Neoclassic.
    M-D.
Konzert 1951 (Schott 1977) 20 min. Allegro; Molto lento; Vivace. Highly chro-
    matic, quartal harmony, thin textures. M-D.
Sinfonisches Konzert Op.21 (Süddeutscher Musikverlag 1144).
Totentanz (Toccata after Holbein) 1978 (Dob 01592). For piano and chamber
    orchestra. 30pp.

Frank Bridge (1879–1941) Great Britain
Beginning as a Romantic, Bridge became increasingly "modern" during the
1930s. His later works show an experimental use of harmony.
Phantasm 1931 (Augener) 27 min. Strong imaginative writing full of potent
    atmosphere and strongly felt logic. Expanded tonality verges on atonality at
    some points. Excellent writing for the piano M-D to D.

Leslie Bridgewater (1893–   ) Great Britain
Concerto (Goodwin & Tabb 1947) 56pp. Tonal, no movement division. M-D.
Concerto I (Novello) 20 min.

Allen Brings (1934–   ) USA
Concerto da Camera I (Seesaw 1976). For piano and chamber orchestra. 10 min.

Estela Bringuer (1931–   ) USA, born Argentina
Concerto I D Op.25 1963 (F. Colombo) 22 min. In three movements (FSF).

Benjamin Britten (1913–1976) Great Britain
Many regard Britten as one of the greatest English composers since Purcell. He has made significant contributions to virtually every area of composition. An eclectic composer with a complete command of technique, Britten had warmth, poetry, and few inhibitions in expressing himself. Although he was attracted to Schoenberg's atonal style as well as to Mahler's post-Romanticism, he did not adhere slavishly to any single style. His piano output, surprisingly, is not large, although he was a marvelous pianist in his own right.
Concerto I D Op.13 1938 (Bo&H) 33 min. Revised 1945, at which time Britten substituted the Impromptu in place of a Recitative and Aria as the third movement. Toccata: brilliant and percussive; ends with a large cadenza. Waltz: graceful; builds to a large climax, which dies away near the end. Impromptu: an imaginative passacaglia set of six variations on a theme first announced by the piano; this movement contains the most interesting piano writing; flows without pause into March: a movement of great brilliance for both soloist and orchestra. Generally fairly dissonant but without a real feeling of atonality. D.
Diversions on a Theme for Left Hand and Orchestra Op.21 1940 (Bo&H) 23½ min. Dedicated to Paul Wittgenstein, the one-armed Austrian pianist who commissioned a number of significant twentieth-century works for the left hand. A marvelously clever set of eleven variations that display various kinds of left-hand technique. No attempt is made to imitate two-handed piano playing. An elaborate and taxing workout for the one hand alone, with trills in the Recitative, widespread arpeggi in the Nocturne, agility over the keyboard in the Badinerie and Toccata, and repeated notes in the final Tarantella. Beautifully tuneful. D.
Scottish Ballad Op.26 1941 (Bo&H). For two pianos and orchestra. 13 min. Britten wrote this work while residing in the United States during the early years of World War II. Although old Scottish tunes are used for thematic material, the work is in no way a medley but rather, in Britten's words, evokes "a sequence of ideas and emotions that have been characteristic of the life of the Scottish people during centuries of stormy history." The three sections are performed without interruption. A short Lento introduction uses the psalm tune "Dundee," which leads into a funeral march based on a Scottish lament, "The Flowers of the Forest." Following a restatement of the

opening psalm tune, which is used as a transition, the work is concluded with an Allegro in the form of a Scottish reel. The linking of a funeral march with a lively reel is typically Scottish, for this type of music was played by pipers returning from a military funeral. The piano writing, although often brilliant and effective, makes only moderate demands on the soloists. M-D.

Hans Bronsart von Schellendorf (1830–1913) Germany
Bronsart studied with Liszt at Weimar from 1854 to 1857. He was the soloist in the first performance of Liszt's *Second Piano Concerto* in Weimar in 1857 with Liszt conducting, and the concerto was dedicated to Bronsart when it was published in 1863. Von Bülow described Eugen d'Albert's *Piano Concerto* in b as "next to Bronsart, certainly the most significant one of the so-called Weimar School."

Concerto f♯ Op.10 1876 (Fritsch; Fl; BPL) 27 min. Allegro maestoso: one theme suggests *Die Meistersinger;* no orchestral interlude between second subject and development section. Adagio ma non troppo: Chopinesque. Allegro con fuoco: impetuous Hungarian character; a tarantella with some intricate double passages. Heroic, Brahmsian, in the sweeping Romantic tradition. Complete authority given to the pianist, but also contains excellent orchestration. D.

Rayner Brown (1912–   ) USA
Concertino (WIM 117 1976). For piano and band. 67pp.
Concerto for Two Pianos, Brass and Percussion (WIM 90 1972) 25 min. Prelude; Allegro; Cadenza; Scherzo; Chorale; Fugue. Adheres to the Classic concerto form except that the SA movement is preceded by a prelude and followed by a cadenza. No pause between movements. Brown has provided a medium for the virtuosity of the pianists in concert, dialogue, and solo with the various and exciting colors of the brass instruments. Pure entertainment is achieved in the various combinations, moods, and rhythms of this feast of musical expression. M-D.

Max Bruch (1829–1920) Germany
Though Bruch lived two decades into the 1900s, he was not of the twentieth century. His compositional esthetic embraced the conservative, tried-and-true ideals espoused by Brahms.
Concerto for Two Pianos and Orchestra Op.88A 1912 (Simrock Elite Ed. 3171) 22 min. A reworking of an unsuccessful orchestral suite begun in 1904; rediscovered in 1971. Andante sostenuto: polyphonically textured in a kind of rigid Bach counterpoint; comes to rest unexpectedly on the dominant and passes into the Andante con moto–Allegro: SA; closes with a short stretto. Adagio: tranquil theme shared by piano and orchestra increases in intensity before subsiding. Andante—Allegro: fanfare opening, fantasy of ideas, triumphant conclusion. Skillful writing for the two pianos; rich orchestration with a certain amount of Tchaikowskian pomp and strong Schumann influence. M-D.

Attillio Brugnoli (1880–1937) Italy
Concerto Op.2 1905 (Ric 1933) 22 min. One large movement with contrasting sections; nineteenth-century idioms and techniques. D.

Theo Bruins (1929–   ) The Netherlands
Concerto 1952 (Donemus).

Ignaz Brüll (1846–1907) Austria
Brüll was a close friend of Brahms.
Concerto I F. Op.10 (Bo&Bo 1884) 26 min.
Concerto II C Op.24 1872 (Bo&Bo) 29 min. Allegro moderato; Andante; Allegro moderato. In the Weber–Schumann–Brahms style; of symphonic proportions; fresh-sounding and charming. More pianistic in some ways than the two Brahms concertos. A solid and enduring work, important enough to become a staple of the standard repertoire. M-D to D.
Rhapsodie d Op.65 1892 (Dob) 14 min. Points to Brahms in more ways than the title. M-D.
Andante and Allegro Op.88 (Bo&Bo 1903; Fl).

Colin James Brumby (1933–   ) Australia
Realizations 1966 (J. Albert) 12 min.

Adolf Brunner (1901–   ) Switzerland
Partita (Br 21024a) 17 min. One large movement, sectionalized. Post-Romantic characteristics, octotonic, freely tonal, corky rhythms in final section, imposing climax. Large span required. M-D.

Evgenii G. Brusilowski (1905–   ) USSR
Concerto d 1947 (USSR 1958) 111pp. Post-Romantic idiom, unusual tempo arrangement in three movements played without breaks. M-D to D.

Joanna Bruzdowicz (1932–   ) Poland
Episode 1973 (PWM) 20pp.

Valentino Bucchi (1916–   ) Italy
Concerto in Rondo 1957 (Forlivesi 12373 1961) 56pp. One movement with contrasting sections that merge into one another. Asymmetrical meters $\left(\dfrac{3+2+2+3}{8} \right)$. Beautifully laid out for the piano; MC. M-D.

Wolfgang Buch (–   ) Germany
Notturno in Blue 1961 (Birnbach 4121) 9½ min. Jazz and blues influence, well written, MC. *Pp* closing. M-D.

Gunnar Bucht (1927–   ) Sweden
Bucht is professor of composition at the Royal Conservatory of Music in Stockholm.
Meditation Op.5 1950 (EC) 6 min. Displays fine craft and a respect for tradition; expressionistic; serious. M-D.

Fritz Büchtger (1903–   ) Monaco, born Germany
Concertino II (Br BE312). For piano and chamber orchestra.

Walter Buczynski (1933–   ) Canada
Berztitula 1964 (CMC 1972) 9 min. One movement with contrasting sections. Flexible meters, octotonic, dramatic gestures, cadenza for piano, *ppp* ending, freely tonal. M-D.
Four Movements 1969 (CMC). For piano and 15 strings. 20½ min. Lento: twelve-tone; quarter-tone inflection for strings; mallets are used on piano strings. Scherzo: pointillistic; "whack effects" created by snapping foot off pedal; hard mallets used inside piano; clusters; wire brush scratches strings. Recitativo: arm on black keys; chromatic figuration. Finale: sweeping gestures, flexible meters, expanded tonal idiom. M-D.

Ryszard Bukowski (1916–   ) Poland
Concertino 1949 (PWM) 15 min.

Revol S. Bunin (1924–   ) USSR
Concerto (USSR 7685).
Concerto (USSR 7710).

Vladimir Bunin (1908–1970) USSR
Concerto (Soviet Composer 1971) 51pp. One large movement with contrasting sections. Large chords move over entire keyboard. MC. M-D to D.

David R. Burge (1930–   ) USA
Burge has done a great deal on behalf of contemporary music. He is an outstanding pianist and teaches at the Eastman School of Music.
Concerto 1956 (MS. in Sibley Library, Eastman School of Music, Rochester, NY 14604). Allegro; Adagio; Allegro.

Henry Burgess (fl.1740–1781) Great Britain
Concerto V g (Hopper—Concordia 97–4825 1968) Full score, 24pp. Andante–Allegro; Largo; Allegro. Can be played with string quartet or full string orchestra. Phrasing marks based on the 1740 J. Walsh London edition. Strong Handel influence. Int.

Norbert Burgmüller (1810–1836) Germany
Robert Schumann valued Burgmüller highly.
Concerto f♯ Op.1 1865 (K&S). Despite its natural immaturity, this Romantic work shows great ability. It has a lovely and effective cello solo in the second movement. An elegiac spirit permeates the work in spite of its being heavy with Chopinesque fioritura. M-D.

Willy Burkhard (1900–1955) Switzerland
Concertino Op.94 (Br 2489). Influences of Scriabin, the French Impressionists, Stravinsky, and Bartók are seen in this work. M-D.

Eldin Burton (1913–   ) USA
Concerto 1971 (CF 1976) 18 min. In three contrasting movements. Freely tonal,

contemporary extension of nineteenth-century pianistic idiom. Finale (Allegro scherzando) is especially exciting. M-D.

Adolf Busch (1891–1952) Germany

Concerto C Op.31 (Serkin—Br&H 5415 1928) 83pp. Allegro non troppo, ma con brio; Adagio tranquillo; Allegro moderato e giocoso. Regerian qualities. Virtuoso technique required. D.

Alan Bush (1900–   ) Great Britain

Concerto Op.18 1938 (LC). For piano and orchestra, with solo baritone and male choir. 57 min. In four movements. Resolutely diatonic, rhythmically propulsive. Chordal conclusion in major keys. Voices used in the last movement only. M-D.

Variations, Nocturne and Finale on an English Sea-song Op.60 (Novello 1973) 21 min. Three movements, all based on the nineteenth-century whalerman's ballad "Blow ye winds." Opening movement consists of thirteen short variations. The Nocturne is quite nostalgic but virtuosic. The Finale is a Giocoso in 12/8. A virtuoso concert piece. D.

Geoffrey Bush (1920–   ) Great Britain

A Little Concerto on Themes by Arne 1966 (Elkin). For piano and strings. 8 min. The sources of this work are the *Harpsichord Concerto* IV, first and second movements, and *Concerto* III, organo solo movement. A gifted teen-ager would enjoy this work. Int.

Ferruccio Busoni (1866–1924) Germany, born Italy.

Busoni made a profound impact on his time as a composer and a musical thinker. He was one of the greatest pianists of all time, but as with Liszt, his career suffered because of a conflict between composition and public performance. He constantly searched for new musical expression, going so far as inventing 113 possible ways of arranging whole and half steps within a seven-note series, experimenting with new systems of musical notation, and working with quarter-tones. His music never fully settles on one style, but centers on a specific problem that explores new musical resources, often at the expense of emotion. Busoni's greatest influence was through the introduction of neoclassicism, with its return to older Baroque formal structures, such as fugue, divertimento, toccata, and concerto grosso. Ultimately Busoni wished to combine Mozart's grace and elegance and Bach's polyphonic logic within a contemporary harmonic and orchestral framework. This musical anticipation of one of the most important developments of musical aesthetics of the twentieth century profoundly influenced Hindemith, Toch, Casella, Pizzetti, and Malipiero.

Konzertstück D Op.31A 1890 (Br&H) 17½ min. Busoni won the Rubinstein prize in 1890 with this brilliant showpiece. Weber's piece by the same title served as model, but Busoni's work owes more to Liszt, pianistically speaking. Its Romantic, post-Lisztian flavor is evident, but it is much more than the work of a young genius working in a then fashionable style. Rather it shows a bold young composer greatly interested in musical freedom. D.

Concerto C Op.39 1904 (Petri—Br&H 2861). For piano and orchestra, with a final chorus for male voices. 63 min. Prologo e introito; Pezzo giocoso; Pezzo serioso; All' Italiana; Cantico. From its opening glimmering murmurings to its choral close, this work is enormously complex and makes severely taxing demands of the soloist, both musically and technically. It is Italian in feeling and actually uses several Italian folk songs. The movements alternate in mood, the first, third, and fifth being tranquil, the second and fourth showing great energy and brilliance. The five movements are conceived as an architectonic pentacle, with the odd-numbered movements symbolizing the apexes of spirituality, while the second movement, a scherzo, and the fourth, a tarantella, represent terrestrial transience. Busoni felt that the last movement with chorus resembled "some original inborn quality in a person which, in the course of years, comes out again in him purified and matured as he reaches the last phase of his transformations." The words to this movement (Hymn to Allah) were taken from the Danish poet Adam Gottlob Oehlenschlaeger (1779–1850). The piano is assigned a double role— solo and obbligato—that is sometimes truly spectacular. This work has never achieved popularity although it has had such champions as Egon Petri and Pietro Scarpini. Its length, difficulty, and large ensemble have discouraged frequent performance. D.

Indian Fantasy Op.44 1913 (Petri—Br&H; Fl) 20 min. Busoni became interested in the rhythms and melodies of the American Indians after having been shown their music by Natalie Curtis, the author of several books on Indians written around the turn of the century. The composer introduced the work publicly in Berlin in 1914, and in Philadelphia the following year. The three parts are played without interruption. Fantasia: theme and variations based on a song of the Hopi Indians. Canzona: poignantly beautiful; based on two Indian songs. Finale: alternations of 3/4 and 4/4. This elaborate, expansively shaped, and brilliant work should be heard more frequently. M-D.

Concertino Op.54 1922 (Br&H) 7 min. for second movement only. First and third movements of this work were composed in 1890 and published as *Konzertstück*, Op.31A. Second movement: Romanza e scherzoso. D.

Nigel Henry Butterley (1935–   ) Australia

Explorations 1970 (J. Albert) 25 min. Uses the full range of contemporary resources; contains some textures of great beauty; offers a musical experience of originality and depth. M-D.

Max Butting (1888–1976) Germany

Konzert Op.110 1964 (Verlag Neue Musik 1971) 21 min. Allegro; Andante tranquillo; Allegro–allegretto. Octotonic, thin textures; percussion usage adds to this work greatly. M-D.

C

Robert Caamaño (1923–   ) Argentina

Caamaño teaches courses in instrumentation, orchestration, and advanced piano at the National Conservatory in Buenos Aires. He is also director of arts of the Colón Theatre in Buenos Aires.

Concerto Op.22 1958 (Barry) 19 min. Three neoclassic movements conceived in the manner of a divertimento. First movement: SA; ironic and somewhat maudlin. Non troppo lento: song form; alternately lyrical and dramatic. Rondo: in nine parts; uses, besides its own themes, those of the first two movements; creates a variety of instrumental and rhythmic combinations. M-D to D.

Charles Wakefield Cadman (1881–1946) USA

Aurora Borealis (Fl). An Impressionistic fantasy.

Dark Dancers of the Mardi Gras, fantasy for piano and orchestra (Edition Musicus 1941; Fl) 10 min. Original title: "Scarlet Sister Mary." "The work takes its name from the Negro side of the Mardi Gras, although no Negro themes have been used. It is built on one theme with extensions. The Negroes of New Orleans have their own Mardi Gras celebration, the same time the white people have theirs. This fantasy is supposed to reflect the fantastic, the grotesque, the bizarre spirit of the carnival" (from the score). M-D.

John Cage (1912–   ) USA

Cage is an experimental composer whose style is difficult to categorize. He has moved along experimental paths first followed by Cowell and Varèse, has assimilated elements of the twelve-tone school, and has also been influenced by facets of Oriental philosophy. Cage has shown a great fascination for rhythm and percussive effects, to the point that rhythms and units of rhythm may even assume roles as his forms. He is perhaps most famous for his invention of the "prepared piano," an activity that occupied his writing for some time. More recently he has shown an interest in the aleatory or "chance" approach to composition. Although his achievements will no doubt be superseded by the experiments now being made in electronically produced sounds, he had a remarkable influence on his generation and pointed to new directions for contemporary music.

Concerto 1950–51 (CFP 6706A). For prepared piano and chamber orchestra. Reproduced from composer's MS. 22 min. Three parts (movements). Tempo indication remains constant; entirely notated; no aleatory elements. The work was constructed with the help of large charts on which the rhythmic structures were drawn up. "I let the pianist (in the first movement) express the opinion that music should be improvised or felt, while the orchestra expressed only the chart, with no personal taste involved. In the second movement, I made large concentric moves on the chart for both pianist and orchestra, with the idea of the pianist beginning to give up personal taste. The third movement had only one set of moves on the chart for both and a lot of silences. . . . Until that time, my music had been based on the traditional idea that you had to say something" (from record jacket notes, Nonesuch H71202). The piano and orchestra have frequent interchanges during the first two movements but coincide closely in the third movement while silences grow longer between sections. The last five bars are completely silent and are marked ritardando! D.

Concert 1957–58 (CFP 6706) 22 min. One of Cage's most elaborate efforts. Introduced on May 15, 1958 in New York, in a program tracing a quarter-century of Cage's evolution as a composer. Combines electronic and percussive sounds as well as "chance" elements. At times the pianist plays the keyboard in a normal fashion, and at others the strings are plucked and strummed and the piano is even thumped from below. The pianist is expected to manipulate various electronic machines occasionally, and the orchestra is also expected to perform in unusual ways. The *Concert* is made up of 84 different compositions that may be played in any sequence, in part or as a whole. Even the number of performers is variable. Much freedom of performance choice is given to each performer, the whole work being a study in chance carried to its ultimate. D.

Giovanni G. Cambini (1746–1825) Italy

Cambini was a pupil of Padre Martini and a prolific composer of instrumental works.

Concerto B♭ Op.15/1 (G. Barblan—Ric 130484 1964) 15 min. Allegro; Rondo. Editor has added appropriate cadenzas. Int.

Concerto G Op.15/3 (Barblan—Ric 1959). For keyboard and strings. 14½ min. Allegro; Rondo—Allegretto. Cadenzas by the editor. Charming, nothing pretentious. Int.

Giorgio Cambissa (1921–   ) Italy

Concerto for Trio and Orchestra 1958 (Ric). For piano, violin, double bass, and orchestra. 19 min. Allegro moderato; Adagio; Allegro. Neoclassic, freely tonal, flexible meters, atmospheric Adagio. The three soloists are generally treated as a unit and are frequently displayed soloistically. M-D.

Charles Camilleri (1931–   ) Great Britain, Malta

Camilleri writes in a style that is essentially new but at the same time very old. He expresses himself in a contemporary approach based on well-tried musical formulas used for centuries.

Concerto I "Mediterranean" (Roberton 95081).

Carlo Cammarota (1905–   ) Italy

Concerto 1958 (Zanibon 4297) 17 min. Andante mosso: SA, fast, three contrast-ing themes, chordal figuration, themes in octaves. Sereno—quasi adagio: slow, two-part form, long orchestral opening, atonal contrapuntal develop-ment; piano adds Romantic figuration. Allegro giusto: fast, neoclassic rondo with SA characteristics, dialogue between piano and orchestra handled well, strong materials and craft. M-D.

Preludio, Adagio e Toccata 1961 (Ric).

Twelve Studi da Concerto (Bongiovanni 2510).

Hector Campos Parsi (1922–   ) Puerto Rico

Duo Tragico to the Memory J. F. Kennedy 1965 (IU) full score, 43pp. Adagio; Allegro. Dramatic opening with sfzordando piano octaves. Octotonic, pref-erence for melodic seconds, textures generally thin, fast-changing chords, orchestration thins to a *pp* ending. M-D.

Bruno Canio (1935–   ) Italy

Concerto da Camera II (SZ). For two pianos and chamber orchestra. 13½ min.

Philip Cannon (1929–   ) Great Britain, born France

Concertino Op.2 1951 (Kronos Press) 12 min. Allegro molto vivace; Andante tranquillo; Presto leggiero. Sparkling; flow of ideas is natural; full of good tunes; plenty of vitality; generally thin textures. Somewhat akin to *Concer-tino* by Jean Français in style and pianistic approach. A gifted teen-ager would enjoy this work. Int. to M-D.

Pierre Capdevielle (1906–1969) France

Concerto (del dispeto) (Leduc 1960) 23 min. Capriccio; Elegia; Rondo. Freely expanded tonality; pianist moves constantly over the keyboard; ferocious conclusion. M-D to D.

Concerto Italien 1969–70 (Amphion). For prepared piano, celesta, electronic or-gan, and vocal and instrumental ensemble. Extensive performance directions in French. Masques; Madrigal; Mouvement. Avant-garde. M-D.

John Alden Carpenter (1876–1951) USA

Much of Carpenter's music might be termed American Impressionism, with an always discernible sentiment and charm allied with a fluent mastery of form and melody. Carpenter combined Impressionistic and conservatively modern com-positional techniques with elements of jazz, and was also successful in capturing elements of urban life in the United States.

Concertino 1915 revised 1949 (GS) 26 min. This pleasantly conservative light-hearted conversation between piano and orchestra is well constructed and has an effective but not overly difficult solo part. Allegro con moto: first main theme is heard in the opening statement of the piano; two other themes and development follow; restatement of the initial thematic material near the end of the movement. Lento: lyrical and poetic; in ternary form. Allegro:

begins with a section in 5/8 time that is based on material stated first in the orchestra; waltz-like section in 3/4 interrupts; opening material returns; final section utilizes material from the 3/4 waltz section; short coda with a flourish of alternating chords in the piano. Effective and accessible work with no drastic demands made on the soloist. M-D.

Patterns 1930–32 (GS) concert piece for piano and orchestra. 18 min.

Elliott Carter (1908–   ) USA

Carter is one of the most significant American composers to develop since World War II. His music reflects a subtle and original mind with great sensibility, and if his style on first hearing seems overly complex and difficult to assimilate, it amply repays the listener's efforts to understand it. Each new work shows Carter using and shaping basic materials in a highly individual way, and he uses dodecaphonic and Stravinskyan elements with a totally independent approach. In combination with a marvelous polyphonic technique, he uses a rhythmic imagination that leads to incredibly complex and expressive results. Carter often uses polyrhythms in a manner that has been described as "metrical modulation" and rhythms that play against each other both horizontally and vertically. But regardless of the level of craftsmanship and compositional complexity in his music, there is always great concern with expressive and imaginative elements. Carter is a slow worker, and has written few works for the piano, although his *Piano Sonata* of 1945 is one of the most important American contributions to that form.

Concerto 1965 (AMP) 26 min. Fantastico; Molto giusto. One of the grandest compositions written in the last fifteen years. Both movements contain a conflict between piano and orchestra. The work is constructed on twelve different three-note groups, six of which are used by the piano and concertino, and six by the orchestra. Each triad has its own particular tempi and expressive characteristics. From these components, Carter builds an incredibly complex, fascinatingly original work, one of the most significant contributions to the concerto literature of this century. The concerto ends softly with the piano by itself for the last five bars. Carter's characteristic metric modulation and thematic evolution are developed to radical lengths. Carter says of this work: "It employs no pre-established form, but is a series of short, usually overlapping episodes, mosaics of fragments that derive from parts of the basic material. . . . (Elliott Carter, in *The Composer's Point of View* [Orchestral Music], ed. R. Hines [Norman: University of Oklahoma Press, 1970], p. 58). The piano writing is contrapuntal, complex, highly dissonant, and full of nervous energy. D.

See: Merion Bowen, "Carter's Piano Concerto," M&M, 18 (May 1970): 60–61.

Irene R. Grau, "Compositional Techniques Employed in the First Movement of Elliott Carter's Piano Concerto," Ph.D. diss., Michigan State University, 1973.

Double Concerto for Harpsichord and Piano with Two Chamber Orchestras 1961 (AMP) 23 min. Introduction; Cadenza for harpsichord; Allegro scherzando; Adagio; Presto; Cadenza for piano; Coda. Continuous accelerations and decelerations are featured. The basic, dynamic concept of diverse elements gradually coming to fusion, then diffusing to the point of maximum diversity again, is the groundplan for this work. The single-movement form has a quasi-symmetrical layout, with the Introduction and Coda presenting the material in a state of maximum differentiation while the two ensembles come closest to fusion in the central Adagio. D.

Dinorá de Carvalho (1905–   ) Brazil
Early works by Carvalho were influenced by the "national music" school of Mario Andrade. Since 1967 her compositions have explored new combinations of timbre and harmony. The following works are available in MS from the composer: Rua Itacolomi, 380—Ap.62, 01239 São Paulo (SP), Brazil.
Fantasia-Concerto 1937 25 min.
Danças Brasileiras 1940 13 min.
Contrastes 1969 20 min.
Concerto II 1972 28 min.

Robert Casadesus (1899–1972) France
Although best known as a concert pianist, Casadesus composed throughout his life, in a mildly contemporary, spirited, Gallic idiom. His writing is pianistic and exploits the piano's possibilities to the ultimate.
Concerto for Two Pianos and Orchestra Op.17 1933 (SACEM) 19 min. Allegro giocoso; Intermezzo; Vivo ma non troppo.
Concerto e Op.37 1944–45 (Durand) 19½ min. Allegro con fuoco: SA; rhythmic; first theme treated contrapuntally; piano enters in a declamatory cadenza; quiet and lyrical second theme; another cadenza near the end; brilliant and toccata-like. Adagio ma non troppo: G, peaceful, lyric, meditative, clear textures, tranquil closing. Allegro moderato: E, rondo, festive and lilting, much pianistic discourse, joyous conclusion. Strongly original rhythmic language; mildly dissonant; witty; slightly modal; neoclassic leanness; eclectic with echoes of Ravel, Honegger, and Prokofiev. M-D to D.
Capriccio for Piano and String Orchestra Op.49 (GS 1975) 15 min. Allegro con fuoco: bristling, capricious, fond of triplet patterns. Vivacissimo scherzando: airy, dainty, and playful. Adagio–Allegro molto: slow atmospheric introduction leads to furious and brilliant finale requiring agile fingers. MC. M-D.
Concerto for Three Pianos and String Orchestra Op.65 1964 (Durand) 15 min. Allegro marziale: *ff* flourish introduced by the three pianos; strings have the main theme; short quiet section turns to rhythmic excitement; recapitulation and a scrumptous coda contains some uncanny cross-rhythms. Andante siciliano: shimmering strings; remarkably airy; pianos enter individually with

a quiet melody that evolves between the pianos; ethereal ending. Presto spagnuolo: strong rhythms, hammered ostinato in bass of one piano, expansive sonorities, dazzling interplay between the various forces, clangorous climax. Pianos are treated percussively in the outer movements. This work has more depth than Op.37. Requires first-rate pianistic ensemble technique. M-D.

André Casanova (1919–   ) France

Casanova "regards Nietzsche and Wagner as the main influences on his musical development" (DCM, 130).

Concertino Op.8 1963 (Jobert). For piano and chamber orchestra. 12 min. One movement; eclectic style. M-D.

Alfredo Casella (1883–1947) Italy

Casella was a strong force in contemporary Italian music through his efforts to further his country's music. He was never a highly original composer himself, possibly because he too easily assimilated the styles of others. Beginning first as a Romanticist, he tried Impressionism, polytonal writing, and finally twelve-tone techniques. His writing seems most at home in the neoclassic style, for as a scholar of old music he was able to combine its features with more contemporary trends.

A Notte Alta 1917–21 (Ric 119059) 12 min. "A programmatic symphonic poem" (so described in the score). Impressionistic. M-D.

Partita 1925 (Rieti—UE) 22 min. One of Casella's best efforts at combining older Classical forms with a more modern idiom. Sinfonia: combines such older models as the bi-thematic sonata form, the seventeenth-century suite, and the instrumental concerto grosso and concerto. Passacaglia: patterned after the old Spanish version of that dance form, with twelve successive variations and a coda. Burlesca: brilliant and lively, with the piano acting mainly in the role of accompanist. Throughout this neobaroque work the orchestral writing takes advantage of the concerto grosso style. Although the piano is given some brilliant solo work, it more often has a subordinate role in the overall orchestral texture. Technical difficulties of the piano part are not great. M-D.

Scarlattiana "Divertimento after the Music of Domenico Scarlatti" 1926 (Stein— UE). For piano and chamber orchestra. 25 min. Sinfonia; Minuetto; Capriccio; Pastorale; Finale. Neoclassic, charming. Contains some tricky spots. M-D.

Concerto Op.56 1933 (Ric; Fl). For piano, violin, cello, and orchestra. 25 min. Largo, ampico, solenne–Allegro molto vivace; Adagio; Rondo: tempo di giga. Thorough integration of solo instruments with full orchestra. At a few places the soloists are spotlighted, but only briefly. Neoclassic and freely tonal around e. M-D.

Concerto Op.69 1937 (UE). For piano, percussion, and strings. 16 min.

Joaquín Cassado (1867–1926) Spain
Hispania (Sal 1914) 51pp. One large movement. Varied sections, colorful, a little
theatrical in places, Romantic idiom. M-D.

Alvaro Cassuto (1937–   ) Portugal
"Cassuto was the first Portuguese composer to write 12-tone music. Since 1961
his approach has broadened to encompass the use of tone color as a primary
structural element" (DCM, 131–32).
Concertino C 1955–65 (MS. available from composer: Av. de Sintra, 826 Cascais,
Portugal). For piano and strings. 10 min. Allegro; Intermezzo; Finale. Neoclassic, flexible meters, lyrical writing throughout, MC. M-D.

Riccardo Castagnone (1906–   ) Italy
Toccata (Ric 1937) 22 min. Varied sections, neoclassic, MC. M-D.

Paolo Castaldi (1930–   ) Italy
Invenzione per pianoforte e orchestra (SZ 1971) 6 min. Reproduced from holograph. May also be performed without the orchestral accompaniment.

Mario Castelnuovo-Tedesco (1895–1968) Italy
Castelnuovo-Tedesco's music has derived from several influences, nonmusical as
well as musical. A neoromantic of considerable taste and imagination, he was
influenced by his native city of Florence, the works of Shakespeare, his Jewish
heritage, and the Bible. Castelnuovo-Tedesco was a pianist of great ability, and
this is reflected in his effective, often difficult, writing for the instrument.
Concerto I G Op.46 1927 (UE 8863) 28 min. Allegro giusto; Andantino alla
Romanza; Vivo e festoso. Brilliant, virtuosic, acrobatic conclusion. M-D
to D.
Concerto II F Op.92 1936–37 (Forlivesi) 26½ min. Vivo: graceful; principal
themes introduced by the orchestra before being developed by the piano.
Romanza: poetic; followed by a cadenza. Vivo e impetuoso: brilliant and
effective finale. A good example of modern (1936–37) Italian Baroque writing. M-D.

René de Castéra (1873–1955) France
Concerto (Sal).

Jacques Castérède (1926–   ) France
Concertino (Leduc 1959). For piano, trumpet, trombone, percussion, and string
orchestra. 13 min. Allegro energico; Andante sostenuto; Allegro. Bright
"Gallic" sonorities, neoclassic, clever, MC. Entertaining for audience, fun
for performers. M-D.
Concerto (Sal). For piano and strings. 23 min.

Niccolo Castiglioni (1932–   ) Italy
Boulez has been a strong influence on Castiglioni's later works, including the
three listed below.

Movimento Continuato (SZ 1961). For piano and chamber orchestra. 5½ min. Spidery textures, snippeted sonorities, fluctuating dynamics, plenty of dissonance. M-D.

Arabeschi 1971–72 (Ric). For piano, flute, and orchestra. 18 min. Reproduced from holograph.

Quodlibet 1975 (Ric 132559). Concerto for piano and chamber orchestra. Facsimile score.

Alexis de Castillon (1838–1873) France

Concerto D Op.12 (Jobert) 70pp. Allegro moderato; Molto lento; Allegro con fuoco. In the Saint-Saëns tradition; symphonic treatment of material; non-virtuosic; interplay of themes is effected fluently and easily; a few sudden tonality changes. M-D.

José Maria Castro (1892–1964) Argentina

Concerto 1941 (Ric; Fl). Predominantly neoclassic, economical style, light and transparent, MC. M-D.

Juan José Castro (1895–1968) Argentina

Castro wrote in an eclectic style that is not easily categorized, for he was cosmopolitan both as a person and as a composer. His harmonic vocabulary "drew on everything from major triads to polytonal chords to unresolved dissonances and strict serialism" (DCM, 132).

Concerto 1941 (Ric Amer) 30 min. Allegro vivo; Tragico; Allegro vivo. Expanded tonality, effective pianistic idioms and whole-tone usage. M-D.

Ricardo Castro (1864–1907) Mexico

Concerto A Op.22 (Hofmeister 1906) 77pp. Allegro moderato; Andante; Polonaise.

Vals Capricho (Hofmeister 1901) 7 min. Originally a solo piano work, then arranged for piano and orchestra. Emphasis on nineteenth-century virtuosic display. M-D.

Georges Catoire (1861–1926) Russia

Concerto Op.21A (Bo&H 1912) 30 min. Moderato, con entusiasmo: cadenza, set of variations. Andante cantabile: Brahmsian figuration. Allegro risoluto: brilliant and festive, post-Romantic style. M-D.

Norman Cazden (1914–1980) USA

Multiple influences have shaped the music of Cazden. His style is characterized by a personal treatment of tonality, widely expanded in concept but carefully controlled. There is a marked rhythmic impulse in his writing, and sometimes he dispenses entirely with time signatures. His thematic treatment consists largely of a sort of evolving variation.

Concerto for Ten Instruments Op.10 1937 (MCA). Features the piano and the viola. 15 min.

Francis Chagrin (1905–1972) Great Britain, born Rumania
Concerto (Lengnick 1948) 25 min. Allegro risoluto; Molto tranquillo; Allegro vivace. Expanded tonality, effective pianistic writing. M-D.

Boris A. Chaikovskii (1929–   ) USSR
Konsert (USSR 1973) 99pp. Five movements. Post-Romantic and Impressionistic idiom. Effective use of piano and orchestra. D.
Concerto (Soviet Composer 1977) 68pp. Toccata; Phantasy. Freely tonal, key signatures used, strong rhythms, many repeated chords, MC. Large span required. M-D.

Julius Chajes (1910–   ) USA
Concerto E 1953 (Transcontinental) 27 min. Allegro deciso; Andante cantabile; Allegro vivace e con fuoco. Expanded tonal idiom, varied pianistic figurations, well-developed ideas. M-D.
Romantic Phantasy (Fl). For piano and chamber orchestra.

Cecile Chaminade (1857–1944) France
Chaminade was described by Norman Demuth in *French Piano Music* as the "moderate performer's Fauré." She had an innate gift for lyricism and the ability to write music that sounds a lot more difficult than it is.
Konzertstück c♯ Op.40 (Enoch 1896; Ashdown). This brilliant, high-spirited, and whimsical one-movement work with flashes of Bizet and Saint-Saëns was premiered by the composer in her American debut in 1908. It is ingratiatingly harmonious throughout, a wholly engaging potpourri, and her pianism is always impeccable. M-D.

Claude Champagne (1891–1965) Canada
Champagne's music always sings. It reflects the richness and color of the Canadian scene the composer lived in.
Concerto d 1950 (BMI Canada) 14 min. Introduction, moderato; Lento; Vif. Strongly contrasted movements in a post-Romantic idiom, in spite of its date. M-D.

John Barnes Chance (1932–   ) USA
Introduction and Capriccio (Bo&H 1966). For piano and 24 winds. 7 min. Neoclassic orientation, freely tonal, octotonic, secco style, tremolo and repeated chords, glissandi, linear textures, *pp* conclusion. M-D.

Julien Chardon (1909–   ) France
Concerto E♭ 1941 (Francis Day) 65pp. One large movement. Freely tonal. M-D.

Jacques Charpentier (1933–   ) France
Charpentier has been strongly influenced by Hindu music and philosophies.
Concerto IV (Leduc 1974). For piano and string orchestra. 14 min. A one-movement work with contrasting sections. Twelve-tone, clusters, cadenza-like passages, freely repeated figures, tremolo chords between alternating hands, widely spaced textures. M-D.

Abram Chasins (1903–   ) USA
Concerto I f Op.14 1928 (Fl) 20 min. Allegro; Andante; Presto. Well constructed.
    Finale is an effective tarantella. M-D.
Concerto II f# 1932 revised 1937 (Fl) 25 min. One continuous movement with
    variations on the themes. M-D.

Carlos Chávez (1899–1978) Mexico
Certain traits in the music of Chávez are derived from native Mexican music and
are fused with harmonic and instrumental techniques from the twentieth century.
In much of his writing there is austerity and starkness, sudden contrasts, archaic
idioms, strong dissonances, and a varied use of primitive rhythms.
Concerto 1938–40 revised 1969 (GS) 96pp. Largo non troppo–Allegro agitato;
    Molto lento; Allegro non troppo. Chávez treats the orchestra and piano as
    equal partners, giving both strongly virtuosic parts. The music is powerfully
    austere, exotic through its use of archaic elements in the middle movement,
    and percussively brilliant in the outer movements. The very rhythmic piano
    writing is basically single notes and octaves, rather than chords. Bartók
    influence is seen in some of the harmonic vocabulary, musical gestures, and
    concepts of concerto style. A highly complex, difficult work for all perform-
    ers concerned, it requires more than one hearing to be understood and
    appreciated. The grandeur of the piano writing is most impressive in the
    toccata-like finale. This work is one of the largest concertos of the twentieth
    century. D.

Charles Chaynes (1925–   ) France
Chaynes studied with Darius Milhaud and Jean Rivier. He won the Prix de Rome
in 1951.
Concerto 1966 (Leduc) 22 min. Lento misterioso–Allegro: the music gradually
    emerges from a short introduction made of wavering calls of the soloist over
    a pianissimo background of the orchestra; this introduction leads, through
    a crescendo, to the rhythmic and vigorous Allegro, which gradually exalts
    itself. Adagio molto espressivo: conceived like a succession of musical ideas,
    linked in increasing depth of feeling—a crescendo of intensity and of lyri-
    cism; ends in an atmosphere of appeasement. Allegro risoluto con esalta-
    zione: overflowing with life, very colorful, features the soloist's virtuosity.
    The work is basically atonal, and uses the orchestra to good advantage.
    M-D to D.

Raymond Chevreuille (1901–   ) Belgium
Music for Chevreuille is an expression of sentiments and psychological states,
where tenderness and poetic freshness dominate. His works achieve balance and
reveal a composer who is animated by a genuine creative urge.
Concerto I Op.10 1937 (CeBeDeM) 22 min.
Concerto Op.34 (CeBeDeM 1946). For piano, alto sax (or viola), and orchestra.
    21 min.
Concerto II Op.50 1952 (ESC; Schott Frères 8964) 23 min. Commissioned for

the Queen Elisabeth Competition. Allegro non troppo; Lento; Presto. Neo-classic. Requires some pianistic acrobatics. M-D to D.

Concerto III Op.88 1968 (CeBeDeM) 20 min. In three movements.

Iurii Mikhailovich Chichkov (1929–   ) USSR

Concerto on Kabardino-Balkarskie Themes (USSR 1965). Three movements (FSF). Expanded tonality, modal and exciting melodies. M-D.

Thomas Chilcot (ca.1700–1766) Great Britain

Chilcot wrote two sets of harpsichord concertos and other works devoted mainly to the instrument on which he was obviously a brilliant executant. These two works are more suitable for performance on a harpsichord but have effective moments on the piano. The keyboardist should extemporize a simple harmonic continuo part in the tuttis, except in short passages of antiphonal writing.

Concerto A Op.2/2 (Langley—OUP) Musica Camera 32. For keyboard and strings. 10 min. Three movements (FSF). Int.

Concerto F Op.2/5 (Langley—OUP) Musica Camera 33. For keyboard and strings. 11 min. Allegro spiritoso; Adagio; Giga. Sequential development, Mannheim-Italianate style, ornate middle movement, delightful. Int. to M-D.

Erik Chisholm (1904–1965) Union of South Africa, born Scotland

Concerto II 1949 (Schott 10180) 31 min. Based on Hindustani themes. Poco maestoso e con fuoco: strong rhythms, free counterpoint, brilliant cadenza. Andante: theme and seven contrasting variations; an effective upward glissando on both black and white keys in Var. 4 adds interest. Rondo Burlesca: dancelike; dramatic and highly exciting conclusion. Presents an artful fusion of Hindu ragas with MC harmonies. M-D to D.

Frederic Chopin (1810–1849) Poland

From the pianist's point of view, the two Chopin concertos are admirable. The *Second Concerto* in f was actually the first in order of composition. Both works were composed when Chopin was between nineteen and twenty-one. The writing for the piano is superb: florid, yet distinguished by brilliance and poetry. The solo parts still constitute a challenge to the technical and interpretive abilities of any pianist. Both works represent an uneasy effort to confine a new and revolutionary technique with the limits of the Classical mold. The piano dominates the texture and places the orchestra in a solely accompanying role.

Variations on Mozart's "La ci darem" Op.2 1827 (PWM; GS; CF) 14 min. Introductory Largo leads to an effective set of five Hummel-inspired variations. Well-developed technique required. M-D.

Concerto e Op.11 1830 (PWM; CFP; Br.&H; Debussy—Durand; Mikuli—K&S; Joseffy—GS; Eulenburg; Augener; Forsyth; Zen-On) 33 min. Unique pianistic writing throughout, long passages of figuration, glittering brilliance alternating with a peculiar expressiveness. Allegro maestoso: soloist reigns supreme; orchestral interruptions only at end of exposition and recapitulation. Larghetto: a lovely accompanied nocturne that reveals Chopin's mastery of expressive ornamentation. Rondo—Vivace: Polish dance influence, bright, strong rhythmic vitality in main theme. Orchestra provides only a harmonic backdrop for the piano. D.

Grand Fantasia on Polish Airs Op.13 1828 (PWM; GS; Mikuli—K&S 1880; Reinecke—Br&H 1880; Leduc; CF) 15 min. Similar to Op.2 but not as deep. The simple tune is decorated with increasingly ornate passagework. M-D to D.

Krakowiak F Op.14 1828 (PWM; GS; Mikuli—K&S 1880; Reinecke—Br&H 1881; CF) 14 min. A Krakowiak is a Polish dance in 2/4 time from the Cracow district. A short introduction leads to a brilliant Allegro with difficult figuration. Requires careful solution of the technical problems. M-D to D.

Concerto f Op.21 1829–30 (PWM; Mikuli—K&S 1880; Reinecke—Br&H 1881; Friedman—Br&H 1914; Pozniak—CFP; Debussy—Durand; Joseffy—GS; Kreutzer—Hug 1927; CF; Eulenburg; Ric; Augener; Zen-On) 30 min. Maestoso; Larghetto; Finale—Allegro vivace. This work demonstrates Chopin's inimitable pianistic writing, unsurpassed penchant for melody, and instinct for tone coloring. The finest orchestration occurs in the second (with its nocturne-type melody) and third movements. The finale is a Hummel-like rondo with mazurka characteristics. Unique demands are made on the pianist; requires great facility in long passages of figuration and technical brilliance. D.

Grand Polonaise E♭ Op.22 1830–31 (PWM; Mikuli—K&S 1880; Friedman—Br&H 1914) 15 min. This concoction is two pieces glued together by Chopin and performed by him at the Paris Conservatoire in 1835. The Polonaise was composed in 1830–31, and the Andante spianato followed in 1834. The Andante ripples along smoothly, while the Polonaise has a lot of youthful energy and bravura but seemingly no deep national feeling. M-D.

The Joseffy (GS) edition of Opp.2, 13, 14, and 22 contains second-piano parts printed separately.

See: Ruth Slenczynska, "On Chopin's Unexpected Invitations to Dance," PQ, 106 (Summer 1979): 24–25. Discusses the dance elements in both concertos as well as the *Etude* Op.25/5.

Chung Yang Yüeh T'uan (Central Music Organization)
See **Yellow River Concerto.**

Jan Cikker (1911–   ) Czech
Initially Cikker wrote "music [that] was a synthesis of Slovak folk-music elements and European concert traditions. Later on he was drawn to the expressionistic music drama stemming from Berg" (DCM, 142).
Concertino 1942 (Simrock).

Johann Cilenšek (1913–   ) Germany
Konzert 1950 (Br&H) 25 min. A well-crafted three-movement (FSF) work in neoclassic style, à la Hindemith with expanded tonal practice. Piano writing

utilizes too much polyphony. The songlike middle movement features the piano prominently. D.

Konzertstück (CFP 9108 1966) 18 min. Fantasie; Adagio; Tokkata. Displays a lively tonal imagination and a flair for melody within the restrictions of twelve-tone technique. Dynamic extremes, flexible meters. M-D.

Domenico Cimarosa (1749–1801) Italy

Cimarosa was a marvelous virtuoso, and his command and knowledge of the keyboard were astonishing. He adapted the prevailing orchestral and operatic styles of his day to the pianoforte, reducing them to a compositional style of extraordinary lightness and subtlety.

Concerto B♭ (Ballola—SZ 1973) full score, 55pp. Revision and cadenzas by the editor. Allegro; Aria; Rondo. Elegant and graceful music requiring modest technique. Operatic influence seen in the Aria. Int. to M-D.

Michel Ciry (1919–   ) France

Concerto II (Schott). For piano, winds, and percussion. 16 min.

Avery Claflin (1898–   ) USA

Pop Concert Concerto 1957 (ACA) 17 min. Allegro con brio; Andantino; Largo—Doppio movimento. Light; saucy; Gershwin and blues influence. Well written for the pianist; effective. M-D.

Philip G. Clapp (1888–1954) USA

Concerto b (Fl). For two pianos and orchestra.

Aldo Clementi (1925–   ) Italy

Stravinsky, Schoenberg, and Webern have had a strong influence on Clementi. His "works of the early 1960's began to incorporate an indeterminancy of detail within fixed gestures" (DCM, 143).

Concerto 1967 (SZ 7293). For piano four-hands and chamber (strings and winds) ensemble. 8 min. Uses an electric harmonium throughout, which sounds a very soft cluster produced by a wooden board held down by a weight. One pianist can perform the work, but two pianists can better differentiate the twelve parts in their durational values. Different registers of the piano are retuned (a quarter-tone below concert pitch, a quarter-tone above, etc.). Avant-garde. M-D.

Concerto 1975 (SZ). For piano, 24 instruments, and carillons.

Muzio Clementi (1752–1832) Italy

Concerto C ca.1790 (Ric 130491) 24 min. Clementi played this concerto in London on February 22, 1790 at one of the "professional" concerts. In 1794 it was published in Clementi's own arrangement for piano solo as Op.36/3. The works are similar; the sonata omits the orchestral accompaniment and interludes. Allegro con spirito: SA; energetic; solo part set off nicely by the orchestral treatment; written-out cadenza. Adagio cantabile e con grande espressione: Italian operatic influence; cadenza called for but not left by Clementi. Presto: rondo; bursting with attractive tunes; a delightful perpetual motion. The outer movements bubble with zest and good humor. Arpeggi, rippling scale passages, and sixteenth-note filigree passages are abundant. Provides a fine introduction to the Beethoven Concertos I and II. Int. to M-D.

Halfdan Cleve (1879–1951) Norway

Concerto I A Op.3 (Br&H 1903; Fl) 29 min. Four movements.

Concerto II b Op.6 (Br&H 1905; Fl) 25 min. Three movements (FSF). Contains some dynamic and effective virtuosity. M-D to D.

Concerto III E♭ Op.9 (Br&H 1907; Fl) 27 min. For piano and four strings. Four movements. Large Romantic gestures. This is really a piano quintet but is listed here because of the title. M-D.

Concerto IV a Op.12 (TONO) 30 min. Three movements.

Concerto V c♯ Op.20 (TONO) 32 min. Three movements.

Henri Cliquet-Pleyel (1894–1963) France

Concerto (Jobert). For piano, right-hand and orchestra. 21 min.

Robert Arnold Clough (   ) Union of South Africa

Concertino 1972 (Cantabilé) 15 min. "The Concertino was designed and written for the young, teenage pianist in mind. It is a one-movement work comprising an Introduction, an Allegro, a slow Middle-section (cantabilé e espress), Recapitulation and a Coda. The content of the work is lyrical and the material is set within a modal framework" (letter from the composer to the author, January 4, 1980). Int. to M-D.

Ruy Coelho (1891—   ) Portugal

Portuguese folk and popular music have been strong influences on Coelho's compositions. The following works are available in MS from the composer: Av. Marquês de Tomar, 106, 2°E, Lisbon, Portugal.

Concerto I 1909 full score, 133pp. Liberamente; Andante; Allegro deciso. A large virtuoso work in late nineteenth-century style and idiom. D.

Concerto II 1948.

Noites nas Ruas da Mouraria ("Nights in the Streets of Mouraria"), Mouraria is a Moorish part of the city. In the same vein as de Falla's *Nights in the Gardens of Spain*.

Rapsódia Portugueza.

James Cohn (1928–   ) USA

Concertino G♯ Op.8 1946 (Fl) 22 min. Four movements.

Avril Coleridge-Taylor (1903–   ) Great Britain

Concerto f (PRS) 30 min.

Giulio Confaloniera (1896–1972) Italy

Concerto (Ric 1961). For piano and strings. 20 min. Poco maestoso; Allegro ben marcato; Poco andante; Allegro festoso. Freely tonal around C, neoclassic, some fugal techniques, very beautiful Andante. M-D.

Marius Constant (1926—   ) France, born Rumania
Constant studied with Messiaen, Boulanger, and Honegger. "His contacts with George Enescu during World War II affected his subsequent musical development" (DCM, 147).
Concerto I (Billaudot) 17 min. In addition to being highly effective writing for the piano, this work fully displays Constant's ability to manipulate orchestral color. M-D.

Dan Constantinescu (1931–   ) Rumania
"Constantinescu's music has been influenced by the late works of Enescu and by Messiaen, Webern and Boulez" (DCM, 147).
Concerto 1963 (Muzicală). For piano and string orchestra.
Concerto (Muzicală). For two pianos and chamber orchestra. 12½ min.

Paul Constantinescu (1909–1963) Rumania
Concerto 1952 (Editura di Stat) 21 min. Allegro: uses ingratiating authentic Rumanian melodies and rhythms. Andante: displays characteristic Balkan rhythmic asymmetry. Presto: thematic material derived from Transylvanian folk dances. M-D.
Triple Concerto (Editura di Stat). For piano, violin, cello, and orchestra. The composer's last work; performed for the first time in Bucharest on Dec. 28, 1963, eight days after Constantinescu's death.

Gino Contilli (1907–   ) Italy
Since 1942 Contilli has taught composition at the Liceo musicale in Messina, Italy.
Suite (UE 1954). For piano, percussion, and string orchestra. Passacaglia; Sarabanda; Galiardo. Twelve-tone. Piano and percussion are used to add touches of color and articulation. Overly explicit and long. M-D.

Frederick Shepherd Converse (1871–1940) USA
Night and Day Op.11 1905 (BMC 1906; Fl) 61pp. Two poems for piano and orchestra. Night: andante, molto sostenuto e tranquillo. Day: allegro con fuoco. Tonal, Impressionistic. M-D.
Fantasy 1922 (Fl).
Concertino 1932 (SB 1940; Western Music Library) 10 min. Allegro vivace e scherzando; Andante cantabile ed espressivo; Moderato e tranquillo.

Eugène Cools (1877–1936) France
Overture Symphonique Poem Op.94 (ESC 1935) 20 min. Tonal, nineteenth-century pianistic idiom, some Impressionistic influences, somewhat in Fauré style. M-D.

David Cope (1941–   ) USA
Cope has a strong affinity for the theater and for dramatic intensity in his large instrumental works.

Variations 1965 (Seesaw). For piano and wind orchestra. 12 min. Employs the piano in a highly effective manner and shows unusual treatment of dynamics. Carefully shaded phrases. M-D.

Aaron Copland (1900–   ) USA
Copland has been one of the strongest influences on the contemporary American musical scene and one of the most respected figures in American music. His style has undergone several transformations, from an early preoccupation with poly-rhythmic music and jazz elements; through a powerful dissonant, percussive, and abstract phase, which changed suddenly to a more popular, accessible idiom; and finally to a number of serial attempts. Recently Copland has composed less and less but has been busy as a spokesman for American music with his books, articles, lectures, and administrative assignments.

Concerto 1926 (Bo&H) 18 min. This youthful masterwork was the last of Copland's attempts to write large works in a jazz idiom. Although not received well initially, it has since proved significant, even though the musical materials are somewhat dated. It makes an effective pianistic impression. The two movements are played without interruption. Andante sostenuto: thematic material of great integrity stated in a short orchestral introduction. Molto moderato: SA design; first theme introduced by the solo piano and the second by a soprano saxophone; followed by development, a piano cadenza, a recall of part of the first movement, and a short coda. The writing is highly dissonant with strong jazz rhythmic elements. A fluent, strong chord technique is demanded of the soloist. Large orchestration. M-D to D.

Piero Coppola (1888–1971) Italy
Coppola was trained in Italy as a composer and conductor and later settled in France. His style is late nineteenth century, suggestive of Liszt and Saint-Saëns.

Poeme (ESC 1931) 30 min. Thoroughly nineteenth-century harmonic technique with a lush Romantic lyricism and texture. Allegro, ma non troppo: traditionally constructed in SA design. Lento: lyrical, with a florid, chromatic piano part. Vivace: brilliant finale featuring much rapid octave display in the solo piano. Essentially a period piece, might merit a re-hearing with the current revival of interest in nineteenth-century music. Requires good octave chord and passage technique; difficulty about the same as in the Saint-Säens *Fourth Piano Concerto*. M-D.

John Corigliano (1938–   ) USA
While making imaginative use of contemporary techniques, Corigliano writes works of unusual accessibility. He teaches at Herbert Lehman College.

Concerto 1968 (GS) 30 min. Molto allegro: SA; contrasts nervous metrical flexibility with a beautiful lyric flow. Scherzo: suggests Bartók; tripartite; many brilliant percussive effects. Appassionato; great leaps and their inversions provide the motivation. Allegro: five-part rondo; uses fugal techniques and clusters. A virtuosic work with genuine impact written in a present-day Romanticism. It has some affinities with the Samuel Barber *Piano Concerto*. D.

Gino Corini (1914–   ) Italy

Concerto 1953 (SZ). Allegro: pleasant but mixed with some effective dissonant voice leading. Second movement: lyrical, straightforward. Finale: many figurations in piano contrast with orchestral melodic ideas. M-D.

Michel Corrette (1709–1795) France

Corrette was a bridge between the last stages of the French baroque tradition and the new, cosmopolitan *galant* style of the later eighteenth century. He seems to point toward the Italian-oriented Johann Christian Bach, and both concertos sound like him much of their merry way.

Concerto II A Op.26/2 (Ruf—Schott 6186) 28pp. Allegro; Adagio; Giga. Int.

Concerto VI d Op.26/6 (Ruf—Nag 210 1959; Billaudot). For harpsichord or organ, flute, 3 violins, viola, and cello, 8 min. Allegro; Andante; Presto. The flute is necessary only if the solo part is played on organ. Skillful and attractive writing. Int.

Philip Antony Corri (1784–1832) USA

Corri was an early American composer whose works deserve reviving. Eugene List performed the following work at his New York recital of September 15, 1979.

Concerto da Camera (Chappell 1812; NYPL). For piano and strings.

César Cortinas (1890–1918) Uruguay

Cortinas's "works show a universalist character and a completely eclectic tendency, of great lyricism and with expressive vehemence within a very free formal line" (*Composers of the Americas,* vol.16 [Washington, D.C.: Organización de los Estados Americanos, 1970], p. 64).

Concierto d (Ric) holograph.

Morris Cotel (–   ) USA

Concerto 1973 (Horn of Gabriel Music Publishers). Directions in English and Italian. "Each score page takes about 10-15 seconds. The conductor gives the beat and each part goes as written" (from the score). Expressionistic, pointillistic. Experimental notation; terribly complex rhythms. Some sections may be played in any order. Avant-garde. D.

Jean Coulthard (1908–   ) Canada

Fantasy 1960 (CMC). For piano, violin, and chamber orchestra, 20 min. Rhapsodic, post-Impressionist style influence, subtle emotional substance, modal shades balanced with atonal harmonies. M-D.

Concerto 1963 (Available from composer: c/o Music Department, University of British Columbia, Vancouver B.C., Canada) 30 min.

Henry Cowell (1897–1965) USA

Cowell was a prolific composer with over a thousand compositions to his credit. His music covers an enormous range of styles and influences, from Irish folk music to American rural hymnology. The music of the Orient and of the Near and Middle East were also a strong creative impetus. He was an important early twentieth-century experimenter, well known for "tone clusters" and the use of the hands directly on the strings to gain unusual sound effects.

Irish Suite (1928–29 (LC) 15 min. The Fairy Bells; The Banshee; The Leprechaun.

Concerto 1929 (Senart) 17 min. Polyharmony: fluent motives are supported by Milhaud-like harmonies; two-octave wide tone clusters played with the forearm. Tone Cluster: secundal harmony is stretched to the limit, uses three-note clusters within the space of a major or minor third, often in a melodic line; wildly rhythmic outbursts in disjunct meters frequently interrupt the otherwise essential cantabile character of this movement. Counter Rhythm: ever-changing groups of ten-note chromatic clusters constitute the main building blocks; shifting metrical patterns; massive three-octave tone clusters at one point. In an Eastman School of Music program for March 24, 1932, Cowell said: "The Concerto is an exploration into a new musical field in the attempt to discover new musical values." The work has an inherent charm and approaches Charles Ives's grandeur. M-D.

Tales of Our Countryside "Four Irish Legends" (AMP 1940) 13 min. Deep Tides; Exultation; The Harp of Life; Country Reel. Originally written as piano pieces between 1922 and 1930, the movements were later joined and expanded into the *Tales*. Each movement was written in a different state: Deep Tides during a stay on the California coast, Exultation in the hills of the Hudson River Valley, The Harp of Life in the Iowa cornfields, and Country Reel in western Kansas. Some tone clusters are used on the piano but for the most part the suite is Romantic, conservative, and immediately accessible. A folk music style is used, however all tunes are original with Cowell. The first, third, and fourth sections have feelings of the Aeolian mode, and the second of Mixolydian. There is no attempt at development of themes, as would be expected in a regular piano concerto. M-D.

Little Concerto (Concerto Piccolo) (LC 1943; Fl) orchestral version. (AMP 1951) for piano and band. 7½ min. Introduction and Step Dance; Rondo: Andante; Hornpipe.

Suite 1943 (AMP; ACA) 10 min. Four movements. Available in piano and strings version and piano and band version.

Edward Cowie (1943–   ) Great Britain
Cowie has been a member of the music staff at Lancaster University since 1973. *Concerto* (Schott).

Johann Baptist Cramer (1771–1858) Germany
A pupil of Clementi, Cramer had a successful career touring as a virtuoso. Beethoven met Cramer in a competition and was quoted by Ries as saying that "Cramer was the only pianist of his time. 'All the rest count for nothing' " (Harold Schonberg, *The Great Pianists* [New York: Simon & Schuster, 1963], p. 60). Cramer was one of the first pianists to feature works by other composers in

his recitals. His own compositions are characterized by solid musical taste. Cramer composed a number of brilliant concertos.

Concerto E♭ Op.10 (Br&H).

Concerto d Op.26/2 (Hofmann—Mannheimer) 24 min.

Concerto IV C Op.38 1807 (Br&H; NYPL). In the first movement the cadenza is placed before the second subject, as Carl M. von Weber did in his E♭ Concerto. M-D.

Concerto V c Op.48 (Clementi) 29 min. A note on the Clementi edition indicates that the work was written "for the Piano Forte As newly Constructed by Clementi & Co. with Additional Keys up to F." Allegro maestoso: dark-hued and dramatic. Larghetto: an elegant nocturne. Rondo a l'hongroise: similar to the last movement of the Haydn *Concerto* D (H.XVIII/11), but with more legato treatment. M-D.

Concerto VI E♭ Op.51 (Br&H; Chappell 1812?). The Chappell edition is at the BPL.

Concerto VIII E Op.56 (Br&H).

Concerto VIII B♭ Op.70 (CFP).

Jean Cras (1879–1932) France

Concerto 1931 (Sal) 25 min. Lent–Modéré; Très lent; Très animé. Freely tonal around B♭, glissandi, colorful. M-D.

Paul Creston (1906–   ) USA

Creston is a fairly prolific composer for the piano. His work, which has generally evolved from traditional compositional procedures, has a strong Romantic feeling colored by Impressionism and modal harmonies. Elements of song and dance have fascinated him and have often influenced the forms his works have taken. His writing for the piano is idiomatic and usually effective.

Fantasy Op.32 1942 (GS) 8 min. In one movement of four contrasting sections. Strong rhythms, freely tonal around D, highly effective, exciting for performer and listener. M-D.

Concerto Op.43 1949 (SP) 20 min. Allegro maestoso: the rhapsodic main theme is presented by the full orchestra, then taken up by the piano; the second theme appears in the cellos and basses; after development of these themes, the movement ending brilliantly. Andante tranquillo: pastoral; two principal themes. Presto: tarantella-like finale maintains a strong rhythmic drive to the end. M-D.

Concerto for Two Pianos and Orchestra Op.50 1951 (SP) 20 min. Allegro energico; Andante pastorale; Allegro vivace.

Janus Op.77 (CF 1959). For piano and strings. A diptych consisting of a lyric prelude and a fast dance with a single theme for both sections. In unvarying triple time but greatly variegated as to rhythms and polyrhythms. M-D.

Ivor Cruz (1901–   ) Portugal, born Brazil

In 1938 Cruz became director of the Lisbon Conservatory and has been a guiding light in the musical activity of that city.

Portuguese Concerto I (Coimbra) 1945 revised 1969 (MS available from composer: % Sassetti) 51pp. Fonte dos Amores; Choupal. Santa Clara-a-Velha.
The titles of the movements refer to areas in the city of Coimbra (site of one
of the oldest universities in Europe). Played without interruption. Style is
similar to that of *Portuguese Concerto* II. M-D.

Portuguese Concerto II (Lisbon) (Sassettti 1958) 47pp. A large one-movement
work in contrasting sections with cadenzas interspersed. Broad Romantic
gestures, glissandi, strong rhythms, colorful. Sophisticated pianism required. M-D to D.

Paul Csonka (1905–   ) Cuba
Cuban Concerto I (PIC; Fl) 8 min.

Arthur Cunningham (1928–   ) USA
Dialogue 1967 (Cunningham Music Corp.; IU) 10 min. Twelve-tone, expressionistic, thin textures, octotonic. Much interplay between piano and orchestra;
lives up to its title. M-D.

Concerto Op.26 1968 (Seesaw) 20 min.

Pataditas 1971 (TP) 5 min. From "Harlem Suite." Freely tonal, dramatic gestures, long trills, shifting meters, octotonic, strong rhythms. Cadenza passages for piano; large span required. M-D.

Michael Cunningham (1937–   ) USA
Cunningham teaches at the University of Wisconsin-Eau Claire.

Concerto 1968 (Seesaw) 20 min. Jive: ragtime and jazz influence; octotonic;
glissandi move over keyboard; triplets with quadruplets; large span required.
Requiem: blues influence; arpeggiated tenth in left hand; legato and lyric;
animated mid-section, freely tonal figuration, *ppp* ending. Toccata: octotonic
rhythmic lines; generally thin textures; tremolo chords in alternating hands
ppp to *fff* close out the work. M-D.

Gonzalo Curiel (1904–   ) Mexico
Concerto I D (Promotoro Hispano Americana de Musica 1960). Four effective
and contrasting movements that owe much to the Tchaikowsky and Khachaturian tradition. Makes a big audience impression and has some fine musical
ideas, but the piece seems tawdry in many ways. D.

Cornelius Czerniawski (1888–   ) Poland
Notturno (Edition Modern) 6 min.

Willi Czernik (1901–   ) Germany
Dionysisches Fest (Ahn & Simrock 1954) 13 min. Contrasting sections and
moods, freely tonal. M-D.

Carl Czerny (1791–1857) Austria
Czerny received a thorough musical education from his father, but also studied
with Beethoven from 1800 to 1803. He was an amazingly prolific composer, and
some of his most effective compositions are in the genre of music for piano and

orchestra. Manuscripts of Czerny's works are in the library of the Gesellschaft de Musikfreunde in Vienna.

Concerto F Op.28 (Diabelli).

Variations on a Haydn Theme Op.73 (Mechetti). "Gott, erhalte den Kaiser," later known as "Deutschland über Alles," is the variation theme of the second movement of Haydn's *Quartet* Op.76/3. Czerny's work has a long, brilliant introduction, a quasi-cadenza, a statement of the theme, the series of variations, and a brilliant coda. Its structure is similar to Chopin's *Variations on "La ci darem la mano."* A charming, skillfully fashioned, and spirited work. M-D.

Concertino C Op.78 (Haslinger).

Concerto C Op.153 (Haslinger). For piano, four-hands and orchestra. A charming tribute to Beethoven's influence. In thematic invention and orchestration this work is worthy of its model, but the development leaves something to be desired. M-D.

Concertino C Op.210 (Musica Obscura; Haslinger).

Concerto a Op.214 (Hofmeister) 28 min. Allegro moderato: binary form, Adagio con moto, cantabile: monothematic. Allegro con anima: rondo. Well constructed; exploits the piano beautifully. M-D.

Quatuor Concert C Op.230 (Diabelli). For four pianos and orchestra.

Concertino avec Orchestre Op.650 (Diabelli).

D

Gordon Dale (1935–   ) Great Britain
Concerto Op.37 (PRS). For piano, percussion, and strings. 14½ min.

Luigi Dallapiccola (1904–1975) Italy
Dallapiccola uses the twelve-tone system in a highly personal manner. He exploits the sensuous qualities of sound more insistently than do most other dodecaphonic composers. He has even "created vocal lines containing elements of the *bel canto* tradition" (DCM, 164).
Piccolo Concerto per Muriel Couvreux 1939–41 (Carisch 20218). For piano and chamber orchestra. Pastorale, Girotondo e Ripresa; Cadenza, Notturno e Finale. Octotonic, repeated chords, figuration in alternating hands, glissandi, four sixteenths with triplets, brilliant figuration, flexible meters, five-second pause between movements, quartal and quintal harmony. Large span required. M-D.

Jean Damase (1928–   ) France
Concerto I 1950 (Sal 15865) 62pp. Allegro; Andante; Allegro. Octotonic, broad gestures. Requires large span, MC. M-D.
Concerto II (EMT 810 1966) 51pp. Effective and fluent piano writing, strong melodic and rhythmic elements. Freely tonal with key signatures in the last two movements. M-D.
Rhapsodie de Printemps 1960 (EMT 353) 45pp. Allegro moderato; Andante; Allegro. No break between movements. Quasi-cadenza sections; post-Romantic style. M-D.

Georges Dandelot (1895–1964) France
Concerto 1932 (ESC) 22 min.

Jean Yves Daniel-Lesur (1908–   ) France
In 1936 Daniel-Lesur founded the group Jeune France with Olivier Messiaen, André Jolivet, and Yves Baudrier. His personal idiom is marked by strong, insistent rhythms (frequently derived from dance patterns) and an almost English pastoral quality.
Variations 1943 (Costallat). For piano and string orchestra. 18 min. Theme and ten variations. Skillful exhausting of the mixed marriage of the piano–strings combination. The conclusion is strongly reminiscent of Messiaen's *Quartet for the End of Time*. M-D.

Passacaille 1950 (Billaudot) 18 min. Each statement of the subject is handled in
a different and colorful manner. M-D.
Concerto da Camera 1953 (Ric 1321) 12 min. Allegro risoluto; Adagio; Rondino
scherzo. Neoclassic, thin textures, charming. M-D.

John Dankworth (1927–   ) Great Britain
Concerto (Novello). For piano and chamber orchestra. 17 min.

Christian Darnton (1905–   ) Great Britain
Concertino (Lengnick). For piano and strings. 18 min.

Thomas Christian David (1925–   ) Austria
Since 1958 David has taught at the Vienna Academy.
Concerto 1962 (Edition Modern 1096) 24 min.

Claude Debussy (1862–1918) France
Fantasia G 1889 (Jobert 1919; CFP; USSR) 22 min. Completed in 1889, this
work was held back from public performance during most of its dissatisfied
creator's lifetime. It is strictly Classical in impulse and is based on the
cyclical principle. It is a three-movement concerto, notwithstanding its title.
Andante ma non troppo: reflects influence of d'Indy *Symphony on a French
Mountain Air* as well as Debussy's late style found in *Pelléas*. Lento e molto
espressivo: murmuring. Allegro molto: cascading, dancing finale. The whole
work has delicacy and a mood of fresh air and humor about it. Lyric melodies
are still apparent. M-D.

Jan Decadt (1914–   ) Belgium
Decadt teaches counterpoint and fugue at the Royal Flemish Conservatorium in
Antwerp.
Concerto I (H. Elkan). In three movements. Displays a rather aggressive contem-
porary style. Spirited rhythms, highly colored orchestration. M-D.

René Défossez (1904–   ) Belgium
Défossez teaches at the Brussels Conservatory.
Concerto 1951 (CeBeDeM 1960) 20 min. Furioso ed marcato: SA; basically c
but freely chromatic and dissonant; rhythmically interesting; fast scales and
arpeggi in the development; large cadenza. Religioso: tries to create "une
grande atmosphère d'elévation"; chantlike melody; triplet arpeggiations.
Allegro giocoso: neoclassic airy feeling; strong pianistic writing and solid
materials. D.
Concerto for Two Pianos and Orchestra 1954 (Editions Cousins, René Défossez,
116 Avenue Franklin Roosevelt, Brussels 5, Belgium).

Helmuth Degen (1911–   ) Germany
Konzert 1940 (Schott 2884) 17 min. Allegro maestoso; Sehr langsam und gross
im Ausdruck; Lebhaft und sehr rhythmisch. Expanded tonal idiom, neoclassic, driving finale. M-D.

Kleines Konzert 1942 (Schott 80–01). For piano and string orchestra. 12 min.
Concertino (Schott). For two pianos and orchestra. 24 min.

Maurice Dela (1919–   ) Canada
Ballade 1945 (BMI Canada) 7 min. SA; lyrical; nineteenth-century idiom and
    style; effective and short. M-D.
Concerto 1946 revised 1950 (CMC 1972) 20 min. Allegro moderato; Adagio;
    Vivo. Freely tonal; fast-moving full chords; harmonic idiom à la Rachman-
    inoff; fully exploits the instrument; dance influence in Vivo. M-D to D.
Concertino 1961–62 (CMC) 16 min. One movement. Neoclassic, contrasting
    sections, freely tonal, freely flowing lines, varied sonorities. Large span
    required. M-D.

Marcel Delannoy (1898–1962) France
In his later works Delannoy leaned toward neoclassicism. "He believed that the
ecclesiastical modes and international folklore would be the most viable bases for
any new systems of music" (DCM, 179).
Concerto de Mai Op.50 1950 (ESC) 72pp. So named because it was begun in
    May 1949 and its orchestration was completed in May 1950. Andante; Al-
    legro scherzando (Cadenza by Jean Hubeau); Final. Expanded tonality, un-
    usual tempo arrangement within the three movements. Piano and orchestra
    are poorly integrated. M-D.
Ballade Concertante Op.59 (ESC 1960) 19 min. One large movement with con-
    trasting sections. Romantic inspiration. Large span required. M-D.

Lex van Delden (1919–   ) The Netherlands
Scherzo 1949 (Donemus) 3 min.
Concerto Op.66 1960 (Donemus) 18 min.

Georges Delerue (1925–   ) France
Concertino (Billaudot 1956). For piano and string orchestra. Neoclassic. M-D.

Frederick Delius (1882–1934) Great Britain
Delius was perhaps the most poetic composer that England has ever produced.
His music is charged with poetry, delicacy, and refinement. His style in some
ways resembles Debussy's, with the use of modal scales, chords moving blocklike
in parallel motion, and an avoidance of complicated thematic work or counterpoint. Yet Delius likes a fuller orchestral sound than does his French counterpart,
and has more open emotionalism and passion. He often has clashing dissonances
and tense harmonic progressions. Everywhere his music is laden with pictorial
allusions and rich emotion.
Concerto c (Bo&H) 25 min. This work began as a three-movement concerto in
    1897. In 1906 the finale was discarded, the first two movements were com-
    bined, and a coda alluding to their ideas was substituted for the original
    finale. It is now in one movement, opening with an Allegro non troppo
    section, followed by a Largo and then a return to the Allegro non troppo
    musical material and a brilliant ending. The work is almost a fantasia, written

in a more out-going style than much of Delius's music. It does not contain much of Delius's unique harmonic idiom but some very beautiful and effective sonorities are present. The writing for the pianist is difficult, with many passages demanding a strong technique in double notes, chords, and octaves. M-D.

Norman Dello Joio (1913–   ) USA
Dello Joio was strongly influenced by his teacher Paul Hindemith. His work is largely neoclassic, but he has been able to blend such old molds as the ricercare, passacaglia, or chaconne with contemporary harmony and rhythm in a strong personal way that immediately communicates. Other influences have been liturgical music, especially Gregorian chant, jazz, and the dance. Most of Dello Joio's writing for the piano is well realized, yet not of overpowering difficulty.
Ricercari 1946 (CF) 20 min. Allegretto giocoso; Adagio; Allegro vivo. The old ricercari form of the sixteenth and seventeenth centuries is retained but is endowed with a contemporary style of writing. A basic idea is presented, then developed in the first movement from a harmonic standpoint, in the second, melodically, and in the third, rhythmically. M-D.
Ballad of the Seven Lively Arts 1958 (CF) 10 min.
Fantasy and Variations 1961 (CF) 24 min. This two-movement work is constructed from a four-note idea: G, F♯, B, and C, and opens with a quiet Fantasy in three parts: Adagio; Allegro vivo; Adagio. The second movement begins in the orchestra, which uses the initial motive but in reverse order: C, B, F♯, G. Six variations of enormous scope follow, and the work ends with extreme brilliance. Dello Joio said of this work: "I approached the *Fantasy* primarily as a vehicle for the piano and I composed it for a virtuoso performer. My goal was music that would be exciting to listen to and demanding to play." D.

Clifford Demarest (1874–1946) USA
Rhapsody (GS).

Jacques De Manasce (1905–1960) Austria
Concerto II (UE). Second movement is an intermezzo. The subject of the finale is based on a Hebrew melody sung during Passover. M-D.

Paul de Marky (–   ) Canada, born Hungary
De Marky studied with the famous Liszt pupil Stephen Thoman (teacher of Bartók, Dohnányi, and Fritz Reiner).
Concerto B "Transatlantique" (MS available from composer: 78A Victoria Avenue, Pointe Claire, Quebec) 25½ min. Ballade: in modified SA design; influenced by World War II and the ominous years leading up to it in Europe. Scherzo: cheeky, with Waltz added. Lyric Interlude: winds tacet, a lied for strings and piano; something of an apology to the strings, which are not featured in the other movements. Fantasia: American; ethnic; sounds like an improvisation; touches of jazz; brief appearance of a harmonica; cadenza

near beginning of movement. Dramatic pianistic gestures, rhapsodic moments, freely tonal, glissandi, some Impressionistic tendencies, effective scoring. Requires advanced pianism. M-D to D.

Peter Deutsch (1901–1965) Germany
The Magic Picture (Concerto for piano and orchestra) (F. Colombo) 10 min.

Frédéric Devreese (1929–   ) Belgium
Concerto Op.5 1949 (Schott Frères) 22 min. One large movement with contrasting sections. Flexible meters; atonal. Piano outshines the orchestra. M-D.
Concerto III 1956 (CeBeDeM) 25 min. Introduction et Allegro; Grave; Quasi Perpetuum. Atonal. Orchestra and piano are well integrated. M-D to D.

David Diamond (1915–   ) USA
Before 1940 Diamond tended to be a Romanticist, using rich harmonic textures and colors. But his writing has become more economical, with increasing concern for rhythmic energy, yet a Romantic lyricism is still present.
Concerto 1950 (PIC) 21 min. Andante–Allegretto–Allegro: a combination of rondo and SA developmental procedures; opens with the main thematic idea played by the strings, while at the piano entry a three-note motive is given; from these two main ideas the rest of the movement is derived and worked out. Adagio, molto expressive: through-composed; thematic material based on the interval of a perfect fifth; opens with the first theme in the strings, followed by a second idea in the piano; after a development of both themes, leading to a large climax, there is a restatement of the opening material. Finale: freely altered seven-part rondo; full of virtuoso display; brilliant. The writing for the piano is moderately demanding, calling for facility in octaves and double notes. M-D.
Concertino 1964–65 (PIC). For piano and chamber orchestra. 12 min. Allegro con brio: highly rhythmic, flowing sections, *ppp* ending. Tema—Adagio: theme and 18 contrasting (mood and tempo) variations, exciting closing. M-D.

Louis Diémer (1843–1919) France
Concertstück Op.31 (Hamelle) 72 pp. Prélude; Finale.

Jan H. van Dijk (1918–   ) The Netherlands
All works are published by Donemus.
Concertstuk 1946. 8 min.
Concertino 1949. 10 min.
Concertino 1949. For two pianos and strings. 11 min.
Concertino II 1953. 7 min.
Concerto 1963. For piano, four-hands and chamber orchestra. 17 min.
Concertino III 1966. 6 min.
Concertino IV 1966. 8½ min. Six short contrasting atonal movements. M-D.
Ad Aquam 1967. For piano and chamber orchestra. 7 min.
2 Résumés 1970. 5 min.

Concertino 1978. For pianola and orchestra. 13 min. (The pianola uses a perforated paper roll.)

Concertino. For two pianos and orchestra. 7 min.

Renato Dionisi (1910–   ) Italy
Concerto for Two Pianos and Orchestra (Zanibon).

Hugo Distler (1908–1942) Germany
Konzert Op.14 1935 (Br 1000). For piano (harpsichord) and string orchestra.
Konzertstück Op.20/2 1937 (Br 2783a) 58pp. This opus posthumous is an arrangment of the *String Quartet* Op.20. One large movement with contrasting moods and tempi, cadenza-like passages, neoclassic. M-D.

Karl Ditters von Dittersdorf (1739–1799) Germany
Dittersdorf was a significant figure in the development of the Classical style. His easy and "correct" style contained a vein of jovial humor as well as bright and fluent melodies.
Concerto B♭ 1773 (Hauer—CFP 9036; Upmeyer—Vieweg) 18 min. Adagio; Presto. This delicious work belongs totally to the Viennese Classic school. J. C. Bach influence is present, especially in the handling of the orchestra. The Presto is a sonata-rondo with a march, and the coda is harmonically daring and full of expression. M-D.
Concerto A 1779 (Upmeyer—Nag 41). For keyboard and strings. Includes cadenzas by C. Döbereiner. Allegro molto; Larghetto; Rondeau—Allegretto. Dittersdorf's melodic fertility and harmonic imagination imbue this work with an unfading charm. The last fifteen bars of the rondo were added by the editor, since the autograph broke off at this point. Int. to M-D.

Ernst von Dohnányi (1877–1960) Hungary
Dohnányi never fully succeeded in establishing a strong personal identity in his writing, and in large measure continued in a nineteenth-century Brahmsian tradition. But even with his avoidance of contemporary directions, his music still has a charm for many, thanks largely to his polished compositional technique, genuine lyricism, and effective instrumentation. And even if his efforts have been overshadowed by his compatriots Bartók and Kodály, his best works still deserve an occasional hearing.
Concerto e Op.5 1899 (Dob) 38 min. Adagio maestoso–Allegro–Adagio; Andante; Vivace. The three movements are bound together by a small number of thematic ideas, all of which appear in the slow introduction of the first movement. Shows a strong feeling for Classical forms, no clichés that mar so much late nineteenth-century Romantic writing. Effective virtuoso piano writing, even if a little heavy-handed. M-D to D.
Variations on a Nursery Song Op.25 1913 (Simrock; Eulenburg; Lengnick; EBM) 22 min. Based on the old French song "Ah, Vous Dirai-Je, Maman," which Mozart also used in a set of variations. In the United States it is known as the alphabet song. After a mock-serious introduction the theme is stated by

the piano in unisons. Eleven clever variations follow, and the set is completed by a robust fugue followed by an altered restatement of the theme. The work is a clever assimilation of virtually every nineteenth-century musical trend. Dohnányi was one of the most famous pianists of his time, so it is not surprising to see this extremely effective and brilliant writing for the solo instrument. The whole work reflects the composer's dedication of this work "to the enjoyment of lovers of humor, and to the annoyance of others." M-D.

Concerto II b Op.42 1947 (Lengnick) 27 min. Allegro; Adagio, poco rubato; Allegro vivace. Ideas are overworked but the pianism is first-rate throughout. Style is not too different from the first concerto, composed 43 years earlier. M-D to D.

Stephen Dodgson (1924–   ) Great Britain
Concerto 1959 (PRS) 25 min.
Concerto da Camera IV (Chappell) 22 min.

Samuel Dolin (1917–   ) Canada
Fantasy (Berandol). For piano and chamber orchestra. 10 min.
Concerto (MS available from composer: 12 Reigate Road, Islington, Ontario M9A 2Y2 Canada) 20 min.

Aleksandr P. Dolukhanian (1910–1968) USSR
Concerto (Soviet Composer 1972) 82pp. Allegro con brio; Andante sostenuto; Allegro grazioso. Freely tonal, similar in style to Kabalevsky. M-D.

Antal Dorati (1906–   ) Hungary
Concerto 1975 (SZ). Three movements. Easily accessible; a Hungarian-flavored lyricism dominates the entire work (influences of Bartók and Kodály). Forceful rhythms, slight dissonance, Puckish sense of humor, unexpected turns of phrase, flashy virtuoso sections. Neatly constructed. M-D.

Felix Draeseke (1835–1913) Germany
Konzert Eb Op.36 1885–86 (Kistner) 32 min. Allegro moderato; Adagio; Allegro molto vivace. In the Liszt tradition; brilliant and effective piano writing. M-D.

Sabin V. Dragoi (1894–1968) Rumania
Concerto 1940–41 (Editura de Stat) 87pp. Largo solenne; Andante; Allegro. A large sprawling work. Freely tonal with colorful moments. D.

Nicholas Dremliuha (1917–   ) USSR
Concerto Db (Musica Ukraina 1967) 104pp. One large-scale movement. Post-Romantic idiom; chromatic; some freely dissonant usage; strong contrast of lyrical and rhythmic elements; effective use of piano and orchestra; transformation of themes is a bit unusual. M-D to D.

Mykola V. Dremluga (1917–   ) USSR
Concerto (USSR 1967) 104pp. One large movement. In Tchaikowsky style but

slightly more contemporary sounding. Cadenza passages; glorifies the piano throughout. M-D to D.

Sem Dresden (1881–1957) The Netherlands
Concerto 1946 (Donemus) 20 min.

Alexander Dreyschock (1818–1869) Bohemia
Dreyschock seems to have been able to play louder and faster than all of his contemporaries. The poet Heine once remarked, "When Dreyschock played in Munich and the wind was right you could hear him in Paris."
Concert-Piece c Op.27 (Schott) 16 min. Nineteenth-century Romantic virtuosity at its peak. Contains some lovely moments of poetic lyricism. After a double exposition a new and haunting cantabile theme in f appears. It is treated throughout the development. A furious coda full of octaves, thirds, and sixths finishes the work (and the performer!). M-D to D.
Salut a Vienne—Rondo Brillant Op.32 (Schott Frères; LC) 17pp. Brilliant and effective pianistically, short on inspiration and craft. M-D.
Concerto d Op.137 (Senff). Eminently enjoyable. An outstanding performance could make this second-rate effort a minor masterpiece. D.

Johannes Driessler (1921–   ) Germany
Driessler has been professor at the Nordwestdeutsche Musikakademie, in Detmold, since 1947.
Konzert Op.27 (Br 2782) 27 min.

Pierre Max Dubois (1930–   ) France
Concerto II (Leduc 1958) 31 min. Three movements (FSF). Expanded tonality. Piano writing is not terribly exciting. M-D.
"Concerto Italien" 1963 (Leduc). For two pianos and orchestra. 21 min. Brillante; Andante; Rondo. Pianistic glitter galore. Most attractive. M-D.
Concertino (Leduc 1964). For piano, violin, and orchestra. 66pp.
Concerto III (Leduc 1967) 20 min. Eglogue; Avec feu; Trés chantant; Rondo diatonique. Gallic, style is in the tradition of the Jean Françaix *Concertino*. Not as overblown as the *Concerto* II. M-D.
Concerto IV (Leduc 1971) 36pp. Allegro giocoso; Andante sostenuto; Rondo allegretto. Neoclassic, thin textures, sparkling instrumentation. M-D.

Théodore Dubois (1837–1924) France
Concerto Capriccioso c (Heugel) 88pp. Allegro–Adagio con fantasia.
Concerto II f (Heugel 1897) 58pp. Allegro; Adagio; Allegro vivo, scherzando; Con molta fantasia—Allegro. In the Saint-Saëns tradition; contains plenty of display for the pianist; sounds dated. M-D.
Suite (Heugel 1922). For piano and string orchestra. 41pp. Moderato; Allegretto; Andante; Allegro vivo. Fluent, facile writing, lovely tunes, more effective than *Concerto* II. M-D.

Vladimir Dukelsky (Vernon Duke) (1903–1969) USA, born USSR
Ballade (Fl). For piano and string orchestra with tympani obbligato.

Concerto C (Heugel 1926) 37pp. One large movement. Freely tonal with much chromatic usage. Well written for the piano. M-D.

Louis Dumas (1877–1952) France

Fantaisie (Ric 1918) 14 min. Sectional, many key changes. Virtuoso writing in late nineteenth-century tradition. M-D.

Jacque-Dupont (1906–   ) France

Concert Op.2 1932 (Leduc) 21½ min. Andante; Presto. Highly chromatic. M-D.

Fantaisie Op.20 (Sal 1948) 26 min. Allegro molto brillante; Lento; Presto. Freely tonal, colorful. Fluid piano writing. M-D.

Concertino (Zurfluh 1961) 11pp. Lento; Souvenirs. Soloist's part is much easier than the orchestral reduction. MC. Int.

Marcel Dupré (1886–1971) France

Fantaisie Op.8 (Leduc 1919) 21 min. Lent; Andante con moto; Allegro giocoso. Freely tonal around b–B. Ideas well developed. Many arpeggios, virtuoso style. Large span required. M-D.

Francesco Durante (1684–1755) Italy

Concerto B♭ (Degrada—Ric 1968). For keyboard and strings. 10 min. Preface in Italian, French, English, and German. Allegro; Grave; Allegro. One of the most striking examples of the eighteenth-century Italian concerto form; surely among the most beautiful of those that have survived. Each moment is built on a basic thematic pattern and has a clear two-part structure. Displays a joyful abandon in the instrumental writing as if the work had developed from free improvisation. Charming throughout. Int.

Concerto (Guerlin—Schott) 9 min.

Zsolt Durkó (1934–   ) Hungary

Durkó's music is primarily contrapuntal, and it often consciously draws on medieval procedures. In the late 1960s, "tone color began to have a more important structural function than before, and another trend became apparent—an attraction toward melody in the classic sense" (DCM, 191–92).

Cantilene 1968 (EMB).

Johann Ladislaus Dussek (1760–1812) Bohemia

Dussek was one of the first composers to exploit the piano. In some ways (harmony and tonality) he anticipated later Romantic traits. In his fifteen keyboard concertos, the Romantic elements of this style are fully developed. It is estimated that Dussek wrote over one hundred works for piano, solo or in combination with other instruments, but there is such confusion in the opus numbers of his works—because of the different systems adopted by French, German, English, and Czech publishers—that only approximations may be made.

See: Howard Allen Craw, "A Biography and Thematic Catalog of the Works of Dussek (1760–1812)," diss., University of Southern California, 1964.

Concerto E♭ Op.15 (OUP).

Concerto F Op.17 (André) 18pp.

Concerto E♭ Op.22 (Corri, Pearce & Co. 1805; Coventry & Hollier ca.1840).

Concerto Op.26 (Br CHF 5170).

Concerto Op.29 [Op.30 in some editions] (Sieber; NYPL).

Concerto C Op.30 (Broderip & Wilkinson 180?) 31pp.

Grand Concerto Militaire Op.40 1799 (Br&H; piano part only at LC and NYPL). Allegro moderato; Rondo—Allegretto militaire. Charming powerfully brilliant in some spots. Should be revived. M-D.

Concerto g Op.49 (Erard) 41pp.

Concerto g Op.50 1802 (C. Reinecke—Br&H; Ruthardt—CFP 3274). The CFP edition contains only the first movement, Allegro, which is extensive enough to stand by itself; SA, delightful figuration. M-D.

Concerto B♭ Op.63/10 (Br CHF 5030; Bo&H). For two pianos and orchestra. 34 min. Composed after 1806. Allegro moderato: pianos have almost continual sunny cadenzas. Larghetto: long lyrical cantilena lines. Allegro moderato: early themes are recalled and resolved; pianos move through some glittering histrionics. Classic forms, brilliant motifs, charming melodies, rich harmonies. M-D.

Concerto III B♭ ca.1800 (Nadermann; NYPL). First movement: unusual harmonic excursions before the climaxes of the exposition and recapitulation. Larghetto: overly sentimental but contains some lovely themes. Rondo: well crafted. Beethoven influence is seen is the piano writing (and Beethoven's piano writing owes something to Dussek). This work has much to recommend it. M-D.

Concerto V (Delioux—Durand 11142).

Rondo "The Ploughboy" (Parkinson—OUP).

See: Harold Truscott, "Dussek and the Concerto," MR 16 (February 1955): 29–53.

Balis D. Dvarionas (1904–1972) USSR, born Lithuania

Concerto g 1960 (USSR). Moderato; Vivo e furioso; Lento; Allegro ma non troppo. According to the composer the music is concerned with the thoughts and feelings of a hero—his aspiration, joys, and sorrows. It abounds in melodic phrases of Lithuanian folk songs. Makes wide use of the technical and timbre potential of the piano. M-D.

Concerto II 1961 (Soviet Composer 1972). For piano and strings. Allegro moderato; Dolente; Molto allegro. Modal, generally thin textures, folktune influence. M-D.

Antonín Dvořák (1841–1904) Bohemia

Concerto g Op.33 1876 (Artia AP786) 28 min. A critical edition based on the composer's MS. Contains a fascinating appendix documenting some of the many revisions Dvořák made in his own piano part. Preface and editor's note in Czech, German, English, and French. Allegro ma non troppo; Adagio ma non troppo; Allegro giocoso, ma non troppo. Lovely melodies, cogent formal dimensions. The piano part is thoroughly capable and exhibits some of the characteristics found in Dvořák's chamber works. Contains some brilliant piano writing with strong rhythmic interest. M-D to D.

Stephen Dydo (1949–   ) USA
Capriccio (ACA) 25 min.

George Dyson (1883–1964) Great Britain
Concertino Leggiero 1951 (Novello). For piano and strings. 20 min. Allegro; Andante; Vivace. Freely tonal; exciting outer movements. M-D.

E

Moneta Eagles (1924–   ) Australia
Autumn Rhapsody 1964 (PRS). For piano and chamber orchestra. 5 min.
Diversions (APRA) 17 min.

Petr Eben (1929–   ) Czech
Eben is an outstanding pianist. He teaches music theory at Charles University in Prague. "An interest in Silesian folksongs has combined with plainchant and medieval music to influence his development as a composer" (DCM, 193).
Concerto 1961 (Panton) 25 min. Preface in Czech, Russian, German, English, and French by M. Nedbal. Allegro risoluto; Tranquillo; Molto con brio. A large symphonic form in neoclassic style. Solo part is well integrated with the orchestra, MC. M-D.

Anton Eberl (1765–1807) Austria
Eberl's symphonies and piano music were praised by Mozart and Gluck.
Grand Concerto C Op.32 (CFP).
Grand Concerto E♭ Op.40 (CFP; LC). Allegro; Andante; Rondo—Vivace. Classic figuration, tuneful melodies. Similar in difficulty to the Beethoven *Concerto* II. Int. to M-D.

Sixten Eckerberg (1909–   ) Sweden
Concerto I 1943 (STIM) 28 min.
Concerto II 1949 (STIM) 35 min.
Concertino 1962 (ES; Fl) 21 min.
Concerto III 1971 (EC; Fl) 20 min.

Sophie Eckhardt-Gramatte (1902–1974) Canada, born Russia
Concerto 1946 (CMC) 30 min. Three movements.
Symphony-Concerto 1967 (CMC) 33 min. In three large contrasting (FSF) movements. Dramatic gestures based on extended nineteenth-century pianistic idiom; chromatic style. Some special effects required, i.e., "like a balalaika," "do not knock the keys; always 'air-tight,' " harmonics. The finale, Vivo, Tempo di Toccata, is a spectacular display for the soloist. Virtuoso pianism required throughout. D.

Helmut Eder (1916–   ) Austria
Eder has taught at the Mozarteum in Salzburg since 1967.
Concerto Semisirio Op.30 1960 (Br 4310). For two pianos and orchestra. 16 min.

Ross Edwards (1943–   ) Australia
Choros 1971 (J. Albert) 15 min.

Klaus Egge (1906–1979) Norway
Egge was greatly influenced by the folk music of his native Norway. His music
is highly polyphonic, with melodic material that is strongly rhythmical. Although
most of his music is tonally based, it is highly dissonant. He was an important
musical figure in his homeland.
Concerto I Op.9 1937 (NK) 24 min. Nordic in character, full of strength and
vitality, ably put together. M-D.
Concerto II Op.21 1944 (Lyche) 20 min. In one compact movement, with an
opening section that is a set of variations on a Norwegian folk song (Sunfair
and the Dragon King). The theme is given at the opening by the cellos,
against an accompaniment on the piano, and is followed by seven variations
and a short concluding cadenza. The writing for the soloist is brilliant, but
not of excessive complexity, and mainly requires a strong octave technique.
A stirring work full of supercharged emotionalism. M-D.

Oleg Eiges (1905–   ) USSR
Concertino 1960 (Soviet Composer). One movement, contrasting sections, tonal.
Int. to M-D.
Concerto (USSR).

Gottfried von Einem (1918–   ) Germany
Since 1963 von Einem has taught composition at the Akademie für Musik und
darstellend Kunst in Vienna.
Klavierkonzert Op.20 1956 (Bo&Bo 1967) 22 min. Molto moderato: SA; recapitulation omits subordinate theme; fast scalar passages; short cadenza.
Adagio: binary; mood and tempo are not successful following the sluggish
first movement but there are effective pianistic sonorities. Con spirito: rondo;
occasional moments of dissonance and polytonality; operatic and dance
influences; exciting pianistic climax precedes coda. Orchestral part over-
shadows piano in first movement, but has weightier effect in last two
movements. The three cyclic movements are written in a neoclassic idiom
spiced with nontoxic dissonances. Eclectic style; elegant, Gallic, airy.
M-D.

Gunnar Ek (1900–   ) Sweden
Concerto b 1944–45 (STIM; Fl) 25 min. Adagio; Allegro marcato; Adagio;
Allegro.

Jan Ekier (1913–   ) Poland
Concerto 1949 (PWM) 26 min.

Hans Eklund (1927–   ) Sweden
Characteristic of Eklund's style are short, rhythmic motives, often in ostinato form, which in works after 1960 are often combined with an attempt at thematic unity.
Concerto (Kammarmusik IV) 1959 (STIM) 14 min. Well-crafted ideas; piano is spotlighted from time to time; subtle sonorities. M-D.

Albert Ellinger (–   ) Germany
Concerto (Mannheimer) 23 min.

Abraham Ellstein (1907–1963) USA
"Negev" Concerto (Belwin-Mills) 18 min. This work is a close relative of the *"Warsaw" Concerto,* both in style and difficulty. M-D.

Jens Laursøn Emborg (1876–1957) Denmark
Concerto Op.72 1930 (Samfundet til Ugivelse af Dansk Musik 1934). For piano and strings. 12 min. Moderato, con fuoco; Andante; Allegro. All movements are attacca. In MC style of early Prokofiev. M-D.

Huib Emmer (1951–   ) The Netherlands
Montage 1977 (Donemus). For piano and chamber ensemble. 15 min.

Einar Englund (1916–   ) Finland
Englund has taught composition at the Sibelius Academy in Helsinki since 1958.
Concerto I 1955 (Fazer 1972) 69pp. Allegro moderato; Larghissimo, Allegro moderato. Reveals strong Stravinsky and folk-song influences. Cadenza-like passages display a strong rhythmic technique. M-D to D.
Concerto II 1974 (Finnish Music Information Center) 24 min. Preludio; Aria; Finale—Allegro assai. Freely tonal, strong chromatic usage, consummate orchestration. M-D.

Donald Erb (1927–   ) USA
Erb is currently Composer-in-Residence at the Cleveland Institute of Music. His music often employs both live and taped electronic sounds in combination with performers on traditional instruments.
Chamber Concerto 1961 (Mercury). For piano and chamber orchestra, 10 min. Andante; Allegro; Adagio; Allegro moderato. Harmonics, thin textures, expressionistic, secco style, flexible meters, strings damped by placing hand on them, long trills, cadenza passages for piano. M-D.

Heimo Erbse (1924–   ) Germany
Erbse studied composition with Boris Blacher. Since 1950 he has been a free-lance composer.
Capriccio Op.4 1952 (Bo&Bo). For piano, percussion, and string orchestra. 13 min. Forceful handling of the piano. Dissonant, flexible meters, driving and rhythmic. M-D.
Dialog Op.11 1958 (Bo&Bo) 12 min.

Klavierkonzert Op.22 (Bo&Bo 1965) 21 min. Sostenuto: expansive, key feeling of G in opening and closing but otherwise highly dissonant. Scherzo: five parts, thin textures. Allegro moderato: thematic materials evolve rather than develop, antiphonal dialogue. The piano part reveals rhythmic and figural complexities and is colorful in its textures and spacing. D.

Triple Concerto Op.32 (Dob). For piano, violin, and cello. 25 min.

Dietrich Erdmann (1917–   ) Germany

Concertino 1957 (Gerig HG279). For piano and chamber orchestra. 15 min. Three movements (FSF). Neoclassic, freely tonal. M-D.

Eduard Erdmann (1896–1958) Germany

Concerto Op.15 (UE) 30 min.

Ulvi Cemâl Erkin (1906–   ) Turkey

Concerto in Three Movements 1951 (UE 11555) 27 min. Allegro; Andante; Scherzo—Andante—Allegro. Well put together; contains some brilliant piano writing; early twentieth-century idiom. Requires large span, MC. M-D.

Andrei Y. Eshpai (1925–   ) USSR

Eshpai studied composition with Golubev, Khachaturian, and Miaskovsky. He concertizes as a pianist throughout the USSR.

Concerto 1954 (Soviet Composer 1958) 85pp. Three movements (FSF). Tonal with some modal usage, effective. M-D.

Concerto (Sikorski 1969). For orchestra with solo piano, trumpet, vibraphone, and double bass. One large movement with fugal cadenza. Relies heavily on syncopation. Brilliant writing for all solo instruments with the piano somewhat favored. M-D.

Concerto II (USSR 1973) 70pp.

Oscar Esplá (1886–1976) Spain

Sonata del sur Op.52 1945 (UME) 22 min. Allegro non molto; Andante liturgico; Allegro alla marcia. Influences of Debussy, Stravinsky, and Spanish popular music. M-D.

Lindley Evans (1895–   ) Australia, born Union of South Africa

Idyll (APRA). For two pianos and orchestra. 9½ min.

Robert Evett (1922–1975) USA

Evett identified himself with the baroque era and described his music as well made and adhering to conservative principles.

Concerto 1956 (ACA; Fl) 18 min. Allegro commodo; Andante con moto; Rondo. Virtuoso piano writing, contains some complex contrapuntal treatment and plenty of dissonance. M-D to D.

Johan Evje (1874–1962) Norway

Quo Vadia, Introduction and Fugue (NK) 25 min.

Orest Evlakhov (1912–1973) USSR

Concerto II Op.40 "Triptych" (USSR 1977). Andante–Allegro giusto; Adagio; Allegro. Strong Schostakovitch influence, freely tonal. Strong piano writing. M-D.

Eberhard Eyser (1932–   ) Sweden, born Poland

Concerto 1974 (EC; Fl) (Tripiko I). For piano and chamber orchestra. 25 min.

F

Richard Faith (1926–   ) USA

Faith writes in a freely tonal and neo-Romantic style. His broad, beautiful melodies naturally unfold into stunning textured sonorities. All of his music deserves performance.

Concerto I 1964 revised 1969 (MS available from composer: School of Music, University of Arizona, Tuscon, AZ 85721) 26½ min. Allegro moderato, sostenuto. Lento: leads directly to Allegro vivace. Freely tonal; long, flowing themes; effective orchestration. Stunning use of the instrument. M-D.

Concerto II 1975 (MS available from composer). Allegro moderato: piano opens with quiet but suspenseful subject that grows to a searing intensity; lyric second subject; cadenza-type passages lead to recapitulation; impressive cadenza; quiet closing. Andantino: cantabile, ornamented lines, glissandi, alternating hands figuration, *pp* closing. Allegro con brio: vigorous opening subject, octotonic, forceful octaves and chords, expressive second subject, parallel moving harmonies, dramatic gestures, stunning closing. Highly pianistic throughout. MC, freely tonal. Strongly recommended. M-D to D.

Both concertos are extremely worthy. Fine performances will ensure not only "crowd pleasers" but "performer pleasers."

Manuel de Falla (1876–1946) Spain

The creative output of Falla was extremely small, for he was intensely self-critical, but most of what he wrote was masterful. The core of his art is the exploitation of Spanish dances and folk music, with sensual flamenco melodies, varied and exciting rhythms that are often imitative of castanets and guitars, and modalities from the church music of Spain. In particular, Falla was influenced by the "cante jondo" of the Andalusian gypsies, with its dark, oriental quality and sinuous ornamentation. Although Falla was a strongly nationalistic composer, he did not borrow directly from existing folk tunes, as did Béla Bartók. His art is unfailingly Spanish, but at the same time of international importance.

Nights in the Gardens of Spain "Symphonic Impressions for Piano and Orchestra" 1915 (ESC; JWC) 25 min. This work has no specific program but contains some of the most poetic music ever written by Falla. In the Gardens of the Generalife: atmospheric; describes the hill garden at Granada, with its beautiful gardens, fountains, and cypresses; two principal themes. A Dance Is

Heard in the Distance: opens with a statement of the principal theme by flute and English horn; another dance tune given by flute and strings follows and leads without break into In the Gardens of the Sierra de Cordoba: Vivo; wild gypsy dance. Although this work is not extremely difficult for the pianist technically, it has severe musical, stylistic, and ensemble problems. M-D.

Guido Alberto Fano (1875–1961) Italy

Andante e Allegro con fuoco (Zanibon 1960) 45pp. Freely tonal, interesting syncopated figuration, MC. Well laid-out between soloist and orchestra. M-D.

Harold Farberman (1930–   ) USA

Paramount Concerto (Belwin-Mills) 14 min.

Harry Farjeon (1878–1948) Great Britain

Phantasy Concerto Op.64 (S&B 1926). For piano and chamber orchestra. 53pp. One large movement, sectionalized. Generally thin textures, Romantic inspiration. M-D.

Ferenc Farkas (1905–   ) Hungary

Since 1949 Farkas has been professor of composition at the Academy of Music in Budapest.

Concertino 1948 (EMB 1955) 15 min. Allegro; Andante; Allegro. A real find; for the talented high school or college student who wants a work that is a little "different." Charming, rewarding, MC. Highly recommended. Requires good octave and chord technique. Int. to M-D.

David Farquhar (1928–   ) New Zealand

Farquhar is presently head of the Music Department at Victoria University, Wellington, N.Z.

Concertino (Price Milburn 1975). For piano and strings. 16 min. Original piano writing in Prokofiev idiom. M-D.

Arthur Farwell (1872–1952) USA

Dawn—Fantasy on Indian Themes Op.12 1901 arranged for piano and orchestra 1926 (Fl) 7 min. The Indian tunes are more effective in the solo piano version, but this is an impressive piece, with the Indian influence permeating the entire work. M-D.

Mountain Vision Symbolistic Study VI 1931 (Fl) 14 min.

Gabriel Fauré (1845–1924) France

Fauré's art is a blend of fastidious workmanship, a sense of proportion, and clarity, all of which go hand in hand with harmonic restraint, personal lyricism, and subtlety of rhythm. Never a composer to wear his heart on his sleeve, Fauré wrote music that is intimate, sober in the best sense of the word, and, above all, French. His output for the piano is considerable; he is one of the nineteenth century's major composers for the instrument.

Ballade F♯ Op.19 1881 (IMC) 13 min. This beautiful one-movement work was originally written for piano solo. The writing for the piano is rich and full but not of excessive difficulty. Beginning quietly with a lyrical cantabile theme stated by the piano alone, the work builds to a fine climax midway in the movement, then fades away to a close in the poetic style of Chopin. A beautiful tone, a sure sense of rubato, and poetry are strong interpretative requirements. M-D.

Fantaisie G Op.111 1919 (Durand) 18 min. Fauré's later writing for the piano is characterized by a sparseness of texture as compared with the more involved, rather figurative writing of thirty or more years earlier. The keyboard writing in the single movement and strangely haunting *Fantaisie* has these characteristics and resembles the textures of Fauré's later chamber music works. The piano opens in an Allegro moderato with the principal theme, which is repeated by the orchestra a tone lower. Following development of this material is an Allegro molto, in which the piano initially states a powerful two-measure motif. The Allegro moderato opening returns in an embellished manner to end the work. M-D.

Samuel Feinberg (1890–1962) USSR

Concerto Op.20 1931 (USSR) 26 min. In one movement in highly contrasting sections. Many parts are reminiscent of Khachaturian. Virtuoso sections. D.

Concerto II 1945 (USSR). First movement: highly derivative, chromatic à la Scriabin. Second movement: lyric in a late-Romantic style. Scherzo: more contemporary sounding than the rest of the work. Allegretto con brio: brilliant and effective, in Scriabin and Rachmaninoff idiom. D.

Morton Feldman (1926–   ) USA

Piano and Orchestra 1975 (UE 16076) 21 min. Everything is blended into one hypnotic, edge-to-edge event, with a dark, rich radiance and transparency that somehow come through. The piano is used as a coloristic solo against the orchestral pallette. Some repeated effects almost become monotonous; a flat surface is sustained with a minimum of contrast. The entire work is quiet and without the feeling of a beat; flexible meters. Large span required. Notes are easy but interpretation and musicianship would place it in the M-D category.

Alessandro Felici (1742–1772) Italy

Concerto F 1768 (Bernardi, Sciannameo—de Santis 1059 1969) 29pp. Allegro moderato; Largo ed espressivo; Allegro assai. All movements are in F. This work helps "support Torrefranca's long-standing view that the origins of the style of Mozart lie in the works of the minor 18th century Italian composers. These calm, smooth-flowing pages of music, with their refreshing melodic line and the suppleness and wealth of their psychological nuances, cannot fail to call to mind moments in the works of the Salzburg composer, even as regards personal ingenuousness" (from the score). Int. to M-D.

Vaclav Felix (1928–   ) Czechoslovakia

Double Concerto 1978 (Czech Music Information Center). For piano, bass clarinet, and string orchestra. 25 min. Classical three-movement construction; middle movement is strongly lyrical; MC. M-D.

Howard Ferguson (1908–   ) Great Britain
Concerto D 1951 (Bo&H). For piano and string orchestra. 25 min. Three movements (FSF). Freely tonal, effective collaboration between pianist and orchestra. The slow movement is an especially appealing set of lyric variations. M-D.

Armando José Fernandes (1906–   ) Portugal
Fantasia Sobre Temas Populares Portugueses 1937 (C. Gulbenkian Foundation) full score, 75pp. One movement, contrasting sections. Tonal, colorful chromaticism, strong rhythms. Piano and orchestra well integrated. M-D.
Concerto B♭ 1951 (C. Gulbenkian Foundation). For piano and strings. Full score, 58pp. Maestoso; Vivace e scherzando; Calmo, con intima espressione; Allegro molto. Broad Romantic gestures require first-rate pianism. M-D to D.

Oscar Lorenzo Fernández (1897–1948) Brazil
Variações Sinfônicas 1948 (PIC) 35 min.

Giorgio Ferrari (1925–   ) Italy
Piccolo Concerto 1965 (Casa Musicale Sonzogno di Piero Ostali). For piano, winds, and percussion. 21pp. One movement in contrasting sections (FSF). Neoclassic, impetuous rhythms in outer sections, thin textures. M-D.

George Fiala (1922–   ) Canada, born USSR
Concerto g 1946 (MS available from composer: 2101 University St., Montreal 2, Quebec, Canada). Tonally oriented.
Concertino Op.2 1959 (BMI Canada). For piano, trumpet, timpani, and string orchestra. 15 min. Three movements (FSF). Appealing Romantic second theme in the opening movement; expressive slow movement; brilliant finale. M-D.
Capriccio 1962 (MS available from composer) 12 min. Shows twelve-tone influence.

John Field (1782–1837) Ireland
Field's first three concertos are available in a modern edition edited by Frank Merrik and published as Vol. 17 (1961) of *Musica Britannica*, available in the U.S. through Galaxy. There are no modern editions of the remaining four concertos.
Concerto I E♭ 1799 (Galaxy; Fl) 17½ min. Allegro: an interesting amalgam of Chopin (who was not yet born) and Hummel; bravura writing; some unusual (for the time) effects, such as in the middle of the movement, after the orchestral tutti. Air ecossais: a theme and variation based on a Scottish song "Within a Mite of Edinburgh Town"; each variation is in the form of a different type of embellishment of the original melody, and is introduced by a short cadenza. Allegro vivace: rondo, shows Clementi influence, unusual

harmonies, sudden key changes. There is a freshness and impish tunefulness about the music. M-D.

Concerto II A♭ 1814 (Galaxy) 30 min. Allegro moderato: one of the most interesting parts follows the second tutti, where piano and orchestra have a unique dialogue and fragments of the first theme are developed by various orchestral instruments. Poco adagio: a nocturne for piano and orchestra. Moderato innocente: rondo, excellent piano and orchestra dialogue, Clementi influence, lengthy. More lyric and rhapsodic than *Concerto* I. Constantly vacillates between Classical decorum and Romantic ardor. Chopinesque figuration and melodies. It is easy to see where Chopin received his inspiration. M-D.

Concerto III E♭ 1816 (Galaxy; Fl) 28 min. Allegro moderato: SA. Tempo di Polacca: rondo. Both movements are fully developed. Extensive passagework, beautiful thematic writing. M-D.

Concerto IV E♭ 1816 (Fl) 25 min. Allegro moderato: rhythmic similarities between this movement and the first movement of Chopin *Concerto* I in e. Adagio: gentle and plaintive. Rondo: lighthearted. M-D.

Concerto V C 1817 (Br&H) "The Conflagration During the Storm." Three movements. Uses a second piano to assist in the thunderous passages! M-D.

Concerto VI C 1823 (Br&H; Fl). In one movement: Allegro moderato–Larghetto–Rondo.

LC has a copy of the Pacini first edition of the first six concertos.

Concerto VII c 1833 (Fl). Allegro moderato. Rondo: in waltz time. Robert Schumann was very enthusiastic about this concerto. In the two-movement concertos, it is possible that Field improvised a "Nocturne" for solo piano for the usual slow middle movement.

See: Geneva Handy Southall, "John Field's Piano Concertos: An Analytical and Historical Study," thesis, University of Iowa, 1966.

Vivian Fine (1913–   ) USA
Fine has taught at Bennington College since 1964.

Concertante 1943–44 (MS available from composer: Music Department, Bennington College, Bennington, VT 05201). 15 min. Andante con moto; Allegro risoluto. The style is tonal and diatonic, with chromatic relief brought about by diatonic alteration rather than preconceived method. The piano writing is nimble and grateful; the musical ideas are clearly stated and effectively worked. The work is a model of structural and expressive clarity. M-D.

Fidelio Finke (1891–1968) Germany, born Bohemia
Capriccio on a Polish Folksong E♭ 1953 (Br&H 5756) 15 min. Humorous writing, clever, strong rhythmic and tempo contrasts. M-D.

David Rufailovich Finko (1936–   ) USSR
Concerto 1971 (Soviet Composer) 47pp. In one movement. Preference for chords

with minor seconds, freely tonal, flamboyant writing for both piano and orchestra. M-D.

Ross Lee Finney (1906–   ) USA

Finney's music is rooted in tonality yet it assimilates twelve-tone techniques and various implications of serialism. Finney is emeritus composer at the University of Michigan, where he taught for many years.

Concerto 1934 (Fl) 20 min. Grave—Allegro moderato; Maestoso con variazioni; Rondo. Originally composed as a piano sonata in 1934, transcribed for piano and orchestra in 1935.

Concertino (MS available from composer: % School of Music, University of Michigan, Ann Arbor, MI 48105) 10 min. In three movements.

Concerto I E 1948 (CFP) 15 min. Allegro marziale; Adagio cantabile; Presto. Less weighty than *Concerto* II, this work scores high, with its charm of sheer sound and its strong rhythmic drive. In its translucency it resembles the music of Henri Dutilleux. Thematically delicate; harmonically rich. M-D.

Concerto II (Henmar 1968) 20 min. Entrance and Crescendo: serial influence, atonal, octotonic, changing meters, effective crescendo throughout. Ornaments and Dialogue: highly chromatic figuration. Cadenza and Climax: builds to tremendous climax. D.

Michael Finnissy (1945–   ) Great Britain

Concerto I 1975 (Edition Modern 1780) 36 min.

Concerto II 1975–76 (Edition Modern 1791) 16 min.

Gerald Finzi (1901–1956) Great Britain

Eclogue Op.10 (Bo&H). For piano and strings. 9 min. Late nineteenth-century idiom, reflectively lyrical, strong formal structure, pianistic and musical. M-D.

Grand Fantasia and Toccata Op.38 (Bo&H) 14 min. Powerful and forthright style; lively Toccata. Very effective piano writing. M-D.

Ertugrul Oguz Firat (–   ) Turkey

Upheaval Op.46 (Piano Concerto) 1969–72 (Seesaw 1977) full score, 159pp. In commemoration of Ataturk. 84 performers are required for full instrumentation. A second piano is placed on stage beside the soloist's. While not generally used as a solo instrument, it gives additional tone, color, and rhythm to the ensemble. Specifically marked places give the impression of a concerto for two pianos. At times two pianists are required for the second piano. Uses techniques such as plucking strings with a metal nail and fingernails, hitting string with mallet, clusters, glissandi on strings. A veritable catalogue of avant-garde techniques. D.

Ernst Fischer (–   ) Germany

Toccata (Gerig 1947). For piano and strings. 5 min. Quiet excitement, perpetual motion, neoclassic, freely tonal around b, *pp* closing. M-D.

Irwin Fischer (1903–   ) USA
Concerto e 1935 (ACA) 17 min. In one movement.

Luboš Fišer (1935–   ) Czechoslovakia
Fišer works as a free-lance composer in Prague, writing functional music (for television, radio, and films) in addition to concert music.
Concerto da Camera 1970 (Artia) 8 min. One movement, contrasting sections.
    Grows out of opening: 4 bars of Vivace, 6 bars of Andante. Lento *pp* closing.
    MC. M-D.

Jerzy Fitelberg (1903–1951) USA, born Poland
"Most of Fitelberg's output consisted of non-programmatic, instrumental music in the classic forms" (DCM, 238).
Concerto (EBM). For piano, trombone, and strings.
Concerto II (PIC) 20 min. New version.

Nicolas Flagello (1928–   ) USA
Flagello's neoromantic style displays a stimulating ingenuity in using harmonic materials (the language is strongly tonal, though not of academic retrocedence) that are basically familiar.
Concertino for Piano, Brass and Timpani 1963 (Gen) 9 min., 11 parts. Theme, seven variations, and a finale. Might be termed "quasi una fantasia," since its construction is interlaced with rhapsodic devices. The Hindemithian cragginess of the opening is paralleled in the brass dectet. Marvelous sonority and dry, taut, chordal percussiveness. M-D.

Robert J. Fleming (1921–1976) Canada
Fleming's style is a pleasant blend of traditional and contemporary musical components.
Short and Simple Suite (OUP 1959). For piano and chamber orchestra.
Concerto '64 1964 (CMC) 12 min. Andante sostenuto; Gently; Allegro. Flexible meters, quartal harmony, chordal syncopation, "bell" effects, neoclassic, tightly controlled forms, excellent craft. M-D.

Erik Fordell (1917–   ) Finland
Concertino I Op.16 1961 (Finnish Music Information Center) 18 min.
Concerto II Op.41 1962 (Finnish Music Information Center) 20 min.
Concerto III Op.42 1962 (Finnish Music Information Center) 20 min.
Concerto IV Op.117 revised 1970 (Finnish Music Information Center) 20 min.
Lasten Savelkuvia (Fazer W13465–0).

Marius Flothuis (1914–   ) The Netherlands
"Flothuis's music has been influenced by his musicological studies of Monteverdi and Mozart and by the compositions of Debussy, Bartók, Willem Pijper, and Bertus van Lier" (DCM, 239).
Concert Op.30 1948 (Donemus). For piano and chamber orchestra. 16 min.

Bjørn Fongaard (1919–   ) Norway
Concertino Op.11 1953 (NK) 11 min.
Space Concerto 1971 (NK). For piano and tape (orchestra microtonalis). 14½ min.

Jacqueline Fontyn (1930–   ) Belgium
Fontyn's style is a kind of modernist Impressionism that finds expression in Romantic emotion. The writing is lucid, warmly colored, and spirited.
Mouvements Concertantes 1967 (Seesaw). For two pianos and strings. 11 min.
   Lento; Allegro. Effective handling of all instruments, especially the two
   pianos. Neoclassic, big sonorities, dramatic gestures. M-D.

Peter Förtig (1934–   ) Germany
Konzertstück 1966 (Edition Modern 1494) 25 min.

Wolfgang Fortner (1907–   ) Germany
Fortner's style has evolved from neobaroque in the 1930s and 40s through free adaptation of the twelve-tone method to an interest in mirror forms and other kinds of symmetry.
Concerto 1943 (Schott 2968) 40 min. Allegro, ma non troppo: strong rhythmic
   first theme, charmingly contrasted second theme; lengthy orchestral introduction is matched with extensive cadenza. Andante: delightful folklike
   theme. Allegro molto: bubbly; short contrasting trio. Adagio–Allegro molto
   energico: brilliant tarantella with lyrical contrasting theme; fugato interrupts;
   bell sonorities add color; brilliant conclusion. D.
Fantasy on BACH 1950 (Schott 4271). For two pianos plus nine solo instruments
   and orchestra. 20 min.
Mouvements 1954 (Schott) 25 min. A concerto in every respect except title.
   Atonal; motoric rhythms; fast chromatic usage (eleven tones at opening) but
   serial technique is apparently not used. Prelude: subtle tempo changes; builds
   to climax, quiet closing; daring pedal effects. Etude I: ABA; B section is a
   toccata for piano with interlocking chords. Interlude: lyrical, calm; piano
   elaborates material. Etude II: perpetual motion in the piano, boogie-woogie
   basses, rumba rhythms. Epilogue: based on inversions of material from the
   Prelude. Requires first-rate musicianship and excellent fingers. D.
"Triplum" 1966 (Schott). For three pianos and orchestra. 25 min. Giuoco; Intermezzo; 4 Variazioni. Proportional rhythmic relationships, pointillistic, expressionistic. M-D.

Lukas Foss (1922–   ) USA, born Germany
The music of Foss revolves around a controlled concept of improvisation based on historical concepts of live performance—creation combined with intentionally used "nonmusical" sounds for drama and expression. He is currently conductor of the Brooklyn Philharmonic and co-director of the Center of the Creative and Performing Arts in Buffalo.

Concerto I 1939–43 (GS) 24 min. Allegro; Andante; Allegro. A large sprawling work with much imitation. Freely tonal, eclectic, versatile instrumentation. Difficult to hold the piece together. M-D to D.

Concerto II 1951 (CF) 34 min. This work is very different from Foss's later idiom. The three movements are in an expanded diatonic style and in extended sonata form. Allegro: long orchestral introduction, brilliant piano writing, free linear lines, mixed meters. Adagietto: slow; the strongest movement; powerful climax. Finale—Allegro vivace: long, toccata-like, varied piano figurations, a good cut is indicated, triumphant concerted conclusion. Dazzling, extroverted writing. D.

Arnold Foster (1898–1963) Great Britain

Concerto on Country Dance Tunes (S&B 1933) 18 min. Allegro vivace; Andante sostenuto, con alcuna licenza; Presto. Part of the thematic material for the outer movements is taken from John Playford's "The Dancing Master." Modal, charming. M-D.

Jean Françaix (1912–   ) France

Françaix's basically urbane style has been strongly influenced by the neoclassic manner of Stravinsky. It has characteristically Gallic irony, grace, clarity, and lightness of touch. In spite of a rather limited harmonic vocabulary, Françaix's works still have a contemporary spice and acidity combined with a sparkling charm.

Concertino 1932 (Schott) 12 min. This early work is thoroughly neoclassic in intent with a great simplicity and directness in the music. Presto leggiero: built entirely on one capricious theme first given by the solo piano. Lent: short (only thirty bars); nostalgic. Allegretto: rather jazzy. Rondo—allegretto vivo: gay and brilliant. A crisp facility for running passagework is demanded. Int. to M-D.

Concerto D 1936 (Schott) 17½ min. This work does not have the large dimensions of a normal piano concerto but is lean in texture, with practically no development of thematic material. Allegro: lighthearted; splashing chords; four themes. Andante: based on one tender, lyrical melody. Scherzo: quick waltz; constructed out of three melodic ideas, each of which is first stated on the piano. Allegro: brilliant Gallic frolic; four basic themes; effective close. M-D.

César Franck (1822–1890) France

Les Djinns (The Spirits) Poème Symphonique 1884 (EC; Enoch; Litolff) 13½ min. Inspired by a Victor Hugo poem, *Les Orientales*. Orchestra is equal to the piano in its thematic importance. Emphasis on treatment of material as well as on piano technique. Begins and ends quietly, contains a memorable unaccompanied melody for solo piano, and some gracious passagework. A very beautiful and little-known work. Highly recommended. M-D.

Variations Symphoniques 1885 (Durand; Philipp—GS; Sauer—CFP; Litolff; Enoch; K; Curci; Eulenburg; Ashdown; CF) 16 min. The opening statement is dramatic and chromatic. The introduction unfolds the theme, played by the piano. Six variations and a finale in F♯. The variation technique of Franck concentrates on the inner, personal qualities he sought under the surface of the melody. Some of Franck's most mature writing, although the orchestra here is more of an accompanist than the piano's equal partner. Requires free rotational technique throughout. M-D.

Johan Franco (1908–   ) USA, born The Netherlands
Serenade Concertante 1938 (ACA; Fl) 12 min. Allegro energico; Adagio molto cantabile; Allegro scherzando. Colorful and effective. M-D.
Symphonie Concertante 1940 (ACA; Fl) 15 min. Allegro elastico; Adagio pesante; Finale.
Concerto Lirico III "Pilgrim's Progress" 1967 (ACA). For piano and chamber orchestra. 20 min. First movement: quarter note = 54. Intermezzo. Third movement: eighth note = 84. Intermezzo. Scherzando. Intermezzo. Alla marcia. Freely tonal, MC. M-D.

Samson François (1924–1970) France
François was an outstanding concert pianist and frequently performed this work.
Concerto (P. Noel 1951) 20 min. One large movement. Eclectic style; cadenza sections show off the piano beautifully; freely tonal, effective orchestration. D.

Marcel Gustave Frank (1909–   ) USA, born Austria
Youth Concerto E♭ (H. Elkan 1963) 10 min. In three movements, played without pause. Written for the talented young pianist, this work contains numerous distinctive rhythmic, dancelike passages as well as broad tunes. Int.

Benjamin Frankel (1906–1973) Great Britain
Serenata Concertante Op.37 (Novello 1961). For piano, violin, cello, and orchestra. Also arranged for violin, cello, and two pianos.

Wim Franken (1922–   ) The Netherlands
Concertino 1952 (Donemus). For piano and string orchestra. 19 min.
Concerto G 1975 (Donemus). Photostat of MS. 23 min.

Emmy Frensel Wegner (1901–1973) The Netherlands
Rhapsody (Donemus) 8 min.

Donald Freund (1947–   ) USA
Freund teaches in the Music Department of Memphis State University.
Concèrto 1970 (Seesaw 1977) 91pp. One large movement, contrasting sections, cadenza-like passages throughout for the piano. Changing meters, neoclassic, freely tonal. M-D.

Peter Racine Fricker (1920–   ) Great Britain
"He is not afraid to think seriously and uncompromisingly," observes London's *Musical Times*, "and he combines this capacity with an ear for novel and ravishing

instrumental sonorities." Fricker is chairman of the music department at the University of California, Santa Barbara.

Concertante Op.15 1956 (Schott). For three pianos, strings, and timpani. A festive work, gaily and exuberantly violent. M-D.

Concerto Op.19 1954 (Schott 10396) 22 min. Allegro moderato; Air and (6) Variations; Allegretto scherzando. Displays uncompromising dissonance and tenuous relationship to key centers, à la Bartók. Strong idiomatic writing for the piano is mixed with flashing spurts of fresh energy and invention. Interesting ornamentation, valid neoclassic style. D.

Toccata Op.33 1959 (Schott 10654) 12 min. Allegro vivace: many octaves, pedal points, large skips, octotonic, linear counterpoint, serial, transparent. A festive show piece for the piano. Large span required.

Géza Frid (1904–   ) The Netherlands, born Hungary
Concert Op.55 1957 (Donemus). For two pianos and orchestra. 20 min.

Wolfgang Friebe (1909–   ) Germany
Slawische Rhapsodie (Ahn & Simrock 1959) 8½ min. Sectional, somewhat akin to the *"Warsaw" Concerto* in style and pianistic usage. M-D.

Günter Friedrichs (1935–   ) Germany
Bewegungen (PIC) 15 min.

Gerhard Frommel (1906–   ) Germany
Concerto b (R&E 1935) 25 min. One large movement. Pianist is constantly moving over keyboard. Freely tonal, overblown. M-D to D.

Gunnar de Frumerie (1908–   ) Sweden
Frumerie is a Classicist with strong tinges of Romanticism. He studied in Paris with Alfred Cortot and teaches piano at the College of Music in Stockholm.
Concerto I b 1929 (ES) 25 min.

Variations and Fugue Op.11 1932 (NMS1942; Fl) 23 min. Freely tonal; large dramatic work. M-D.

Concerto II a 1935 (ES) 40 min.

Symfonisk Ballad Op.31 1944 (GM; Fl) 29 min. In three movements; opens with cadenza between piano and orchestra. Vigorous and sensitive writing, well-contrasted sections. Tends toward the dramatic. Freely tonal using post-Romantic pianistic techniques. M-D.

Concerto 1953 (ES). For two pianos and orchestra. 20 min.

Robert Fuchs (1847–1927) Austria
Concerto b♭ Op.27 1881 (K&S) 47pp. Allegro maestoso ed energico; Andante sostenuto; Finale. Freely tonal around b♭, strong Brahms influence. The slow movement is beautiful and effective. M-D.

Sandro Fuga (1906–   ) Italy
Toccata 1952 (Ric 128919) 23 min. Sectional, chromatic, neoclassic. M-D.

Concerto (EC 9236 1970) 94pp. Moderato, all marcia; Andantino tranquillo;

Danza. Expanded tonality, neoclassic, strong rhythms in the outer movements. Facile pianism required. M-D.

Anis Fuleihan (1901–1970) USA, born Cyprus

"Fuleihan's early recollections of and subsequent research into Mediterranean music were influential on his development as a composer" (DCM, 258).

Concerto I 1937 (PIC). For piano and string orchestra. 21 min. Allegro moderato; Andante con moto; Allegro. Interesting tonal writing throughout. Contrasting sections, brilliant cadenza in finale. M-D.

Concerto II 1938 (GS). For piano and string orchestra. 21 min. Allegro moderato; Andante; Presto. Expanded tonality with some polytonal counterpoint. The final two movements are connected. M-D to D.

Concerto 1940 (PIC). For two pianos and orchestra, 22 min. Allegro moderato: melodic, effective concerted scoring. Slowly: lyric; broad sweeping midsection. Lively: dancelike, brilliant. M-D.

Epithalamium 1941 (GS). Variations for piano and string orchestra. 12½ min.

Concerto for Piano, Violin and Orchestra 1944 (PIC) 20 min.

Wilhelm Furtwängler (1886–1954) Germany

Symphonic Concerto 1937 (Alkor 285).

Werner Fussan (1912–   ) Germany

Music for Strings, Piano, Percussion, and Timpani (Br&H) 16 min.

Karl Heinz Füssl (1924–   ) Austria, born Czechoslovakia

Refrains Op.13 1972 (UE 1973). Reproduced from holograph. 22 min. Expanded tonality, mid-twentieth-century idioms, cadenza. M-D.

G

Jenö Gaál (1906–   ) Hungary
Concertino 1945–59 (EMB) 14 min. One large movement, neoclassic, some
nationalistic flavor, much activity throughout, MC. M-D.

Kenneth Gaburo (1926–   ) USA
Gaburo teaches at the University of California, San Diego. He directs the New
Music Choral Ensemble, which performs experimental twentieth-century
repertory.
Sinfonia Concertante 1949 (Sibley Library, Eastman School of Music). Largo,
Allegro meno mosso; Adagio; Allegro molto.

Bogdan Gagić (1931–   ) Yugoslavia
Koncert II 1972 (Drustvo Hrvatskih Skladatelja) 11 min. Serial influence, pointillistic, expressionistic. M-D to D.

Henri Gagnebin (1886–1960) Switzerland, born Belgium
"Gagnebin considered himself a classicist and, as a young man, was influenced
in his harmonic thinking by the French impressionists" (DCM, 259).
Concerto C Op.57 (Br&H) 32 min.
Concerto 1951 (Ric 129293 1957) 25 min. Allegro non troppo; Notturno; Finale.
Tonal, has some effective moments, especially the middle movement. M-D.

Marius François Gaillard (1900–1973) France
Images d'Epinal 1929 (ESC). For piano and brass orchestra. 34pp. Preface; Ab-
del-Kader; Geneviève de Brabant; Fanfan la Tulipe; Cul de Lampe. A few
contemporary techniques are sprinkled in lightly. Requires a strong chord
technique. M-D.
Tombeau Romantique, Concerto pour la piano avec orchestra (Choudens 1955).
Three movements (FSF). Expanded tonality. M-D.

Hans Gál (1890–   ) Great Britain, born Austria
Gál was a co-editor of the complete edition of Brahms.
Concertino Op.43 1934 (Simrock 3125). For piano and string orchestra. Intrata;
Siciliano; Fuga. Tonal, chromatic, neoclassic. Cadenza at end of the Sicil-
iano leads directly to the Fuga. M-D.
Concerto Op.57 1947 (Br&H).

Blas Galindo (1910–   ) Mexico
Segundo Concierto 1962 (EMM) 23 min. Allegretto: free adaption of SA, twelve-
tone, changing meters, dramatic sweeping gestures with big chords, fast
octaves, octotonic, Andantino mid-section. Largo: ABA, broad cantabile
lines, builds to climax, subsides. Allegro: brilliant and rhythmic, marchlike
section, some cyclic usage, rousing conclusion. Neoclassic influence seen
in entire work. D.

Gérard Gallo (–   ) France
Concerto (Technisonor EFM 1518 1974). First two movements are untitled, third
is called Décidé. Complex, expressionistic, pointillistic, dynamic extremes,
rhythmic problems. D.

Baldassare Galuppi (1706–1785) Italy
Motivic development and "galant" melodic treatment characterize Galuppi's
works.
Concerto VI c (Ric). Outer movements in SA design; middle movement full of
melodic ideas and richly ornamented. M-D.
Concerto F (Henmar). For keyboard and strings. 14 min. The right hand has all
the interest; the left hand winds up with Alberti bass most of the time. Int.
Concerto F (Farina—Zanibon 4865). For keyboard and strings. Full score, 32 pp.
Allegro, non tanto; Grave; Presto. May be played with the accompaniment
of a string quartet (if one wishes, even without the viola). However, the most
suitable performance is with a small string orchestra, with the double-bass
added to the cellos. A few small cadenzas are suggested by the editor. Int.
to M-D.

German G. Galynin (1922–1966) USSR
Galynin was a disciple of Miaskowsky and Shostakovitch.
Concerto C 1946 (USSR 1956) 75pp. Allegro; Andante; Allegro vivo. Influences
of Les Six and Shostakovitch are seen in its light-neoclassic style. Contains
a few dissonances and some tendency to polytonality. Superficially brilliant
pianism, especially in the cadenza to the first movement. M-D to D.

Nikolai Karlovich Gan (1908–   ) USSR
Concerto III (Concerto-Poem) (USSR 1979).

Gerardo Gandini (1936–   ) Argentina
Since 1970 Gandini has been on the faculty of the American Opera Center at the
Juilliard School.
Fantasie-Impromptu 1970 (MS available from composer: % The Juilliard School,
Lincoln Center, New York, NY 10023) 11½ min. An imaginary musical
portrait of Chopin, based almost entirely on thematic material of Chopin.
The use of small melodic fragments (sonic atoms) and the simultaneous use
of several fragments, however, often make the material unrecognizable. For

example, the piano prologue, reminiscent of the piano miniatures of Schoenberg's Op.11 or Op.19, is actually based on fragments of Chopin's b♭ Mazurka. The main body of the work consists of eleven sections or "moments." Orchestral writing is contrapuntal, aleatory, and dense. A long piano cadenza precedes the climax of the work of the tenth section, where the orchestra plays dozens of fragments from the Preludes, Etudes, Polonaises, and other works of Chopin simultaneously, à la Ives. Chopin's influence is also seen in the improvisatory nature of the piano cadenza, the passagework, and the overall lyricism of the work. M-D to D.

Contrastes (Bo&H) Concerto for two pianos and chamber orchestra. 15 min.

Rudolf Ganz (1877–1972) USA, born Switzerland

Konzertstück B Op.4 1892 (A.P. Schmidt 1902) 32pp. One large movement; eminently pianistic. M-D.

Concerto E♭ Op.32 1941 (CF) 23 min. March-like; Song-like; Scherzo; Finale. Bravura writing including a chromatic glissando at the end of the Scherzo. Scherzo is constructed from the numbers of Ganz's 1940 and 1941 automobile license plates and Frederick Stock's 1940 automobile license. First performance, February 20, 1941, with the Chicago Symphony, Frederick Stock conducting and the composer as soloist. M-D.

John L. Gardner (1917–   ) Great Britain

Concerto I B♭ Op.34 (OUP) 25 min.

Terenzio Gargiulo (1903–1972) Italy

Concerto (EC 1940) 38pp. One large movement, contrasting sections, virtuosic, MC. M-D.

Lucija Garuta (1902–   ) USSR

Concerto f♯ 1966 (Musika 1970) 116pp. Lento, pesante; Grave; Maestoso. Written in a "neo-Tchaikowsky" virtuoso style. M-D to D.

Irena Garztecka (1913–1963) Poland

Concertino 1959 (PWM). For piano and chamber orchestra. 20 min.

Gotfrid A. Gasanov (1900–   ) USSR

Concerto 1949 (USSR 1958) 31 min. Three movements (FSF). Tonal, moderately effective, late 19th-century idiom. Some brilliant pianistic writing. M-D.

Concerto II (USSR 1960).

Heinrich Gattermeyer (1923–   ) Austria

Concertino Op.53 (Dob).

Mario Gaudioso (1906–   ) Italy

Capriccio (EC 1941; Fl) 20 min.

Hans Gebhard (1882–1947) Germany

Konzert Op.25 (Schott) 23 min.

Konzert Op.62 (Br&H 1958). For piano, strings, and percussion. 19 min. Three
movements (FSF). Early twentieth-century idioms, clever use of instrumentation. M-D.

Heinrich Gebhard (1878–1963) USA, born Germany
Divertissement (ECS 1932; LC). For piano and chamber orchestra. 44pp. Andante
con moto; Allegro. Freely tonal; nineteenth-century pianistic idiom; drives
to a strong conclusion. M-D.

Fritz Geissler (1921–   ) Germany
Konzert (CFP 9368 1974) 26 min. One large movement. Complex expressionistic
writing throughout; exploits sonorities of the instrument thoroughly. Requires virtuoso pianism. D.

Harald Genzmer (1909–   ) Germany
"Genzmer's style combines the contrapuntal writing of Hindemith's middle period with a certain amount of expressive colouring" (GD, III, 596).
Concertino I 1946, new version 1957 (Schott 5854). For piano, flute, and string
orchestra. 15 min.
Konzert 1948 (Schott 5278 1963) 25 min. The influence of Hindemith (Genzmer's
teacher) is obvious, especially in the expanded diatonic usage. First movement: SA and rondo combined; moderato opening section followed by the
vivace main theme; effective use of orchestra. Adagio: a number of themes
add interest; etudelike double note figuration in the episodes. Finale: rondo;
left hand has an Alberti accompaniment figure; delightful interplay between
piano and orchestra, toccata-like interlocking chords in the coda. Ingenious
reworking of standard forms in all three movements. M-D to D.
Concertino II 1963 (CFP 5973 1969). For piano and strings. 21 min. Andante
tranquillo–Allegro; Largo; Burleske; Finale—Adagio–Presto: C ending.
M-D.

Earl George (1924–   ) USA
Concerto (OUP) 23 min. In three movements. Freely tonal, traditional pianistic
figuration, flexible meters. M-D.

Jaap Geraedts (1924–   ) The Netherlands
Concerto da Camera 1956 (Donemus). For piano, violin, cello, and orchestra. 23
min.

Fritz Christian Gerhard (1911–   ) Germany
"*Rhapsodisches Konzert*" 1950 (Br&H 3850). For piano and strings. 12 min.
Kraftvoll beginnend, lebhaft; Ruhig; Schnell. Flexible meters, strong Hin-
demith influence, freely tonal. M-D.
Concerto con Unisono (Br&H). For piano, strings, and timpani. 11 min.

Roberto Gerhard (1896–1970) Great Britain, born Spain
Gerhard's music represents a blend of dodecaphonic with neoclassical and Spanish
elements.

Concerto 1951 (Belwin-Mills 1970). For piano and string orchestra. 24 min. Tiento; Diferencias; Folia. Thin textures, flowing arpeggios in Diferencias, cadenza-like passages, octotonic, glissandi, tremolo chords. Iridescent colors and fine mood contrasts. Gerhard's first consistently twelve-tone work and also the first in which he renounced "classical" twelve-tone technique. "The liberties . . . were Schönbergian rather than Bergian. The traditions of early Spanish keyboard music were drawn upon, and the Spanish feeling, though still unmistakable, was universalized" (DCM, 265). M-D to D.

Edwin Gerschefski (1909–   ) USA
Concerto in One Movement Op.5 (ACA) 8 min. Neoclassic, varied moods and contrasting tempi, MC. M-D.

George Gershwin (1898–1937) USA
Gershwin was unquestionably one of the most gifted American composers in terms of sheer native endowment. Out of the elements of jazz, ragtime, and the blues he wove a musical language that is fresh, spontaneous, and above all, American. He was a born lyricist; and his complex rhythms, changing meters, and original modulations indelibly stamp his music. Compared to his achievements, his technical flaws in construction and orchestration pale to insignificance. In his short life Gershwin not only made American popular music respectable but also influenced such composers as Ravel, Copland, Weill, Krenek, and Walton.
Rhapsody in Blue 1923 (Warner Brothers) 16 min. Written at the request of Paul Whiteman for a concert of popular music given at Aeolian Hall, New York, February 12, 1924. Orchestrated by Ferde Grofé. Few serious works of the twentieth century have achieved such success in such a short time, for the *Rhapsody* set in motion a whole new trend of writing serious works in a jazz idiom. The music sums up the 1920s as much as a Johann Strauss waltz does the Vienna of a hundred years ago. The work begins with an ascending line of the clarinet, followed by the first theme, which sets a jaunty mood for the whole piece. A second theme appears first in the winds, then in the piano, and leads to the central section, which contains material from the opening. The work ends brilliantly with a brief coda. The piano part requires above all a strong sense of rhythm, to project the music properly. M-D.
Concerto F 1925 (Warner Brothers) 30 min. Through the enormous success of the *Rhapsody in Blue*, Gershwin was commissioned to write the *Concerto* in F by the New York Symphony Society. Although flawed by some formal defects, it has proved to be one of the most popular American works of the twentieth century. Allegro: principally made up of material from two themes. Andante con moto: poetic opening leads to a large climax, after which the music fades away to an ending of mystery. Allegro con brio: utilizes Gershwin's most brilliant rhythms and jazz themes. A secure technique and great rhythmic projection are needed for a proper performance. Uses a full Romantic orchestra. M-D to D.

Second Rhapsody 1931 (Warner Brothers) 14 min. Gershwin came to Hollywood in 1930 to write screen music for a musical entitled *Delicious*. Included was a six-minute orchestral sequence that described the sounds of a city and in particular emphasized the rhythm of riveting. Gershwin decided to use this material in a symphonic work that he intended to call *Rhapsody in Rivets,* but he later changed the title to *Second Rhapsody*. An initial "rivets" motif is stated at the beginning in the solo piano and is followed by development by the orchestra. After a rumba melody, the heart of the composition is reached with a blues song in the strings. A recapitulation of the opening section ends the work. Although this work does not have the inspiration of the *Rhapsody in Blue,* it deserves more frequent hearings. M-D.

Variations on "I Got Rhythm" 1934 (Warner Brothers) 8½ min. Gershwin's song "I Got Rhythm," from his musical comedy "Girl Crazy" of 1930 catapulted Ethel Merman to fame. In 1934 Gershwin went on an extended tour of one-night stands with the Leo Reisman orchestra performing programs of his own works. For this tour he composed the *Variations*. He changes not only the rhythm, structure, and melody of the original song but also the mood in each variation. An effective performance work. M-D.

Ottmar Gerster (1897–1969) Germany

Konzert A 1955 (CFP 4908) 21 min. Allegro; Largo; Vivace. Freely tonal around A; Vivace is in C. Neoclassic, strong rhythmic usage. Reminiscent of Stravinsky of the 1920s and 30s. M-D.

Giorgio F. Ghedini (1892–1965) Italy

Concerto 1946 (Ric PR221) 26 min. One large movement, contrasting sections. Freely tonal, MC. M-D to D.

Fantasia (Ric). For piano and strings. 17 min.

Concerto 1947 (SZ 4418). For two pianos and orchestra. 19 min.

Concerto dell' albatro, da "Mody Dick" di Hermann Melville (SZ 1949). For piano, violin, cello, narrator, and orchestra. 28 min. Italian, English, and French words. The narrator's words in the fourth and fifth movements are from *Moby Dick*.

Valentin Gheorghiu (1928–   ) Rumania

Concerto 1961 (Editura Muzicală a Uniunii Compozitorilor) 72pp. Allegro molto e con brio; Andante tranquillo e semplice; Presto, selvagiamente. Freely tonal, hard-driving rhythms. Impressionistic middle movement, barbaric finale. M-D.

Concerto 1973 (Editura Muzicala a Uniunii Compozitorilor) 130pp.

Cecil·A. Gibbs (1889–1960) Great Britain

A Simple Concerto 1955 (OUP). For piano and string orchestra. 10 min. A gifted teen-ager would enjoy this work. Tonal, effective, rewarding. Int. to M-D.

Concertino Op.103 (Bo&H 1944). For piano and strings. 15 min. Three short movements. Unpretentious but solid pianistic treatment. Folk-like theme of the second movement and strong dance rhythms in all movements add much interest. Int. to M-D.

William Wallace Gilchrist (1846–1916) USA
Suite (Fl) 109pp. Idyll; Rondo grandioso.

Alberto Ginastera (1916–   ) Argentina
Ginastera is a nationalistic composer who combines the colorful, often primitive and savage, sonorities and rhythms of Argentinian folk music with the most advanced techniques of composition. After an early, rather parochial nationalism in his writing, he proceeded to neoclassicism, serialism, and ultimate use of sounds produced by electronic means. Never a prolific composer for the piano, Ginastera has achieved extraordinary popularity with his *Sonata for Piano,* 1952.
Concierto Argentino 1941 (Fl) 115pp., full score. Allegretto cantabile; Adagietto poético; Allegro rustico. This early work seems to have little in common with the other two concertos. M-D to D.
Concerto I Op.28 1961 (Barry 1964) 25 min. "Cadenza e varianti: begins with the exposition of the main row presented in the form of a rotating polychrome chord; afterwards the piano develops the melodic transposition of the same row. On these basic elements is built the whole movement, in which piano and orchestra alternate with violent contrasts. The 'varianti' are ten micro-structures in different moods, they are a sort of variations of the original elements. Scherzo allucinante: very fast and it is played throughout with the dynamics 'pianissimo'. The composer uses a pointillist instrumentation and the arch form in five sections: three central symmetrical sections framed by an introduction and a coda. The third movement, Adagissimo, is an intense lyrical interlude formed by three sections which resemble the ternary form, reaching in the middle part a climax of passionate character. This movement ends in a dodecaphonic chord played by the whole string section, until it vanishes. Some solo notes in the piano emphasize the sensation of distance. The fourth and last movement, Toccata concertata with strong and vigorous rhythms, is a real piece of 'bravura' in which there is a constant dialogue between piano and orchestra. The form recalls the seven section rondo form, preceded by a short introduction and followed by a coda" (composer, quoted in the score). Score contains a formal bar-by-bar analysis. This twentieth-century masterpiece is an exciting vehicle for the virtuoso. D.
See: Eui Hyun Paik, "An Analysis of the First Piano Concerto (1961) by Alberto Ginastera," DM diss., Indiana University, 1979, 30pp.
Concerto II 1972 (Bo&H). First movement: consists of 32 variations based on a chord from the last movement of Beethoven's *Ninth Symphony.* Scherzo: for left hand alone; Bartók-like. This mood carries into the slow third movement. Finale: based in part on a theme from the finale of Chopin's b♭ *Sonata* Op.35. Infused with intense emotion, rich in variety, and exciting instrumental timbres. Ginastera describes the work as "tragic and fantastic." The refer-

ence to Chopin's "wind over the graves" in the last movement is skillfully handled. The entire work is a brilliant showpiece in the grandest Lisztian tradition. Daring sonorities are mixed with more traditional contemporary tonal and harmonic devices. More difficult than *Concerto* I. D.

Tomasso Giordani (ca.1730–1806) Italy
Giordani's style is similar to Johann Christian Bach's and consists of *galant* traits, simple left-hand figures, graceful melodies, and flowing passage work. The three works listed are for keyboard and strings.
Concerto III C Op.14/3 (Castagnone—Ric 130483; Fl) 13 min. Allegro spirito; Larghetto; Presto. Int.
Concerto V D Op.14/5 (Castagnone—Ric 130477; Fl) 10 min. Allegro; Rondo— Spiritoso. Int.
Concerto G (Bittner—Nag 157) 27pp. Giordani is the supposed composer. Int.
These three works are composed in the easy style of the amateur concertos. The orchestra consists of two violins and bass. The keyboard writing is thin and an Alberti bass livens the sustained harmonies. "Pocket-sized" concertos.

Walter Girnatis (1894–   ) Germany
Rondo-Bolero (Süddeutscher Musikverlag 1928).
Concert Retrospectif (Sikorski 1955) 37pp. Moderato; Lento; Allegro con fuoco. Neoclassic, much activity, freely tonal. M-D.

Gaetano Giuffré (–   ) USA, born Greece
New York Concerto (Seesaw 1978) 36pp. One movement, contrasting sections. Fast repeated parallel chords, quick octaves, post-Romantic section à la Rachmaninoff (Andante con anima), full chords move over keyboard, neoclassic with nineteenth-century pianistic techniques. M-D.

Gunnar Gjerstrøm (1891–1951) Norway
Concerto I f 1931 (NK) 28 min. Three movements.
Concerto II "Sea Moods" (NK) 20 min. Five movements.

Peggy Glanville-Hicks (1912–   ) USA, born Australia
Etruscan Concerto 1954 (CFP; ACA) 16 min. Inspired by D.H. Lawrence's "Etruscan Places" and "The Painted Tombs of Tarquinia." Promenade— molto spiritoso (with glee); Meditation—lento misterioso e tranquillo; Scherzo—allegro con spirito. Written in neo-archaic modalities purported to reflect the ethos of the ancient Etruscans. M-D.

Werner Wolf Glaser (1910–   ) Sweden, born Germany
Capriccio III 1964 (ES) 20 min. Strong Hindemith influence. M-D.
Arioso e Toccata II 1969 (ES) 18 min.

Louis Glass (1864–1936) Denmark
Fantasi Op.47 (WH 1924) 23½ min. One large sectionalized movement. Nineteenth-century style, effective pianistic treatment. M-D.

Aleksandr Glazunov (1865–1936) Russia

Glazunov was a master craftsman whose music sometimes lacked direction even though beautiful melodies and original harmonic treatment abound at every turn.

Concerto I Op.92 f 1911 (Belaieff; Bo&H; USSR) 27 min. Allegro moderato; Tema con variazioni (nine variations). The theme and variations movement serves as the slow movement, Scherzo, and finale. This impressive work has more character and invention than its almost total neglect would suggest. M-D to D.

Concerto II Op.100 B (Muzyka 1976) 17½ min. This rhapsodic single-movement work (the nucleus of which originated in 1894) is built on a cyclical model and couched in a network of erudite polyphony. M-D.

Benjamin Godard (1849–1895) France

Concerto a Op.31 (Bo&Bo 1879; Fl). Four movements. The Scherzo emulates the scherzos of Litolff. Ingratiating. M-D.

Introduction and Allegro Op.49 (Durand 1880; Fl) 29pp. In Saint-Saëns tradition, tuneful, colorful harmonies, facile rhythms. M-D.

Concerto II g Op.148 (Hamelle 1899; Fl) 43pp. Con moto; Andante; Scherzo; Andante maestoso. Conservative throughout; sounds dated although there are some lovely moments. M-D.

Hugo Godron (1900–1971) The Netherlands

Aubade Guadeamus, suite environ D 1968 (Donemus) 29 min.

Concertsuite 1947 (Donemus). For piano and string orchestra.

Seven Miniatures 1935 (Scenes paedagogiques) (Donemus).

Roger Goeb (1914–   ) USA

Concerto 1954 (ACA; Fl) 18 min. Allegro molto; Lento; Allegro. Freely atonal. M-D to D.

Fantasy (ACA). For two pianos and strings. 8 min.

Alexander Goedicke (1877–1957) USSR

Concertstück b Op.11 (Jurgenson 1900; Fl) 73pp. Awarded the Rubinstein Prize, Vienna, 1900. In Liszt tradition; piano writing is richly conceived; elaborate textures, dramatic themes, and thunderous octaves; picturesque harmony; imposing ending. M-D to D.

Alexander Goehr (1932–   ) Great Britain

Goehr uses a high degree of dissonance and complex rhythmic procedure. Serial writing has strong appeal for him.

Konzertstück Op.26 1969 (Schott 11093). For piano and chamber orchestra. 12 min. One movement, expressionistic, piano part well integrated with orchestration. M-D.

Concerto Op.33 (Schott) 32 min.

Hermann Goetz (1840–1876) Germany

Goetz was obviously influenced by Brahms, Chopin, and Schumann, but he speaks with his own voice.

Concerto B♭ Op.18 1867 (Music Treasure Publications; K&S) 31 min. Mässig bewegt; Mässig langsam; Langsam, lebhaft. While not a show piece for a virtuoso, this work does contain moments of sweeping brilliance and irresistible appeal; and challenges in the solo part demand the highest artistry and control. Clarity of form, engaging elegance, and affecting sonorities seem to point back to Mozart to a far greater degree than does other music written at the same time. M-D.

Marin Goleminov (1908–   ) Bulgaria

Prelude, Aria, and Toccata 1947 (Science and Artistic) 50pp. MC; ideas flow naturally; nineteenth-century inspiration. Pianist is kept busy, especially in the outer movements. M-D.

Stan Golestan (1857–1956) France, born Rumania

Sur les cîmes Carpathiques 1935–38 (Durand) (Concerto pour piano et orchestra) 20 min. 1. Jour de fête—Voix dans la nuit. 2. Solitude. 3. Joies des foules. Tonal, Impressionistic influences, fluid piano writing, programmatic tendencies. M-D.

Marta Naumovna Golub (–   ) USSR

Concerto (Soviet Composer 1963). For piano and string orchestra. 12 min. Allegro non troppo; Andante; Allegro moderato. Freely tonal in a sort of Prokofiev style, strong lyric element. M-D.

Yevgeny Golubev (1910–   ) USSR

Concerto I Op.24 (Soviet Composer 1960) 97pp. Andante mosso–allegro appassionato; Andante con moto; Allegro con fuoco. MC, similar in style to early Kabalevsky, pianistic. M-D.

Concerto II Op.30 (Soviet Composer 1958). Andante cantabile; Allegro con fuoco. Tonal, strong nineteenth-century influence, dramatic gestures, similar to Scriabin without the ecstasy. M-D.

Concerto III g Op.40 1954 (USSR 1959). First movement: impassioned material; dramatic; piano completely dominates. Second movement: lyrical warmth, saccharine themes. Third movement: folk gestures, widely spread arpeggiation, effective pianism, obvious Rachmaninoff influence. D.

Carlos Gomez Barrera (–   ) Mexico

Fantasia (EMM 1964) full score, 33pp. A one-movement work, rhapsodic, chromatic. Cadenza for piano in middle of the piece; many octaves and large chords with grand gestures. M-D to D.

Eugene Goossens (1893–1962) Great Britain

Phantasy Concerto Op.60 1942 (JWC) 27 min. Moderato con moto; Allegro; Andante; Finale. Played without a pause between movements. Interesting dissonances arise from linear chordal treatment; clever rhythmic transformations of opening four-note idea; expert craft. M-D to D.

Otar M. Gordeli (1928–   ) USSR

Concerto Op.2 1952 (USSR 1975) 24½ min. Allegro moderato; Andante sostenuto; Vivace. Modal; interesting rhythmic usage. M-D.

Gino Gorini (1914–   ) Italy

Concerto 1948 (SZ) 26 min. Allegro ritmico; Andante sostenuto; Allegro spig-
liato. Expanded tonality, MC. Effective, especially the lively and brilliant
finale. M-D.

Studi 1960 (SZ). For piano and string orchestra.

Sandro Gorli (1948–   ) Italy

Flottaison Blême 1977 (SZ) 15 min. Requires a large percussion section. Strong
dissonance. M-D.

Louis Moreau Gottschalk (1829–1869) USA

Gottschalk was one of the most flamboyant figures in nineteenth-century American music and the first American to rank with the European virtuosos. His piano
compositions require a solid technique (many demand virtuosity of the highest
degree), and all are well laid-out for the piano. Gottschalk drew on Afro-American
and Creole sources for much of his inspiration.

L'Union Op.48 (Adler—GS 1972). Arranged for piano and orchestra and two-
piano reduction by Samuel Adler. "*The Union* was written as a 'battle piece'
for piano solo in 1862 and dedicated to General McClellan, whom Gottschalk
admired. It begins with a typical battle piece rumble which was traditionally
delegated to cannon shots, but which the composer foregoes in favor of a
muscular virtuoso passage of interlocking octaves. Out of the 'bombardment'
emerges a beautifully harmonized and imaginative arrangement of the 'Star-
Spangled Banner.' After this remarkably personal treatment of our National
Anthem, Gottschalk further introduces two or more familiar tunes and combines them to form a brilliant and rambunctious ending. If one considers that
'The Union' was written twelve years before Charles Ives was born, it may
seem a prophetic piece, and certainly as much of a 'tour de force' of the art
of the Civil War era as the impassioned forensic oratory of anything by Daniel
Webster" (from the score). M-D.

Grand Tarantelle Op.67 1868 (H. Kay—Bo&H 1964) 7 min. Big, one-movement,
exuberant virtuoso piece. Orchestral score reconstructed by Kay. The first
such work by a native-born American, it still retains its power to charm and
delight. It requires a pianist who can dash off the roulades and figurations
with nimbleness and aristocratic grace. M-D.

Morton Gould (1913–   ) USA

Gould has been successful in giving serious form to popular styles of American
music, often in a genuinely distinctive manner. He is prolific, with a fine compositional technique that rarely shows haste or sloppiness. A fine pianist himself,
his writing for the instrument is idiomatic and effective.

Chorale and Fugue in Jazz 1935 (CF). For two pianos and orchestra.

Interplay (American Concertette) 1943 (Belwin-Mills) 13 min. Gould wrote this
work for a radio concert, with José Iturbi performing the piano part and
Gould conducting the orchestra. The score was soon afterward used for a
ballet by Jerome Robbins, and in that form achieved repeated successes in
the Ballet Theater touring repertoire. With drive and vigor: extremely
rhythmic. Gavotte: a short, light dance. Blues: in a slow, nostalgic mood.
Very fast: a brilliant, rapid finale. M-D.

Concerto 1944 (Belwin-Mills) 20 min. Moderately fast with drive and gusto;
Chant; Fast with gusto.

Dance Variations 1953 (Chappell). For two pianos and orchestra. Brilliant, witty,
and charming. A set of variations made up of dance forms. In the Style of
a Chaconne: quasi-Baroque chaconne. Arabesques: introduces several dance
forms, including the gavotte, pavane, polka, quadrille, minuet, waltz, and
can-can. Pas de deux—Tango: interjects a distinct South American flavor.
Tarantelle: virtuosic. M-D.

Inventions 1954 (Chappell). For four pianos, brass, winds, and percussion, 17½
min. Warm Up; Ballad; Schottische; Toccata. Clever, effective, harmonics,
freely tonal. Pianos are generally used as a group in contrast to the rest of
the instrumentation. M-D.

Dialogues 1956 (GS). For piano and string orchestra. 22 min. Recitative and
Chorale: linear, cadenza-like passages, harmonics; Chorale is in 5/4 and is
treated in various ways. Embellishments and Rondo: flexible meters, thin
secco textures, perpetual motion. Dirge and Meditation: slowly—with meas-
ured tread, widely spread arpeggiated chords, intense climax before quiet
ending. Variations and Coda: freely tonal, varied figurations, rhythmic
chords, contrasting moods with variations, effective ending, dodecaphonic
procedures used. M-D.

Charles Gounod (1818–1893) France

Fantaisie sur l'hymne national russe 1886 (Leduc). Based on the theme "God
Preserve the Tsar," which is used in the finale of Tchaikowsky's *1812 Overture* and *Marche slav.* Treated in the manner of Liszt, tempered with Gottschalk, and even echoes Tchaikowsky. M-D.

Suite Concertante A (Saint-Saëns—Leduc 1890) 25 min.

Paul Graener (1872–1944) Germany

Concerto a Op.72 (Simrock 1925) 47pp. Allegro moderato; Adagio; Allegro.
Neoclassic, effective syncopation, MC. M-D.

Ulf Grahn (1942–   ) USA, born Sweden

Grahn holds degrees from the Stockholm City College and The Catholic University of America. He lives in Washington, D.C.

Ancient Music 1970 (Seesaw). For piano and chamber orchestra. 14 min. "Deals
with different aspects of music in its physical space and the relation between
performers in such space" (from a letter to the author, 26 December 1979).

Concertino 1979 (STIM). For piano and string orchestra. 14 min.

Hector Gratton (1900–   ) Canada
Coucher de Soleil 1947 (CMC). For piano and strings. 12½ min. Suite in four movements based on a tale by Felix Leclerc. MC. M-D.

Karl Heinrich Graun (1704–1759) Germany
Graun cultivated the older form of the concerto, which had not advanced very far past Vivaldi.
Concerto F Op.2/4 (Ruf—Müller SM 1103 1959). For keyboard and strings. 35pp. Allegro non tanto; Largo; Allegretto. Displays a high degree of contrapuntal craftsmanship as well as facile melodies. Contains a beautiful slow movement. Int. to M-D.

Johann Gottlieb Graun (1703–1771) Germany
Brother of Karl Heinrich Graun and briefly a teacher of W. F. Bach, the only Bach to receive instruction outside the family. Later, for nearly thirty years, Graun was an associate of C. P. E. Bach in Berlin.
Konzert c (Hoffmann—Möseler). For keyboard and strings. 24pp. A nice work with interesting melodies and solid construction; witty finale. Int. to M-D.

Arthur de Greef (1862–1940) Belgium
Concertino G 1928–29 (JWC) 16 min. Allegro; Scherzo. Somewhat in the style of the Français *Concertino*. M-D.

Ray Green (1909–   ) USA
Green's music has been greatly influenced by early American hymn-tune harmony and counterpoint and by the rhythmic vitality of jazz. Green has been active in supporting American music through his American Music Editions.
Concertino (AME 1973) 25 min. Allegro con moto; Scherzo I; Intermezzo; Scherzo II; Finale. Orchestration includes electric guitars.

Cestmir Gregor (1926–   ) Czechoslovakia
Concerto Semplice 1958 (Panton) 19 min. Con moto: SA. Moderato: ABA, expanded with a development section. Con brio: a large rondo with a development section. Imitative technique brings about polytonality and at times atonality. Closing chords are always tonal. Thin textures. M-D.

Artur Grenz (1909–   ) Germany
Manhattan-Capriccio Op.13 (Sikorski 1957) 23pp. Neoclassic, octotonic, double glissandi, fast octaves. M-D.

Edvard Grieg (1843–1907) Norway
Concerto a Op.16 1868 (CFP; Grainger—GS; Eulenburg; K; CF; Zen-On) 29 min. Allegro moderato; Adagio; Allegro marcato. This Romantic, fresh, and charming work was influenced by the Schumann piano concerto in the same key but the form of the Grieg concerto is simpler. Enchanting melodies, frequent orchestral interludes. Liszt's influence is especially notable in the extensive three-part cadenza concluding the first movement. Power and good octaves are required but otherwise there are no excessive technical demands.

The GS edition contains numerous alternatives in the piano part that were sanctioned by Grieg. M-D.

See: Edwin Smith, "Grieg's Piano Concerto," *Music Teacher* 57 (July 1978): 17–18.

Karl-Rudi Griesbach (1916–   ) Germany
Konzertante Musik (Br&H 1966) 10 min.

Romualdo S. Grinblats (1930–   ) USSR
Concerto 1963 (Musica 1968). Four untitled connected movements; serial and based on a twelve-tone row. The row of each movement is slightly different but there are subtle relationships between the rows. First movement: jazz influence, tango rhythm in first theme, thin piano textures. Second movement: more rhapsodic, colorful. Third movement: scherzo-like, canonic writing for piano, most effective movement. Finale: slow statement of broad theme, dramatic piano cadenza, quiet closing. One of the most imaginative Soviet concertos yet produced. D.

Cor de Groot (1914–   ) The Netherlands
De Groot is best known as a pianist. He has concertized throughout the world and has recorded extensively. His piano works require much facility.
Concertino 1941 (Edition Modern) 14 min.
Capriccio 1955 (Edition Modern) 8 min. Sparkling MC writing, has much to recommend it. M-D.
Miniature Concerto 1950 (Donemus) 11 min.
Variations Imaginaires (Henmar). For piano, left-hand and orchestra. 22 min.
Bis (Evocation) 1972 (Donemus) 2 min.

Wilhelm Grosz (1894–1939) Austria
Symphonischer Tanz Op.24 1928 (UE 9783) 20 min. One movement. Opalescent orchestration; grotesque touches are a part of the style. M-D.

Eivind Groven (1901–   ) Norway
Concerto I 1950 (Lyche) 29 min. Three movements. Tonal, neoclassic. M-D.

Rudolph Gruen (1900–1966) USA
Alpine Concerto Op.50 1962 (ACA) 27 min. Allegro marcato; Adagio sostenuto; Moderato.

Louis Gruenberg (1884–1964) USA, born Poland
Concerto II Op.41 1938 revised 1963 (Fl) 30 min. Slowly, gently and flowingly; Slow, sustained and mysteriously; Somewhat faster; Broad and expressively.
Concerto for Strings and Piano 1955 (Fl) 20 min. Flowingly; Vivaciously; Vigorously.

Jean-Jacques Grünenwald (1911–   ) France
Concert d'été 1947 (Sal). For piano and strings. One of the most enchanting works from this period. The writing is fresh, original, and distinctly personal. M-D.

Concerto (Sal 1956). Lento moderato; Adagio expressivo; Allegro molto vivace. Neoclassic, freely tonal, cadenza passages, interesting sonorities. M-D.

Carmine Guarino (1893–1965) Italy

Concerto (Carisch 21390 1959) 24 min. Allegro vivace; Molto lento; Molto vivo. Neoclassic, thin textures, freely tonal, Stravinsky influence. M-D.

Mario Guarino (1900–   ) Italy

Concerto (SZ 1951) 43 min. Allegro impetuoso; Allegro vivo e leggero; Andante. Ideas are overworked, and the excessive padding does not help. Some lovely thematic material is the redeeming feature of this involved work. M-D to D.

Concerto II (Le Chant du Monde 1954) 24 min. Allegro; Moderato; Vivo. Expanded tonality, early twentieth-century techniques, neoclassic tendencies. M-D to D.

Camargo Guarnieri (1907–   ) Brazil

Guarnieri's music is largely nationalistic and makes extensive use of polyphonic textures. Most of the works listed below required advanced pianism.

Concerto I 1931 (AMP) 18 min. Selvagem; Saudosamente; Depressa.

Concerto II 1946 (AMP; Fl) 22 min. Deciso: first subject (Deciso) and toccata-like treatment of the piano provide the thematic and developmental material; brilliant cadenza leads directly into the second movement. Affettuoso: ABA, lyric, Chopin-like; mid-section is a Scherzando. Vivo (Rondó): vigorous rhythmic devices, secco, playful, octotonic, large chords, skips, brilliant dance. D.

Variations on a Theme of the Northeast 1953 (Ric). MS copy. 22 min.

Chôro 1956 (Ric). MS copy. 17 min Cômodo; Nostálgico; Alegre.

Concertino 1961 (Ric) 18 min. Festivo; Tristonho; Alegre (Rondó).

Concerto III 1964 (Ric) 17 min. Alegre deciso; Magoado; Festivo.

Seresta 1965 (Ric) 14 min. Decidido; Sorumbático; Gingando.

Concerto IV 1968 (Ric) 16 min. Resoluto; Profundamente triste–Vivo–Profundamente triste; Rápido.

Concerto V 1970 (Ric) 18 min. Improvisando; Sideral; Jocoso.

Carlos Guastavino (1914–   ) Argentina

Native folk rhythms permeate Guastavino's writing.

Romance de Santa Fe 1952 (Ric BA 11194) 12 min. One movement, sectional. Dance-like; basically thin textures become thicker near the conclusion. M-D.

Emilia Gubitosi (1887–   ) Italy

Concerto (Carisch 1963) 58pp. One large movement in contrasting sections. Varied pianistic figurations, nineteenth-century inspired, MC. M-D.

Guido Guerrini (1890–1965) Italy

Two Concerto Movements (Ric 1937) 19 min. Lento e doloroso; Allegro gaio–non troppo mosso. Nineteenth-century pianistic style. Atmospheric Lento, rhythmic Allegro, MC. M-D.

Tema con Variazioni 1954 (Ric 128757) 26pp. Theme and six variations, with variation 6 being the climax and the most exciting. Dramatic pianistic gestures, freely tonal. M-D.

Richard de Guide (1909–1962) Belgium

Concerto "Le Temeraire" ("The Daring") Op.26 1952 (CeBeDeM 1965) 16 min. Allegro: bland piano material, poor orchestral integration, cadenza with many sequences. Largo: slow repetition of many parallel chords, block quartal harmonies. Finale: unbroken reiterated patterns, habanera rhythms. M-D.

Jean Guillou (1930–   ) France

Guillou is best known in the U.S. as an organist, but his works display a firm and colorful compositional craft.

Concerto (Leduc 1974) 37 min. Molto cantabile; Vivace. Colorful, highly chromatic, atonal at spots, brilliant piano cadenza at end of last movement. Piano writing is superb. M-D to D.

Albrecht Gürsching (1934–   ) Germany

Gürsching teaches at the Hochschule für Musik in Hamburg.

Konzert 1972 (Edition Modern 1098: PIC) 16½ min. Lento; Adagio; Allegro molto. Clusters, avant-garde notation, many "free" sections, expressionistic. M-D.

Gene Gutche (1907–   ) USA, born Germany

Gutche "makes use of contemporary resources such as microtones, polytonality, and 12-tone procedures. He always aims at communicating to a wide audience" (DCM, 292).

Concerto Op.24 1955 (Highgate 1970; Fl) 43 min. Half note = 76; Quarter note = 92; Eighth note = 184. Twelve-tone. D.

Rites in Tenochtitlàn Op.39/1 1965 (Highgate 1970; Fl) 14 min. Sacrifice; Incantation; Festival. Contains program notes. Colorful, serial influence, thin textures. M-D.

Gemini Op.41 1965 (Highgate 1970; Fl). For two pianos and orchestra. 15½ min. 9..8..7..6..5..4..3..2..1..0; Walk into Space (written in microtones); Earthbound.

Symphonic Poem 1965 (ACA).

Jacques Guyonnet (1933–   ) Switzerland

Guyonnet studied composition and conducting with Pierre Boulez. In 1967 Guyonnet organized the Electronic Music Studio A.R.T. (Art, Recherche, Technique) in Geneva.

En 3 Eclats! 1964 (A.R.T.). For piano and chamber orchestra.

Janos Gyulai-Gaál (1924–   ) Hungary

The Fountain (Symphonic Picture) 1961 (EMB) 8 min. One large movement, long flowing lines, MC. M-D.

Concertino (EMB) 12 min.

H

Alois Hába (1893–1972) Czechoslovakia

Around 1920 Hába evolved a system of quarter-tone and sixth-tone music based on equal temperament. He never abandoned tonality, for many successions of tones and chords contain features of functional harmony.

Symphonic Fantasy Op.8 1920 (Ceský Hudebni Fond) 24 min. Folk-inspired melodies are used alongside more complicated harmonic and polyphonic structures; aggressive dissonance. M-D to D.

Henry Hadley (1871–1937) USA

Concertino B♭ Op.131 1932 (Birchard 1937; LC) 12 min. In one movement with contrasting sections. Brahms-inspired; moves over the keyboard nicely. M-D.

Edvard Hagerup Bull (1922–   ) Norway

Divertimento Op.15 1954 (Billaudot 1969). For piano, percussion, and orchestra. 16 min. Energico, allegro giusto; Adagio; Allegro. Piano, percussion, and orchestra are treated equally. Adagio is calm and stately, contrasting with the propulsive rhythms in the last movement. M-D.

Reynaldo Hahn (1874–1947) France

Concerto 1930 (Heugel) 31 min. Improvisation; Danse; Rêverie; Toccata et Finale. Graceful and neatly constructed. The work is divided into sections bearing titles that indicate clearly what to expect: charm, a desire to please, winning Romanticism, and exquisite craftsmanship. M-D.

Alexei Haieff (1914–   ) USA, born USSR

"Haieff's music is neoclassic in the best sense of that 'school.' It moves with clean crispness and a boundless vitality and natural attractiveness" (GD, 4, 17).

Concerto 1950 (Bo&H; Fl) 24 min. Moderato: SA; development is composed of new material, therefore it does not really develop. Vivace: Scherzo; introduced with a Lento libero section that returns later in the movement. Lento–Vivace: a kind of free fugal fantasy; clever contrapuntal usage; contains two Andante sections and a cyclical coda that summarizes earlier material. Some jazz influence in first two movements. Fast octaves, fluent figurations well designed. Skillful and peppy, yet controlled in its kineticism.

Centered freely around C with many pandiatonic ramifications and cyclical treatment. D.

Concerto (Gen 950). For piano and chamber orchestra. 14 min.

Cristobal Halffter (1930–   ) Spain
Halffter has been director of the Madrid Conservatory since 1964. Since the mid-1950s he has used serial techniques in his writing.

Processional 1973–4 (UE 15995). For two pianos and orchestra of winds and percussion. 23 min. Explanations in German. Reproduced from holograph.

Ernesto Halffter (1905–   ) Spain
Halffter was inspired by de Falla's Spanish classicism and by Domenico Scarlatti. Later he worked with Ravel, and the influence of this association can be heard in the *Portuguese Rhapsody*.

Portuguese Rhapsody 1939 (ESC 1952) 20 min. Dedicated to Ravel. Firmly based on folk music themes and formulas. Ampio e sostenuto: opening melodic idea bristles with figuration; cadenza-like passage moves into development of opening idea. Allegretto vivace: dancelike; provides the piano with an opportunity for decorative filler in the upper register; very rhythmic. Bridge leads to the Andante (mormorato) section, an Allegretto vivace (a cadenza), vivo con allegrezza, and a return of the piano in the earlier dancelike material. Allegro brioso: Iberian overtones; exciting conclusion. Highly pianistic. D.

Rodolfo Halffter (1900–   ) Mexico, born Spain
Halffter's early compositions stem from the tradition of de Falla. He began using twelve-tone techniques in 1953.

Obertura Concertante 1932 (Ediciones del Consejo Central de la Musica; Fl; LC) 15 min. One movement in contrasting sections. A nice display piece for the piano; MC. M-D.

James Nicolas Haliassas (1921–   ) Greece
Concerto 1977 (MS available from composer: Patroclou Str. 4, Haladri, Athens, Greece) 24 min. Three movements.

Richard Hall (1903–   ) Great Britain
Concerto (Hin) 35 min.

Bengt Hallberg (1932–   ) Sweden
Lyrisk Ballad 1968 (STIM). For two pianos and orchestra. 20 min.
Ivory Concerto 1976 (ES).

Hermann Haller (1914–   ) Switzerland
Concerto I (Henmar) 23 min. In three movements.
Concerto II (Henmar) 19 min. In three movements.

Hilding Hallnäs (1903–   ) Sweden
"In his early works Hallnäs used rich harmonies and melodies for expressive purposes" (GD, 4, 26). Since the mid-1950s he has used twelve-tone technique in a personal manner.

Konsert 1956 (STIM) 19½ min.

Triple Concerto 1972–73 (ES). For piano, violin, clarinet, and orchestra. 24 min.

Iain Hamilton (1922–   ) USA, born Scotland

During Hamilton's early years, Bartók, Hindemith, and Stravinsky were the dominant influences on his writing. His works from this period "were praised for their thrusting vigor, seriousness, dark-tinged scoring, formal innovations, and individual flavors of rhetorical and sometimes harsh beauty. By the late 1950s Hamilton had become a serialist" (DCM, 298).

Concerto 1960 revised 1967 (TP 1974) 20 min. Reproduction of composer's MS. Contains many titled sections: Wild; Solo cadenza: Capriccious; Fantastico; Brillante; Lento Presto [piano part is Lento, orchestra part is Presto]; Cadenza: Piacerole; Largo—Notturna; Cadenza: Ancora drammatico; Quodlibet; Coda: molto drammatico. Clusters, pointillistic, proportional rhythmic relationships. Large span required; ensemble problems. D.

Howard Hanson (1896–1981) USA

Hanson is a neoromantic and uses clear forms.

Pan and the Priest Op.26 1926 (CF) 10 min. Symphonic Poem with piano obbligato. In one movement, ingeniously and economically structured. Direct and melodic. M-D.

Fantasy Variations on a Theme of Youth Op.40 1941 (CF; Fl). For piano and string orchestra. 11 min. One movement. Bold rhythms, appealing use of thematic material, modal harmony, melodically oriented, *pp* closing. M-D.

Concerto G Op.36 1948 (CF; Fl) 20 min. For younger pianists. Lento molto e tranquillo: sonatina form (without development, ABCABC with a prologue and epilogue). Allegro molto ritmico: scherzo, strong materials. Andante molto espressivo: monothematic, lyrical. Allegro giocoso: part form; ends with a cyclical return of main theme from the first movement. Much octotonic writing throughout. Very little pianistic technical interest. Ideas good but treated ineffectively. No cadenzas. M-D.

Roy Harris (1898–1979) USA

Harris's best works have a deep meditative quality combined with exuberance. Even without citing folk materials they exude an American air. His music is work of distinction and reflects high artistic aims. The thematic, harmonic, and instrumental usage is sophisticated, and the texture is frequently of great beauty.

Concerto 1942 (Belwin-Mills). For piano and band. 10 min. One movement.

Concerto for Two Pianos and Orchestra 1946 (CF) 25 min.

Fantasy 1954 (AMP) 16 min. Rooted in three folk songs, which appear in highly variegated patterns. One is given to the strings, one to the winds, and the third to piano. They are woven into a thick, muscular tapestry of sound that builds with increasing force and fervor to a busy, noisy, and exhilarating climax. M-D.

Concerto 1968 (AMP). For amplified piano, brasses, percussion, and string basses. 20 min. Motoric opening toccata contains amusing quotes from Debussy and others; whimsical use of prepared-piano effects near end of movement. Slow movement recalls the similar movement of Harris's *Fifth Symphony*. The finale is a brilliant three-way tug-of-war between solo piano, brass, and timpani; a real "slam-bang" conclusion. M-D.

Concerto (GS). For piano and strings. 20 min. A note-for-note orchestration (minus a couple of solo cadenza passages) of the strong *Piano Quintet* of 1936. Interlaced with brooding tension and tenderness. M-D.

Lou Harrison (1917–   ) USA

Harrison has been strongly influenced by serial and aleatory procedures, by medieval and Renaissance polyphony, and by Asian cultures.

Suite 1951 (AMP). For piano, violin, and chamber orchestra. 16 min. Six contrasting movements. Free contemporary style; strong in rhythmic variety, polytonal harmonies, atonal melodic lines. Gives flights of fancy and intricate duet passages to the soloists. Graceful and joyous style is reminiscent of India—of both sacred and secular modes. M-D.

Tibor Harsányi (1898–1954) France, born Hungary

Harsányi's melodies stem from Hungarian folk melos; his rhythms are sharp, often with jazzlike syncopation, and his harmonies are largely polytonal.

Konzertstück (Senart 1931) 15 min. Lento; Allegro vivace. MC, fluid pianistic features. M-D.

Concertino (Sal 1932). For piano and strings. 25 min.

Heinz Friedrich Hartig (1907–1969) Germany

Concerto Op.30 (Bo&Bo) 21 min.

Walter S. Hartley (1927–   ) USA

Hartley uses traditional forms, contrapuntal textures, and an expanded tonal idiom. Bartók, Busoni, Hindemith, Honegger, and Stravinsky were the major influences on his music.

Concertino 1950–52 (Fema 1969). For piano, two winds, eight strings, and one percussion. 13½ min. Andante–Allegro moderato; Molto lento, liberamente; Scherzo: Vivace; Chaconne. A true contemporary chamber concerto. Not difficult technically but requires ensemble experience. M-D.

Concerto 1952 (Fema; Fl) 19 min. Allegro con brio; Adagio; Allegro grazioso.

Emil Hartmann (1836–1898) Denmark

Concerto F Op.47 (WH 11155 1894) 55pp. Allegro; Canzonetta; Finale. Solid writing in a post-Brahms tradition. Glissandi, varied figuration. M-D.

Karl Amadeus Hartmann (1905–1963) Germany

Concerto 1958 (Schott 4421). For piano, winds, and percussion. 16 min. Short introduction leads to the main body of the first movement, which is a set of rondo-variations based on a melody and interlude. The second movement, Melodie, is fantasia-like with the piano predominating. The finale also uses variations. Virtuosity is required of the pianist and of the large percussion section. M-D to D.

Koh-Ichi Hattori (1933–   ) Japan
Concertino for Small Hands (Bo&H 1968). For piano, strings, and drums. 10 min.
   Allegro moderato; Adagio ma non troppo; Vivace. Octotonic, scalar, contemporary "Alberti bass" treatment, quartal harmony, MC. Solo part requires no reach larger than a seventh. Int.

Josef Matthias Hauer (1883–1959) Germany
Klavierkonzert Op.55 1928 (UE 1977) 13 min. Twelve-tone, expressionistic. D.

Herbert Haufrecht (1909–   ) USA
Suite 1934 (ACA). For piano and string orchestra. 14 min.

Hans Haug (1900–1967) Switzerland
Concertino II 1962 (EC). For piano and chamber orchestra. 23 min. Allegro
   giocoso; Andante; Rondo. Neoclassic, thin textures, sprightly throughout
   most of the outer movements. M-D.

Franz Joseph Haydn (1732–1809) Austria
Although Haydn was a late bloomer, by his late twenties he had learned how to
write well enough for keyboard and strings. This involved knowing how to keep
thin textures from developing holes, how to manage effective modulations, and
how to handle the strings (usually three) so that they corroborate, punctuate, and
provide a framework for the keyboard. Pianists often refer to the *Concerto* in D
(Hob. XVIII/11) as "the" Haydn concerto but the list below makes us aware of
how many piano (harpsichord) concertos Haydn actually composed. The definitive numbering of Haydn's works follows the catalogue of Anthony van Hoboken
(Hob.), who was to Haydn as Köchel was to Mozart: *Joseph Haydn: Thematisch-
bibliographisches Werkverzeichnis*, Vol. I: *Instrumentalwerke* (Mainz: Schott,
1957).
Little Concerto C Hob. XIV/3 (Kreutzer—BMC; Anson—CFP 6282, called *Con-
   certino-Divertimento*). Originally a divertimento for piano, two violins, and
   cello, arranged by Haydn as a concerto for two violins and bass. Three short
   movements: Allegro moderato (with a cadenza suggested by the editor);
   Menuetto and Trio; Allegro di molto. Attractive, vintage Haydn. Int.
Concerto C Hob. XIV/4 1764 (Wertheim—Bo&H 1955) 11 min. Allegro; Menuet; Allegro. In spite of its simplicity, this work evinces the charming and
   gracious spirit of Haydn. It is still one of the most popular Haydn concertos
   for intermediate students.
Concertino Hob. XIV/11 1760 (Landon—Dob 1959) 11pp. Here published for
   the first time. No.21 in DM series. Preface in German and English. Moderato; Adagio; Allegro. Can be performed as chamber music (one player to
   each part) or as a miniature concerto. Int.
Concerto C Hob. XIV/12 ca.1760 (Landon—Dob 1969) 19pp. No.323 in DM
   series. Allegro; Adagio; Allegro. Int.
Concerto–Divertimento G Hob. XIV/13 ca.1765 (Lassen—Schott 4653) full
   score, 11pp. Here published for the first time. Schott (4959) has the same

edition with cadenzas by H. Schröter. Allegro moderato; Adagio; Presto. Int.

Concertini (Walter—Henle 188). Contains Hob. XIV/11, 12, 13; XVII F2.

Concerto C Hob. XVIII/1 1756 (Schneider—Br&H 1953). Allegro moderato. Large; Allegro moderato. Charming and unpretentious writing. Int.

Concerto F Hob. XVIII/3 ca.1765 (Schott 4959). Allegretto; Largo; Presto.

Concerto G Hob. XVIII/4 composed before 1782 (Schubert—Nag; IMC; CFP; PWM; K; Castagnone—Ric 2589; Fl). Allegro moderato; Adagio; Presto. One of the most popular Haydn concertos. This piece is typical of the change from the old to the new classic style. The fact that the choice of harpsichord or piano is left optional indicates the transitional period. Short cadenzas are required just before the end of the first and second movements. Int. to M-D.

Concerto C Hob. XVIII/5 composed before 1763 (Heussner—Nag 200; Bo&H; Br&H). Allegro moderato; Andante; Allegro. An early work that exhibits a somewhat naive sincerity with playful emotions. Falls between concerto and chamber music in style and content. Very effective as a piano quartet. Excellent preface in Nag edition. Int.

Double Concerto F Hob. XVIII/6 composed before 1766 (Schultz—Br 3839; Fl). For piano, violin, and strings. 20 min. Allegro moderato; Largo; Allegro. This work was probably intended for the composer to play with his concertmaster, the same artist for whom he wrote so many solos in the symphonies of this early Esterházy period. Int. to M-D.

Concerto F Hob. XVIII/7 composed before 1766 (Ka-We; Weelink—Cuypstr 1962; Fl; NYPL). Moderato; Adagio; Allegro.

Concerto G Hob. XVIII/9 composed before 1767 (Brusotti—Schott 5313). Allegro; Adagio; Tempo di Menuetto.

Concerto C Hob. XVIII/10 ca.1760 (Walter—Henle 202) 20pp., parts. Moderato; Adagio; Allegro. Represents the type of easily playable, small solo concerto accompanied by a string trio (two violins and cello). Markings missing from the source are printed in square brackets. This edition is from the *Collected Haydn Edition* of the Joseph Haydn Institute, Cologne, Germany. A realization of the figured bass is inserted in small type. Int. to M-D.

Concerto D Hob. XVIII/11 composed before 1782 (CFP 4356; PWM; Eulenburg). Vivace; Un poco adagio; Rondo all'Ungarese—Allegro assai. By far the most popular of all the Haydn piano concertos. Int. to M-D.

Kinder Concerto Hob. XVIII/11 (Robyn—O. Ditson). The Hungarian Rondo (last movement) from the popular *Concerto D*, Hob. XVIII/11. Int.

Concerto C Hob. XVIII/12 (Landon—Dob) 19pp. DM No.323.

Concerto F Hob. XVIII/F1 (Veyron-Lacroix—IMC; Lenzewski—Vieweg). Allegro moderato; Andante; Presto. Cadenzas by the editor in the IMC edition. Int. to M-D.

Concerto F Hob. XVIII/F2 ca.1760 (Landon—Dob) DM No.324. Moderato; Adagio; Allegro assai. Important as a rare specimen of Haydn's early style; trim and accomplished writing, charming and graceful. Int.

Children's Concerto C (Werner—Curwen 1964) 2½ min. No identification listed.
Allegro moderato; Andantino; Allegro. Delightful. Easy to Int.

Michael Haydn (1737–1806) Austria
Brother of Franz Joseph Haydn. Michael Haydn was a prolific composer, but
most of his works were sacred compositions.
Concerto C P.55 (Angerer—Dob 1970) DM No.182. For keyboard, viola, and
string orchestra. 46pp. Allegro moderato; Adagio; Prestissimo. Could be
performed with four strings plus soloist. Cadenza supplied by editor. Simple
and direct in its construction. Int. to M-D.

Anthony Hedges (1931–   ) Great Britain
Concertante Music 1968 (UE) 9 min. One movement, tonal, neoclassic, corky
rhythms. M-D.

Bernhard Heiden (1910–   ) USA, born Germany
Concerto 1957 (AMP). For piano, violin, cello, and orchestra. 27 min. Commissioned by the Beaux Arts Trio. Allegro; Adagio; Allegro molto–Vivace.
Strong and very beautiful neoclassic writing; a whale of a score that surely
deserves more hearings. The soloists come to the fore at places, then are
artfully fused with the full instrumentation. M-D.

Werner Heider (1930–   ) Germany
Capriccio (Edition Modern 1955). Neoclassic. M-D.
Bezirk 1969 (CFP 8109) holograph reproduction. Contains precise and approximate notation; performance directions in German and English. "Four large
fringe areas or divisions surround four main areas varying in size and each
differing specifically in pitch (treble, bass, nonspecific), dynamics and instrumental sequence. Forming the central point of the work is the 'Cadenza,'
which appears in the form of an orchestral obelisk, the point of culmination"
(from the score). Avant-garde; clusters. M-D to D.

Paavo Heininen (1938–   ) Finland
Heininen teaches composition at the Sibelius Academy in Helsinki.
Concerto I Op.13 1964 (Finnish Music Information Center) 28 min. A three-
movement work divided into smaller sections by improvisatory wedges, in
which the brilliant piano part is underlined especially by percussion instruments. D.
Concerto II Op.15 1966 (Finnish Music Information Center) 27 min. Sonata;
Nocturne; Ricercata. Dynamic, extroverted writing; displays adroit use of
the piano. Difficult for the pianist in both the intellectual and the technical
sense. D.

Mikko Heinio (1948–   ) Finland
Heinio teaches in Helsinki University's Department of Musicology.
Concerto I Op.4 1971 (Finnish Music Information Center) 25 min. Expanded
tonality; dramatic and virtuosic. M-D to D.
Concerto II Op.13 1973 (Finnish Music Information Center) 24 min. Introdu-

zione—Allegro tumultuoso; Largo; Allegretto con moto; Cadenza; Coda— Presto. All movements are played attacca. Expanded tonality, neoclassic, fluent pianistic gestures. M-D.

Hermann Heiss (1897–1966) Germany
Double Concerto (Br&H). For piano, violin, and orchestra. 21 min.

Gustaf Heintze (1879–1946) Sweden
Konsert I f (STIM) 30 min.
Konsert II e (STIM) 25 min.
Konsertstycke f♯ (STIM) 17 min.
Konsert a (STIM). For two pianos and orchestra. 25 min.

Walter Helfer (1897–1959) USA
A Fantasy on Children's Tunes 1935 (CF) 12 min.
Concertino Elegiaco 1939 (CF). Andantino; Allegro con amore; Andante cantabile.

Everett Helm (1913–   ) USA
Helm's style blends linear clarity with dissonant counterpoint and lively rhythmic treatment.
Concerto I G 1951 (Schott; Fl) 24 min. Allegro moderato: SA, slow contrasting second theme evolves from the active first theme, cadenza at beginning of recapitulation. Molto adagio: ABA with the second "A" freely altered. Allegro moderato con brio: five-part rondo, built on two unrelated subjects, one angular and busy, the other chordal and lyric; begins with a pseudo-cadenza. Expanded tonality, driving rhythms. A broad virtuosic work requiring full orchestra. D.
Concerto II 1956 (Bo&Bo; Fl) 15 min. Three compact movements played without pause. More intimate than *Concerto* I; displays wit and imagination. Formal procedures are based on the principles of organic growth—that is, the development of new material and relationships from material already presented—thus creating variety within a unified structure. M-D to D.

Robert Helps (1928–   ) USA
Helps studied piano with Abby Whiteside and composition with Roger Sessions. He is a professional pianist and performs much contemporary music.
Concerto 1968 (CFP 6608) 20 min. Largamente: cadenza, attacca Toccata: cadenza, *pp* ending. Andante. Thin textures, effective pianistic handling, atonal. D.

Oscar van Hemel (1892–   ) The Netherlands, born Belgium
Concerto 1941–42 (Donemus 1949) 20 min.

Eugene Hemmer (1929–   ) USA
The Voice of the Grand Piano 1955 (AME) 25 min. For narrator, piano, and orchestra. In the first section the narrator describes the construction of a grand

piano while a mock piano is built on the stage. The second section is a one-movement Concertino exhibiting a wide range of piano techniques. M-D.

Concerto 1956 (AME). For two pianos and orchestra. 20 min. Fanfare; Nocturne; Scherzo; Finale.

Gerard Hengeveld (1910–   ) The Netherlands
Concert 1957 (Donemus).
Concertino (Br&VP 803).

Hans Henkemans (1913–   ) The Netherlands
Henkemans's style is strongly Impressionistic with rich chromatic harmonies supporting melodic lines of a diatonic, often modal, character and occasional bitonality.
Concerto 1932 (Donemus) 14 min.
Concerto 1967 (Donemus). For piano and strings. 12 min.
Passacaglia and Gigue (Donemus) 15 min.

Albert Henneberg (1901–   ) Sweden
Konsert Op.8 (STIM) 20 min.

Adolph Henselt (1814–1889) Germany
Konzert f Op.16 1839–47 (Reinecke—Br&H; Music Treasure; Musical Scope; Ruthardt—CFP; Paragon) 27 min. Allegro patetico; Larghetto; Allegro agitato. Contains pianistic difficulties not readily apparent to the listener. A splendid virtuoso vehicle, with charming tunes and sonorous piano writing; brilliant and effective. "An entertaining exhibition of the pianist's prowess and of the piano's possibilities" (Raymond Lewenthal, from record jacket of Columbia MS-7252). Lewenthal has written a most interesting preface for the Music Treasure edition. "The Henselt F Minor is a magnificent work, strong and sure, brilliant, technically inventive, and to be touched only by super-virtuosos of grand sweep and romantic style" (Harold C. Schonberg, in the *New York Times;* quoted on Columbia MS-7252). The work is strongly influenced by the piano writing of Chopin and Liszt. M-D to D.

Hans Werner Henze (1926–   ) Germany
Henze is a major figure in recent German music, best known for his operas. His musical heritage comes from Berg, but in the 1960s Henze rejected dodecaphonic themes but continued to use inversion, retrograde, and other variation processes. More recently he has become involved in radical politics, and this influence shows in his later works by the incorporation of "counter-culture" music.
Concerto I 1950 (Schott 4931) 20 min. Movement titles are inspired by the dance. Entrée: march tempo, forceful main theme followed by involved rhythmic treatment. Pas de Deux: slow 7/8, ternary form, quiet pastoral material works to a dramatic romantic climax, soft closing. Coda: toccata style, fugal, brilliant and dissonant with chords of opposite tonalities. Excellent thematic and textural invention although the work reveals an immature craft and dodecaphonic tendencies. D.

Concerto II 1967 (Schott 5957) 45 min. Three movements played without pause. Originally subtitled a "Psychodrama," this work is a major addition to the large-scale piano concerto repertoire. Contains twelve-tone materials. First movement: lyrical, angular lines, strongly built. Second movement (Scherzo): a wild dance, bold, some will-o-the wisp ideas. Finale: contrasting tempi, savage climaxes, intricate textures. One of the most important piano concertos yet written in this century. D.

Tristan 1973 (Schott). Preludes for piano, electronic tapes, and orchestra. 44 min. This work is many things: a set of piano preludes, a personal preoccupation with music from Wagner's *Tristan und Isolde* and with the Tristan legends, thoughts about death and violence and nightmares, a pianola roll of Chopin's "Funeral March," old musical instruments, a prepared piano, and a syntesizer. It is a six-movement work involving all of this, and much of it adds up to an impressive musical experience. The piano preludes serve as a unifying device throughout and are heard sometimes in the solo piano and sometimes with other instrumentation. M-D.

Concertino for Piano, Wind Orchestra and Percussion (Schott 1977) 18 min.

Robert Herberigs (1886–   ) Belgium
Concerto II 1953 (H. Elkan).

Hugo Herrmann (1896–1967) Germany
"Herrmann's musical style was influenced by Catholic mysticism and the compositional techniques of the middle ages" (DCM, 317).
Konzert Op.76 1930 (Bo&Bo) 25 min. Praeludium und Fuge; Partita mit Variationen (Theme and seven variations). Freely tonal, neoclassic, MC. M-D.

Peter Herrmann (1941–   ) Germany
Kleines Klavierkonzert für die Jugend (DVFM 1973) 39pp. Catchy tunes, much repetition, plenty of rubato. Active piano part, colorful orchestral part. Would make a good substitute for the Kabalevsky *Youth Concerto* Op.50. Int. to M-D.

Henri Herz (1806–1888) Austria
Herz acknowledged that he courted the popular taste. He was highly regarded as a fashionable teacher and composer. "The bravuras that Herz writes," wrote a critic in the *Allgemeine Musikalische Zeitung* (no.144, 1836), "sound good, are easy to listen to, have a fresh lustre, make for mechanically dextrous fingers and fascinate by their clever endings—the utmost bliss attained by many players."
Concerto Op.34 (Simrock 1828?; NYPL).
Concerto III Op.37 (Schott; NYPL; LC) 43pp. Allegro moderato; Andantino sostenuto; Finale. Outer movements are exuberant while the middle movement is a cantabile-like nocturne with some unusual octave and filigree treatment. M-D.
Concerto V Op.180 (Schott ca.1857; NYPL; LC) 29pp. Allegro moderato; Andantino; Finale.

Concerto VI Op.192 (Schott 189?; NYPL).
Concerto VII Op.207 (Schott 189?; NYPL).
Concerto VIII Op.218 (Schott ca.1874; NYPL).
Grand Fantaisie Militaire (Pond 1849; LC). Based on a theme from Donizetti's
    La Fille du regiment. M-D.

Hans Joachim Hespos (1938–   ) Germany
Blackout (Edition Modern 1467).

Kurt Hessenberg (1908–   ) Germany
Hessenberg evolved an effective idiom, basically classical, but containing Wagnerian elements in dramatic passages.
Concerto Op.21 revised 1956 (Leuckart) 27 min.
Concerto Op.50 1950 (Schott 37740 1977). For two pianos and chamber orchestra.
    21 min. Allegro con fuoco. Larghetto: varied tempi, concludes with a vivace
    section. Has many affinities with Stravinsky; imitation, thin textures, neo-
    classic. M-D.

Jacques Hetu (1938–   ) Canada
Concerto (Berandol 1976) 20 min. Sostenuto–Allegro; Adagio–Vivace–Adagio;
    Presto. Atonal, thin textures, expressionistic, subtle writing. M-D to D.

Edward Burlingame Hill (1872–1960) USA
Concertino Op.36 1931 (GS; Fl) 12 min. In one movement.

Ferdinand Hiller (1811–1885) Germany
Concerto f Op.5 (Simrock).
Concerto f♯ Op.69 1860 (GS; Cranz; Br 3849) 17½ min. Moderato, ma con
    energia e con, fuoco: vigorous. Andante espressivo: less interesting than
    the outer movements but does contain some very beautiful melodies. Alle-
    gro con fuoco: dashing finale. Mendelssohn's influence is noted in the form.
    M-D.
Konzertstück C Op.113 (Cranz) 21 min. Alla marcia—Allegro energico con fuoco:
    the marchlike opening theme is immediately appealing but it seems to go
    nowhere. Andante religioso, ma con moto: introspective and sensitive. Al-
    legro: a tarantella with attractive tunes and effective orchestration. M-D.

Lejaren A. Hiller (1924–   ) USA
Hiller studied with Milton Babbitt and Roger Sessions at Princeton while earning
his Ph.D. in chemistry. A great deal of his most recent composition is *inter-media*
in nature.
Concerto Op.6 1949 (MS available from composer: % Department of Music,
    State University of New York, Buffalo, NY 14214).

Paul Hindemith (1895–1963) Germany
Hindemith was one of the major international figures in twentieth-century music
with a prolificness that encompassed virtually every possible medium and form.
Because of his commitment to neoclassicism, his work emphasizes linear writing.

He was influenced strongly by the music of Brahms, Reger, and Richard Strauss, but he moved from a harmonic approach to the contrapuntal art, which descended from Bach. Although Hindemith adheres to the principle of tonality, his harmony is constructed from the free use of twelve notes around a tonal center, and at times it has a modal feeling. His melodies emphasize intervals of the fourth and fifth, having as their basis the popular songs of medieval Germany. Rhythmically his writing tends to have a steady quality that recalls the Baroque, rather than the energy and excitement of a Bartók or a Stravinsky. His approach to form is traditional, and Hindemith used as models such Baroque molds as the concerto grosso, toccata and fugue, passacaglia and chaconne. There is always clarity and sturdiness in his formal constructions. Above all, his music is serious, intellectually objective, idealistic and inexorably logical and purposeful.

Kammermusik II *Concerto for Piano and Twelve Solo Instruments* Op.36/1 1924 (Schott 1857; Fl) 20 min. Sehr lebhafte Achtel: opens with the piano playing the main theme, from which the whole first movement is derived, a rapid perpetual motion figuration stated canonically between the hands; piano is seldom silent and usually plays in two parts with occasional octave doubling. Sehr langsame Achtel: ternary; main theme of the first part is stated by the solo instruments, and piano soon follows with embellishing figurations; cadenza passages in the piano punctuated by instrumental commentary lead into the middle doppio movimento section; ends with a shortened restatement of material from the opening section. Kleines Potpourri—Sehr lebhafte Viertel: short; scherzo-like; opens with a repeated-note theme that is used as a basis for the entire movement. Finale—Schnelle Viertel: opens with the main theme stated by the solo instruments, then taken up by the piano; a second thematic area, based on triplet figurations follows, and leads into a fugato, which combines material from the opening part; coda sums up much of the preceding material. Intellectually difficult, with a piano part that demands facility in passagework. M-D.

Concert Music for Piano, Brass and Two Harps Op.49 1930 (Schott) 21 min. The quarters in quiet walking tempo: a short introductory movement; leads without pause into Lively: aggressive; march-like; opens with a lengthy piano solo that states the main theme of the entire movement; final fugato section leads into a brilliant coda. Variations—very quiet: theme stated in the piano, followed by two variations and a coda; most of the material in this beautifully expressive movement is heard in the piano. Moderately fast, vigorous: lively finale ends with a serene coda. Pianistic demands not excessive; challenge is more intellectual than physical. M-D to D.

The Four Temperaments 1940 (Schott 1625) 28 min. Theme and Variations for Piano and String Orchestra. Theme; Melancholy; Sanguine; Phlegmatic; Choleric. Shows an increase in virtuosity as regards techniques of orchestration and composition over the two previous works. Also displays a greater profundity of polyphony. This work depicts "in spacious neo-Baroque modalities the four 'humors' of medieval biology—melancholy (in muted violins, followed by a manic-depressive march), sanguine (a hedonistic waltz), phlegmatic (in turgid motion), and choleric (in vigorously impassioned rhythms)" (MSNH, 788). M-D.

Concerto 1945 (Schott 3838) 26 min. Moderately fast: has three main ideas; the first is heard at the opening by the clarinet, the second more lyrical theme is given by the bass clarinet and two clarinets, and the third by a muted trumpet; ends quietly with beautifully transparent writing. Slow: ternary; melodically appealing; complicated counterpoint treatment of the two main themes. Medley on "Tre Fontane": a series of sections entitled Canzona, March, Valse lente, Caprice, and Medieval Dance; all based on a fourteenth-century dance tune that Hindemith found in *Archiv der Musikwissenschaft*, Vol.I; final statement of the theme returns at the finish, stated by both piano and orchestra, to end the movement in a simple yet effective manner. M-D to D.

Wells Hively (1902–1969) USA

Priscilla Variations 1939 (ACA). "For Concert Orchestra with a Junior Pianist for Soloist." 5 min. The seven variations are generally of the decoration type and require a fine "Junior" pianist. Modal, MC. Int. to M-D.

Concerto 1958 (ACA) 28 min.

Bolko Graf von Hochberg (1843–1926) Germany

Concerto c Op.42 (Simrock 1906; IU) full score, 97pp. Sostenuto; Larghetto; Vivace. Post-Reger style with the Vivace having a kinship with the Richard Strauss *Burleska*. M-D.

Alun Hoddinott (1929–   ) Wales

The following works show Hoddinott to be a far finer composer than is generally recognized.

Concerto for Piano, Winds and Percussion Op.19 1961 (OUP) 20 min. Four movements. Instrumentation is like Stravinsky's, for wind and percussion. Set in a traditionally dissonant modern idiom. A grand, rhetorical piece that contains one of the most completely imagined and successful palindromic movements (the Scherzo) in all of Hoddinott's output. Grateful and effective. M-D.

Concerto II Op.21 1960 (OUP 1968) 15 min. Moderato; Adagio; Allegro molto. Neoclassic; thin textures in outer movements; chromatic arpeggio passages add color to the Adagio. M-D.

Concerto III Op.44 1966 (OUP) 23 min. A strong work that distributes material evenly between piano and orchestra. Cadenza: solos alternate with ritornellos. Scherzo: rondo; theme is varied in subsequent appearances; many repetitions and syncopations. Notturno: atmospheric, short motives. Finale alla marcia: "straightforward march with two intervening sections" (from note in score). Freely dissonant, sometimes atonal with imaginative piano writing. D.

Richard Hoffman (1925–   ) USA, born Austria
Hoffman studied with Schoenberg and teaches at Oberlin College.
Concerto 1953–54 (Boelke-Bomart) 17 min. Theme is based on a dodecaphonic
    row and contains a rhythmic serialization in international Morse code
    (._...._.__) of Mozart's scatological letter to his father, dated 17 October
    1777, and other verbal serialisms. Every element of the music—intervals,
    meters, rhythms, timbres, and dynamics—is highly organized. D.

Josef Hofmann (1876–1957) USA, born Poland
Chromaticon (Kunwald 1916). "At every turn, the *Chromaticon* unleashes the
    least expected in phrase structure, in harmonic progression, in orchestration.
    Sinewy stuff, austere and sardonic, it reminds one of the leaner styles of
    Prokofieff and Busoni. These qualities appear in bold relief when a theme
    of compelling warmth and immediacy is borne aloft for a few moments. And
    few composers have devised a more acerbic ending" (Frank Cooper, from
    notes in recording "Josef Hofmann, Golden Jubilee Concert—November
    28, 1937," International Piano Library). M-D.

Franz Anton Hoffmeister (1754–1812) Germany
Hoffmeister, a music publisher in Leipzig, issued works by Haydn, Mozart, and
Beethoven, among others. His business was taken over in 1813 by C.F. Peters.
Hoffmeister was popular all over Europe, for his many works were typical of the
style then in vogue.
Concerto B♭ Op.16 (Zobeley—Mannheimer) 22 min. Allegro; Adagio; Rondeau
    Allegro. Charming, displays a facile craft that sometimes overworks the
    diminished seventh chord in the Rondeau. Int. to M-D.
Concerto D Op.24 composed before 1784 (Edition Kneusslin 1964) 52pp. First
    modern edition. Allegro brioso; Adagio; Allegretto. An atrractive work,
    rarely striking, but often pretty. The soloist is to accompany the tutti parts
    in a "continuo" style. Int. to M-D.

Lee Hoiby (1926–   ) USA
Hoiby's style displays lyric melodies and an ability to suggest mood, character,
and dramatic situation through music.
Concerto Op.17 1958 (GS) 25 min. First movement: lyrical first theme; tempo
    giusto second theme; in clear a minor tonality; piano cadenza. Lento: forceful
    opening tutti; embellished cadenza in early part of movement; in turn lyrical,
    contemplative, and rhapsodic. Allegro vivo: sonata-rondo form evolves from
    opening 7/8 dance figure; the last pages are marked by steadily increasing
    momentum leading to a *ff* close. Unabashedly lyrical throughout. M-D.

Josef Holbrooke (1878–1958) Great Britain
Concerto I Op.52 "The Song of Gwynn ap Nudd" 1908 (JWC) 59pp. A sym-
    phonic poem; chaotic; bombastic; many nineteenth-century clichés. Daunt-
    ingly virtuosic piano part. M-D.
Concerto II Op.100 "L'Orient" (Modern Music Library 1936).

David Holden (1911–   ) USA
Music for Piano and Strings 1936–37 (GS) 18 min. With virile accent; Veiled;
    Boisterously ("Sumer is icumen in"). M-D.

Hans Holewa (1905–   ) Sweden, born Austria
Holewa was the first Swedish composer to adopt Schoenberg's serialist tech-
niques. His musical language seems closest to Alban Berg's *Violin Concerto* fused
with cool Scandinavian lyricism.
Variations 1943 (ES).
Concerto 1975 (EC). For two pianos and orchestra. 17 min.
Concerto 1972 (ES; Fl) 17 min. In the form of a French overture (S-F-S move-
    ments). The slow outer movements give this very intense and frequently
    expressive work a bleak, somewhat sparse sound. The first two moments are
    played without a break. Logic and precision reminiscent of much of Ernst
    Krenek's serial writing. M-D to D.

Peder Holm (1926–   ) Denmark
Concertino II (WH 4298 1975). For piano and strings. 12 min.

Vagn Holmboe (1909–   ) Denmark
Holmboe's music is strongly influenced by Carl Nielsen and Béla Bartók. Holm-
boe leans toward linear textures.
Chamber Concerto IV Op.30 1940 (WH). For piano, violin, cello, and orchestra.
    No big emotional gestures; the music grows consistently from the initial
    germ material; subtle and haunting atmosphere. M-D.

Arthur Honegger (1892–1955) Switzerland, born France
The writing of Honegger was never in sympathy with the French "Les Six,"
although he was ostensibly a member of that group. Much of his music is conceived on a grand scale, with a fondness for sonata structure and extended development of material that is in the German, rather than the French, tradition. His
great model was Johann Sebastian Bach, for Honegger sought polyphonic textures
and linear writing. He utilized most of the twentieth century's musical materials,
and at one time or another he made use of polychordality, atonality, and polytonality. His last works contain a deep sense of mysticism and religious conviction.
Concertino 1924 (Sal 6886; USSR) 13 min. One of the few works of Honegger's
    that attempt to imitate the atmosphere of the popular music hall. There is
    always a refreshing lyricism and jaunty rhythm plus a touch of the mischie-
    vous. Allegro molto moderato: a dialogue between piano and orchestra, with
    an ensuing brief fugal section and a return to the opening. Larghetto soste-
    nuto: lyrical; utilizes material from a melody first heard in the piano. Allegro;
    brilliant finale; many syncopated passages. All three movements are played
    without pause. M-D.

Joseph Horovitz (1926–   ) Great Britain, born Austria
Jazz Concerto 1965 (Novello). For harpsichord or piano, drums, string bass, and
    small string orchestra. 15 min. The outer movements (Allegro and Vivace)

reflect the influence of J. S. Bach in the structure and part-writing combined with that of Duke Ellington in the harmonies. The middle movement, a Slow Blues, is a purple smoulder with a crackling, elegant cadenza for piano. M-D.

Zoltan Horusitsky (1903–   ) Hungary

Concerto II (EMB 1966) 24 min. Allegro giubilato; Andante disperanto; Allegro vivace. Exciting writing, brilliant handling of the piano part, tonal with many chromatic inflections, strong rhythms in the finale. M-D.

André Aminoullah Hossein (1907–   ) France

Concerto I Op.24 (EMT 1957)

Concerto II Op.45 (EMT 1958) 15 min. Allegro vivo; Andante quasi lento; Allegro scherzando. Interesting rhythms and harmonies, many parallel chords with added tones. M-D.

Concerto III (EMT 1974) 13½ min. A one-movement work with a lyrical mid-section and a final section that relies on scales and broken-chord figures. Repeated notes overworked. Orchestral role is very secondary. M-D.

Pierick Houdy (1929–   ) France

Concerto 1961 (Leduc). For harpsichord or piano and string orchestra. 13½ min. Allegro: octotonic, neoclassic, freely tonal. Largo: germinal opening idea is basis for movement, flowing. Allegro: contemporary Alberti bass, thin textures, chromatic but tonal. M-D.

Alan Hovhaness (1911–   ) USA

Hovhaness has developed a style that combines traditional Western materials with elements from other countries, especially those of Armenia, South India, and the Far East. Rhapsodic improvisation characterizes most of his music.

Lousadzak Op.48 1944 (Coming of Light) (PIC 1960; Fl). For piano and strings. 18 min. Imitates the tar, kanoon, and saz. Noble and majestic opening; repeated figures in the cadenza; dancelike sections; contrasting moods; brilliant conclusion. M-D.

Zartik Parkim Op.77 1949 (Awake My Glory) (PIC 1964; Fl). For piano and chamber orchestra. 15 min. Zankag (Bell)—Moderato; Tmpoug—Allegretto (dancelike); Srynk—Andante. Modal color in large contrasting panels! M-D.

Janadar Op.81 1950 "Five Hymns of Serenity" (PIC 1964; Fl). For piano, violin, trumpet, and strings. 40 min. Fantasy; Yerk; Prayers; Sharagan; Tapor.

Concerto V Op.108 (Fl). For piano and strings.

Symphony VIII "Arjuna" (CFP 1963). For piano, timpani, and orchestra. 25 min. Written in the Carnatic classical style. Uses the Indian instrument maidangam. M-D.

Frank Hruby (1918–   ) USA

Concertino 1941 (Fl) 19 min. Allegro; Andante con moto; Allegro–slowly–Allegro.

Jean Hubeau (1917–   ) France

Concerto Héroïque B on Two Hymns (*Concerto* I) (Durand 1946) 25 min. Allegro
   moderato; Andante maestoso: leads to Allegro vivo, quasi presto and numerous other tempo and mood changes that serve as the final movement.
   Brilliant writing, not always controlled, formally speaking. M-D.

Gerald Humel (1931–   ) USA

Chamber Concerto (Bo&Bo). For piano, horn, and strings. 16 min.

Ferdinand Hummel (1855–1928) Germany

Concerto B Op.35 (K&S 1884).

Johann Nepomuk Hummel (1778–1837) Hungary

Hummel was often mentioned in the same breath with Mozart by nineteenth-
century writers. His works represent the highest concerto achievements among
Beethoven's contemporaries. There are many moments of genuine inspiration in
these compositions, which were highly esteemed by Chopin and others of his
time.

Double Concerto G Op.17 (reconstructed by Helmut Riessberger, Gesellschaft
   der Musikfreunde Library, Vienna; Costallat). For piano, violin, and orchestra. 29 min. The two instruments are generally used in imitation, in contrast,
   and in combination. The melodic craft is fine, with the violin writing as
   facile as that for the piano. Allegro con brio: material unfolds gracefully;
   cantilena sections; imaginative cadenza for both instruments. Andante con
   variazioni: graceful; dolce character; writing becomes more involved as
   movement proceeds. Rondo: spirited, has some brilliant moments. M-D.

Concerto C Op.34 1813 (Schlesinger; LC) 40pp. Listed as Op. 36 in some publications. Allegro con spirito; Adagio; Vivace assai. Heavy figuration and
   ornamentation; themes are suffocated under all the scales and passage work.
   M-D.

Rondeau Brillant A Op.56 (Simrock; CFP; LC) 16½ min. A prominent example
   of the virtuoso piano style of Hummel's time, as well as proof of the composer's poetical feeling and musical temperament. M-D.

Concertino G Op.73 (Rihm—Steingräber; LC). Allegro moderato; Andante grazioso; Rondo. Delightful. M-D.

Concerto a Op.85 1821 (CFP; GS; Br&H; Paragon) 31 min. This well-crafted
   work influenced Chopin's e minor *Concerto*. Themes in the first movement
   (Allegro moderato) and last movement (Rondo) have an early-Romantic
   quality and are profusely ornamented. The middle movement, Larghetto, has
   a dreamy, Chopinesque quality about it; this movement in particular requires
   graceful and rhythmic execution of the decorations. D.

Concerti Op.85 and 89 (Ruthardt—CFP 714) 87pp.

Concerto b Op.89 1819 (Paragon; CFP; GS; Br&H; Heugel; Steingräber; Cranz)
   32 min. Some publishers list this work as Op.90. Allegro moderato; Larghetto; Finale. Hearing this work for the first time, if the composer's name
   were concealed, one would be tempted to think of very good Mozart, of

Beethoven at the period of the "Rasumovsky" *Quartets,* or of a sketch for the Chopin *Second Piano Concerto.* Or the hearer might imagine this is the kind of music Mozart might have written had he lived longer. An altogether attractive work, especially the impressive outer movements. M-D.

Concertos Opp.35 and 89 (Cranz).

Rondo Brillant on a Russian Folk Theme Op.98 1822 (LC) 29pp. The folk song "Zemlyanichka Yagodka" talks about the delights of raspberries. This work is a souvenir of Hummel's Russian tour of 1822 and bears a dedication to the Princess Gertchakoff. It is a slight piece but charming, although the Slavic flavor is pretty well dissipated after the first statement of the theme. M-D.

Concerto E Op.110 "Les Adieux" (Heugel; LC) 39pp. Allegro pomposo e spiritoso; Andante con moto; Rondo.

Concerto A♭ Op.113 (Reinecke—Br&H). Allegro moderato; Romanza; Rondo.

Variations Brillantes "Das Fest der Handwerken" Op.115 1830 (LC) 17pp.

Oberons Zauberhorn—Grosse Fantasie Op.116 1829 (Schlesinger; LC) 29pp. Hummel pays homage to Weber's *Oberon* in this fantasy, "Oberon's Magic Horn." It is a mixture of the Konzertstück and an operatic fantasy, a form that was popular at the time. M-D.

Gesellschafts Rondo D Op.117 (Schlesinger; LC) 21pp. M-D.

Le Retour de Londres—Grand Rondeau Brillant Op.127 1830 (LC) 27pp. M-D.

Klavierkonzert A (D. Zimmerschied—Hofmeister FH 3107 1971) 34pp. Without opus number. Allegro moderato; Romanze; Rondo. Based on the autograph in the British Library. M-D.

Klavierkonzert I F Op. posth. (Br&H 1839). Allegro moderato; Larghetto; Finale—Allegro con brio.

See: Francis H. Mitchell, "The Piano Concertos of Johann Nepomuk Hummel," diss., Northwestern University, 1957.

Andrzej Hundziak (1927–   ) Poland

Concertino 1972 (PWM). For piano, children's percussion, and three-part children's or female chorus. 14½ min. One movement. Four sixteenths with three eighths; cadenzas for piano. Chorus has spoken and sung parts. MC. M-D.

Karel Husa (1921–   ) USA, born Czechoslovakia

Husa writes music that is highly emotional and uses serial techniques and advanced harmonies. In 1954 he came to the USA, to Cornell University, where he still teaches.

Concertino Op.10 1949–50 (Schott) 15 min. Allegretto moderato; Quasi fantasia—moderato molto; Allegretto moderato. Makes use of appealing devices developed in recent years, which are well integrated into the fabric. Octotonic, flexible meters, flowing lines, effective use of trills, dramatic conclusion. M-D.

Henry Holden Huss (1862–1953) USA

Rhapsody C Op.3 1886 (LC).

Concerto B Op.10 (GS 1898; LC) 66pp. Allegro maestoso; Andante con senti-
mento; Final—Allegro vivace. Thick textures, strong Germanic Romantic
characteristics. More difficult than Brahms, Liszt, and Schumann concertos;
awkwardly involved. D.

Scott Huston (1916–   ) USA

Concerto 1952 (MS at Sibley Library, Eastman School of Music, Rochester, NY)
24 min. Molto moderato; Larghetto; Allegro con poco malizia.

I

Rustem Mukhamet-Khazeevich Iakhin (1921–   ) USSR
Concerto f (USSR 1959). Three movements in an unabashedly Romantic idiom.
   Sounds as though it could have been used in a Hollywood movie of the
   1940s or 50s. Heroic and sentimental themes; pianistically effective; well
   crafted. Especially fine use of piano and orchestra, both singly and together.
   M-D to D.

Andrew Imbrie (1921–   ) USA
Imbrie's style is marked by formal clarity, lucid polyphonic texture, and sharp
melodic line where the harmony arises from the counterpoint.
Little Concerto 1956 (SP). For piano, four-hands and orchestra. 12 min. In one
   movement. Flexible meters, twelve-tone influence; piano textures are generally thin and tend to be octotonic. Requires first-rate ensemble experience
   and superb musicianship. M-D.
Concerto I 1973 (Malcolm) 17 min. Maestoso; Andante; Allegro. Expressionistic,
   thin textures, strong dissonance, playful, provocative, witty. M-D.
Concerto II 1974 (Malcolm) 22 min. This difficult score is skillfully wrought and
   brings to mind techniques of the jazz era. It is sterner in mood than *Concerto*
   I. M-D.

Herbert Inch (1904–   ) USA
Concertino (Fl). For piano and strings.

Carlo de Incontrera (1937–   ) Italy
Concerto 1965 (Ric). For piano and chamber orchestra. 15 min. Performance
   directions in Italian. Graphic notation, pointillistic, clusters, avant-garde.
   Improvisation required. M-D.

Vincent d'Indy (1851–1931) France
D'Indy's music does not indulge in powerful dramatics or extravagances, nor is
it highly colored or overpowering in sonority. Rather it has a subtle appeal to the
intellect with a characteristic detachment, objectivity, and clarity. D'Indy sought
an amalgamation of the German tradition with French musical culture. He had
varying degrees of success in attempting to fuse his own lyric gifts with German
counterpoint.
Symphony on a French Mountain Song Op.25 1886 (Hamelle; IMC). For orchestra

and piano concertante. 24 min. Three movements based on a simple folk melody. First movement: SA. Second movement: freely sectional. Third movement: variations. The piano is essentially a member of the orchestra, although its part in each movement is considerable. It is used for effect but not for virtuoso effect. Except for the authenticity of the French folk tune itself, the *Symphony* has no other programmatic implications. M-D.

Jour d'Été à la Montagne (Summer Day on the Mountain) a Rhapsody for Piano and Orchestra Op.61 1905 (Hamelle). Dawn; Day; Night. This impression-istic and pictorial symphonic triptych is perhaps d'Indy's masterpiece of programmatic music, being a French Pastoral Symphony. Although the piano has a definite solo role, the orchestra is equal if not slightly dominating rather than acting in an accompanying capacity. Based on a theme from the Cévennes mountain region of France, which d'Indy uses throughout. This cyclic treatment is borrowed directly from Franck. The piano is frequently used with the harp. Technical demands not excessive. M-D.

Triple Concerto for Piano, Flute, Cello and String Orchestra Op.89 1927 (Sal) 30 min. Modéré mais bien decidé; Lent et espressif; Mouvement de rond française. D'Indy wrote this work during the last decade of his life, when he was leaning more and more toward neoclassicism. This tendency can be seen in the restrained, lean score of this work. There is a definite relationship to the eighteenth-century concerto grosso, with the concertino group of soloists being used in contrast to the tutti orchestra. M-D.

John Ireland (1879–1962) Great Britain

Ireland combines Impressionistic and post-Romantic qualities with such elements of English folk song as modal and pentatonic harmony. His writing is polished, and his harmonic style is mildly conservative. Much of his work was influenced by the mystical writings of Arthur Machen. A teacher for many years at the Royal College of Music in London, Ireland numbered among his pupils Benjamin Britten and Humphrey Searle.

Concerto E♭ 1930 (JWC) 24 min. The colorful orchestration of this work includes five percussion instruments in addition to the regular timpani. In tempo moderato: no regular concerto form. Lento espressivo: opening Lento is full of irregular meter changes; Allegretto giocoso section has a lively theme that keeps doubling back on itself; the opening Lento returns briefly before the brilliant coda. Both main themes of the first movement are used in the second half of the concerto. The piano writing is brilliant and effective, and requires solid virtuoso equipment. D.

Legend 1933 (Schott) 15 min. This single-movement work has a form that cannot be analyzed according to classical models. Opening with a general tonal sense of e♭, the piece ends in a feeling of d. The "Dies irae" is quoted in the section marked "Quasi recitando." Throughout, the writing for the piano is comparatively restrained, and the piano acts as a partner with the orchestra.

Dedicated to Arthur Machen, the work has a mystical and pastoral quality about it. M-D.

Yoshino Irino (1921–   ) Japan, born USSR

Irino has used twelve-tone technique since 1951.

Doppelkonzert 1955 (Ongaku no Tomo 1957). For piano, violin, and orchestra.

Mioslav Istvan (1906–   ) USSR

Concerto-Symphony (Soviet Composer 1962). Adagio; Allegro. Expansive. Allegro has numerous tempo and mood changes, and a large cadenza. Tonal, much chromatic color. M-D to D.

Janis Ivanos (1906–   ) USSR

Concerto (Soviet Composer 1960) 71pp. Moderato maestoso; Andante; Allegro. Freely tonal around C, strong rhythms, nineteenth-century oriented. M-D.

Charles Ives (1874–1954) USA

Calcium Light Night 1907? (Fl). For two pianos, six winds, and two drums. 2½ min. Pianos mainly add coloristic atmosphere (clusters) and some rhythmic push. Large span required. M-D.

J

Carlo Jachino (1887–1971) Italy

In his early compositions Jachino followed the Romantic Italian style. Later he adopted a modified twelve-tone method.

Concerto 1952 (EC) 23 min. Mosso; Largo; Mosso. Contains an analysis in Italian. Twelve-tone. M-D.

Concerto II 1957 (Ric) 26 min. Un poco agitato; Calmo (La Savana di Bogotà); Vivace: based on a popular tune of Boyacà. Colorful. Advanced pianism required. M-D to D.

Gordon Jacob (1895–   ) Great Britain

Concerto I (OUP 1927). For piano and strings. 46pp. Allegro assai; Adagio; Allegro risoluto. Freely tonal, a little Impressionistic; contains some brilliant piano writing. A gifted teen-ager would enjoy this work. Int.

Concertino (OUP 1955). For piano and strings. 12 min. In three movements.

Concerto II 1957 (OUP) 30 min. Three movements. Freely tonal, effective use of piano and orchestra. Second movement is a set of four highly contrasted variations. Could be a knock-out for a teen-ager who has well-developed technique and musicianship. Int. to M-D.

Concerto (Nov). For piano, three-hands and orchestra. 20 min.

Frederick Jacobi (1891–1952) USA

Jacobi was a student of Joseffy in piano and Ernest Bloch in composition. He taught at the Juilliard School from 1936 until 1950. His style generally represents a synthesis of classic, Romantic, and modern styles and was influenced by the music of the American Indian (of whom he was a scholar) and by Jewish sources.

Ave Rota 1939 (Fl) 14 min. Three pieces in multiple style. La Balançoire; The Merman; May Dance.

Concertino C (EV; Fl 1946) 17 min. Allegro: mainly rhythmic. Andante: lyrical and meditative. Tarentella: brisk and humorous. The writing throughout is tonal, bright, and effective. Contains fine neoromantic tunes. Not of excessive difficulty. M-D.

Serenade (MCA) 10 min.

Wolfgang Jacobi (1894–   ) Germany

Capriccio 1954 (Edition Modern) 24pp., holograph. Neoclassic, tricky spots, more difficult than it looks. M-D.

Hyacinthe Jadin (1769–1800) France
Concerto I (Ozi).
Concerto II d (Erard).
Concerto III (Erard).

Robert H. Jameson (1947–   ) USA
All three concertos show a fluid handling of the piano writing and effective orchestration. These works deserve performance.
Concerto I 1965 (LC). Allegro giusto; Andante grazioso; Allegro non troppo. M-D.
Concerto II 1967 (MCA) 22½ min. Allegro moderato; Andante cantabile; Allegro non tanto. M-D.
Concerto III 1969 revised 1970–71 (MCA) 22 min. Allegro moderato; Andante; Allegro ma non troppo. M-D.

Leoš Janáček (1854–1928) Czechoslovakia
Janáček's music is extremely indebted to Moravian folk music and uses cadences, rhythms, and contours that are peculiar to this music. The influence of the Bohemian language is important, for Janáček endeavored to construct his melodies out of its speech patterns. He was sometimes called "the Moravian Mussorgsky." His musical language is essentially post-Romantic with a mobile, always tonal, harmony. His form is like a mosaic structure and is based on variation treatment of a few basic motives; and his melodic lines tend to be broken up into short, oft-repeated phrases similar to speech patterns. Janáček was not always a sophisticated craftsman, but his work at its best is filled with power and intensity.
Concertino 1925 (Artia) 16½ min. This work is mainly pastoral in feeling and is built from a series of preludes, each of which is related thematically to the preludes of the other movements. The first three movements are in ternary form. Moderato: opening figure given by the piano is heard throughout, accompanied by a melodic line in the horn. Più mosso: the clarinet and piano divide the principal material. Con moto: greater utilization of full ensemble writing. Allegro: freer in design; opens with running passages in the piano from which the principal theme is derived; might almost be described as an accompanied cadenza. M-D.

Johann Gottlieb Janitsch (1708–1763) Germany
Concerto (McGinnis & Marx). For keyboard and strings.

Hanns Jelinek (1901–1969) Austria
Jelinek studied with Schoenberg and adopted the twelve-tone technique in the 1930s.
Phantasie 1951 (UE). For clarinet, piano, and orchestra. 12 min. Pays homage to classicism by including the BACH motive in the Introduction and at the conclusion. M-D.
Rai Buba Op.34 1962 (Edition Modern 1065) 18 min. Etude for piano and orchestra.

Donald Jenni (1937–   ) USA
Concertino 1955 (ACA) 18 min. Animato na non troppo vivo; Larghetto semplice
    ma espressivo; Energetico.

Jaroslav Ježek (1906–1942) Czechoslovakia
Fantasie 1930 (Panton) 13 min. Composed for Ježek's own graduation concert;
    full of youthful imagination. A main idea is used throughout. Alternates
    Allegros with less-rapid passages. Orchestral part interspersed with piano
    solos. M-D.
Concerto 1927 (Panton 1961) 17 min. Introduction in Czech, Russian, German,
    English, and French. Adagio quasi andante: SA; Foxtrot introduced. Tango:
    ABA, large cadenza connects with the last movement, Allegro vivace: rondo;
    uses the Charleston. A good example of the charm and dancing mood at the
    close of the 1920s. M-D.

Carlos Jimenez-Mabarak (1916–   ) Mexico
Concerto C (EMM) 14 min.

Karel Boleslav Jirak (1891–1972) USA, born Czechoslovakia
Concerto Op.55 1949 (Orbis) 74pp. One large movement. Strong writing, ex-
    panded tonality, expressive lyric lines, dissonant free counterpoint. Brilliant
    pianistic treatment. D.

Ivan Jirko (1926–1978) Czechoslovakia
Concerto III G (Panton 1961) 20 min. Allegro; Andante tranquillo; Allegro vivo.
    The Andante speaks the language of an expressive national character; its
    meditatively lyric conception leaves its mark on the whole work. M-D.

Sven-Eric Johanson (1919–   ) Sweden
Concerto III "Concerto Gothenburgese" 1970 (ES) 30 min. Blithely mixes var-
    ious musical styles and quotes from well-known musical works. M-D.

Bengt Johansson (1914–   ) Finland
Johansson is on the staff of the Finnish Broadcasting Corporation.
Concerto 1951 (Finnish Music Information Center) 25 min. Three (FSF) move-
    ments. Romantic–neoclassical tendencies; bass line is connected to the tonal-
    ity bitonally through a second interval; modal melodies. M-D.

Björn Johansson (1913–   ) Sweden
Concerto 1965 (ES) 30 min.

Hunter Johnson (1906–   ) USA
Concerto 1936 (Fl). For piano and chamber orchestra. 17 min. Maestoso; Allegro.

André Jolivet (1905–1974) France
Jolivet was a student of Edgar Varèse and was heavily influenced by Schoenberg
and Berg. His writing shows great harmonic freedom, which borders on atonality,
and wide use of asymmetric and often complex rhythms and imaginative dynamic
effects. Combined with these qualities is a personal lyricism that makes much of
his music accessible. Jolivet was drawn to mystical religious ideas and considered

the universe to be made up of invisible psychic forces inherent in all things, with music a sort of magical incantation. Many of his works try to capture this mystical feeling.

Concerto 1950 (Heugel) 23½ min. Allegro deciso: SA characteristics; opens brilliantly and almost immediately goes into a dialogue between the piano and percussion instruments, with much of the piano writing being of a chordal, percussive nature à la Bartók. Senza rigore—Andante con moto: broad, rhapsodic, ternary form. Allegro frenetico: arch design, brilliant, effective coda. Rhythms and timbres suggestive of Asia and Polynesia add an exotic element. In addition to the usual orchestral personnel, an unusually large number of extra percussion instruments is demanded. Throughout, the writing is complex for both soloist and orchestra, and requires complete pianistic equipment. D.

Marinus de Jong (1891–   ) Belgium
De Jong teaches at the Royal Flemish Conservatorium in Antwerp.
Concerto I Op.21 1924 (CeBeDeM) 21 min. In one large movement.
Concerto II Op.80 1952 (CeBeDeM) 20 min. Highly chromatic and complex idiom. D.
Concerto III Op.105 1956 (CeBeDeM) 18 min. More tonal than *Concertos* I and II, but still the chromatic element is strong. Three movements (FSF). M-D.

Joseph Jongen (1873–1953) Belgium
Jongen wrote animated and expressive music, harmonious in its very dissonance and always supple. His preference for bright sonorous colors is seen in both these works.
Pièce Symphonique Op.84 1928 (CeBeDeM) 24 min. Reproduced from holograph. Many nineteenth-century pianistic idioms, some Impressionistic moments, contrasting sections, Franck influence. M-D.
Concerto Op.127 1943 (Lemoine 1956) 30 min. Dramatic, virtuosic, freely tonal. M-D to D.

Sverre Jordan (1889–   ) Norway
Jordan makes liberal use of folk songs in his works.
Concerto e Op.45 1945 (NK) 30 min. Three movements.
Concerto Piccolo F Op.77 1963 (NK) 17 min. Three movements.

Wilfred Josephs (1927–   ) Great Britain
Concerto I Op.48 (Weinberger 1967) 26 min. Three movements. Nonserial. The finale, a brilliant Passacaglia, provides the most drive and is pianistically the most rewarding. Contains some unusual orchestral effects and brilliant piano writing. M-D.
Concerto II (Novello) 25 min.

Werner Josten (1885–1963) USA, born Germany
Concerto Sacro I, II 1927 (Birchard; H. Elkan; Fl) No. I, 22 min. No. II, 20 min. No. I: Annunciation; The Miracle. No. II: Lament; Sepulchre and Resurrec-

tion. "This work was originally conceived by the composer as one Concerto in four movements. The character and musical balance of those movements, however, make it feasible to perform either half of the work as an entity in itself. To facilitate this division and two parts have been entitled collectively *Concerto Sacro I—II*" (from the score). Modelled after the *Brandenburg Concertos* of Bach and couched in a Romantic German style. Strong counterpoint underneath expansive harmonies; colored with a few Impressionistic sonorities. "Lament" refers to the verses in the book of Luke describing the crucifixion. The MC harmonies and lines add to the primitive simplicity and directness of the piece. M-D.

John Joubert (1927–   ) Great Britain, born South Africa
Concerto 1958 (Novello 1964). For piano and string orchestra.
Concerto Op.25 (Novello 1964; Fl) 35 min. Allegro; Lento; Lento–Allegro vivace. Freely tonal, octotonic, moves over entire keyboard. Allegro vivace is propulsive, with an effective closing cadenza. M-D to D.

Helge Jung (1943–   ) Germany
Klavierkonzert Op.11 (DVFM 1973). A student concerto. Ballade: story develops in interesting manner. Four Variations: based on a Ukrainian folk song; contrasting. Toccata: rhythmic; has a few glissandi. Attractive MC writing for the student of average ability. Int.

Paul Juon (1872–1940) Germany, born Russia
Concerto Op.45 (Schlesinger 1912). For piano, violin, cello, and orchestra. Allegro moderato; Lento; Allegro non troppo. Classic forms and treatment. M-D.

Simon Jurovský (1912–1963) Czechoslovakia
First Symphony for Concertant 1954 (Slovenské Ludobné Vydavatel Štvo).

K

Dmitri Kabalevsky (1904–   ) USSR

All of Kabalevsky's concertos are conceived in the traditional forms. His writing is designed for immediate utility and popular consumption.

Concerto I a Op.9 1929 (UE) 33 min. Moderato quasi andantino; Tema—Moderato; Vivace marcato. Written in a lyric–heroic style with recurring eruptions of kinetic energy in an optimistic tonal ambience. Brilliant outside movements; slow middle movement (5 variations plus coda) based on a Russian folk song. Late nineteenth-century eclectic idiom. M-D.

Concerto II g Op.23 1935 (MCA) 23½ min. Allegro moderato: lyrical quality but also brilliant and rhythmic. Andante semplice: philosophical; dirgelike; develops to a dramatic climax. Allegro molto: concatenations of consecutive triads; instant modulation; unresolved dissonances; engaging writing for piano and woodwinds in combination; coda represents an enlargement of the opening theme of the first movement. Highly contrasted movements in a neoromantic style with pianistic display and effective musical ideas. Flamboyant array of emotional patterns. M-D.

Concerto III Op.50 "Youth" 1952 (MCA; K; IMC) 18 min. Allegro molto; Andante; Presto. The last of a trilogy of "Youth" concertos, the others being the *Violin Concerto* Op.48 and the *Cello Concerto* Op.49. All three are in the classical three movements, pose no problems, and make for delightful listening. Perhaps because he himself is a pianist, Kabalevsky has always had a special love and affinity for the piano. His writing is strongly rhythmic and tonal and interlaced with a variety of effective pianistic devices. Int.

Rhapsody on a Theme of the Song "School Years" Op.75 1964 (MCA; USSR) 14 min. Ten variations, cadenza, coda. The contrasting variations unfold parallel to the words of the song. Transparent yet colorful and supple orchestration make this a welcome contribution to the virtuoso repertoire of young musicians. Inventive and exciting solo part. Int.

Prague Concerto (USSR 1979). For piano and string orchestra. Vol. 13 of "Piano Music for Children and the Youth." For young pianists.

Pal Kadosa (1903–   ) Hungary

Concerto I Op.15 1931 (EMB) 21 min. Three movements (FSF). Propulsively percussive style; consanguineous with the music of Bartók. M-D.

Concertino II Op.29 1938 (EMB) 17 min. Preludio (Toccata); Romanza; Tarantella. Neoclassic, sparkling, highly appealing. M-D.

Concerto III Op.47 1953 (EMB) 26 min. Vivo: SA. Sostenuto: ABA. Allegro con
brio: rondo; zippy figurations; Bartók influence but carried out on a less-
inspired level; lacks pianistic expertise; figures and scalar passages not handled in an exciting manner. Only some of the linear collision adds interest.
M-D.

Concerto IV Op.63 1966 (EMB) 15 min. Allegro: SA. Sostenuto: ABA. Vivace:
SA. Bartók-inspired. Tertian sonorities, well-defined thematic material, dull
piano part. M-D.

Simon Milhailovich Kagan (1909–   ) USSR

Concertino 1963 (Soviet Composer) 72pp. For piano and dance orchestra (uses
saxophones, guitar, and accordian) plus regular orchestra. One movement.
Jazz influence; similar to Shostakovitch style; freely tonal around G♭; piano
textures generally thin. M-D.

Viktor Kalabis (1923–   ) Czechoslovakia

Concerto Op.12 1954 (Panton) 20 min. Introduction in Czech, Russian, German,
English, and French. Three movements (FSF). Chromatic dissonance provides expanded tonality; neoclassic piano aesthetic; lyric lines are intellectually varied; virtuosity absent; echoes of Menotti and Copland. M-D.

Friedrich W. M. Kalkbrenner (1785–1849) Germany

All the music listed below is demanding and at times beautifully written for the
instrument. The salon style displays Weber arabesques, Chopin mannerisms, and
touches of Schubert lyricism. Generally the material is not convincingly organized, and it is too lengthy for the content.

Grand Rondo Brillant Op.60 (LC) 23pp. Introduction precedes the Rondo.

Concerto Op.61 (Simrock; Br&H; LC; NYPL 1824?) 39pp. Allegro maestoso;
Adagio di molto; Rondo. Salon style, beautifully written for the instrument.
M-D.

Gage d'Amitié Op.66 (Kistner).

Effusio Musica; Grande Fantaisie Op.68 (Probst 1827; NYPL; LC) 22 min. Brilliant, suave, beautifully pianistic. Reminds one of Mozart, Beethoven, and
Hummel.

Les Charmes de Berlin Op.70 (Schlesinger). Grande Rondo Brillant.

Fantaisie et Grandes Variations sur un Thême Ecossais Op.72 (Pleyel; LC) 24pp.
Elaborate introduction followed by theme, the Fantaisie, and the contrasting
variations.

Concerto II Op.80 (LC) 47pp. Allegro maestoso; La Tranquillité; Rondo.

Grande Polonaise Op.92 (LC 1827). For piano and strings. Introduction and
March precede the Polonaise.

Introduction et Rondeau Brillant C Op.101 (LC). The attractive tunes are handled
with imagination and craftsmanship and roll along on the support of a lively
rhythmic foundation.

Concerto III Op.107 (Kistner 187?; BP:) 34pp. The piano has all the best lines!
Variations Brillantes Op.112 (Kistner).
Le Rêve. Grand Fantasie Op.113 (Kistner).
Grand Concerto Op.125 (Kistner ca.1835; NYPL). For two pianos and orchestra.
    Material is poorly organized, quiltlike!
Concerto IV Op.127 (CFP 1835; NYPL). NYPL version is arranged for piano and
    string quintet. LC has a version for piano and orchestra. LC copy has Op.125
    for this work. Rhythmic scansion (harmonic rhythm) is constantly vacillat-
    ing. Abrupt changes of tempo and dynamics. Robert Schumann called this
    work "manufactured pathos and affected profundity."

Edvin Kallstenius (1881–1967) Sweden
Konsert C Op.12 (Sinfonia Concertata) (Fl; STIM) 30 min. Written in the spirit
    of late German Romanticism. M-D to D.

Martin Kalmanoff (1920–   ) USA
Concerto III "Climax" (Rosarita).

Manolis Kalomiris (1883–1962) Greece
Rapsodie Op.22 (Fl).

Dmitrii R. Kaminski (1907–   ) USSR
Concerto I 1948 (State Publishers of the White Russians 1955; LC) 115pp. Three
    movements. Tonal, unusual rhythms. M-D.
Concerto IV (USSR 1977) 79pp. One large movement, two cadenzas. More ex-
    panded tonal idiom than in *Concerto* I. M-D.
Concertino (Soviet Composer 1970) 63pp. Three movements (FSF). Mainly thin
    textures, but full parallel chords are exploited in the first movement; MC.
    M-D.

Heinrich Kaminski (1886–1946) Germany
Orchesterkonzert mit Klavier (Schott 2974 1937) 26 min. Toccata; Tanz; Finale.
    Freely tonal around C, many figurations, polyphonic, neoclassic. Ideas seem
    labored. M-D.

Arno Kapp (1913–   ) Germany
Concertino 1952 (Br&H 3719). For piano and strings. 12 min. Allegro; Andan-
    tino; A tempo giusto. Neoclassic, contemporary Alberti bass, similar to
    Françaix *Concertino*. Int. to M-D.

Dezider Kardos (1914–   ) Czechoslovakia
Koncert Op.40 (Czech Music Information Center 1974) 138pp.

Maurice Karkoff (1927–   ) Sweden
From the largely Romantic style of his earlier works, Karkoff has developed a
more expressionistic language. However, the basic Romantic flavor is still fully
distinguishable.
Konsert Op.28 1957 revised 1960 (GM) 22 min.

Erhard Karkoschka (1923–   ) Germany
Polyphonic Studies for Orchestra with Piano Obbligato (Br 3579).

Leon Kartum (1895–   ) France
Poème Rhapsodie (Choudens). For piano and jazz orchestra.

Lucrecia R. Kasilag (1918–   ) Philippines
Kasilag studied at the Philippines Women's University and the Eastman School of Music. She is president of the Cultural Center of the Philippines, Roxas Blvd., Metro Manila, Philippines.

Concertante 1979 (MS available from composer). For piano, strings, brasses, and percussion. 8½ min. Allegretto; Molto adagio; Più vivo. Octotonic; rhythmic chords move over keyboard; plucked strings; driving octaves; MC. M-D.

Divertissiment 1960 (MS available from composer). Allegro moderato: neoclassic, octotonic, parallel scales an eleventh apart. Poco andante: "play right hand slightly after left hand"; simulates plucking of strings; glissandi. Allegro vivace: quartal and quintal harmony, grandiose effective closing, MC. M-D.

Howard Kasschau (–   ) USA
Concerto C 1940 (Schroeder & Gunther) 7 min. Allegro; Canzonetta; Allegretto. Technically easy and musically satisfying. Int.
Concerto Americana 1950 (Schroeder & Gunther). For piano and band.
Candlelight Concerto 1957 (Sam Fox). For piano and band.
The Legend of Sleepy Hollow (A Program Concerto) 1964 (GS) 10 min. Andante; Moderato; Presto. Contains the story by Washington Irving. Int.
Country Concerto (GS 1971). Three movements (FSF). For young pianists. Int.

Rudolf Kattnigg (1895–1955) USA, born Austria
Konzert Op.15 (Müller SM1159) 87pp. Allegro; Allegro; Lento; Vivace. Much work is required to bring this piece up to performance level, and it might not be worth it to the performer. MC. M-D.
Exotische Hirtenballade (Ahn & Simrock 1972) 36pp.

Walter Kaufmann (1907–   ) USA, born Czechoslovakia
Concerto 1950 (Moldenhauer Archives, 1011 Comstock Court, Spokane, WA 99203).

Milko Kelemen (1924–   ) Yugoslavia
Transfigurationen 1961 (Litolff) 15 min. Textures, rather than harmonies and melodies, are juxtaposed. Fragmented melodies, polyrhythms. Well put together; expressionistic. M-D.
Compose 1967 (CFP). For two pianos and three orchestral groups. Put together in an intricate web in two moods, in which figuration and basic color vary. Powerful musical outbursts; folkish and primitive effects. In five parts. About midway through an improvisation section begins. Following this the piano parts are fired with an iridescent quality that brings relief and leads to the

ending. During the monstrous cadenza heavy chains are dropped onto a gong
lying on the floor. Avant-garde. D.

Homer Keller (1915–   ) USA
Concerto (CF; Fl) 15 min.

Rudolf Kelterborn (1931–   ) Switzerland
Concertino 1959 (Br 3909). For piano, percussion, and strings. 12 min.

Talivaldis Kenins (1919–   ) Canada, born Latvia
Fantaisies Concertantes 1970 (CMC).

Kent Kennan (1913–   ) USA
Concertino 1946 (MS available from composer: % Music Department, University
    of Texas, Austin, TX 78712) 13 min. Revised for piano and wind ensemble
    1963.

Minuetta Kessler (–   ) USA
Alberta Concerto 1947 (MS available from composer, 30 Hurley St., Belmont,
    MA 02178) 88pp. Moderato; Adagio; Presto. Post-Romantic tonal vocabu-
    lary, sweeping, impassioned pianistic gestures, buoyantly joyous finale.
    M-D.

Aram Khatchaturian (1903–1978) USSR
The Soviet-Armenian composer Khatchaturian was much closer to the Romantic
heritage of the nineteenth century than either of his colleagues Prokofiev or Shostakovitch. He drew from the folk art of the trans-Caucasian peoples, with its
characteristic rhythms, oriental color, and strong emotional contrasts.
Concerto 1935 (Bo&H; Br&H; IMC; K; Sikorski; USSR) 30 min. Allegro ma
    non troppo e maesto; Andante con anima; Allegro brillante. Khatchaturian's
    writing always has an impact on first hearing, and this is particularly true of
    this work, which solidified his position as a composer. The first movement
    is introduced by a theme which is characteristically Armenian in its structure
    and which is brought back in the finale. The first and last movements are full
    of brilliant virtuoso writing with an electrifying rhythmic momentum that at
    times suggests Liszt. The second movement, by way of contrast, has an
    exotic oriental mood, full of brooding poetry and introspection. The work
    concludes with a triumphant Caucasian dance that requires brilliant finger
    technique. M-D to D.
Concert-Rhapsody 1969 (Soviet Composer 1975) 78pp. An Allegro non troppo
    piano solo introduction with much octotonic usage leads to an Andante soste-
    nuto with huge heavy chords joined by the orchestra. This material develops
    colorfully and is followed by a lyric cantabile section. An Allegro vivace
    with driving rhythms leads to a Feroce section that brings back some of the
    opening (Tempo I) material but with the orchestra. A Maestoso e pesante
    dramatic closing wraps up this brilliant extraganza. M-D to D.

Leon Aleksandrovich Khodzha-Einatov (1904–1954) USSR
Concerto I (USSR).
Concerto II f (Music Fund of USSR 1947; LC) 61pp. One large freely tonal movement, general-purpose Soviet modernity. M-D.

Tikhon Khrennikov (1913–   ) USSR
Khrennikov studied with Shebalin and Miaskovsky. In 1948 he became first secretary of the Union of Soviet Composers, and since 1949 he has been its chairman. He is a formidable pianist.
Concerto I F Op.1 1932–33 (Soviet Composer 1970) 71pp. Allegro: resembles Prokofiev. Andante: has a certain anonymity. Andante–Molto allegro: somewhat brash finale. Well laid out for the medium. Ideas flow naturally and are intelligently developed. M-D.
Concerto II C Op.21 1971 (USSR) 56pp. Moderato. Allegro con fuoco; Giocoso. Has an incontestable dramatic effect, many fortissimos. More overtly effective than *Concerto* I; strong Prokofiev influence noted. Opens with a twelve-note row though the work is firmly in C. Fluent, facile, permeated with a lyrical touch. M-D.

Bruno Kiefer (1923–   ) Brazil, born Germany
Kiefer came to Brazil in 1935. He is a Professor at the Art Institute of the Rio Grande do Sul University.
Diálogo 1966 (Radio MEC. Servico de Radio di fusaõ Educativa do Ministério da Eduçacão e Cultura Proça da República, 131-A 20,000 Rio de Janeiro [RJ] Brazil) 15 min.

Valerii Grigorevich Kikta (1941–   ) USA
Concerto I (USSR 1970) 51pp. Allegretto non troppo; Lento; Allegro. Much imitation and many octaves, MC. M-D to D.
Concerto II (USSR 1979).

Wilhelm Killmayer (1927–   ) Germany
Concerto (Schott) 18 min.

Earl Kim (1920–   ) USA
Dialogues (EBM) 12 min.

Leon Kirchner (1919–   ) USA
Kirchner's music is written in a tradition stemming from central European expressionism. His style reflects the impact of Bartók, Schoenberg, and Stravinsky. Much of his music has great emotional impact and power, strong rhythmic propulsion, and personal lyricism. His work leans towards the atonal, with serial techniques and austere linear writing in his later works. He is one of the most significant American composers now writing.
Concerto I 1953 (AMP) 30 min. The soloist's part is of incredible difficulty although virtuosity is never used as its own end. Harmonically much of the work is influenced by the tritone, with use of extreme chromaticism. Allegro: grows organically from material stated in the opening orchestral tutti and

closes with an extended piano cadenza of great imagination. Adagio: a "night music" piece with striking writing; lyrical passages in the piano alternate with outbursts from the orchestra, somewhat reminiscent of the second movement of Beethoven's *Fourth Piano Concerto*. Allegro ma non troppo: full of explosive energy; seems at times to be a battle between the orchestra and piano, as each of their timbres are pitted against one another. Kirchner's work is a significant one, but should only be approached by the most advanced virtuosi. D.

Concerto II 1963 (AMP) 30 min. In two movements, to be played without break. Constant meter and tempo changes. Solo piano writing stresses linearity. As in the *Concerto* I, the writing is almost atonal and of enormous complexity. The material is rhapsodic, fragmented, and kaleidoscopic in instrumentation. Ends quietly on a gentle atonal chord. D.

Ivo Kirigin (1914–1964) Yugoslavia
Concertino 195? (Muzička Naklada) 38pp. Allegro; Andante con moto; Presto. Neoclassic, attractive, clever writing, MC. M-D.

Johann Philipp Kirnberger (1721–1783) Germany
Concerto c (Eickemeyer—Schott 2165). Attributed to J. S. Bach at the top of the MS in the Bachsammlung Manfred Gorke in Eisenach, and to W. F. Bach by the present editor, but composed by Kirnberger, according to Breitkopf's 1763 thematic catalogue of MSS. Cf. *Zeitschrift für Musik*, 1932, 891. Int. to M-D.

Richard Rudolf Klein (1921–   ) Germany
Chamber Concerto III (Möseler). For piano, fourteen winds, cello, and double bass.

Leon Klepper (1900–   ) Israel, born Rumania
Concertino (IMP 1962; Fl). For piano, flute, and strings. 14 min. Title page in Hebrew and English.

Concertino 1964 (Ahn & Simrock). For piano, four-hands and orchestra. 33pp. Allegro sciolto; Andante con moto; Allegro moderato, giocoso. Neoclassic, octotonic, driving rhythms, solo parts and orchestra beautifully integrated, a rewarding work. M-D.

Paul Kletzki (1900–1973) Switzerland, born Poland
Concerto Op.22 d (Br&H 1930) 70pp. Allegro, ma non troppo; Andante sostenuto; Allegro agitato. Big, dramatic, nineteenth-century gestures, post-Brahmsian idiom. Requires a superb octave technique. M-D to D.

Arno Knapp (1913–1960) Germany
Concertino 1952 (Br&H 3719). For piano and strings. 12 min. Allegro; Andantino; A tempo giusto. Strong neoclassic tendencies, bitonal implications, flexible meters, MC. M-D.

Marcelo Koc (1918–   ) Argentina, born Russia
Concertino (EAM). For piano and ten instruments. 15 min.

Erland von Koch (1910–   ) Sweden
Koch has been Professor of Harmony at the Royal Music Conservatory in Stockholm since 1953.
Concerto I Op.11 1936 (STIM).
Concerto II 1962 (PIC) 23 min. Allegro moderato; Andante espressivo; Molto vivace. Expanded tonality; strong rhythmic usage; melodies flow naturally. M-D to D.
Concerto Lirico 1970–72 (STIM). For piano and band, also for piano and orchestra. 22 min. Strikingly musical, lively rhythms. M-D.
Concerto 1974 (ES). For piano, violin, and orchestra. 22 min.

Frederick Koch (1923–   ) USA
Suite Op.48 1961–2 (LC). Toccata. Ballad. Finale.
Short Symphony I 1965 (Gen) 15 min. Allegro; Lento; Theme and Variations.
Concerto Sonica 1977 (Seesaw). For two pianos and orchestra. 15 min. Three movements.

Günter Kochan (1930–   ) Germany
Konzert Op.16 1957–58 (CFP 4948) 18 min. Allegro; Andante; Allegro con brio. Freely tonal around F, flexible meters, octotonic. Finale has some glittering moments, à la toccata. M-D.
Variationen über eine venezianische Canzonetta 1966 (CFP 9174) 35pp.
Mendelssohn's Variations for Piano and Orchestra 1971–72 (CFP 9559) 22 min. Twenty variations, two codas. Strong dissonance, expressionistic. D.

Charles Koechlin (1867–1950) France
Koechlin's style displays great clarity and subtle nuances.
Ballade Op.50 1919 (Technisonor EFM169 1974). One large movement in eight sections. Beautifully flowing and supple lines, haunting melodies, modal flavor, cool and transparent harmonies. Where has this work been? Highly recommended. M-D.

René Koering (–   ) Germany
Combat T3N (Ahn & Simrock) 12 min. Large orchestration requiring four percussion groups in addition to strings and winds. Strings of the piano are strummed; clusters; keyboard is violently attacked; dynamic extremes; proportional rhythmic notation; large piano cadenza. Avant-garde. M-D to D.
Triple et Trajectoires 1965 (Ahn & Simrock). For piano and two orchestras. Directions in French, requires two conductors. In two movements. Graphic notation, espressionistic, avant-garde. M-D to D.
Jeux et Enchantements (Technisonor 1974) 29pp.

Jan Koetsier (1911–   ) The Netherlands
Kreisleriana 1965 (Donemus). For two pianos and orchestra. 20 min.
Homage to Gershwin 1969 (Donemus).
Concerto Capriccioso 1975 (Donemus) 18 min.

Jaan Koha (1929–   ) USSR, born Estonia
Concerto Op.6 1958 (USSR 1974) 75pp. Largo—Vivo scherzando; Allegro.
   Strong Prokofiev influence. Allegro has moments of real excitement. M-D
   to D.

Karl Kohn (1926–   ) USA, born Vienna
Kohn is professor of music and composer in residence at Pomona College.
Sinfonia Concertante 1951 (CF) 20 min.
Concerto Mutabile 1962 (CF). For piano and chamber orchestra. 13 min.
Episodes 1966 (CF) 11 min. "The instrumentation of this work aims to extend
   the possibilities of an essentially classical orchestra by adding piccolo and
   tuba to emphasize the extreme ranges and four horns to enrich the central
   register. The harp, glockenspiel, vibraphone, and triangle, used with piano,
   achieve, by modest means, a broader spectrum of tone colors, creating a
   variety of plucked and struck sounds. The piano is used both as a member
   of the orchestral body and as soloistic obbligato to it. The work is composed
   in sections of varying tempo, character, and sonority. The sections themselves convey a sense of development rather than of exposition. The title
   therefore alludes, in part, to this particular formal characteristic. The total
   shape of *Episodes* depends on the balance and poised order in which the
   varied sections succeed each other" (from the score). Includes performance
   notes. Extreme range, chordal tremolo, pointillistic, flexible meters, clusters, harmonics, aleatory. D.
Interlude II 1969 (CF). For piano and string orchestra. 7 min.

Ellis B. Kohs (1916–   ) USA
Kohs is chairman of the Theory Department in the School of Music, University
of Southern California, Los Angeles.
Concerto 1945 (ACA) 16 min. I. Quarter-note = 126; II. Quarter-note = 84;
   III. Quarter-note = 138. Neoclassic varied figurations. Outer movements
   are highly rhythmic; middle movement is nocturnelike. Pianistic. M-D
   to D.

Michal Kondracki (1902–   ) Poland
Concertino C 1945 (PWM) 20 min.

Paul Kont (1920–   ) Austria
Concertino des Enfants (Dob 1960). For piano and chamber orchestra. 16 min.
   Sectionalized, charming, neoclassic, thin textures. Int.

Herman David Koppel (1908–   ) Denmark
Concerto I Op.13 1932 (WH) 49pp. Allegro moderato; Andante quieto. Many
   parallel chords, flexible meters, skipping figuration, MC. M-D.
Concerto III Op.45 1948 (Imudico) 25 min. Allegro; Andante; Rondo. Expanded
   tonality. D.

Juri N. Kornakov (1938–   ) USSR
Concerto Op.20 1967–68 (USSR) 87pp. Con moto; Lento; Allegro assai. This work seems to be much more in line with international twentieth-century techniques than most Russian concertos. Such devices as asymetrical meters and rhythms (Bartók influence?), pointillistic techniques, dissonance, orchestral percussion, and clusterlike sonorities make this work more interesting from a musical and a pianistic point of view. M-D.

Erich W. Korngold (1897–1957) Austria.
Konzert Op.17 (Schott). For piano, left hand and orchestra. 25 min. Korngold's warm, sumptuous Romanticism comes through brilliantly. Lyrical richness sometimes reminds us of Richard Strauss or even Gustav Mahler. M-D.

Karl Korte (1928–   ) USA
Concerto 1976 (ECS). For piano and winds. 26 min.

Sergei A. Kortes (1935–   ) USSR
Concerto 1969 (USSR 1973) 51pp. One large movement. Clusters, asymetrical rhythms, exciting writing if a little brash at spots. M-D.

György Kósa (1897–   ) Hungary
Concerto (Bo&H). For piano, violin, and orchestra. 30 min.

Anatolii Iosypovich Kos-Anatolsky (1909–   ) USSR
Concerto f (Mistetsvo 1963) 65pp. Rubato e pesante; Andante tranquillo e cantabile; Allegro gioioso. Freely tonal, nineteenth-century pianistic idiom. M-D.

Boris Koutzen (1901–1966) USA, born Russia
Concertino 1959 (Gen). For piano and strings. 15 min. Neoromantic, polyphonic, unencumbered by any noticeable excesses of sentimentality. M-D.

Hans Kox (1930–   ) The Netherlands
Concert voor Piano en Orkest 1962 (Donemus) reproduced from composer's MS. 21 min. First movement: fast; suggests SA but is monothematic; piano introduction in brilliant octaves; quick contrapuntal lines; splendid coda. Second movement: slow; ABA; attractive thematic material; lyrical theme emphasizes mordents. Finale: fast; subtle formal treatment; ABA; octaves in wide skips; motoric ostinato figures; cadenza (octave etude?); colorful orchestration. One of the finest concertos to appear in the Netherlands. Atonal. D.

Leopold Anton Kozeluch (1747–1818) Bohemia
Kozeluch wrote fourteen piano concertos and contributed considerably to the formation of the classic style. In 1792, Kozeluch succeeded Mozart as composer to the Imperial Court in Prague.
Concerto I G (Janet).
Concerto II F Op.12 (Sieber).
Concerto III Op.13 (Nadermann).
Concerto IV (André).

Concerto V (Nadermann).

Concerto VI (Nadermann).

Concerto VII D Op.25 1784 (Meyland—Br&H 6340 1963) 25 min. Allegro: SA. Andantino con (7) variazioni. Allegretto. Makes much use of ornaments. Would be a fine substitute for the overworked Haydn *Concerto* D, Hob. XVIII/11. Characterized by fluency of discourse and solid musicianship. Int. to M-D.

Concerto Bb (Novak—Zanibon 1978). For piano, four-hands and orchestra. 59pp. Note in Italian and English.

David Kraehenbuehl (1932–   ) USA

Rhapsody in Rock 1974 (CF) 7 min. One movement. Based on rock and roll idiom. Bears many formal resemblances to a famous jazz concerto. Effective audience music with which young musicians, even those who cannot reach octaves, can make a brilliant impression.

A Short Piano Concerto for Young People (CF 1978). In the form of three marches, derived from each other to aid in memory. Twelve-tone style with clear tonal orientation. Marches can be played separately or together as a complete concerto. Sounds more difficult than it is; pianistic. Int. to M-D.

William Kraft (1923–   ) USA

Kraft describes his works as having been influenced by his background as a jazz performer and arranger and by his acquaintance with Stravinsky and Varèse. He is currently percussionist with the Los Angeles Philharmonic Orchestra.

Concerto 1973 (Belwin-Mills) 22 min. A one-movement, three-sectioned work. Percussive in both its piano and orchestral parts. Arm clusters, trills for alternating hands, single-note sforzandi. The piece depends on the composer's special sensitivity to the ingenuity with timbre and on the acute perceptions of the soloist. M-D to D.

Johann Ludwig Krebs (1713–1780) Germany

Krebs took lessons along with C.P.E. Bach from the latter's distinguished father and subsequently became the younger Bach's friendly rival in Leipzig musical circles.

Concerto (Janelzky—Süddeutscher Musikverlag 1976). For keyboard and string orchestra. 67pp. Memorable opening movement in a "modern" style for the period. The other movements are less strong but the overall impression is positive. The whole work is a good example of the merging of baroque and rococo early-classical styles. M-D.

Concerto a (Br DV8102). For two keyboards and orchestra. The two keyboards refer to a two-manual harpsichord. The second movement is related in style to the music of the Bach sons, while the finale is more cheerful and bravura than would probably be attributed to any of the Bachs. M-D.

Ernst Krenek (1900–   ) Austria

Although his music now is severely intellectual, uncompromising, and often of extreme complexity, Krenek did not always write in so severe a manner. His first compositions are of a post-Romantic style, which later evolved into an idiom influenced by jazz. Finally by 1931 he had begun to use twelve-tone techniques. Total serialism, combined with experiments with electronic techniques and musico-mathematics, have enveloped his style in more recent years. He is a composer who makes no concessions to his public. An extremely prolific writer, Krenek has influenced many younger composers, and is an authoritative and important contemporary figure.

Concerto I F♯ Op.18 1923 (UE) 30 min. This is Krenek's youthful protest against the Romantic concerto. A simple minuet rhythm makes an ironic appearance in the Tempo di Minuetto movement. M-D.

Concerto II Op.81 1937 (UE) 22 min. More serially strict than *Concerto* I. In four movements without pause. Contrasting moods and tempi, complex contrapuntal texture. Piano part often recedes into the orchestral fabric. M-D to D.

Little Concerto 1940 (MS in Vassar College Library, Poughkeepsie, NY 10023). For piano, organ, and chamber orchestra. 10 min. Andante sostenuto; Andantino; Allegro energico; Andante; Adagio; Allegretto.

Concerto III Op.107 1946 (Schott) 17 min. Allegro con passione; Andante sostenuto; Allegretto scherzando; Adagio; Vivace. Unlike most of Krenek's works of this period, this *Concerto* does not use the twelve-tone system, but is written in a basically tonal idiom. Nonetheless it is an uncompromising and austere work. As an unusual feature, Krenek uses a different section of the orchestra as background for the soloist in each movement. The first uses the brass and tympani; the second uses the strings as a fugal background; the third has woodwinds; the fourth has harp and percussion, with a lengthy piano cadenza; and the rondo finale uses full orchestra. A cyclic approach is used, with thematic material from the earlier movements being recalled in the final movement. A difficult work to assimilate. D.

Concerto IV 1950 (Br 1962) 22 min. Allegro; Molto adagio; Allegro.

Double Concerto 1950 (EBM). For piano, violin, and chamber orchestra. 16 min. In seven short movements.

Concerto 1951 (Br 1962). For two pianos and orchestra. 13 min. Allegro vivace; Andante; Allegro vivace; Adagio.

Jan Krenz (1926–   ) Poland

Concertino 1952 (PWM 1965) 40pp., 20 min. Lento e rubato; Andante sostenuto; Allegro vivace. Neoclassic, charming, appealing, MC. Int.

Conradin Kreutzer (1780–1849) Germany

Concerto Op.42 (CFP 1819? NYPL). Could pass for minor Schubert, many early Romantic characteristics. M-D.

Vladimir Kriukov (1902–1960) USSR

Concerto Op.55 (USSR 1959). Three movements (FSF). Tonal with some modal influence; good handling of piano materials. M-D.

Gustav Křivinka (1928–   ) Czechoslovakia
Concerto Grosso I Op.3 1949 revised 1960 (Panton) 15 min. Allegro moderato;
Largo; Allegro molto. Neobaroque style, fluent musical flow, inventive fresh-
ness plus firm technical skill. M-D.

Karl Kroeger (1932–   ) USA
Five Bagatelles 1967 (CFE). For piano and chamber orchestra. 8 min. Alla marcia;
Andante dolente; Scherzando; Larghetto; Allegro con spirito.

Georg Kröll (1934–   ) Germany
Cerchi 1960 (Edition Modern 1078) 6 min.

Gail Kubik (1914–   ) USA
Kubik's style is relatively simple in texture and dramatic in tone. The composer
feels that the essential expressivity of music lies in the melody.
Symphonie Concertante 1952 revised 1953 (Ric). For piano, trumpet, viola, and
orchestra. 24 min. Won the Pulitzer Prize in 1952. This work "represents an
effort to reconcile the large-scale expressive demands of a symphony with
the virtuoso exhibitionistic demands of the concerto form" (from the score).
Fast, vigorously: modified SA. Quietly: a long, increasingly dramatic song
with a reflective epilogue. Fast, with energy: a clear-cut rondo, with, however, many "development techniques" superimposed. The piano adds color,
tension, and excitement. M-D.

Friedrich Kuhlau (1786–1832) Denmark, born Germany
Concerto C Op.7 1810 (Til Udgivelse af Dansk Musik 1961; Fl) 30 min. Allegro;
Adagio; Rondo—Allegro. Straightforward classical treatment. Resembles
Clementi in some ways although a little more chromatic and ambitious in
scope, thematic individuality, and instrumental imagination. Int. to M-D.

Max Kuhn (1896–   ) Switzerland
Klavierkonzert "Concierto de Tenerife" (Hug).

Theodore Kullak (1818–1882) Germany
Concerto c Op.55 (Br&H 1851?; BPL).

Alfred Kullman (–   ) France
Poème Concertante (Senart 1930) 53pp., full score. Mildly Impressionistic, a
colorful tone-poem. M-D.

Rainer Kunad (1936–   ) Germany
Concerto "Conatum 45" (DVFM 1973) 65pp. One movement. Much percussive
use of the piano. D.

Edvard Künneke (1885–1953) Germany
Concerto A♭ Op.36 (Birnbach 1935) 67pp. Allegro, un poco moderato; Moderato;
Lebhaft. Nineteenth-century orientation. M-D.

Meyer Kupferman (1926–   ) USA

Kupferman has worked with twelve-tone materials since 1947, but not exclusively.

Concerto 1948 (Gen) 13 min. In one movement.

Mario Kuri-Aldana (1931–   ) Mexico

Pasos 1963 (IU). For piano and chamber ensemble. 74pp., full score. A colorful nationalistic work, especially noted for the use of native percussion instruments. Energetic rhythms, quartal harmonies. M-D.

Robert Kurka (1921–1957) USA

Concertina Op.31 (Weintraub). For two pianos, trumpet, and string orchestra. 15 min. Three movements.

Siegfried Kurz (1930–   ) Germany

Konzert Op.32 1964 (DVFM) 30 min. Three movements (FSF). Expanded tonality; moves over keyboard quickly. M-D to D.

L

Felix Labunski (1892–   ) USA, born Poland
Music for Piano and Orchestra 1966 (MS available from composer: 2324 Park
Ave., Cincinnnati, OH 45206). One large movement with contrasting sections. Full chords, preference for seconds in chords, freely tonal. Piano has
main idea at opening; ideas well-developed. M-D.

Wiktor Labunski (1895–1974) USA, born Poland
Concerto C Op.16 1937 (MS copy at University of Missouri—Kansas City; Fl)
21 min. Krakowiak; Nocturne; Mazurka. Inspired by Polish dance forms.
Generally thin textures, beautifully laid out for the soloist, colorful. Large
span required. Fl also has a copy arranged for two pianos and orchestra.
Op.16B (1937–1951). M-D.

Helmut Lachermann (1935–   ) Germany
Klangschatten—Mein Saitenspiel 1972 (Gerig 1978). For three grand pianos and
48 strings. 54pp. Reproduced from holograph. Preface in German and
English.

Ezra Laderman (1924–   ) USA
Laderman studied composition with Stefan Wolpe, Otto Luening, and Douglas
Moore. He has contributed many articles on contemporary music to the *New York
Times*.
Concerto I 1940 (Regaldi) 20 min.
Concerto II 1957 (TP) 17 min. Atonal-chromatic idiom. Thematic ideas are used
as the basis for a continuous process of development. M-D to D.
Concerto III 1979 (Regaldi). Three movements. Broadly scored, influences of
Webern and Rachmaninoff in the lush romanticism and pointillistic treat-
ment. The first movement is a series of variations. Laderman seems to favor
tonal and lyric elements, in the first movement especially. Contains some
gargantuan piano writing. D.

Edouard Lalo (1823–1892) France
Lalo's musical personality exudes charm, vigor, and virile candor. It emerges in
bold strokes in this concerto. Lalo can write exceedingly persuasive melodies,
and his orchestral idiom is both ravishing and original.
Concerto F 1889 (Choudens; Hartmann—Heugel) 22½ min. Lento–Allegro:

varies two themes presented in the introduction; the second one is used in the other two movements. Lento: E♭. Allegro. Displays formal balance, polished craft, influences of Franck and Massenet. The cyclic idea is used but subtly modified; Romantic gestures are displayed in the melodic inspiration. Requires a muscular and lyric pianist who has plenty of virtuosity in reserve. D.

Constant Lambert (1905–1951) Great Britain
Lambert was a pupil of Vaughan Williams. The dance was a decisive influence in his life, and much of his activity included writing and conducting for the ballet. From 1928 to 1947 he was musical director of Sadler's Wells. Many of his compositions show a great contrapuntal skill, as well as an assimilation of the jazz idiom.

Concerto 1931 (OUP). For piano and nine players. 25 min. Overture: heavily syncopated with such rhythms as 7/4, 11/8, 13/8; lengthy cadenza. Intermède: more expressive, but has similar rhythmic treatments; flute, trumpet, and trombone are given lyrical solos. Finale: written in memory of Lambert's friend Philip Heseltine, who died in 1930; tempo indication "lugubre"; elegiac mood is kept to the end, with a quiet close. The work is original and well constructed; exhibits jazz influence. Exotic effects through the use of unusual instruments: flute-piccolo, 3 clarinets, trumpet, tenor trombone, cello, double bass, and percussion. M-D.

John La Montaine (1920–   ) USA
La Montaine's style is a combination of post-Romantic idioms and influences from the French school.

Concerto Op.9 1958 (Galaxy; Fredonia Press) 25 min. Won the 1959 Pulitzer Prize. Romantically flavored with contemporary condiments; lyric yet contains sonorous writing without bypassing artistic content. Moderately fast— decisive: bold, heroic, classic in form (SA), Romantic in content, well-constructed cadenza. Elegy: sensitive; slow and introspective; perhaps the peak of the work; written in memory of the composer's sister. Rondo: brilliant and marchlike; both main themes come from the opening movement. Fluent lyrical writing throughout based on a strongly conservative formal Romanticism. Transcendental technique required. D.

Birds of Paradise Op.34 1966 (CF; Fredonia Press) 13 min. Prologue; twelve variations; theme; Epilogue. Colorful; birdlike sonorities; tremolo clusters on white and black keys simultaneously; long pedals. M-D.

Serge Lancen (1922–   ) France
Concertino (Hin 1953) 13 min. Allegro: diatonic, light textures, reminiscent of Jean Françaix *Concertino*. Andante: free opening, accompanied melodic writing. Final—Allegro: toccata-like, C center, many chromatics. M-D.

Fantaisie Creole (Technisonor 1969) 73pp. Moderato; Allegro; Adagio; Allegro vivo; Andante–Allegro Brillante. Creole rhythms, chromatic harmonies, twentieth-century Gottschalk! Fun, but a little strange. M-D.

Concerto-Rapsodie (Technisonor 1974) 55pp. One large movement with contrasting sections. Dramatic pianistic gestures, blues influence, freely tonal, virtuoso ending. M-D.

Concerto (Hin) 18 min.

Marcel Landowski (1915–   ) France

Piano Concerto "Poème" 1939 (Choudens) 37pp. Andante–Allegro deciso; Andante; Allegro, bien rythmé. Colorful, Impressionistic. M-D.

Concerto II (Choudens 1963) 23 min. Moderato: neobaroque, polyphonic writing for piano. Calme: many "sluggish" quarter notes. Allegro vivace: persistent rhythms overused. M-D.

Pierre Lantier (1910–   ) France

Concerto (Lemoine 1953) 70pp. Three movements (FSF). Expanded tonality, fluent figuration for the piano. M-D.

Concertino F (Leduc 1954) 14 min. Allegro marcato; Andante sostenuto; Allegro. Neoclassic, charming, appealing. M-D.

Concertinetto (Zurfluh 1960) 12pp. A delightful MC work for the high school student. Int.

Alcides Lanza (1929–   ) Argentina

Lanza is head of the Electronic Music Studio and professor of composition at McGill University in Montreal. He is an outstanding pianist.

Concerto 1964 (Barry) 16 min. Cómodo; Piccole variante; Cadenza; Allegro. Uses serial and aleatory procedures, clusters, pointillistic effects, and original notation. Employs a large percussion section. D.

Claude Lapham (1890–1957) USA

Concerto Japonesa c Op.35 1935 (Fl; LC) 18 min. Colorful, much pentatonic usage. Requires some energetic octave passage work. M-D.

Lars Erik Larsson (1908–   ) Sweden

Larsson's style during the 1930s displayed clear classicistic features but more recently it has shifted into Nordic late Romanticism, neoclassicism, and twelve-tone technique.

Concertino Op.45/12 1957 (GM). For piano and string orchestra. 15 min. This work gives both pianist and orchestra (amateur) a modern piece of a reasonable degree of difficulty. Displays concentration, clarity, and immediacy. Int. to M-D.

Alexander Laszló (1895–1970) USA, born Hungary

Hollywood Concerto 1944 (Guild Publications of California 1950) 14 min. In one movement, six parts. Extensive program notes contained in score. Jazz influence, many added-note chords associated with popular music. M-D.

Marc Lavry (1903–1967) Israel, born Lithuania

Concerto II 1947 (IMP 607 1965) 22 min. Allegro; Andante; Allegro vivo. Modal, strong rhythms, parallel chords, bitonal descending octaves at conclusion. M-D.

Filip Lazar (1894–1936) France, born Rumania

Concerto II Op.19 (Durand 1933) 59pp., 19 min.

Henri Lazarof (1932–   ) USA, Bulgaria

Concerto 1957 (MS available from composer: % Music Department, University of California, Los Angeles, 405 Hilgard Avenue, Los Angeles, CA 90024).

Concerto 1961 (MS available from composer). For piano and 20 instruments. Eclectic, broadly defined gestures; much energy and technical competence. M-D.

Textures 1971 (AMP). For piano and five instrumental groups. 23½ min. A catalogue of various sonorities, pointillistic, some indeterminate notation, avant-garde. M-D to D.

Daniel Lazarus (1898–   ) France

Concerto 1928 (Schott) 60pp. Allegro moderato; Largo; Allegro con brio. Lighthearted style is reminiscent of Poulenc; tonal around D; nineteenth-century pianistic gestures. M-D.

Jacques Leduc (1932–   ) Belgium

Concerto Op.31 1971 (CeBeDeM) 17 min. Required piece for the Queen Elisabeth Competition, 1972. Allegro energico; Andante espressivo; Vivace e giocoso. Atonal, changing meters, glissandi, neoclassic. Large span required M-D.

Noel Lee (1924–   ) USA

Caprices sur le nom de Schönberg 1975 (MS available from composer: 4 Villa Laugier, Paris 75017 France) 23 min. Annonce; Exhortation; Stance; Interpellations; Tiquetures; Striures; Synchronies; Desinence. Serial, pointillistic, tremolo, octotonic, harmonics, glissandi. Piece concludes with a final horizontal statement of the row by the piano. Virtuoso writing for all instruments; dramatic, inspired orchestration. Large span required. D.

Benjamin Lees (1924–   ) USA

Declamations (Weintraub 1955). For piano and string orchestra. 9½ min. One dramatic movement, contrasting sections; could be the first movement for a concerto. Freely tonal, *fff* closing. M-D.

Concerto I 1956 (Bo&H) 23 min. Allegro con moto; Adagio maestoso; Allegro marcato. Neoclassic style and texture laced with routine twentieth-century dissonances. M-D.

Concerto II 1966 (Bo&H) 25 min. Allegro enfatico: SA design, three main parts in the exposition, development extended with many melodic fragments and a cadenza, Bartók and Stravinsky influence. Adagio vago: suggestive of the "night music" in some of Bartók's slow movements. Allegro tempestoso: highly intense with an extended recapitulation and coda based on the opening (marked Presto). A review by Martin Bernheimer says that this work is "a sure fire audience pleaser" (*American Musical Digest* 6, 4: 30–31, 1970). Economical ideas. Uses a standard orchestra with triple winds and a large number of percussion players. Piano and orchestra complement rather than oppose each other. M-D to D.

Five Etudes for Piano and Orchestra (Bo&H 1974). Etude 1: harmony uses minor seconds and major sevenths in a sharply dissonant manner; 3/8. Etude 2: more triadic. Etude 3: emphasizes parallel triads linked chromatically; concludes polytonally. Etude 4: a Scherzo in jazzy dialogue with some of the colorful percussion in the orchestra. Etude 5: recalls the minor seconds and major sevenths but this time they are coupled with minor thirds; a waltz feeling emerges, and the final chord pulls the thematic major sevenths together. Has immediate appeal and challenge for the pianist. Alternates between thrust and intense lyricism. Plenty of rhythmic drive and tone color in piano and orchestra. Style is conservatively modern but certainly of our time. Has the long, lyrical line and the big form. M-D.

Variations for Piano and Orchestra 1976 (Bo&H). Propulsive rhythms. M-D.

Victor Legley (1915–   ) Belgium

Bartók and Hindemith are strong influences in Legley's style.

Concerto Op.39 1959 (CeBeDeM) 18 min. Three movements (FSF). Freely atonal. Piano and orchestra are carefully integrated. One of the finer contemporary Belgian concertos. M-D to D.

Franz Xaver Lehner (1904–   ) Germany

Little Concerto (Br BE 303). For piano, strings, and percussion.

René Leibowitz (1913–1972) France, born Poland

Leibowitz's study with Schoenberg and Webern grounded his style in twelve-tone technique.

Concerto Op.5 1941–2 (Boelke-Bomart). For piano, violin, and 17 instruments. 22 min.

Concerto Op.32 1954 (Boelke-Bomart) 15 min.

Kenneth Leighton (1929–   ) Great Britain

Leighton teaches at Edinburgh University.

Concerto I Op.11 1951 (Novello) 23 min. Strong influences of Bartók, Hindemith, and, to a lesser degree, Dallapiccola. M-D.

Concerto II Op.37 1960 (Novello) 25 min. Expanded tonality, strong mood contrasts (sadly beautiful vs. nervously energetic). M-D.

Concerto III Op.57 1969 (Novello) 33 min. Orchestration is brilliant and both it and the piano writing are handled with complete ease. M-D.

Jeanne Leleu (1898–   ) France

Suite Symphonique (Leduc 1926). For piano and wind instruments. Prélude; L'Arbre plein de chants; Mouvements de foule; Bois sacré; Joie populaire. Freely tonal, Impressionistic tendencies. M-D.

Heinrich Lemacher (1891–1966) Germany

Konzertduo Op.149 (Gerig 1956). For piano, four-hands and string orchestra. 15

min. Energico; Cantabile, con moto; Con anima. Neoclassic, freely tonal around D, thin textures. M-D.

Kamilló Lendvay (1928–   ) Hungary
Concertino 1959 (EMB). For two pianos, winds, percussion, and harp. 10 min. Allegretto; Adagio cantabile; Allegro furioso. Neoclassic, flexible meters, freely tonal, fast octaves in alternating hands, piano cadenza at end of Allegretto. Effective instrumentation that shows off the piano like a jewel. M-D.

Alfonso Leng (1884–   ) Chile
Leng is a representative of post-Romantic tendencies.
Fantasia 1936 (IEM; IU) 15 min. Poetic; sectional; shows influence of Rachmaninoff in orchestration and pianistic treatment. M-D.

Jacques Lenot (1945–   ) France
Concerto 1975 (SZ) 22 min.

Nicolaas Lentz (1720?–1780) The Netherlands
Concerto I (Heuwekemeijer 1961; Fl) 31pp.

Argeliers León (1918–   ) Cuba
Concertino 1948 (Cuadernos de Música; IU 1967). For piano, flute, and strings. 48pp. Andantino; Allegretto–Andante sostenuto; Andantino molto cantabile con espressione–Allegretto. Freely tonal, many chordal added-note seconds and sixths, MC. M-D.

Tania León (–   ) USA
Concerto Criollo 1977 (LC) 20 min. Commissioned by the National Endowment for the Arts. Allegro moderato; Andante Rubato; Allegro. Expanded tonal idiom, octotonic, parallel chords, neoclassic orientation. Requires fine octave technique. M-D.

Franciszek Lessel (1780–1839) Poland
Lessel studied with Joseph Haydn in Vienna. He could not make a living as a musician on his return to Poland, and he wound up an architect who refused to stop composing.
Concerto C Op.14 (PWM 1951) 24 min. Three movements (FSF). The finale (the best movement) is half rococo and half Romantic; it is energized by rhythms with a mazurka flavor. The whole work is about one cut above a typical salon piece at the turn of the nineteenth century. M-D.

Alfonso Letelier (1912–   ) Chile
La Vida del Campo Op.14 1937 (IEM) 24 min. SA design; displays influences of Impressionism; folk rhythms; and piano writing à la Rachmaninoff. M-D.

Toni Leutwiler (1923–   ) Switzerland
"An eine Geliebte," Reminiscence 1966 (Birnbach).
Fantasia Romantica Op.56 (Edition Modern 1954) 7½ min. One movement, nineteenth-century oriented. M-D.

Gnomentanz Op.91 (Edition Modern 1957). Clever, picturesque, MC. M-D.

Konzert (Edition Modern 1957). For piano and jazz and symphony orchestras. The two orchestras are divided. The piano primarily serves as the bridge between them. MC. M-D.

Harold Levey (1898–1967) USA
Concerto I (Witmark) 15 min.

Zara Aleksandrovna Levina (1906–   ) USSR
Concerto 1948 (Soviet Composer 1975) 116pp. Allegro; Andante; Allegro. Freely tonal, in a style closely related to Prokofiev. Piano and orchestra are treated cohesively. M-D.

Iurii A. Levitin (1912–   ) USSR
Concerto Op.40 (USSR 1958) 52pp. Three movements (FSF). Tonal, effective, reminiscent of Rachmaninoff *Concerto* III. M-D to D.
Concerto (USSR).

Marvin David Levy (1932–   ) USA
Concerto I 1969 (Bo&H) 22 min. In one movement. Premiered on December 3, 1970, with the Chicago Symphony Orchestra, George Solti, conductor, and Earl Wild, soloist. One movement, contrasting sections. Expressionistic. Improvisation required of soloist and orchestra. D.

Alfred Lewis (1925–   ) USA
Classical Concerto Op.13 1939 (Fl) 20 min.

Sergei Liapunov (1859–1924) Russia
Concerto I Op.4 e♭ (Bo&Bo 1892) 47pp. In one continuous movement with contrasting tempi. Brilliant piano writing, mellifluous themes. In Liszt tradition; symphonic style. M-D to D.

Ukrainian Rhapsody Op.28 1908 (Zimmermann) 16½ min. One broad movement with contrasting sections or episodes. Rich and brilliant in color; makes no pretense at formal security. Written in an expansive Lisztian manner without loss of the lyric and rhythmic flavor of the Ukrainian songs used as basic material. M-D to D.

Concerto II Op.38 E 1909 (Zimmermann; USSR) 50pp. Themes well developed; cadenza passages; effective. Virtuoso technique required. M-D to D.

Boris N. Liatosynski (1895–1968) USSR
Slavonic Concerto Op.54 1953 (USSR 1956) 89pp. Three movements (FSF). Tonal; strong melodic material. M-D.

Ingemar Liljefors (1906–   ) Sweden
Liljefors uses Swedish folk music in his compositions, especially with regard to rhythm.
Rapsodi Op.5 1936 (ES; Fl) 17 min.
Konsert Op.11 1940 (ES; Fl) 22 min.
Concertino Op.22 1949 (ES) 20 min.

Ruben Liljefors (1871–1936) Sweden
Concerto f Op.5 1899 (Raabe & Plothow).

Bo Linde (1933–1970) Sweden
Linde's style displayed a warm, lyrical strain. The two concertos listed below
show his raucous humor.
Concerto I Op.12 1954 (ES). For piano and strings. 23 min.
Concerto II Op.17 1956 (EC) 22 min.

Osmo Lindeman (1929–   ) Finland
Lindeman teaches at the Sibelius Academy in Helsinki and has written the first
book in Finnish on the technology of electro-acoustic music.
Concerto I 1963 (Finnish Music Information Center) 13 min. One movement with
    contrasting sections. Twelve-tone; cluster sonorities; cadenza. M-D to D.
Concerto II 1965 (Finnish Music Information Center) 14½ min. One movement,
    cadenza passages for piano. Twelve-tone; expressionistic; pointillistic. Mo-
    bile sections can be arranged by pianist. Requires a virtuoso octave technique
    and great stamina. D.

Jiri Ignac Linek (1725–1791) Bohemia
Concerto F (Goebels—Heinrichshofen 1960) 12 min. Allegro moderato; Andante;
    Allegro. Experts and admirers both may take pleasure in this little concerto,
    which is, according to Mozart, something "between too difficult and too
    easy, pleasant to the ear, natural, without being mundane. Now and again
    even experts can be satisfied, and also the layman without knowing why"
    (from the score). Elegant classic style. Int. to M-D.

Norbert Linke (1933–   ) Germany
"Linke's musical development has passed from atonality to (in 1961) post-
serialism, then to composition centered on timbres and textures, graphic notation,
and collage" (DCM, 426).
Concerto (Gerig).

Dinu Lipatti (1917–1950) Rumania
Concertino im Klassischen Stil Op.3 1936 (UE 11546). For piano and chamber
    ensemble. 16 min. Allegro maestoso; Adagio molto; Allegretto; Allegro
    molto. Freely tonal around G; Bach and Scarlatti influence; clever; thin
    textures; strong syncopations; rippling dissonance; *pppp* ending. Attractive,
    MC. M-D.
Trois Danses Roumanines 1945 (Sal) 18 min. Vif; Andante; Allegro vivace. Strong
    rhythms, energetic. Folk melodies are attached with penetrating dissonances.
    Fast passage work; requires advanced pianism. M-D to D.

Alexander Lipsky (1901–   ) USA, born Poland
Concertino (ACA).

Franz Liszt (1811–1886) Hungary
Liszt's two concertos are highly imaginative in their formal structure and in their

orchestration, particularly in the use of percussion. The material is colorful and has a notable rhythmic vitality. Both concertos were sketched out by 1840 but were extensively revised and did not see performance until 1855 and 1857 respectively at Weimar. Throughout both works, the listener is always aware of Liszt's complete mastery of piano technique. "S." refers to the Humphrey Searle catalogue, which was published in the fifth edition of *Grove's Dictionary* in 1954 and updated by Gregg Press in 1966.

Concerto I E♭ S.124 (Sauer—CFP 3602C; Joseffy—CFP 3606; Joseffy—GS L1057; Sauer—GS L1057; d'Albert—Haslinger; Pauer—Litolff; K; Rosenthal—Hug; Eulenburg; Durand; Augener). This one-movement work is sectionalized to give the impression of a four-movement plan. Liszt uses thematic transformation as a unifying device from section to section. Outstanding characteristics of the piano writing involve the colorful antiphonal octaves in response to the orchestra's opening motto theme, a beautiful cantabile for solo piano, a scherzo that emerges smoothly from the slow movement, and a final summing-up that ends in a blazing accelerando. D.

Concerto II A S.125 (EMB; Joseffy—CFP 3607; Joseffy—GS L1058; d'Albert—Schott; Rosenthal—Hug; Hughes—GS; K; Durand; Eulenburg; CF). This work is constructed in a hybrid form which is closest to Sonata-Rondo, with the Allegro moderato lyrical section serving as the central episode. Three slow-fast sections are evident. Themes are transformed and varied. The piano writing has characteristics similar to those of *Concerto* I: elaborate figuration, brilliant octaves, and expressive cantabile. The richly varied final climax, in a "marziale" guise of the opening theme, glitters with unusual effectiveness. D.

Malédiction S.121 (Br&H; Sauer—CFP; Musica Obscura). For piano and strings. 14½ min. Sketched 1830? revised ca.1840. The title is not Liszt's. The word *malédiction* ("under a curse") was attached to the work because Liszt scribbled it over the opening theme. This work is a succession of mood pictures: poetic, Romantic, and emotional. Five or six basic motives are interrelated in a mosaiclike fashion. Bold harmonies and many broken octaves. M-D.

Fantasy on Themes from Beethoven's "Ruins of Athens" S.122 (Joseffy—GS; Siegel 1865) 11 min. Beethoven composed his incidental music to Kotzebue's festival play *The Ruins of Athens* (Op.113) in the summer of 1811. The Overture and Turkish March are the only parts of the score that are performed with any frequency today. The Turkish March was actually adapted by Beethoven from an earlier work, a set of variations for solo piano, Op.76, which he composed in 1809. Liszt composed a *Capriccio alla turca* on motives from Beethoven's incidental music in 1846 for solo piano. But the *Fantasy* listed here is an entirely different work and was composed between 1848 and 1852 for piano and orchestra and was dedicated to Nicholas Rubinstein. Liszt also arranged the work for piano solo and for two pianos. This short, brilliant work is one of the most effective Liszt ever arranged. The orchestration is well meshed with a masterful solo piano part. M-D.

Hungarian Fantasia S.123 1852 (CFP; GS; K; UE; Durand; Hug; CF; Augener; Eulenburg has a miniature score) 15½ min. This work uses the same material as the *Hungarian Rhapsody* No. 14. It is appealing and has the same technical and character requirements as the solo version. Liszt intended it to be a brilliant instrumental concert piece with dazzling colors, and he achieved that purpose magnificently. M-D.

Totentanz (Dance of Death) S.126 (EMB; Sauer—CFP; K; Br&H; Paragon; Eulenburg) 17 min. This set of variations on *Dies Irae* (Day of Wrath) was planned in 1838, finished in 1849, and revised in 1853 and again in 1859. It was inspired by a series of wall paintings in Pisa thought to have been done by Andrea Orcagna. Liszt creates an unearthly atmosphere of mingled horror and fantasy. The virtuosity of the piano part underscores the grotesque and savage character of the entire work. Glissandos for both hands are not difficult, and there are no excessive technical demands in this highly effective work. M-D.

Spanish Rhapsody S.254 arranged by Busoni (GS; K; Siloti—K&S; CFP). This arrangement of Liszt's solo piano work enhances its effectiveness. Following a short cadenza for the pianist, a series of variations emerge based on the *Folies d'Espagne* theme. They build to a strong climax and then subside into a lively Jota aragonese. A piano cadenza leads to the second theme, which is developed before the first Jota tempo returns. These two contrasting themes are worked together with increasing excitement and lead to a dramatic statement of the *Folies d'Espagne*. Lisztian fireworks close the piece. D.

Concerto Pathétique e S.258 (Darvas—EMB; CF). This work began life as a *Grosses Konzertsolo* in 1849, the year after Liszt retired from active concertizing. A year later he arranged it for piano and orchestra under the title *Grand Solo de Concert* and dropped the central slow section. In 1856 the piece surfaced once again, with the middle section restored, in two-piano form. It is a sort of precursor of the b minor *Sonata* and is in some ways related to the "Dante" *Sonata*, which is highly rhetorical. M-D.

Wanderer-Fantasia C Op.15 (D.760) S.366 (Joseffy—GS; UE; Cranz) 22 min. Schubert composed his *Wanderer-Fantasia* in 1822, and Liszt made this concerted setting in 1850 or 1851. Liszt did a great deal to make the music of Schubert better known. He took a great interest in this piece since both the piano writing and the form of the work show a strong affinity with his own aims. Tovey called this "the earliest and best of all symphonic poems," although Schubert did not know he was writing a symphonic poem! Schubert had achieved what Liszt was attempting, even to the metamorphosis of whole sections. Liszt did not change the formal construction of the original work; only the transition to the second subject was enriched by a cadenza. The form is that of a sonata in four movements played without pause: Allegro con fuoco–Adagio–Presto–Allegro. The slow movement is a series of variations on Schubert's own song *Der Wanderer* Op.4/1 (D.493) composed in 1816. Liszt also made an arrangement for two pianos. D.

Polacca Brillante E Op.72 1819 S.367 ("L'Hilarité") (GS L1382; CF). A transcription of one of Weber's most brilliant pieces for the piano, which Liszt made about the same time as he transcribed the Schubert *Fantasia*. It is dedicated to Liszt's fellow virtuoso Adolph von Henselt. (A version for solo piano was subsequently produced by Liszt.) The style is similar to that of Chopin, who was only nine years old when the piece was written. Liszt has preserved this quality in his transcription and has given the orchestral writing a suitably Weberesque character. He changed the shape of the work slightly by adding a Largo from an earlier *Polonaise* (Op.21) by Weber as a prelude. Following the prelude, the work continues on its strutting and delightful course with only a short respite for a languourous cantabile episode before the buildup to the glittering conclusion. M-D to D.

Henry Litolff (1818–1891) Great Britain
The "English Liszt," Henry Litolff was born in London and became famous on the continent as composer and pianist. He had a strong influence on Liszt's playing and piano writing. His concertos are firmly in the late-Beethoven/Brahms mold of large-scale, lavishly orchestrated works in which the piano functions almost as an obbligato. But the piano parts are always brilliant as is Litolff's orchestration. Litolff was the first to use the title *Concerto Symphonique*, associating the concerto with the symphony. His concertos contain truly symphonic writing for both piano and orchestra. He must be given credit for having radically reformed the concerto style, making it into a bold, expressive art.
Concerto Symphonique II b Op.22 (Schlesinger; LC) 47pp. Maestoso; Scherzo; Andante; Rondo. M-D.
Concerto Symphonique III Eb Op.45 "National Hollandais" (MTP; Litolff; LC) 51pp. Maestoso; Presto; Andante; Allegro vivace. Contains several Netherlands folk tunes. The MTP edition contains the Scherzo from the *Concerto Symphonique* IV. M-D.
Concerto Symphonique IV D Op.102 1851 (MTP) 37 min. Allegro con fuoco; Scherzo—Presto; Adagio Religioso; Allegro impetuoso. Strong orchestral backing, bold, sweeping, in the grand Lisztian style. Pianistically effective with much interplay between piano and orchestra; elegant and sparkling. M-D. Available separately: Scherzo (Ashdown). This movement was very famous in the nineteenth century. Contains virtuoso writing, lush harmonies, and cantabile melodic usage.
Concerto Symphonique V c Op.123 (Litolff; LC) 57pp. Allegro maestoso; Interméde; Finale. The Interméde is a scherzo. Berlioz especially admired the last three of these "symphonic concertos."

Gerald Lloyd (1938–   ) USA
Concertino 1965 (MCA) 18 min. Andante–Allegro moderato; Eulogy (Adagio); Allegro molto.

Norman Lockwood (1906–   ) USA
Concerto 1973 (ACA) 25 min. Allegro: cadenza in middle of movement. Adagio:

cantando; tender; expressive; "glassy" figuration decorates lines in the orchestra. Scherzoso: moves to a subito adagio in 4 for a time before gradually returning to Tempo I; allargando broadening at conclusion. Expanded tonality. D.

Charles M. Loeffler (1861–1935) USA, born France

A Pagan Poem Op.14 (after Virgil) 1901 revised for piano and orchestra 1906 (GS). Cast in a neo-archaic vein. Masterful orchestration; fluid streams of Impressionistic arpeggi; whole-tone scale; ninth-chords. Interstitial chromatics add color to a basically tonal framework with a key signature of two flats. Probably Loeffler's greatest work. M-D.

Nikolai Lopatnikoff (1903–   ) USA, born Russia

Concerto I Op.5 1921 (MS available from composer: % MCA) 30 min. Three movements (FSF). Vigorously diatonic and rhythmically propulsive style. M-D.

Concerto II Op.15 1930 (Schott 2138) 25 min. Allegro energico: propulsive. Andantino: angularly lyric. Allegro molto: neobaroque. Dissonant idiom. M-D.

Concerto for Two Pianos and Orchestra Op.33 1949–50 (MCA; Fl) 20 min. Allegro risoluto; Andante; Finale—Allegro molto vivace. Strong lyric episodes are contrasted with energetic figurations; freely dissonant counterpoint and harmonizations; percussive neobaroque style. D.

Fernando Lopes-Graça (1906–   ) Portugal

Concerto I 1940 (MS available from composer: Vivenda El Mio Paraiso, 2° Avenida da Republica Parede, Portugal). Bartók and Stravinsky influence. M-D.

Concerto II 1942 (MS available from composer). Second movement is reminiscent of the slow movement of the Ravel *Concerto* in G. M-D.

Concertino 1954 (Santos Beirão) 15 min. One movement with contrasting sections. Neoclassic, effective. M-D.

Folk influence is strongest in the last movements of all three works.

Antonio Lora (1899–1965) USA, born Italy

Concerto 1948 (ACA) 23 min. Written while Lora was a member of the faculty at Ohio State University. Maestoso–Allegro; Andantino, quasi andante; Burlesco. Freely tonal; Impressionistic influences show up more in the accompaniment than in the melodic line; chromatic harmony. Cadenza passages; virtuoso technique required in a few places, but piano writing in general lacks brilliance. M-D.

Danilo Lorenzini (1952–   ) Italy

Concerto 1976 (SZ). For piano and orchestra with one soprano voice. 20 min.

Jean Louël (1914–   ) Belgium

Louël's style is concentrated and unromantic. Its energetic nature is sometimes expressed succinctly and sometimes with virile emotion.

Concerto II 1948 (CeBeDeM) 18 min. No pause between movements. Expanded
   tonality; Ravel influence seen in the slow section; highly effective piano and
   orchestral writing. M-D to D.

Prince Louis Ferdinand (1772–1806) Germany
Louis Ferdinand was an excellent amateur musician and a great admirer of Bee-
thoven, whose influence is everywhere noticeable in the prince's works.
Rondo B♭ Op.9 (Fl).

Vladimir Lovec (1922–   ) Yugoslavia
Concerto a (DSS) 30 min.

Juliusz Luciuk (1927–   ) Poland
Concertino 1973 (PWM 1977). For piano and chamber orchestra. 41pp., 10 min.
   Maestoso; Adagio; Animato. Twelve-tone influence, pointillistic, octotonic,
   strong rhythms, broken triads in Animato. M-D.

Stepan Lucky (1919–   ) Czechoslovakia
Concerto 1971 (Panton). For piano, violin, and orchestra. 15 min. Three movements. Bartók influence; derivative but lively and economical; neatly put
   together (at least in the second and third movements). M-D.

Ray E. Luke (1928–   ) USA
Concerto 1968 (OUP) 20½ min. In three movements. Bitonal usage in an expanded tonality, strong rhythmic treatment, thin textures, cadenza passages
   for soloist. M-D to D.

Leopold Genrikovich Lukomskii (1898–   ) USSR
Concerto in the Classical Style A (USSR 1960) 59pp. Three movements (FSF).
   Effective. Prokofiev set the pattern (and more effectively) in his *Classical
   Symphony*. M-D.

Per Lundkvist (1916–   ) Sweden
Mountain Rhapsody 1960 (Reuter & Reuter) 15pp. Flamboyant theatrical style,
   contrasting sections. M-D.
Concerto I (ES) 28 min.
Concerto II 1976 (ES) 30 min.

Torbjörn Iwan Lundquist (1920–   ) Sweden
Hangar Music (Piano Concerto I) 1967 (ES) 18 min.

Anatolii B. Luppov (1929–   ) USSR
Concerto-Toccata (USSR 1971) 44pp. Allegro energico. One large movement,
   propulsive rhythms, colorful and effective. M-D.

Elizabeth Lutyens (1906–   ) Great Britain
Lutyens was influenced by Schoenberg and Webern, but in recent years she has
worked in a free atonal idiom.
Music for Piano and Orchestra (Schott) 10 min.

Symphonies Op.46 1961 (Schott 10907). For solo piano, brass, harp, percussion, and orchestra. 17 min. Twelve-tone, flexible meters, dynamic extremes, pointillistic, intricate rhythmic patterns. D.

David L'vovich L'vov-Kompaneets (1918–1974) USSR

Concert Waltzes (Soviet Composer 1957) 42pp. The waltzes evolve, one into another. Contrasting moods, tonal. M-D.

Concertino (Soviet Composer 1957). One movement, tonal. Int. to M-D.

M

Robert McBride (1911–   ) USA

Ill Tempered (ACA) 3 min. "Apologies to J.S.B." A take-off on Prelude c from *Well Tempered Clavier,* vol.I. The Bach Prelude is played intact, with only a few added syncopations, but the orchestra is very much in the twentieth century, with obvious blues influence (snare drum and guitar added to a traditional orchestration). Int. to M-D.

John McCabe (1930–   ) Great Britain

McCabe studied composition with Harald Genzmer and is an accomplished pianist.

Concerto Op.43 1966 (Novello) 30 min. Largo; Vivo; Lento (multisectional); Giocoso. Atonal, varied material, fantasy-like development, good use of orchestra, cyclic characteristics present. The Giocoso sparkles in a light bravura style. M-D to D.

Concerto II (Novello). For piano and double orchestra. 22 min.

Concertino 1968 (Novello). For piano, four-hands and orchestra. 10 min. One movement in (FSF) arrangement. Flexible meters, neoclassic. Well-written short show piece for this medium. M-D.

Harl McDonald (1899–1955) USA

Concerto for Two Pianos and Orchestra 1936 (EV) 23 min. Molto moderato; Theme and Variations; Juarezca. Freely tonal; both pianists get a good work-out; one piano carries most important idea(s), other piano tends to accompany. Finale is an exciting dance that works to an acrobatic conclusion. M-D.

Edward MacDowell (1861–1908) USA

Concerto a Op.15 1882 (GS; Br&H; K; CF) 30 min. A youthful work dedicated to Liszt. Maestoso, Allegro con fuoco: SA. Andante tranquillo: strophic form (monothematic). Presto–Maestoso–Molto più lento–Presto: five-part rondo form (ABACA with the C section a recall of material from the first movement; this finale is influenced by the last movement of the Grieg *Concerto.* Contains effective passage work for the soloist. The first movement cadenza at the end of the recapitulation employs rapid double-note passages in the right hand. A revised version appeared posthumously in 1910 with a more massive, embellished version of the opening ten-bar piano solo being the only change. Expert technique required. M-D.

Concerto d Op.23 1885 (GS; Br&H; CF; USSR; Da Capo) 26 min. This work was performed by MacDowell (shortly after his return to America) with Theodore Thomas in New York on March 5, 1889. It was also played by Teresa Carreño (to whom the work is dedicated) with Theodore Thomas on his Summer Night Concerts in Chicago on July 5, 1888. Larghetto-calmato–Poco più mosso: SA. Presto giocoso: rondo. Largo–Molto allegro: three-part sectional form. This work is more intricate than the *Concerto* Op.15. Thematic material from the first movement returns in several spots in the third movement. Three different cadenza passages occur in the first movement. The perpetual-motion figures in the second movement require a highly developed finger technique. Obvious Liszt influence. This brilliantly cohesive and logical work is one of the major piano concertos by an American in the established concert repertoire. M-D.

Aleksei Machavariani (1913–   ) USSR
Concerto 1943 (USSR 1966) 100pp. Andante–Moderato; Andante amoroso; Allegro con brio. Freely tonal, propulsive rhythms. M-D.

Tadeusz Machl (1922–   ) Poland
Concerto 1967 (PWM).

Paul P. McIntyre (1931–   ) Canada
Concerto (MS available from composer: 4285 Mitchell Crescent, Winsor, Ontario, Canada N9G 2G1). 22 min.

Quinton MacLean (1896–1962) Canada, born Great Britain
Concerto 1953 (CMC).

Elizabeth Maconchy (1907–   ) Great Britain
Maconchy writes in an expressionistic style. Her music is tense and concentrated.
Concertino (Lengnick). For piano and chamber orchestra. 16 min.
Concertino (Belwin-Mills). For piano and strings. 14 min.
Concerto 1930 (OUP). For piano and chamber orchestra. 16 min.
Dialogue 1940 (Lengnick) 16 min.

Colin McPhee (1901–1964) USA
Concerto 1928 (AMP). For piano with wind octet. 12 min. Allegretto: pastoral 6/8; dissonant lines produce polytonal chordal figuration. Chorale: clever, free counterpoint, veiled pointillistic texture. Finale: brilliant, toccatalike. Neo-classic style with the piano treated throughout as a virtuoso instrument, but always closely integrated with the supporting octet. Brilliant orchestration also calls for a virtuoso ensemble. M-D.
Tabuh-Tabuhan Toccata 1936 (Fl). For two pianos and orchestra.

Bruno Maderna (1920–1973) Italy
Concerto 1959 (SZ) 17 min. Serial, indefinite pitch notation, effects inside the

piano, aleatory, twitching rhythms, pointillistic, percussive effects, varied
sonorities. Continuous, but roughly divisible into two parts, each culminat-
ing with a solo cadenza. Work dissolves into a whisper. Large orchestration. D.

Concerto 1948 (SZ). For two pianos and chamber orchestra. Three movements.
Strong Bartók and Hindemith influence, neobaroque style. M-D.

Boguslaw Madey (1932–   ) Poland
Madey is professor at the State College of Music in Warsaw and conductor of the
Warsaw Opera.
Concerto Op.12 1957 (PWM) 30 min.

Antoon Maessen (1919–   ) The Netherlands
Concertino 1962 (Donemus) 12 min. Reproduced from the composer's MS.

Mikhail I. Magidenko (1915–   ) USSR
Concerto (Soviet Composer 1972) 52pp. One large movement with cadenza in the
middle. Freely tonal; Tchaikowsky influence. M-D.

Konstantin D. Makarov-Rakitin (1912–1941) USSR
Concerto Op.8 (Soviet Composer 1976) 90pp. Andante–Allegro; Andante; Allegro maestoso. Freely tonal, colorful, strong pianistic gestures. M-D.

Artur Malawski (1904–1957) Poland
Symphonic Studies for Piano and Orchestra 1947 (PWM 1977) 18 min. Intrada—
Scherzino; Romanza; Capriccio; Notturno; Burlesco; Finale—fugato. Written in a luscious quasi-Rachmaninoff virtuoso idiom. M-D.
Toccata et Fugue en Forme de Variations 1949 (PWM) 8 min. Toccata consists of
a brief introduction and nine variations. Fugue is also treated to variation
technique. Catalogue of mid-twentieth-century pianistic techniques. M-D.

Wilhelm Maler (1902–   ) Germany
Trio Concerto (Schott). For piano, violin, cello, and orchestra. 40 min.

Gian Francesco Malipiero (1882–1973) Italy
"An extended concept of tonality underlies all of Malipiero's works: the early
ones betray the influence of Debussy; those of the 1920s were strongly attacked
for their dissonant 'modernism'; those of the 30s and 40s are frequently modal
and predominantly diatonic; and the later works tend towards greater chromaticism and sharper dissonance, sometimes bordering on atonality" (DCM, 447).
Variazioni senza tema 1923 (Ric 119580) 15 min. The piano is used more as an
instrument of the orchestra than as a solo instrument. The title was selected
"not for the sake of a paradox, but because the component parts of this work
actually possess the character of variations on an absent theme" (from the
score).
Concerto I 1934 (Ric; Fl) 18 min. In one continuous movement in three distinct
sections. Piano is treated in a translucent Baroque idiom enlivened by modernistically percussive effects. M-D.

Concerto II 1937 (SZ) 15 min. Allegro molto marcato; Lento; Allegro. Fluid neoclassical writing throughout, repetitious rhythms, expanded tonal idiom. M-D.

Concerto III 1948 (Ric) 16 min. Allegro; Lento; Allegro agitato. Movements played without pause. Transparent contrapuntal style. Thematic developments display no virtuoso writing; antirhetorical discourse. In the third movement the solo is entrusted with a kind of parenthesis without any acrobatics attached. Pianistic interest is minimal. M-D.

Concerto IV 1950 (Ric) 16 min. Allegro; Lento; Allegro. Written in a bright and compact neoclassic style with little dissonance; piano and orchestra alternate contrasting themes. Third movement is in ternary form with a solo cadenza built on new material in the middle section. M-D.

Concerto V 1958 (Sal) 16 min. Represents a departure in the composer's established idiom. More dissonant in chord combinations and rhythmic variety than the earlier concertos. Materials are shared between piano and orchestra. M-D.

See: John Weissman, "Venice 1958," MR 20 (February 1959) :78.

Concerto VI "Delle macchine" 1965 (Ric) 18 min. In three cyclic movements: Allegro; Lento; Allegro. Ends with a stroke on the bass drum. M-D.

Quinta Sinfonia (Concertante, in Eco [Echo]) 1947 (Ric). For two pianos and orchestra. 18 min. Four movements in which "there are two pianos in pursuit, they superpose, they yield one to another, from time to time they rest only to resume afresh their chase without ever joining each other. It is not a concerto but the character of the work is 'concertante' " (from the score). Neoclassic. M-D.

Concerto for Two Pianos and Orchestra 1957 (Ric) 17 min. Written in a grand pandiatonic style. M-D.

Dialoghi (Ric 1957). For two pianos and orchestra. 17 min.

Concerto a tre (SZ 642Z 1939). For piano, violin, cello, and orchestra. 15 min. Allegro; Lento; Allegro. Equal treatment of solo instruments and orchestra make for a highly successful neoclassic work. M-D.

Riccardo Malipiero (1914–   ) Italy

In 1945 Malipiero adopted the twelve-tone technique and repudiated most of his music written before then.

Piccolo Concerto (Carisch 20351 1946). For piano and chamber orchestra. 30pp. Decisamente marcato; Piuttosto lento; Energico. Strong Stravinsky influence; neoclassic. M-D.

Concerto for Piano and Chamber Orchestra (SZ 5193 1955) 17 min. Vivace: delightful mixed meters. Adagio molto: expressive, Impressionistic piano devices. Allegro con moto: highly rhythmic and charged with invigorating effects, virtuosic coda. Atonal; thin textures. M-D.

Concerto per Dmitri 1960 (SZ 5755 1962) 25 min. Two austere movements. Serial, opens with the row; pointillistic; two-voice effect. Lyric sections contain expressive melodic writing; cadenzalike passages; cross rhythms; polytonal and diatonic sections vie with each other; rondo elements present in both movements, careful balance of dissonant sections with those more lyrical. D.

Witold Maliszewski (1873–1939) Poland
Maliszewski studied with Rimsky-Korsakov.
Concerto b♭ Op.29 1932 (PWM) 32 min. A large virtuoso work in late nineteenth-century style. D.

Nariman Mamedov (–   ) USSR
Concerto (USSR).

Alex Manassen (1950–   ) The Netherlands
Double Helix 1978 (Donemus). For piano, clarinet, and orchestra. 11 min.

Mana-Zucca (1887–   ) USA
Concerto I Op.49 1907 (Congress) 16 min. In one tonal movement, Romantic characteristics. M-D.
Concerto II (Congress).

Christian Manen (1934–   ) France
Concertino (Zurfluh 1968) 20pp. Gai et très rythmique. Aimable et avec souplesse (followed immediately by a Final—Presto, all part of the second movement). A well-put-together MC work for high school students. Int.

Vincenzo Manfredini (1737–1799) Italy
Concerto B♭ (Toni—Carisch 21280 1957; Fl) 46pp. Allegro; Grave; Allegro. Written in Russia for performance at the court of the Empress Catherine. First two movements are well written, but the cheerful finale is the finest. Int. to M-D.

Henning Mankell (1868–1930) Sweden
Konsert D (STIM) 31 min.

Franco Mannino (1924–   ) Italy
Concerto (de Santis 1954) 37 min. Three movements (FSF). Expanded tonality. M-D.
"Music for Angels" 1965 (Ric). For piano and string orchestra. 7 min. Fleet arpeggi, tremolo chords, octotonic, long trills. Piano adds atmosphere and at some points carries the melodic line. M-D.
Concerto II Op.100 (EC 1974) 42pp. Allegro moderato; Allegro (tempo di Scherzo); Andante; Allegro energico. Dramatic, chromatic, freely tonal. Piano is on prominent display. M-D.

Vincenzo Mannino (1913–   ) Italy
Concerto (F. Colombo DS 935).

André-François Marescotti (1902–   ) Switzerland
Concerto 1956 (Jobert) 23 min. Dedicated to Lottie Morel, Marescotti's pianist

wife. Moderato; Adagio; Allegro ostinato. Neoclassic, freely atonal, twelve-tone influence, strong thematic material. Thin piano textures; cadenza in first movement replaces the development; excellent use of orchestra. M-D.

Tera de Marez Oyens (1932–   ) The Netherlands
Concertino "In Exile" 1977 (Donemus). For piano and chamber orchestra. 51pp., 9 min. Reproduced from holograph. One movement. Proportional rhythmic relationships, some unusual notation, serial influence, pointillistic, expressionistic. M-D.

Franco Margola (1908–   ) Italy
Concerto I 1943 (SZ 4478) 20 min. Vibrante e teso; Sereno e cantabile; Vivo assai. Neoclassic, beautiful slow movement, brilliant cadenza at end of work. M-D.
Kinderkonzert (Ric 1954) 12 min. Three movements (FSF) that require a well-developed musical *Kind*! Int. to M-D.
Terzo Concerto 1969 (EC 9030) 62pp. Allegro assai; Andante disteso; Vivo con spirito. Expanded tonality. M-D.
Concerto di Oschiri (Bongiovanni 195?). For two solo pianos and orchestra.
Doppio Concerto 1960 (EC 7296). For piano, violin, and orchestra. 18 min. One large movement with contrasting sections. Freely tonal, chromatic, neoclassic characteristics. Cadenza for both instruments together. M-D.

Ljubica Marić (1909–   ) Yugoslavia
Concerto Byzantin 1959 (Secrétaire de la Section des Beaux-Arts et de la Musique de l'Académie Serbe des Sciences et des Arts Belgrade, Yugloslavia 1976) 72pp. Preludio quasi una toccata; Aria; Finale. Based on the second, third, and fourth modes of the Oktoéchos, from the eight modes of the ancient Serbian popular spiritual chants. Modal, fascinating sonorities. Advanced pianism required to be able to handle the melodic freedom. M-D to D.

Igor Markévitch (1912–   ) Switzerland, born Russia
Concerto 1930–1 (Schott) 14 min. Three vivaciously lyric movements, written in a Gallic neobaroque polytonal style. Rhythm is inspired by Bach and Stravinsky, punctuated with barbaric dissonance. M-D.
Partita 1930 (Schott 2160). For piano and chamber orchestra. 17 min.

Henri Martelli (1895–   ) France
Concerto Op.56 1948 (Choudens) 31 min. Three movements (FSF). Expanded tonality. M-D.
Fantaisie sur un Thème Malgache (TP) 19 min.

Frank Martin (1890–1974) Switzerland
After much experimentation, Martin evolved a personal language that combined twelve-tone and tonal elements. This reconciliation of dodecaphonic with the older harmonic functions has been his specific contribution to contemporary style. He was one of the most important representatives of the modern Swiss school.

Concerto I f 1934 (UE 13850Z) 17 min. Lento; Largo; Allegro molto. Written in a post-Romantic style marked by propulsive rhythms. M-D.
Ballade 1938 (UE). For piano, alto sax, and strings. 13 min.
Ballade 1939 (UE 11556) 16 min. Reproduction of holograph. Molto Andante introduction followed by a 3/4 Allegro vivace of tarantella character with En Valse solo part; brilliant ending. Distinguished and elegiac writing. M-D.
Ballade 1939–41 (UE 11318). For piano, flute, and string orchestra. 6½ min.
Petite Symphonie Concertante 1945 (UE; Ph 385; Fl). For piano, harp, harpsichord, and two string orchestras. 22 min. Martin's most widely played work; a true masterpiece of its genre. The piano, harpsichord, and harp are used as solo instruments. Two large movements: Introduction; Allegro. The second movement is in SA form; the second theme and the further development again take up the essential elements of the Introduction. "This Allegro resembles a concerto, with its solo parts (and two always accompanying the other), and the continually recurring orchestral part. The second movement is carried forward by the spontaneous movement of the music. The melodious main theme, introduced in a slow movement by the harp and taken up by the piano, suddenly develops into a lively march. In contrast to the first part, and despite numerous episodic elements, there is only one main theme. It rises to a climax and then concludes with a short coda" (from the score). The unusual instrumentation enables Martin to spin a luminescent texture of fluent counterpoint that is mysterious and ethereal yet also fully logical and coherent. The piano part is octotonic, chordal, and chromatic; uses full arpeggiated chords, glissandi, and strong syncopations; and is neoclassically oriented. M-D.
Concerto for Harpsichord and Chamber Orchestra 1952 (UE 12364) 20 min. Edition for harpsichord or piano.
Concerto II 1968–69 (UE 14955Z 1975) 22 min. Con moto; Lento; Presto. Fingering added by Paul Badura-Skoda. Much more austere than *Concerto* I. Straightforward melodic development. Two fast outer movements emphasize obsessive motor rhythms and attractive ideas. Passacaglia influence felt in the Lento. M-D.

Jean-Louis Martinet (1912–   ) France
Divertissement Pastoral 1955 (Editions Françaises de Musique). Twelve-tone procedures integrated with a variety of more traditional techniques. M-D.

Giovanni Battista Martini (1706–1784) Italy
Concerto C (Piccioli—SZ 5275).
Concerto D (Bernardi, Sciannameo—de Santis 1968). For keyboard and strings. 47pp. Allegro; Andante; Allegro. Practical performing but clean edition, figured bass realized, ornaments clarified. Int. to M-D.
Concerto G 1752 (Desderi—Zanibon 4066 1955). For keyboard and strings. 15 min. Third movement is in SA design. Finale (a fourth movement, unusual for the time) is a quasi minuet with a minore mid-section. Int. to M-D.

Concerti per cembalo e orchestra (Agosti—Classici musicali italiani 1943 [see bibliography]) 103pp. Vol.11. Contains concertos E, G, and F.

Donald Martino (1931–   ) USA
Martino was a student of Milton Babbitt and Luigi Dallapiccola and has taught at Yale and the New England Conservatory. His work utilizes serial techniques and pays close attention to details of structure.
Concerto 1958–65 (Ione; Dantalian) 26 min. Moderato; Presto; Adagio molto. Played without pause; connected by notated cadenzas. A stunning work of great complexity and difficulty. Uses serial procedures. Frequent changes of meter and tempo contribute to the work's challenges. Uses an unusually large percussion section. The work is in conventional notation, but presents large physical and mental demands on the soloist. In many ways, it is a full blown "Romantic" Concerto. D.
See: Arthur Custer, *NOTES* 28 (June 1972):777–78 for a review.

Jean Martinon (1910–1976) France
Symphoniette Op.16 1936 (Sal 1952). For piano, harp, percussion, and string orchestra. 17 min. Lento–Allegro molto; Allegretto–Vivo. Percussive use of the piano in some sections is controlled with flowing legato soft lines; glissandi. MC, attractive. M-D.

Bohuslav Martinů (1890–1959) USA, born Czechoslovakia
Martinů's work has a French precision, economy, and clarity that is also influenced by stylistic characteristics of Czech folk music. His music is facile in the best sense and his harmonic language, although often complex, is usually based on orthodox procedures while his use of form is indebted to the Baroque concerto grosso. Martinů is a copious writer whose work always maintains the supremacy of expression over mere technique.
Concerto I 1925 (Ars Polona 1733). Allegro; Andante; Rondo.
Concertino 1926 (Br CHF 5200). For piano, left-hand and chamber orchestra. 20 min. Allegro moderato; Andante; Allegro con brio. Virtuoso treatment of the left hand. Utilizes entire keyboard. M-D to D.
Concertino 1933 (Melantrich 1949). For piano, violin, cello, and string orchestra. 15 min. Allegro con brio; Moderato; Adagio. Written in a neobaroque style with the thematic elements permeated by vigorous Bohemian melodies and rhythms; more in the spirit of a concerto grosso. Jovial and always sophisticated. Intensely concentrated energy dominates the motoric outer movements and provides an undercurrent of tension in the two inner ones. M-D.
Concerto II 1934 (Ars Polona 1511; Panton) 22 min. Allegro moderato; Poco andante; Allegro con brio. Orchestra part consists of sweet and strong melodies; piano part is strongly dissonant and uses clusters. The two approaches are worked out carefully and successfully. D.
Concertino 1938 (Panton 1967) 21 min. Allegro moderato; Lento; Allegro.
Double Concerto 1938 (Bo&H; Fl). For piano, timpani, and two string orchestras. 20 min. Poco allegro; Largo; Allegro. Neobaroque style with searching

atonal melodic leaps; impatient yet restrained rhythmical pulse; tonal and bitonal sections; triadic harmony though no key signatures are used. The first two movements conclude on major triads while the last movement ends on an effective but agonizingly polytonal chord. M-D.

Sinfonietta Giocosa 1940 (Bo&H) 32 min. Poco allegro; Allegretto moderato; Allegro; Andantino–Allegro. This jolly work has a catchy neoclassic tune that is worked out with rigor and precision. Busy, contrapuntal texture. The finale. has constantly shifting bar lengths. Demands are not overly taxing; first-class workmanship throughout. M-D.

Concerto for Two Pianos and Orchestra 1943 (AMP) 25 min. Allegro non troppo: a brisk toccata; contrapuntal; brilliant sixteenth-note figurations in the piano parts. Adagio: lyrical contemplation permeates this movement; soloists are heard for the most part unaccompanied; Szymanowsky-like with post-Impressionistic chords and figuration; diatonic mid-section is especially appealing. Allegro: propulsive; rondolike; dance influence; has a cadenza for both pianists; complex textures. This work is evocative of the poignant melodies and rhythms of Moravian folk music. Generally the orchestra part tends to accompany rather than act as an independent partner for the soloists. Formally the work has characteristics of the concerto grosso. Much virtuoso writing for the pianists. D.

Toccata e due Canzoni 1946 (Bo&H; Fl) 24½ min. Basically a concerto grosso in modern garb, à la Bloch. Toccata: neobaroque; a rhythmically obsessive Bach-like Allegro; opens sounding like Hindemith and closes sounding like Françaix. Canzone I: grows from the fragile entry of the solo piano, which quietly unwinds and provokes the orchestra to follow; a slow, chromatic dirge. Canzone II: three-part melancholic outside sections with another Toccata in the middle; becomes reflective and ends softly. M-D.

Concerto III 1948 (Panton) 25 min. Allegro: brilliant with much virtuoso writing for the piano; two principal ideas, the first stated in the piano and the second, more lyrical one given by the flutes. Andante poco moderato: stately; occasionally recalls themes from the first movement. Moderato–Allegro (poco): polka-like finale recalls the principal theme of the opening movement near the end. Throughout there is a tendency to present long stretches of sequential figuration material with relatively little development of themes in a traditional sense. The piano writing is idiomatic but not of unreasonable difficulty. M-D.

Sinfonietta La Jolla 1950 (Bo&H) 18 min. Poco allegro; bright; breezy; chromatic; contains fairly large part of the main theme of the Finale of Martinů's *Symphony* V (1946); nervous dramatic ostinatos give way to bright cadences. Largo–Andante moderato: reflective, wistful, numerous repeated notes and phrases. Allegro: ideas are tossed back and forth between piano and orchestra; bubbles along until the music becomes ecstatic; then abruptly ends. Neoclassic; pithy musical vocabulary. Piano part is like an obbligato. M-D.

Incantation, Fourth Piano Concerto 1955–56 (Supraphon 4318a) 20 min. Poco allegro; Poco moderato. Second movement has a cadenza in the middle and concludes with an Allegro section. Czech polka influences come through from time to time, especially in the opening movement. M-D to D.

Fantasia Concertante (Piano Concerto B♭) 1957 (UE) 20 min. Poco allegro risoluto: SA; brilliant syncopated main theme is given first by the orchestra, then by the piano; second theme is played by the orchestra alone, then accompanied in figurations given in the piano; the two themes are developed, then finally return in abbreviated form, followed by a coda. Poco andante: rondo; piano has many passages of accompanying figurations to the lyrical writing in the orchestra. Poco allegro: rondo; opens with thematic material in rapid sixteenth-note figurations given by the orchestra and later taken up by the piano; contrasting middle section with upward-moving scale passages in the piano; return to the opening perpetual-motion material; brilliant ending. Martinů's writing for the piano is not usually idiomatic and demands a sense of color and rhythm to project the music properly. This work is closer to French Impressionism that to Bohemian folk music, whose idiom is only occasionally to be detected in the rhythmical features. Demands a fluent octave and tremolo technique. M-D to D.

Tauno O. Marttinen (1912–   ) Finland
Marttinen is director of the Institute of Music at Hämeenlinna, Finland.

Concerto I Op.23 1964 (Seesaw) full score, 76pp. Allegro; Adagio; Allegro molto. Freely tonal, clever elaboration of thematic ideas. Based on nineteenth-
century pianism, which employs many octaves and full chords; large span required. M-D.

Concerto II Op.74 1972 (Finnish Music Information Centre) full score, 92pp. Allegro; Adagio; Allegro molto. Based freely on the twelve-tone system but contains some versatile musical expression. Preference for half-step usage is strong. M-D to D.

Giuseppi Martucci (1856–1909) Italy

Concerto b♭ Op.66 (K&S 1886). Three large movements (FSF). Strong Brahms influence. M-D to D.

Concerto II d (SZ 7699).

Tema con Variazioni (Fl). For piano and chamber orchestra.

Joseph Marx (1882–1964) Austria

Romantisches Klavierkonzert E (UE 6017 1920) 87pp. ". . . in three movements exuding the aroma of tardigrade romanticism. . . " (MSNH, 352). Not very much in the concerto style in the sense of a dualism of partners. Colorfully chordal. M-D to D.

Castelli Romani (UE 8233 1930) 30 min. Three pieces for piano and orchestra. Villa Hadriana; Tusculum; Frascati. Picturesque writing, many tempo and mood changes. Requires bravura pianism. M-D to D.

Karl Julius Marx (1897–   ) Germany
Konzert Op.9 (Bo&Bo) 29 min. Passacaglia; Presto e leggiero; Adagio; Rondo.
   Tonal, neoclassic, always does what you expect it to do! M-D.
Konzert C Op.24 (Br&H) 20 min.

Daniel Gregory Mason (1873–1953) USA
Prelude and Fugue Op.20 1921 (JF; LC) 11 min. Prelude: a passacaglia related
   to the fugue subject. Fugue: subject is decorated with many figurations;
   passacaglia theme returns at the close and provides added counterpoint.
   Mason also arranged this work for two pianos, and for piano and organ.
   M-D.

Jules Massenet (1842–1912) France
Concerto E♭ 1902 (Heugel) 80pp. Andante moderato: opens with a long cadenza;
   develops into a cheerful Hungarian dance with furious octaves and fast passage work; hints at Hummel. Largo: *bien chanté*; flowing melody throughout.
   Airs slovaques: rhythmic; many embellishments; evolves into a Hungarian
   rhapsody. M-D.

Jan Masséus (1913–   ) The Netherlands
Concerto 1945 (Donemus) 20 min.
Symphonic Variaties Op.9 1949 (Donemus) 13 min.
Concerto Op.37 1966 (Donemus).

Gerard Massias (1933–   ) France
Concert Bref 1956 (Jobert). For piano, wind instruments, and percussion. 13 min.
   Modéré; Très lent; Modérément animé. Strong rhythms, expanded tonal idiom, proportional rhythmic notation, dissonant. Requires much ensemble
   experience. M-D.

Eduardo Mata (1942–   ) Mexico
Mata is conductor of the Dallas Symphony Orchestra. "His current musical language is a free mixture of polytonal, twelve-tone, serial, and aleatory techniques
in which timbre and other textural elements are a major concern" (DCM, 458).
Improvisaciones II 1965 (EMM). For two pianos (one played by a percussionist),
   strings, percussion, and orchestra. The percussion pianist plays only inside
   the instrument, on the strings. This works best on a Steinway. Performance
   directions in Spanish and English. Clusters, plucked strings, aleatory, unusual sonorities, avant-garde. M-D.

Bruce Mather (1939–   ) Canada
Concerto 1958 (CMC). For piano and chamber orchestra. In one concertante
   movement. Except for the middle piano solo, the piano is integrated into the
   orchestral texture. Luxurious sonorities; complex textures. M-D.

William Mathias (1934–   ) Great Britain
Concerto I Op.2 1955 (PRS) 21 min.
Concerto II Op.13 1961 (OUP 1964) 23 min. Molto moderato, sempre flessibile:

modified SA; lyrical first theme, contrasting second idea; quiet coda returns opening theme; freely diatonic. Allegro molto vivace: five-part; varied meters and material. Lento molto e flessibile: open form; two main ideas worked together in counterpoint; fast accompanied cadenza leads to the Finale—Allegro alla danza: SA; thematic construction related to first and third movements (cyclic); strong piano domination. D.

Concerto III Op.40 1968 (OUP) 25 min. Allegro energico; Adagio, sempre flessibile; Allegro con brio. Freely tonal; much figuration alternating between the hands; thin, steely-edged textures; requires outstanding octave technique. M-D.

Yoritsune Matsudaira (1907–   ) Japan

Tema e Variazioni 1951 (SZ 5770) 15 min. Theme and six variations. Expanded tonality; virtuoso figuration, *ppp* closing. M-D to D.

Tre Movimenti 1963 (SZ). First movement: six preludes, the order to be determined by the conductor; piano and harp involved in all six. Second movement: Japanese *Bugaku* (originally an accompaniment to a dance) is inspiration for this movement; texture is elaborated and thickened at center of movement (dynamic arch form!) and thinned at conclusion; piano part is fairly active; cadenza (in three sections) uses an aleatory set of choices. Finale: six variations; only numbers 1 and 6 are fixed; the conductor may select the order of the others; vigorous rhythms and counterpoint. Aleatory. Virtuosity for the pianist is mostly avoided, even in the cadenza that separates the second and third movements. D.

Concerto 1965 (SZ). In three movements. Inspired by ancient Japanese court music, but constructed according to dodecaphonic techniques, lubricated by quarter-tones and diversified by aleatory devices. M-D.

Tobias Matthay (1858–1945) Great Britain

Concert Piece a Op.12 (Ric 1922) 18 min. A concerto in one movement that uses post-Brahmsian techniques and idioms, flowing lines. M-D.

Siegfried Matthus (1934–   ) Germany

Konzert 1970 (DVFM 1415) 17 min. Four contrasting movements played without pause. Improvisation for soloist and orchestra, ultracontemporary techniques, avant-garde. Development of the work is not conditioned by themes and motives but by certain structures that constitute the source material of each movement. Thus, the first movement is based on an eight-voice harmony; the material of the second movement is a whole-tone scale stretched through three octaves; the third is based on a twelve-note series; and the fourth on diatonic material. Virtuoso cadenza. D.

Roger Matton (1929–   ) Canada

Matton's style is characterized by vibrant rhythms, a good sense of symphonic writing, and an idiom that—while entirely modern—retains tonal centers.

Concerto 1954–55 (MS available from composer: % Archives du Folklore, Université Laval, Rue Sainte Famille, Québec, P.Q. Canada). For two pianos and percussion. 17½ min. Three movements.

Concerto 1964 (CMC). For two pianos and orchestra. 20 min. Allegro: two basic themes are transformed both melodically and rhythmically. [Untitled]: an idyllic and emotional song. [Untitled]: brilliant toccata in which themes of the previous movements are reexamined. Expanded tonality; cadenzas; rhythmic vitality and exciting driving force with sharply contrasted sweeping lyrical lines. M-D.

Paule Maurice (1910–) France

Concerto 1950 (Lemoine) 20 min. Three movements (FSF). Early twentieth-century techniques. M-D.

Suite (EV). For two pianos and orchestra. 13½ min.

William Mayer (1925–) USA

Octagon 1967 (MCA) 29pp. Moderato interrotto; Cantilena; Scherzo; Toccata; Fantasia; Clangor; Points and Lights; Finale. This brittle eight-movement showpiece stresses chordal and instrumental sonorities; themes are pitted against each other. Bravura writing for both soloist and orchestra; alternates gentle with the abrasive; exciting. Requires virtuoso technique; each movement features a different facet of the piano. M-D to D.

Johann Simon Mayr (1763–1845) Germany

Mayr is best known for his operas, about eighty in all. Donizetti was his pupil. The MSS of the two concertos are located in the Donizetti Conservatory in Bergamo, Italy.

Concerto I C 17½ min. Allegro moderato: orchestra sets the stage for the piano, which promptly takes over the spotlight and generates very little conflict with the accompanying group; sudden down-stepping key shifts are, however, unexpected. Andantino grazioso: tender; transparently scored. Rondo: smart, brief, wastes no time and notes. Int. to M-D.

Concerto II.

Toshiro Mayuzumi (1929–) Japan

Pieces for Prepared Piano and Strings 1957 (CFP 6325B) 13 min. Prologue; Interlude; Finale. Score includes preparation directions with diagrams. Two pieces of rubber, bolts, and screws are required for the preparation, which creates sounds similar to the ancient Japanese gong and lute. The music is fragmentary: the piano part has many repetitions of the same note and figures that look rather conventional on paper, but which produce imaginative sounds. The three sections are performed without a break. Metronome markings indicate the tempo and distinguish the three movements. M-D.

Nicolas Medtner (1880–1951) USSR

Medtner is sometimes termed a "Russian Brahms." His own powers as a piano virtuoso are in evidence in his complex and demanding writing for the keyboard. His compositions are filled with complex rhythms and thick contrapuntal textures.

At its best, Medtner's music is capable of much grandeur, with intellectual concentration coupled with poetry and imagination.

Concerto I c Op.33 1918 (CFP) 33 min. In one SA movement. Following a short introduction by the piano, the principal theme is given by the violins. The cellos give the second theme as the piano plays an upward-moving passage consisting of chords and octaves. Following a piano cadenza, the two main themes are used in nine variations, which constitute the development. A recapitulation and coda end the work in a brilliant fashion. The writing for the piano is complex with much use of contrapuntal textures; it demands full virtuoso and musical equipment. D.

Concerto II c Op.50 1927 (Zimmermann) 85pp. Dedicated to Sergei Rachmaninoff, who finished his not too-dissimilar *Fourth Concerto* in the same year. Toccata; Romance; Divertimento. All three movements have spacious and formal designs. Weak orchestration. The style sounds like complicated Rachmaninoff without the melody. M-D to D.

Concerto III e Op.60 1942–43 "Ballade" (Zimmermann) 30 min. Con moto largamente: freely modulating, numerous piano cadenza-like passages. Interludium: a short diptych of variations on previously stated themes. Finale—Allegro molto, svegliando, eroico: rondo; culminates in a heroically rhetorical declaration of musical faith in E. The entire work is conceived in an ascetically restrained contrapuntal idiom. D.

Henryk Melcer (1869–1928) Poland

Melcer studied with Moszkowski and Leschetizky.

Concerto I e 1895 (Dob; PWM) 30 min. A significant and individual work in the style of Liszt and Chopin. M-D.

Henrik Melcher Melchers (1882–1961) Sweden

Konsert I (STIM) 30 min.

Konsert II (STIM) 32 min.

Felix Mendelssohn (1809–1847) Germany

Mendelssohn's two mature piano concertos (Opp.25 and 40) are interesting in that they are built on a small scale and yet beautifully display characteristics of the Romantic style. The orchestral scoring suits the material but lacks some of the grandeur and power of the fully developed Romantic concerto.

Concerto for Two Pianos and Orchestra E 1823 (Kohler—DVFM 4251a 1971; Fl) 28½ min. Allegro vivace; Adagio non troppo; Allegro. Mendelssohn composed this double concerto in the autumn of 1823, when he was fourteen years old. It was apparently performed only twice during his lifetime. It contains all the style characteristics we associate with *Concerto* g. M-D.

Concerto for Two Pianos and Orchestra A♭ 1824 (DVFM 4252a 1963) 31 min. Allegro vivace; Andante; Allegro vivace. More ambitious than *Concerto* E. M-D to D.

These two early works display good taste, appealing form, and astonishing finish. Both are conceived along strictly Classical lines with solid musical substance. Mendelssohn made few concessions to the virtuoso in the finales, for good taste was as important to him as bravura technique. He cast a gay, scintillating surface over finales as naturally as he wove a tender, deep-toned meditation into his slow movements. His music is at all times gracious and natural. Above all he has the precious gift of melody, romantically spirited and romantically warm. M-D to D.

Concerto d 1823 (DVFM). For piano, violin, and string orchestra. 38 min., with cuts about 28 min. The piano part was probably intended for Mendelssohn and the string part for his violin teacher, Eduard Rietz. Some judicious cuts are desirable as the uncut version is too long for the material. Soloists frequently have display passages. Allegro: numerous contrasting duet episodes; cadenza contains plenty of fire and sweetness. Adagio: a "song without words"; extended passages for soloist while orchestra is quiet. Allegro molto: an energetic rondo full of charm and bravura. M-D.

Concerto a (DVFM 1967). For piano and strings. Allegro; Adagio; Allegro ma non troppo. This early work is in the style of Hummel, but it already contains characteristics that show up in the two later piano concertos. No pause between the Adagio attaccas and the finale. The outer movements contain brilliant pianistics. M-D.

Capriccio Brillant b Op.22 (GS; CFP; Br&H; Schott; Eulenburg; K; Augener; Hug). An introduction, similar to the one in the *Rondo Capriccioso*, Op.16, leads to an Allegro with technical characteristics similar to the first movement of *Concerto* g, Op.25. The second subject is a jestful march, which is cleverly worked together with the main subject in a delightful development. Efficiently designed. M-D.

Concerto g Op.25 1832 (CFP; GS; PWM; CF; K; Augener; Hug; Eulenburg; Zen-On). Three movements played without break. Brilliant and idiomatic piano writing, cogent form and orchestration. The first movement departs from the classical concerto form by skipping the ritornello before and after the opening piano solo. The slow movement has a Romantic theme, which is later given to the orchestra with the piano decorating with airy arpeggios. The bravura finale utilizes rotational passages with octaves and staccato chords. A high degree of thematic unity graces this work. M-D.

Rondo Brillant E♭ Op.29 1834 (GS; CFP; K; Eulenburg; Augener; Hug) 12 min. A brilliant display piece for the pianist, full of dazzling staccato octaves, chords, and broken chords. Effective scoring throughout. Displays charm, delicacy, and a cool elegance. Deserves much more playing. M-D.

Concerto d Op.40 1837 (GS; CFP; Br&H; K; Augener; Eulenburg; Hug; USSR). Not as successful as *Concerto* Op.25; the material is less inspired. But the Finale is one of the most brilliant displays of Mendelssohn's high-spirited fancy. A trace of Weber is present. The work is always astonishingly competent. M-D.

Serenade and Allegro Giocoso b Op.43 1838 (Simrock; CFP; Br&H; Augener). A short and effective work. The Serenade serves as a dialogue (piano and orchestra) introduction to the lively Allegro, which is delightfully efficient. Strong inspiration seems to be lacking. M-D.

Duo Concertant en Variations Brillantes sur la Marche Bohémienne from the Melodrama Preciosa de C. M. de Weber Op. 87B (Kistner ca.1849: LC) 14½ min. This work is for two pianos with optional orchestral accompaniment. It was jointly composed by Mendelssohn and Ignaz Moscheles. Mendelssohn wrote the Introduction and the first two variations, Moscheles the third and the fourth, and they shared efforts in the extended Finale. "In April of 1833, just three days before a scheduled London concert (arranged by the enterprising Moscheles), the two friends decided to create a new work in which they could share as composers, performers and improvisers. They chose a well-known theme. Two days later, with the aid of some sketched-out notation, they held a rehearsal. The following day the work was presented, in all earnestness, as a finished composition, played on a new Erard pianoforte before a distinguished and delighted audience" (from record jacket, Orion, ORS 79343). Introduzione in c has syncopated chords, arpeggi; leads directly into Allegretto Tempo di Marcia, where theme is presented. Four contrasting variations and a finale follow, using chromatic runs, chords, and octaves. Brilliant and effective writing. Tuneful, occasionally wistful and playful, charming, and witty. M-D.

Rudolf Mengelberg (1892–1959) The Netherlands
Capriccio (Donemus) 15 min.

Peter Mennin (1923–   ) USA
Concerto 1958 (CF; Fl) 26 min. Maestoso–allegro; Adagio religioso; Allegro vivace. A busy virtuoso piece with the piano pitted against the orchestra. Intricate piano writing requires a performer with extraordinary technical ability. The music contains an enormous pulsating drive, expressive power, and natural harmonic and contrapuntal flow. United in a lofty, poetic grandiloquence. D.

Gian Carlo Menotti (1911–   ) USA
Concerto F 1945 (Ric) 30 min. Allegro; Lento; Allegro. Long, diffuse work that exudes the baroque aura of the Italian classical period. Stark concentrated writing, especially in the outer movements. Virtuoso technique required. D.

Sophie Menter (1846–1918) Germany
A pupil of Tausig and Liszt, Menter was one of the major female piano virtuosos of the nineteenth century. She was Liszt's favorite female pupil, and her writing reflects his style in most respects. Her music is interesting only as a period piece.
Ungarische Zigeunerweisen (Hungarian Gypsy Airs) 1909 (GS). This work is similar in treatment to Liszt's *Hungarian Fantasy* for piano and orchestra. After an orchestral introduction in a reflective slow tempo, the piano is given a brilliant opening solo cadenza. The work builds to a final brilliant Presto. Throughout, the writing is brilliantly virtuosic and requires a typical Lisztian

technique of rapid octaves, double notes, and fleet passage work. The orchestral accompaniment is by Tchaikowsky. With the interest in minor figures of the nineteenth century, this work would merit a hearing simply as a curiosity, as the piano writing is extremely effective. M-D.

Siegfried Merath (1928–   ) Germany
"Concerto d'amore" 1964 (Birnbach) 6 min. One tonal movement. The melodic treatment is the most interesting element. M-D.

Usko Meriläinen (1930–   ) Finland
Meriläinen is a composer of energetic and brilliant instrumental music. He is a symphonist, but the form of the concerto is even more congenial to him. In a decade of new simplicity and neotonalism in Finland, he stands close to a group that in this milieu could be called neo-expressionistic, although his starting point was neoclassic rather than Romantic.
Concerto I 1955 (Edition Pan) 20 min. An unlyrical style reminiscent of Hindemith in regard to tonality and polymodal counterpoint and of early Stravinsky with respect to rhythmic vivacity. D.
Concerto II 1969 (Fazer) 17 min. Forms are built of large blocks; less-complex rhythms than in *Concerto* I; extreme intervallic tensions. Neoclassical rhythmic elasticity; an almost Romantic warmth and continuity of sound. D.
Dialogues 1977 (Edition Pan) 25 min. Themes undergo character metamorphosis; strong figurations. D.

Olivier Messiaen (1908–   ) France
Messiaen has attempted, and in many ways succeeded, in enlarging the frontiers of music. He has produced an entirely new concept of musical time, which has had an enormous influence on contemporary composers, including Pierre Boulez and Karlheinz Stockhausen. Messiaen's music is colorful, and his piano style is varied. It features multiple modality, free use of dominant discords that often produce fresh sonorities, and orchestral treatment of the piano. Birdcalls and Hindu ragas have also influenced Messiaen, whose emphasis on sonority is striking. His musical gestures are generous and almost ritualistic in the obsessive use of characteristic rhythmic procedures.
Turangalîla-Symphonie 1946–48 (Durand) 80 min. Pour piano principal et grand orchestre. Ten sections. The piano is used thematically and not merely for harmonic splashes. This uneven and problematic work represents the *ne plus ultra* of the concertante style. There are many solo passages, but they do not alter the position of the piano in relation to the general ensemble. M-D to D.
Reveil des Oiseaux "The Awakening of the Birds" 1953 (Durand) 20 min. Birdsong patterns in piano and orchestra provide the basic material. This ornithological symphony, whose melodic ideas are drawn from an aviary of 37 songbirds, exhibits a remarkable similarity of atonal intervallic structures among such different species as a robin, a thrush, and a blackcap, with a preference for major sevenths and minor ninths. Elements of rhythm and sonority combine to produce an almost hypnotic effect. Demonstrates the

composer's "strange charm of impossibilities in the domain of mode and rhythm." Messiaen's "theological rainbow" permeates this piece in a beautiful manner. D.

Oiseaux Exotiques 1955–56 (UE). For piano and chamber orchestra. 14 min. Conjures up in sophisticated idealization the tweets, chirps, warbles, twitters, and trills of 40 polychromatic birds of Asia and America. These are combined with involved rhythmic patterns. Messiaen achieves dazzling sonorities, often by compiling layers of sound with sustaining instruments. D.

Sept Haïkaï: Esquisses Japonais 1962 (Leduc). For piano and chamber orchestra. 20 min. Composed after a trip to Japan. Uses the electronic keyboard instrument the Ondes Martenot in the orchestration. Seven short movements like the Japanese haiku poems. Notes in French. Introduction; The Park of Nara and the Stone Lanterns; Yamanaka—Cadenza; Gagaku; Miyajima and the Torii in the Sea; The Birds of Karuizawa; Coda. M-D.

Couleurs de Cité Céleste (Colors of the Celestial City) 1963 (Leduc). For piano and chamber orchestra. 16 min. These "inner colors" spring from five quotations from the Apocalypse (given in the score). The form of each piece depends entirely on colors. Themes (melodic or rhythmic), complexes of sonorities, and timbres evolve like colors. Greek and Hindu rhythms, permutations of note-values, birdsong of different countries, plainsong *Alleluias*, are all used. The work ends the way it begins, by juxtaposing flamboyant colors against bland ones. M-D.

Des Canyons aux Étoiles (From the Canyons to the Stars) 1971–74 (Leduc). For piano, horn, zylorimba, glockenspiel, and orchestra. 102 min. Study score available in three volumes: I, 1–5; II, 6 and 7; III, 8–12. Preface in French. A big theological cycle that glorifies God in all his creation, that creation including the canyons (of Utah) and stars of the title as well as a brilliant and exotic aviary. Twelve sections each with an inscription from the Bible or various mystical writers. There are two solo piano sections of birdsong mosaic. Marvelous mixture of sonorities in the orchestral part. M-D.

See: Norman Demuth, "Messiaen's Early Birds," MT, 101 (1960):627–29.

Adrian C. Evans, "Olivier Messiaen in the Surrealist Context: A Bibliography," *Brio* 11 (Spring 1974): 2–11. Most extensive bibliography.

Arthur Meulemans (1884–1966) Belgium

Concerto I 1941 (Uitgave Artur Meulemansfonds 1968; LC) 25½ min. Allegro; Andante poco con moto; Allegro con brio. Mainly tonal with a few biting dissonances mixed in; Impressionistic overtones. Virtuosic orchestral palette. M-D.

Ernst Hermann Meyer (1905–   ) Germany

Konzertante Sinfonie 1961 (Verlag Neue Musik) 34 min. Andante larghetto; Allegro moderato; Adagio maestoso. Freely tonal, ideas overworked, *ppp* closing. M-D.

Konzert Für Orchester mit Obligatem Pianoforte 1974 (CFP 9735) 116pp., full score. Allegro con brio; Larghetto; Allegro con fuoco. Observes the primacy of melody; marked by consistency of texture and intensity of expression. Fine sense of craft stems from composer's study with Hindemith. M-D.

Alexander Meyer von Bremen (1930–   ) Germany
Konzert 1953 (UE 12431) 30 min. Andante: has a driving toccata in the main section. Adagio: dirgelike. Cadenza: partly improvisatory; for piano solo with only a timpani roll at conclusion. Epilogue: parallel chords, octotonic, tonal ending. Some triadic harmonies, highly chromatic, many octaves. Effective and brilliant piano writing if not highly imaginative. D.

Jean de Middeleer (1908–   ) Belgium
Concerto 1953 (CeBeDeM) 14 min. Three movements (FSF). Freely tonal. M-D.
Concerto (CeBeDeM).

Peter Mieg (1906–   ) Switzerland
Concerto 1956 (Bo&Bo). For harpsichord or piano and orchestra. Energetic opening movement, cantabile slow movement with double-note patterns, cheerful and brilliant finale with Bartók influence. M-D.

Costin Miereanu (1943–   ) Rumania
"Miereanu's serial music has been influenced by Webern and Boulez; later he began working with electroacoustics and with John Cage's aleatory procedures" (DCM, 485).
Finis Coronat Opus 1966 (Sal). For pianist and six groups of instruments. Directions in French. Clusters, new notation; one pianist plays two pianos. Five sections, piano cadenza at end of section three. Avant-garde. D.
Espaces II 1967–9 (Sal). For piano, tape, and twenty strings.

Francisco Mignone (1897–   ) Brazil
Portuguese, Indian, and Negro elements are combined in Mignone's music. His piano style is Romantic in conception and full of rich sonorities. Mignone is considered the dean of living Brazilian composers.
Fantasia Brasiliera I 1929 (Ric) 15 min. One large movement. Primitive Afro-Brazilian rhythms; orchestral and pianistic glitter; tonal; virtuoso passages; cadenzas; strong rhythms. M-D.
Fantasia Brasiliera II 1931 (Fl; MS available from composer: R. Pompeu Loureiro, 148, Apto.1002 [Copacabana] 20.000 Rio de Janeiro RJ Brazil) 14 min.
Fantasia Brasiliera III 1934 (Fl; MS available from composer) 18 min.
Fantasia Brasiliera IV 1936–39 (MS available from composer) 14 min.
Burlesca e Toccata 1958 (MS available from composer) 13 min.
Concerto 1958 (MS available from composer) 32 min. Allegro moderato; Andante; Allegro con spirito.
Concerto 1965–66 (MS available from composer). For piano, violin, and orchestra. 25 min. Moderato; Andante; Allegro.

Georges E. Migot (1891–1976) France
"The harmonic vocabulary in Migot's music is modal, and harmony and rhythm derive from, rather than direct, an intertwining of melodic lines" (DCM, 485).
Suite 1925–26 (Leduc) 18 min. Prélude; Pastorale; Conclusion. M-D.
Concerto 1962 (Editions Françaises de Musique) 17 min. Three movements, freely tonal, many syncopated figurations. M-D.

Marcel Mihalovici (1898–   ) France, born Rumania
Toccata Op.44 1938–40 revised 1949 (Heugel) 18 min. Two sections, brilliant and colorful with modal influence, Enescu influence, MC.

Andras Mihály (1917–   ) Hungary
Mihály has taught chamber music at the Budapest Academy since 1950.
Concerto 1954 (EMB) 23½ min.
Concerto 1959 (EMB). For piano obbligato, violin, and orchestra. 15 min. Allegro; Andante; Presto. The piano plays an important part even though it is secondary to the violin. Modal, clever cross-rhythms, chromatic. M-D.

Slavko Mihelčič (1912–   ) Yugoslavia
Concertino (DSS). For piano and strings. 10 min.
Fantasy (DSS 1957). For piano and strings. 7 min. One movement, freely flowing rhythms, tonal around B. M-D.

Darius Milhaud (1892–1974) France
Milhaud used a variety of techniques, both old and new. Polytonality, contrapuntal textures, folk song, and jazz are all utilized in generous measure. In addition, contrasting moods of tenderness and gaiety were popular with this prolific composer.
Ballade 1920 (UE 9649) 12 min. Short; polytonal; the same vigorous syncopation and Latin-American dance rhythms as are found in Milhaud's *Saudades do Brazil*. Impressionistic orchestration. Requires span of a ninth. M-D.
Five Etudes 1920–21 (UE) 89pp. Vif; Doucement; Fugue; Sombre; Romantique. The composer's most extreme sample of polytonality. Fugue is the most dissonant; four separate and conflicting fugues by woodwind, brass, strings, and piano are heard simultaneously. M-D to D.
Le Carnaval d'Aix (Fantaisie pour piano et orchestre) 1926 (Heugel) 15½ min. Suite of twelve short pieces. Fairly dissonant and somewhat humorous. Contains effective dance rhythms and an entertaining march. Milhaud's most popular work for piano and orchestra. M-D.
Concerto I 1933 (Sal) 12 min. Très vif; Barcarolle; Finale. Neoclassic. Outer movements contain much rhythmic interest; middle movement uses a persistent barcarolle rhythm. Most of the writing fits the hands well, but the finale (a hedonistic rondo) contains some awkward spots. M-D.
Fantaisie Pastorale 1938 (Sal) 10 min. Flowing, double glissando in thirds, octotonic, freely tonal. M-D.
Concerto II 1941 (Heugel) 17 min. Animé: toccata-like, à la Poulenc with a

ragtime second theme. Romance: rhapsodic, lilting, like a barcarolle, bluesy. Bien modérément animé: South American patterns. Pandiatonic. Fine interplay between piano and orchestra. Requires facile pianism. M-D.

Concerto III 1946 (AMP; Fl) 52pp. Alerte et avec élégance: pastorale-like, charming; requires alertness and elegance. Lent: dirge-like, colorful figurations, forceful climax. Avec espirit et élégance: dancelike, to be played with continued elegance and "esprit." Rhythmic, dissonant; pianist is kept very busy. M-D to D.

Concerto IV 1949 (Heugel) 19 min. Animé; Très lent; Joyeux. Acrid; contains a superabundance of pianistic acrobatics. Conceived in contrasting meditative and joyous moods; reaches polytonal polyphony at recurring climaxes. Demands a maximum of pianofortitude! The most dissonant and complex of the five piano concertos. D.

Suite Concertante 1947–52 (Enoch) 18 min. Animé; Lent; Vif. An arrangement of Milhaud's marimba *Concerto* (1947). Many pedal indications (unusual in the piano and orchestral works), clever ensemble writing. M-D.

Concerto V 1955 (ESC) 19 min. Alerte: sonatina design (no development section). Nonchalant: a hybrid SA design (development and recapitulation telescoped together), an excellent discourse on a quiet tender theme. Joyeux: free rondo. Not as much pianistic activity as in Concertos III and IV. Challenging piano writing with fast, virtuosic double-note passages; quick octaves; and rapid, wide leaps. D.

Concerto for Two Pianos and Orchestra 1941 (EV; Fl) 20 min. Animé: heavy piano style; figuration of broken ninths; tuneful; builds to big conclusion; effective cadenza; large span required. Funèbre: dirgelike, widespread figuration, glissando. Vif et précis: rhythmic and bouncy, many chords, effective closing. Free, dissonant counterpoint; atonal harmonization. All movements are in 4/4 time. Calls for virtuoso playing from ensemble as well as pianists. D.

Suite for Two Pianos and Orchestra Op.300 1951 (Heugel) 18 min. Entreé; Nocturne; Java; Fuguée; Mouvement Perpétuel; Finale. Extended, appealing, but not Milhaud's strongest writing. The *Java* is a popular French dance in an alternating 3/4 and 2/4 time. M-D.

Concertino d'Automne (Heugel 1952). For two pianos and eight instruments (winds and strings). 11 min. One movement. Sober, introspective, dark-hued instrumentation. Pianos have a virtuoso cadenza that concludes in four-part canons. Demanding for the pianists. M-D to D.

Concerto II for Two Pianos and Percussion 1961 (ESC). Four percussion parts requiring four performers. While not a true work for piano and orchestra, this is one of the most important and significant piano works by Milhaud. It invites comparision with the Bartók *Sonata* in the same genre. Upper range of pianos exploited at beginning; unusual and effective sonorities throughout; strong rhythmic treatment. M-D to D.

Chamber Concerto for Piano and Ten Instruments (ESC).

See: Forrest Robinson, "The Music of Darius Milhaud for Piano and Orchestra," AMT 18 (November-December 1968): 20–21, 47.

Charles Mills (1914–   ) USA
Concerto 1949 (ACA) 23 min. Allegro moderato; Adagietta con moto; Allegro vivace. Neoclassic, well-developed ideas, beautiful orchestration. D.

Akira Miyoshi (1933–   ) Japan
Miyoshi teaches at Tokyo University of the Arts.
Concerto 1962 (Kawai-Gafuku).

Ernest John Moeran (1894–1950) Great Britain
Rhapsody F♯ (JWC 1943) 18 min. The piece has stylistic inconsistencies and tends to wander, but there is a certain strength and character that make it worth checking into. M-D.

Albert Moeschinger (1897–   ) Switzerland
Concerto II Op.23 (Schott 3272 1933) 50pp. Allegro scherzando; Langsam; Allegro con spirito. Neoclassic, highly chromatic, very few cadences, thorny. M-D to D.
Concerto IV Op.96 1953 (Edition Modern 1219) 16 min.

Richard Mohaupt (1904–1957) Germany
Concerto 1938 revised 1942 (AMP 1952) 22 min. Largo–Allegro; Lento; Allegro molto; Vivace. Strong rhythms; thematic development lacking. M-D.

Robert Moevs (1920–   ) USA
"Moevs has been influenced by the theoretical ideas of Pierre Boulez and describes his compositional procedure as 'systematic chromaticism,' a modification of serial techniques in which a pitch collection is systematically exhausted but not in a rigidly ordered way" (DCM, 493).
Concerto 1960 (MS available from composer: Blackwell's Mills, Belle Mead, N.J. 08502). For piano, percussion, and orchestra. 19 min.

Philipp Mohler (1908–   ) Germany
Konzert Op.16 (Müller 676) 23 min.

Henry Mollicone (–   ) USA
Fantasy 1967 (ACA). For piano and chamber orchestra. 10 min. Neoclassic, freely tonal, bell-like sonorities, varied sections and moods, colorful use of Chinese temple blocks, *ppp* closing. M-D.

Spartaco V. Monello (1909–   ) USA
Concerto (Fl). For piano and string orchestra.

Georg Matthias Monn (1717–1750) Austria
Monn's works marked a transition from the classic to the modern instrumental style along the lines perfected by Johann Stamitz.
Concerto G (DTOe 19, 2, 1912). An arrangement of a cello concerto; thus it has an origin similar to those of the concertos of J. S. Bach. Int.
Concerto (Fl).

Marius Monnikendam (1896–1977) The Netherlands
Concerto 1973–74 (Donemus) 18 min. Three movements (FSF). Expanded tonalities including polytonality. M-D.

David Monrad Johansen (1888–   ) Norway
Concerto E♭ Op.29 1955 (NK) 30 min.

Nicola A. Montani (1880–1948) USA
Fantasia (Ric 1956).

Xavier Montsalvatge (1912–   ) Spain
Concerto Breve 1952 (PIC) 24 min. Energico: driving parallel chords, varied figuration and tempi. Andante rubato (cadenza): free section leads to toccata-like chords. Vivo: exciting closing. One large movement divided into sections. MC harmonic language; eclectic; themes varied interestingly. M-D.

Emanuel Moor (1863–1831) Hungary
Concerto I D 1886 (Simrock). Allegro moderato; Molto andante; Finale.
Concerto II c Op.46 1888 (Rozsavölgyi).
Concerto III D♭ Op.57 1906 (K&S) 20 min. Busy figurations, Regerian characteristics. M-D.
Concerto Op.70 1907 (K&S). For piano, violin, cello, and orchestra.
Concerto IV E♭ Op.85 1911 (Sal) 59pp. Allegro moderato; Adagio; Allegro moderato. Has a formal element related to the Liszt *Concerto* I E♭. M-D.
Concertstück Op.88 1908 (Sal) 31pp.

Oleg A. Moralev (1922–   ) USSR
Concerto (USSR 1968) 90pp. Three movements (FSF). Freely tonal. M-D.

Oskar Morawetz (1917–   ) Canada, born Czechoslovakia
In his early works Morawetz favored a neoromantic style, but lately has adopted a more progressive style of writing, without, however, identifying himself with any single school of contemporary composition.
Concerto I 1963 (Leeds) 19 min. One movement (Allegro moderato; Adagio; Allegro) written in an expanded diatonic idiom with the neoclassic spirit. Smooth idiomatic piano writing, no virtuosic excitement, well crafted. M-D.

Makoto Moroi (1930–   ) Japan
Moroi teaches at Osaka University of the Arts.
Concerto I 1966 (Nippon Hōsō Kyōkai).

Henrique de Curitiba Morozowicz (1934–   ) Brazil
Since 1976 Morozowicz has been coordinator of the artistic curriculum of the Federal University of Paraná.
Divertimento 1969 (MS available from composer: R. José Bruzzamolin, 77 Parque São Lourenco, 80.000 Curitiba [PR] Brazil) 12 min.

Harold Morris (1890–1964) USA
Concerto 1927 (Birchard 1932) 27 min. Allegro moderato, marcato: free version

of SA. Variations on the American Negro Pilgrim Song ("I'm a Poor Way-farin' Stranger"): jazz and blues techniques used. Rondo—Allegro giusto: includes part of the opening movement; large orchestra. Distinguished by a somber, evocative, quasi-Impressionistic style, with an American sentiment in the melodies and rhythms; Scriabin influence. M-D.

Virgilio Mortari (1902–   ) Italy
Concerto 1961 (EC 7283) 15 min. Allegro; Romanza; Variationi.
Concerto a Due (EC 8939). For piano, violin, and orchestra.
La Padovana (Zanibon 5418). For piano and strings.

Finn Mortensen (1922–   ) Norway
"Bach, Bruckner, and Stockhausen have been the most important composers in Mortensen's development" (DCM, 498).
Concerto Op.25 1963 (NMO) 10 min. Performance directions in English. Palm and forearm clusters, pointillistic, dynamic extremes, expressionistic, cadenza. Written in that "international style" of the 1960s that sounds like so many other works composed at that time. M-D.
Fantasy Op.27 1965–66 (NMO) 13 min.

Ignaz Moscheles (1794–1870) Bohemia
Moscheles was Mendelssohn's teacher and among the first to perform Beethoven's sonatas in public. Moscheles wrote eight concertos for piano and orchestra and was one of the finest musicians of his era.
Concerto I F Op.45 1819? (Boosey & Sons 1860; Schott 549) 33pp. Allegro maestoso; Adagio; Rondo—Allegro vivace. Brilliant figuration that is constantly turning and moving to new (related) keys. Charming. M-D.
Concerto II E♭ Op.56 (Steiner 1824) 45pp. Passionate recitative in the middle movement is highly Romantic in character. M-D.
Concerto III g Op.58 1820–21 (Music Treasure 1971) 67pp. Preface in German and English. Allegro moderato; Adagio; Allegro agitato. This work remained in the repertoire as an important piece for a long time. It was originally issued as Op.60 but most succeeding publications designate it Op.58, and it is known under this opus number today. It is classically conceived throughout and has much to recommend it. M-D.
Concerto IV E Op.64 1823 (Steiner). Allegro maestoso; Adagio; Rondo. Elegant and brilliant, a direct ancestor of Schumann's *Concerto* a. M-D.
Concerto V C Op.87 1826 (Haslinger) 32½ min. Allegro moderato; Adagio non troppo; Allegro vivace. Has the classic format of Beethoven, brilliant passage work like Hummel, and the elegance of early Chopin. Always pleasing and crisply defined; reveals a wide scale of emotions. M-D.
Concerto VI B♭ "Fantastique" Op.90 1833 (Cramer).
Concerto VII c "Pathetique" Op.93 1835–36 (Cramer). Hans Engle, in his *Die Entwicklung des deutschen Klavierkonzert von Mozart bis Liszt*, p.138, praises this work, in which he finds the virtuosic character receding in proportion to content, with Romantic pessimism as well as cyclic references,

which are said to have influenced Liszt. Perhaps Moscheles' best concerto. M-D.

Concerto VIII D "Pastorale" Op.96 1838 (Cramer; Haslinger). Dedicated to Mendelssohn. Represents a village idyll; somewhat feeble. M-D.

Anticipations of Scotland Op.75 (J. B. Cramer 1827) 19pp. A grand fantasia in which are introduced the favorite airs Kelvin Grove, Auld Robin Gray, and Lord Moira's Strathspey.

The Recollections of Ireland Op.69 (J. B. Cramer 1827) 29pp. A grand fantasia in which are introduced the favorite airs, The Groves of Blarney, Garry Owen, and St. Patrick's Day.

Rudolf Moser (1892–1960) Switzerland

Concerto e♭ Op.61 (Steingräber 1935) 28pp. Allegro moderato; Poco sostenuto; Presto. Tonal; post-Brahms idiom. M-D.

Mihaly Mosonyi (1815–1870) Hungary

Mosonyi was largely self-educated. He became well known as a bass player and composer in his homeland. Mosonyi was one of the most important figures in the revival of Hungarian national music and wrote many articles on the subject.

Concerto e 1844 (Karoly—EMB 1966) 19½ min. Allegro moderato; Adagio con moto; Allegro. Three movements played without pause. Themes from the first movement reappear in the last. The finale, a rondo, is more eighteenth-century oriented than the other two. Free-flowing, rhapsodic, appealing, and virtuosic writing. M-D.

Piotr Moss (1949–   ) Poland

Concertino 1973 (AA). For piano and chamber orchestra.

Moritz Moszkowski (1854–1925) Poland

Concerto E Op.59 1898 (CFP 2872; CF; K) 36 min. Moderato; Andante; Scherzo—Vivace; Allegro deciso. A virtuoso kind of salon writing, with fluid melodic lines and exhilarating rhythms, highly pianistic and brilliantly effective. This work was extremely popular in England for many years. It deserves more attention—it is sparkling, witty and often distinguished. Requires facile pianism. M-D.

Diether de la Motte (1928–   ) Germany

Concerto 1965 (Bo&Bo) 18 min.

Georgii A. Mouchel (1909–   ) USSR

Concerto II a (USSR). Andante pesante; Presto energico.

Concerto VI (Sokolov—USSR).

Raymond Moulaert (1875–1962) Belgium

Concerto 1938 (CeBeDeM) 22 min. Franck and Wagner influence, some modal usage. M-D.

Wolfgang A. Mozart (1756–1791) Austria

Mozart was the first great composer of concertos specifically designated for the piano. His body of piano concertos is one of the greatest heritages in all piano literature, an imperishable testimony to a feeling about the world, the times, and style—a feeling that until the last few years was being buried under each succeeding epoch. We are finally realizing the great legacy Mozart left us in these works. Most of his original concertos, including K.175, are more advanced than Haydn's in orchestration, organization, and technical demands. A liquid smoothness of tone and articulation—*jeu perlé*—is required to make his melodies "sing." There are treacherous passages in almost all the concertos, and the transparent texture exposes the least unevenness. It should be remembered when performing Mozart that runs should be played non legato or staccato—legato playing of passages that are not explicitly slurred is incorrect. Mozart made thorough use of the orchestra. Köchel's original numbers (and Einstein's revisions) are used below.

EDITIONS:

Konzerte für ein oder meherer Klaviere und Orchestra mit Kadenzen (Marius Flothuis—Bärenreiter) Neue Mozart Ausgabe, 7 vols. This edition represents the most scholarly and up-to-date thinking.

Vol. 1, V/15/1 (Br 4563) contains the solo concertos K.175 and 238, *Concerto for Three Pianos* K.242, and a later setting of the latter for two pianos K.382. Preface in German.

Vol. 2, V/15/2 (Br 4571) contains K.246, 271, and 365 (316a).

Vol. 3, V/15/3 (Br 4575) contains K.414 (386a), 413 (387a), and 415 (387b).

Vol. 4, V/15/4 (Br 4572) contains K.449, 450, and 451. Preface in German. Autographs for K.449 and 451 are no longer available. They were sent eastward for safety in 1941 and have never been recovered. Secondary sources for K.449 and 451 have been discovered in a set of parts that Nannerl copied from the autographs loaned to her by her brother in May 1784. Some very interesting features found in these copies have been incorporated into this edition. Leopold made some marks in his daughter's copy so this edition throws light on Mozart's Vienna performances as well as his sister's in Salzburg. Superb urtext edition. Also contains three sketches from K.450.

Vol. 5, V/15/5 (Br 4542) contains K.453, 456, and 459.

Vol. 6, V/15/6 (Br 4528) contains K.466, 467, and 482.

Vol. 7, V/15/7 (Br 4519) contains K.488, 491, and 503.

Concertos 17–22 (Dover 1978) in full score, with Mozart's cadenzas for nos. 17–19, from the Br&H (1877–79) complete works edition, 370pp. Contains K.453, 456, 459, 466, 467, and 482.

Concertos 23–27 (Dover 1978) in full score, with Mozart's cadenzas for nos. 23 and 27 and the *Concert Rondo* D, from the Br&H complete works edition. Contains K.488, 491, 503, 537, and 595.

These two collections are reprinted from the old Mozart *Gesamtausgabe* (Collected Edition).

Other editions with arrangement of the accompaniment for second piano:

G. Schirmer: K.175, 238, 242, 246, 271, 413, 414, 415, 449, 450, 451, 453, 456, 459, 466, 467, 482, 488, 491, 503, 537, 595.

Breitkopf & Härtel: K.175, 238, 246, 413, 415, 450, 451, 453, 459, 466, 467, 482, 491, 537, 595.

C. F. Peters: K.175, 238, 271, 413, 414, 415, 449, 450, 453, 456, 459, 466, 467, 482, 488, 491, 503, 537.

International Music Co.: K.271, 414, 449, 450, 453, 456, 466, 503, 595.

Kalmus: K.271, 414, 450, 466, 467, 482, 488, 491, 537.

Kalmus miniature and study scores: K.37, 39, 40, 41, 175, 238, 242, 246, 271, 382, 413, 414, 415, 449, 450, 451, 453, 456, 459, 466, 467, 482, 488, 491, 503, 537, 595.

Broude Brothers, orchestral scores: K.271, 413, 414, 415, 450, 453, 459, 466, 467, 482, 491, 503, 537, 595.

Eulenburg miniature scores: K.271, 450, 453, 459, 466, 467, 482, 488, 491, 503.

Bärenreiter study scores: K.466, 467, 482, 488, 491, 503, 537, 595.

Carl Fischer: K.271, 467, 488, 491, 503.

CADENZAS:

A thorough investigation of the cadenzas available for any given concerto is both an interesting and profitable task and certainly contributes to a better understanding of the work as a whole. This writer also recommends composing your own cadenza(s). It is a humbling but learning experience. Mozart wrote 36 cadenzas for the following concertos: K.175, 271, 382, 414, 415, 449, 450, 451, 453, 456, 459, 488, and 595. There are no original cadenzas for K.37, 39, 41, third movement to 175, 238, 466, 467, 482, 491, 503, and 537.

Thirty-six Original Cadenzas by Mozart (Br&H; K; BB).

Original Cadenzas (Auclert—EMT 1973). Mozart's original cadenzas for the solo piano concertos and the two-piano and three-piano concertos.

The Complete Original Cadenzas by W. A. Mozart for his Solo Piano Concertos with Supplementary Cadenzas by Beethoven and Krauss (Lily Krauss—Belwin-Mills). The Beethoven cadenzas are for K.466.

Anda (Bo&Bo) for K.466.

Badura-Skoda (Br 4464) for K.175, 238, 415, 449, 453, 456, 466, 467, 482, 491, 503, 537, and 595.

Casadesus (IMC) for K.482.

E. Fischer (Schott 4947) for K.365, 453, 466, 482, 491, 503, and 537.

A. Foldes (Br) for K.453, 467, 482, and 503.

M. Flothuis (Br&VP) for K.467, 482, 503, and 537.

L. Godowsky (CF) for K.365.

P. K. Hoffmann, edited by A. H. King (CFP) cadenzas and elaborations for K.467, 482, 488, 491, 503, and 595. From original editions of 1802 and 1803.

W. Kempff (Bo&Bo) for K.246, 466, 467, 482, and 491.

W. Landowska (BB) for K.271, 413, 414, 415, 450, 453, 466, 482, 488, and 537.

N. Magaloff (EC) for K.415, 466, 467, 482, 491, and 503.

F. Mannino (EC) for K.467.

Cadenzas to Eight Concertos (A. E. Mueller [1767–1817]—CFP) for K.456, 459, 466, 482, 488, 491, 503, and 537.

Reinecke (IMC) for K.365 and 466.

A. Rubinstein (Schott) for K.466.

C. Saint-Saëns (Durand) for K.491.

P. Sancan (Durand) for K.466.

C. Schumann (CFP 3629) for K.466, first and third movements.

Eighteen Cadenzas and Four Fermatas (S. Stravinsky—CFP) for K.175, 238, 246, 365, 413, 466, 467, 482, 491, 503, 537, and 595.

H. Zilcher (Verlag von Holm Pälz) for K.467, 488, and 491.

CONCERTOS:

Concertos K.37, 39, 40, and 41 (A. Balsam—OUP 1966) are arrangements made in Salzburg in 1767 by Wolfgang and his father, Leopold, of movements by other composers known to the Mozart family. An introduction by A. Hyatt King explains the background surrounding these works, which were put together for Wolfgang's tours. They are by far the easiest of the concertos and provide excellent preparation for the more mature works.

Concerto F K.37. 15 min. Arrangement of sonata movements by Raupach and Honauer. Allegro: classic figuration, broken chords, triplets. Andante: a short-long figure forms the basic idea; cadenza by editor. Rondo: sparkling, dashing, cadenza by editor, not easy but effective. Int.

Concerto B♭ K.39. 14½ min. Arrangements of sonata movements by Raupach and Schobert. Allegro spiritoso: fine rhythmic interest, Alberti bass, cadenza by editor. Andante: short introductory prelude, effective triplet figuration. Molto allegro: brilliant figuration, cadenza by the editor. Int.

Concerto D K.40. 12½ min. Arrangement of sonata movements by Honauer, Eckart, and C. P. E. Bach. Allegro maestoso: trill important, one cadenza by editor and one by Mozart. Andante: ornate melody over broken-triplet accompaniment. Presto: scalar, broken octaves, based on the C. P. E. Bach movement. Int.

Concerto G K.41. 14½ min. Arrangement of sonata movements by Honauer and Raupach. Allegro: Alberti bass, cadenza by editor. Andante: one of the finest movements in all four of these early concertos. Molto allegro: equal emphasis of hands; cadenza by editor. Int.

Three Concertos D, G, E♭. K.107 (Wollheim—Schott; Hoffmann—Mösler). Available separately for piano and three string parts. Can be performed as piano quartets. After the piano sonatas of J. C. Bach, *Six sonates pour le clavecin ou le piano forte,* Op.5. Written in London or Holland in 1765. Cadenzas by W. Jacobi in the Möseler edition. These are apprentice works.

The slight orchestrations added by Mozart serve only as accompaniments. The solo parts are more or less literal adaptations of Bach's original with the exception of the short cadenzas that need to be added by the performer. No.1 D, 13 min. Allegro; Andante; Tempo di Minuetto. No.2 G, 8 min. Allegro; Allegretto (with 4 variations). No.3 E♭, 9½ min. Allegro; Allegretto (Rondeaux).

See: Niels Krabbe, "Mozart's KV 107 and Johann Christian Bach's opus V," *Dansk aarbog for musikforskning* 6 (1968–72):101–12. In English. Mozart's admiration of J. C. Bach can be seen from both his letters and his music. The earliest purely musical proof of this admiration is K.107, three piano concertos, based on J. C. Bach's Op.5/2, 3, and 4. A comparison between the two shows that the long-held view that Mozart rather mechanically copied the sonata by J. C. Bach could be challenged. Krabbe contends that both bibliographic facts and a direct musical analysis indicate a more reflective attitude of the part of Mozart to his source, the more so since these facts hint that Mozart did not compose his concertos under the direct influence of the encounter with J. C. Bach in London 1764–65, but probably about five years later.

Hans Moldenhauer, "A Newly Found Mozart Autograph: Two Cadenzas to K. 107," JAMS 8 (1955):213–16.

Edwin J. Simon, "Sonata into Concerto: a Study of Mozart's First Seven Concertos," *Acta Musicologia* 31 (1959):170–85.

Theodore Price Walstrum, "The Influence of J. S. Bach on Mozart's Keyboard Concerto Style," Ph.D. diss., Indiana University, 1962, part two of a three-part diss.

Concerto D K.175 1773. Mozart's first attempt at a full-scale keyboard concerto is orchestrated more heavily than his previous works in this form, adding timpani and trumpets. Of all his concertos, it was the greatest popular success throughout Mozart's life. Allegro: dashing; ample display for the soloist; form is held tightly in tow. Andante ma un poco Adagio: lightly scored in contrast to the first movement; built on a sustained melody. Allegro: SA; employs much imitation, fast broken chords, and broken octaves; fiery tunes. Mozart wrote cadenzas for the first and second movements. This enchanting work is unjustly neglected and deserves much more performance. It is a definite "crowd pleaser" (P. Badura-Skoda in the Eulenburg full score). M-D.

Concerto B♭ K.238 1776. Mozart also used this concerto on the road, playing it in Augsburg and Mannheim. Written in a mood of unsophisticated freshness. Allegro aperto: delicate figuration mixed with brilliance, syncopation in the second subject (latter part), precise structure. Andante un poco Adagio: tender thoughts slowly expressed, interesting phrase groupings. Rondo: brisk, fresh episodes; great variety with one idea growing from another. M-D.

Concerto F K.242 1776 (Badura-Skoda—Eulenburg: Full score, includes the original cadenzas; Br&H: contains an alternate arrangement for two pianos). For three pianos and orchestra. This work is related in chamber music style to the concertos of J. C. Bach. Uncomplicated writing for the instruments (especially piano III) and comfortable ensemble throughout. Allegro: the three instruments open in unison, decorate and continue the material as a team, constantly passing the main melodic material to one another. Andante: in delicate and excellent taste if a little too long. Rondeau: a languid minuet; no fast tempi; cadenzas offer the most challenge. The entire work is amiable and pleasing to play but reaches no great heights of inspiration. M-D.

Concerto C K.246 1776 (P. Badura-Skoda—Eulenburg; Steingräber; PWM). Written on a smaller scale than K.238. A delightful work full of inventive and imaginative touches. Prominent and subtly expressive piano part throughout. Allegro: more rhythmic intricacies here than at first meet eye or ear; see the unusual three bars just before the cadenza. Andante: aristocratic and gracefully ornamented. Tempo di menuetto: a rondo on a menuet theme; piano states the theme at each recurrence and orchestra dutifully answers, sometimes with a touch of humor. M-D.

Concerto E♭ K.271 35 min. Mozart's first masterpiece and one of his most startlingly original works. Alfred Einstein compared this "monumental" concerto with Beethoven's "Eroica" *Symphony* for its "originality and boldness." Allegro: opens with a six-bar dialogue between orchestra and soloist, brilliant pianistic writing, cross-hand technique, fast modulations, masterful condensation of themes in the recapitulation, magnificent cadenza. Andantino: c, long and somber, simple short developments and imitations, effective cadenza, imaginative coda in dialogue between soloist and orchestra. Presto: rondo in almost a perpetual motion style, interrupted by a charming Menuetto in place of the third section, which is followed by a cadenza and leads back to the extended opening perpetual motion subject. This is a daring work on a majestic scale. One of the greatest of all the concertos. M-D.

See: Marian W. Corbin, "Aspects of Stylistic Evolution in Two Mozart Concertos: K.271 and 482," MR, 31 (February 1970):1–20.

Concerto E♭ K.365 1779 (CFP; GS; IMC: K; cadenza by R. Casadesus—Sal; B. Bartók—Bartók Archive, for the third movement). For two pianos and orchestra. The two solo parts are evenly balanced, somewhat similar to Mozart's *Sonata* for two pianos, D, K.448, with the same smiling euphony and a wealth of short, pretty tunes. The orchestra has little to do since most of the dueting is between the pianists. Allegro: the two pianos make a strong opening and then decorate and play with the material in leisurely dialogue; stream of melody between the two instruments with sequences and connecting passages. Andante: an expressive unfolding of short melodic materials and then decorations. Rondo: all gaiety and sparkle. Technical demands are comparable to the two-piano sonata K.448. M-D.

Concert Rondo D K.382 1782 (Badura-Skoda—Eulenburg; CFP 893; Br&H;

IMC) 10 min. Composed as a new finale for K.175. A *galant* set of simple variations set to a light staccato theme. Seven variations lead to a transition section with a cadenza followed by a short codetta. The final section, Allegretto grazioso, restates the original theme and adds a few other simple variations with effective acciaccaturas. A striking climax with a coda ends this "applause catcher." Int. to M-D.

Concert Rondo A K.386 1782 (reconstructed by P. Badura-Skoda, C. Mackerras— Schott 5187; Einstein—UE 10766). A delightful, delicate, and well-formed work; the Badura-Skoda reconstruction seems more convincing. This is believed to be an alternate for the finale of *Concerto* A, K.414, to which it is closely related in style and spirit although the instrumentation is different. K.386 is more subtly developed than its mate but has no cadenza. Int. to M-D.

Concerto F K.413 1782–83 (Hoffmann—Möseler). The first of three concertos (K.413, 414, 415) written with the main purpose of raising subscriptions for their publication. They are very brilliant, pleasing to the ear, and natural, without being empty. K.413 is the brightest and cheeriest and is written on the smallest scale. Allegro: engaging themes, triple meter, brilliant crossed-hand figuration. Larghetto: 4/4, flexible rhythmic treatment of a songlike melody, little orchestral involvement. Tempo di Menuetto: main theme repeated three times, with the material reshuffled on each return. M-D.

Concerto A K.414 1792 (Hoffmann—Möseler). Themes are more attractive in this work than in K.413, and the solo part is handled more individually. Written shortly after the death of J. C. Bach. As a memorial tribute to his departed friend, Mozart based the slow movement on a theme from one of J. C. Bach's orchestral works. Mozart was very fond of this work and often taught it to his pupils. Allegro: tuneful opening, sunny mood, lengthy and well-defined first and second tonal areas, crossed-hand figuration. Andante: the full chords in the piano at the opening are unusual; haunting modulations; main theme is decorated by variations, which sweep the movement along in a stream of fresh invention. Allegretto: the subject of this rondo is a sparkling, playful tune; clever; whimsical and fun. Mozart wrote two cadenzas for each movement. M-D.

Concerto C K.415 1782–83 (Redlich—Eulenburg; Hoffman—Möseler). Larger orchestra than in K.413 and 414. Allegro: most of the brilliance in this concerto is contained in this movement; fugal interplay; daring modulations; march rhythms; shows off the soloist effectively. Andante: ABA; requires a light and easy pace; subsequent embellishment is added when the A section returns. Allegro: jolly tune in 6/8; interrupted twice by adagio sections; bravura passages will capture the layman's applause; finale fade-out is magical. Of all the concertos, K.415 is perhaps the most undervalued by pianists, conductors, and managers. M-D.

Concerto E♭ K.449 1784 (Eulenburg; Hoffmann—Möseler). Described by Mozart as "a concerto of quite another kind" (compared with the three following it), composed for a small orchestra. Allegro vivace: after the long tutti exposition, piano and orchestra proceed hand in hand in a duet of give and take; contrasting moods in themes; many trills; operatic overtones; no clearly defined first ritornello and middle section. Andantino: a calm and distinctly tender song, developed and embellished; the turn is very evident, a large part of the mid-section is transposed from B♭ to A♭. Allegro ma non troppo: most venturesome of the three movements and the crowning glory of the work; lighthearted staccato theme; brilliant contrapuntal integration underscored by contrast of legato and staccato; more difficult than rest of the work; unique among concerto rondos; consistently inspired. M-D.

Concerto B♭ K.450 1784. One of the most difficult and ebullient of the concertos: the first and last movements especially have tricky passage work. In a letter to his father of May 24, 1784, Mozart wrote: "I cannot come to a decision between those two concerto in B♭ and D (K.451). I consider them both to be concertos and concertos that are bound to make the performer sweat. From the point of view of difficulty, the B♭ concerto beats the one in D." Allegro: pianist dominates throughout (as well as in the finale) with every sort of running figure, but the orchestra is not really subordinate but sounds symphonic; winds alternate with strings; piano writing gives a new freedom to the left hand; nothing is developed in the mid-section but the pianist's technique; masterly recapitulation. Andante: a serene melody, two variations, and a coda; ornamental figures in 32nd notes cease to be decorated and are now moving melodies; requires no rubato (can quickly become sentimental). Allegro: a lilting and romping 6/8 theme, more spacious in its invention and bolder than any before; endless surprises in transition; contrast and chromatic manipulation; remains virtuosic to the end. This work will quickly distinguish the real musician from the good technician. M-D to D.

Concerto D K451 1784 (Eulenburg) 24 min. Spontaneous writing that displays orchestral brilliance, with trumpets and timpani, and full pianistic expertise in the first and last movements. This is probably the first Mozart concerto that can be played with a modern concert grand and an orchestra of seventy and still keep its true character. Allegro assai: majestic opening; symphonic style; marchlike character; synthesis and interplay of ideas; solo speaks clearly both through and with the augmented orchestra. Andante: of the Romanza type used in later concertos; a simple rondo; charming orchestration with elegant writing for the wind instruments. Allegro di molto: opened by the orchestra, and not, as usual, by the solo instrument; high-spirited; piano plays a decorated role in *perpetuum mobile*; interesting rhythmic transformations in the coda. Mozart's cadenza for this movement is more satisfying than the one for the first movement. M-D.

Concerto G K.453 1784 (E. and P. Badura-Skoda—Br, study score based on the New Mozart Edition) 31 min. One of the most unusual of the concertos, emotionally searching; exacts an unusual musical intelligence from its performers. Requires only a small orchestra; technical demands are moderate.

Allegro: opens quietly, never attempts to stun with brilliance, exhibits a variety of moods and treatment. Andante: a true, spacious symphonic slow movement in variation form, one of Mozart's most sublime creations; piano and orchestra are treated equally and move through a golden haze, interrupted by the two minore sections from the piano. Allegretto: big, theatrical, and fast; a witty theme is followed by seven variations; a presto buffa operatic finale rounds off the movement. Mozart's cadenzas to the first and second movements are especially effective. This writer also likes the Andor Foldes cadenzas. M-D.

Concerto B♭ K.456 1784 (E. and P. Badura-Skoda—Eulenburg; Cotta'sche; Hamelle) 31 min. This concerto is not very difficult or very showy, but it has many charms. Allegro vivace: opening march rhythm was a favorite of Mozart's; it is freshly developed and at last dismissed with an especially delightful coda. Andante un poco sostenuto: five variations and coda on a plaintive theme g; coda, of haunting beauty, is long enough for a sixth variation; intense poignancy. Allegro vivace: rondo-sonata design; expectedly cheerful until interrupted by a B episode, a magic transition; but we are soon brought back to delightful symmetrical tunes and all ends well. Mozart's cadenzas to the first and second movements are especially satisfying. M-D.

Concerto F K.459 1794 (E. and P. Badura-Skoda—Br; Rehberg—Steingräber) 27 min. A joyous and popular work but it offers little opportunity for soloistic display. It is more chamber-music-oriented. Has no true slow movement. Allegro: cheerful; one long melody holds the movement together; it sometimes reappears in its entirety, sometime in parts, sometimes in small fragments. Allegretto: theme is divided into segments and used for integral development in a binary SA design without a middle section. Allegro: two main subjects and some broad symphonic writing; difficult contrapuntal textures rushing at full speed. This concerto is only for a performer who loves Mozart at least as much as his own prowess in glittering cascades. M-D.

Concerto d K.466 1785 (Gerig; Ric). The best known of Mozart's concertos and the first in a minor key. It contains pathos, broad dynamic range, conflict of mood, and sudden contrasts. Beethoven was fond of this work and composed cadenzas for it, as did Brahms. Increasing emphasis on motivic discourse is found here. Allegro: soft and mysterious opening; accumulates power; pianist enters with a new and contrasting theme, which sets up the struggle between the piano and the orchestral threat of violence; deep bass broken octaves, accompanied by bright, high treble chords, enrich the texture and provide some startling effects; requires precise broken octaves and broken chords. Romance: simple; charming; flows peacefully in the valley between the massive movements on either side of it, except for the agitated minore g section in the middle. Rondo: magnificent and strenuous finale; contains some of Mozart's most enchanting tunes. Figuration makes strong demands on fingers and brain. Other cadenzas by Beethoven (Dob 01205); Flothuis

(B&VP); Doyen (Leduc); R. Casadesus (EV); Beethoven, Brahms, and Reinecke (IMC); Brendel (Dob 01211); Chajes (Transcontinental); Sancan (Durand). M-D.

Concerto C K.467 1785 Perhaps Mozart's happiest and most carefree concerto and surely the most consistently satisfactory. Very elaborate piano part. Allegro maestoso: dominated by march tunes; pianistic bravura in constant interplay with orchestral themes; generates new ideas as it develops. Andante: solo begins, and passes from phrase to unequal phrase with many a mood and many a modulation, yet never with any sudden, dramatic, or momentous change of key, time, or mood; sustained lyricism; unusual scoring. Allegro vivace assai: an adventure in modulation; surprises; happy invention; open and straightforward; the humorous theme is developed in an ingenious way, as in the passage following bar 287, where it appears in a new chromatic garb in a dialogue between the piano's bass and the double reed instruments. Other cadenzas by Casadesus (EV); Flothuis (B&VP); Wührer (Dob 01214). M-D.

Concerto E♭ K.482 1785 35 min. Mozart was writing *The Marriage of Figaro* during this same time, and a *buffo* spirit spilled over into this work. K.482 contains a large number of theatrical themes and a showy part for the soloist. Allegro: grandeur and dignity in the opening gives way to a long movement filled with gracious lyricism; of special interest are the blazing solid chords in both hands that announce the b♭ theme. Andante: one of the most beautiful movements in all concerto literature; three variations; opening theme has a truly Mozartian second strain; especially effective serenade-like section given to the winds; chain trill exploits the piano beautifully; haunting coda. Allegro: lively rondo tunes in 6/8; mild contrasting section in 3/4 in which the woodwind choir affords new delights before the swift close. Demands perfect flexibility, sheer independence of fingers, and a perfect legato technique. Pianist also needs plenty of strength for the music is entirely masculine in treatment and concept. Other cadenzas by Hummel (CFP); Badura-Skoda—(Dob); Casadesus (IMC); Flothuis (B&VP); Britten (Faber). M-D. See: Marin W. Corbin, "Aspects of Stylistic Evolution in Two Mozart Concertos: K.271 and K.482," MR, 31 (February 1970):1–20.

Concerto A K.488 1786 (Beck—Br; Gerig). Gracious and popular. Allegro: relatively simple and unpretentious; presents little technical difficulty; Themes join into a continuous melodic flow. Adagio: a siciliano in 6/8; poignant; profoundly expressive; beautiful instrumentation generously endowed with winds; some passages are presented in skeleton and invite elaboration. Allegro assai: a swift and happy rondo; strong and broad movement; many themes; fleet fingers required for the tricky passage work. Other cadenzas by Godowsky (CF); Casadesus (IMC); Flothuis (B&VP). M-D.

Concerto c K.491 1786 (E. Badura-Skoda—Br 4741a; Boethius Press 1979). The Boethius edition is a facsimile of Mozart's autograph score (now in the Royal College of Music, London) showing his method of working, and incorpo-

rating a number of "second thoughts." Contains an introduction by Denis Matthews. Einstein wrote concerning this work that here Mozart "evidently needed to indulge in an explosion of dark, tragic, passionate emotion." This work is generally considered his most independent and challenging, the most prodigious in this form. Written quickly, some passages in the first movement are merely indicated by a single note to a measure, the actual figures in sixteenths having to be filled in by the soloist. Allegro: strenuous activity; chromatic succession of phrases with upward skips of diminished sevenths; varied treatment of the opening tutti; thematic material rearranged in the development and recapitulation; cadenza presents a lengthy coda that ends pianissimo. Larghetto: rondo with three elegant, childlike themes; in the same simple Romance mood as K.466; independent wind accompaniment. Allegretto: one of Mozart's finest sets of variations; on two subjects, the second of which opens the way for astonishing chromatic development. Brilliant and highly technical piano writing. Other cadenzas by Foldes (Lyche); Brahms (Br&H), in the Collected Edition; Wührer (Dob 01215); Badura-Skoda (Dob); Flothuis (B&VP); Godowsky (CF); Babin (LC). M-D to D.
See: John A. Meyer, "Mozart's *Pathetique* Concerto," MR, 39 (1978): 196–210.
H.F. Redlich, "Mozart's C minor Concerto (K.491)," MR, 9 (1948).

Concerto C K.503 1786 (Beck—Br 4742a; Kerman—Norton Critical Scores). One of the largest, most impressive, and most contrapuntal of the concertos. It has been aptly called "Olympian" and Mozart's "Emperor" concerto. It is broad and ample throughout. Allegro maestoso: achieves majestic proportions through the addition of two new orchestral sections; dwells in broad chord successions and unhurried cadences; contrapuntal display especially obvious in development; clever transitions lead through a number of keys. Larghetto: a serene, reflective aria; ornate decoration in the solo part; binary form with a small transitional section instead of a development section. Allegretto: cheerful and brilliant with much variety of material and exceptional freedom in the rhythmic structure; some of the most interesting material is found in the transitions rather than in the thematic material. Other cadenzas by Badura-Skoda (Dob); Gulda (Dob 01212); Flothuis (B&VP); Hoffmann (Hin).
See: Hans Keller, "K.503: The Unity of Contrasting Themes and Movements," MR 17 (1956): 120–29. An in-depth analysis of the compositional process.

Concerto D K.537 ("Coronation") 1788. Performed by Mozart in Frankfurt during the festivities for the coronation of Leopold II in 1790. The solo part has a limpid beauty and avoids glittering passage work. The piano part was not completely written out by Mozart. Allegro: ceremonious and formalistic opening theme; second theme more lyric; dignified and sonorous throughout; more frolicsome third theme, brought in by the piano, is built around a double dotted-note idea. Larghetto: melody creates its own dreamy atmosphere. Allegro: dance rhythm adds much playful quality, shows off the soloist's delicacy and vigor; brilliant and effective; a happy choice for a festive occasion. Other cadenzas by Gulda (Dob 01213); Wührer (Dob 01216); Flothuis (B&VP).

See: R. G. Reynolds, "K.537: Regression and Progression," MR 35 (1974): 142–48.

Concerto B♭ K.595 1791. Composed at the beginning of Mozart's last year. In an almost chamber music style, it no longer aims at reaching the general public; it has no noisy virtuosity and evokes a gentle and loving atmosphere. Allegro: themes are characteristic and agreeable rather than striking, but as they are developed Mozart's invention takes a firm grip; rhythmic and harmonic subtleties everywhere; solo cadenza followed rapidly by conclusion, which is prolonged by the piano's ending to the first orchestral exposition. Larghetto: rondo form; unpretentious; melodic; increased in beauty as it unfolds; happy conclusion. Allegro: dance character affords soloist opportunity for display of vitality and delicacy; most ideas derived from the main theme; rich in invention; fantasy and improvisation show most clearly in the extended cadenzas. Other cadenzas by Casadesus (Sal).

See: Frank John Adams, Jr., "The Place of the Piano Concerto in the Career of Mozart: Vienna 1782–1786," Ph.D. diss., Harvard University, 1972.

Clarence Adler, "The Piano Concertos of Mozart," MTNA Proceedings 1944, pp.357–61.

Eva and Paul Badura-Skoda, Interpreting Mozart on the Keyboard (New York: St. Martin's Press, 1957). While largely concerned with the piano concertos, this work also contains much that is relevant to the instrument, ornamentation, and style.

Alfred Einstein, Mozart, His Character, His Work (New York: Oxford University Press, 1945).

Denis Forman, Mozart's Concerto Form (New York: Praeger Publishers, 1971).

Cuthbert Girdlestone, Mozart and His Piano Concertos (London: Cassell, 1948).

Dika Golovatchoff, "A Study of Cadenzas to Mozart's Piano Concertos K.466 and K.491," DM document, Indiana University. Demonstrates that the majority of cadenzas written for these two Mozart concertos are stylistically inappropriate. Recommends twentieth-century cadenzas by Brendel, Casadesus, Badura-Skoda, and S. Stravinsky.

Truman Daniel Hayes, "Some Aspects of Mozart's Thematic Unity Based upon a Study of Selected Piano Concerto Allegros," DMA diss., University of Illinois, 1966.

Arthur Hutchings, A Companion to Mozart's Piano Concertos (London: Oxford University Press, 1948).

Robert D. Levin, "Improvisation and Embellishment in Mozart's Piano Concertos," Musical Newsletter, 5/2, (Spring 1975):3–14.

Henry G. Mishkin, "Incomplete Notation in Mozart's Piano Concertos," Musical Quarterly 61 (July 1975):345–59.

Philip Radcliffe, *Mozart Piano Concertos* (Seattle: University of Washington Press, 1978). Uses more description than analysis.

Hans Tischler, *A Structural Analysis of Mozart's Piano Concertos* (Brooklyn, NY: Institute of Medieval Music, 1966). A bar-by-bar analysis.

Robert Muczynski (1929–   ) USA
Muczynski has a fundamentally neoromantic orientation, and he has a penchant for large instrumental forms. He teaches at the University of Arizona in Tucson.
Concerto I Op.7 1954 (SP 1971) 16½ min. Short; full of good themes and interesting rhythms; exploits upper register with octotonic writing; sparse harmony in piano part. Maestoso: imitation between piano and other instruments; first theme is folklike, the second is a mountain air. Allegretto pastorale: minimum orchestra; piano part emphasizes simplicity of the music; limpid; remote quality. Vivace: energetic; clownish eccentricity; terse themes take unexpected directions; rhythms and accents shift and vary; closes in a climax of high spirits. M-D.

Jan Mul (1911–   ) The Netherlands
Concerto 1962 (Donemus). For piano, four-hands and orchestra. 17 min. Reproduced from holograph.
Divertimento (Donemus) 15 min.

Herman Mulder (1894–   ) The Netherlands
Concert Op.37 1943 (Donemus) 30 min.
Concertino Op.131 1964 (Donemus) 28pp.
Concert Op.151 1969 (Donemus). For two pianos and orchestra.

Johann Gottfried Müthel (1728–1788) Germany
Müthel was a North German composer of the *Sturm und Drang* generation and the last pupil of J. S. Bach. He also worked with C. P. E. Bach, who very much influenced his style.
Two Concertos (Robert G. Campbell, "Johann Gottfried Muthel, 1728–1788," Ph.D. diss., Indiana University, 1966). Contains piano concertos in c and d, both published in 1767, as well as a thematic catalogue. The concertos are each in three movements. The keyboard writing is not too far removed from J. S. Bach's, but as a whole, the style is more reminiscent of C. P. E. Bach's concertos. Charles Burney, in 1773, rightly counted these works, so full of novelty, good taste, and grace, among the greatest achievements of the age. M-D.

Joseph Myslivecek (1737–1781) Bohemia
Mozart greatly admired Myslivecek's pianoforte sonatas.
Concerto II F (Fendler—Bo&H) 15 min. Allegro con spirito. Larghetto. Tempo di Menuetto. Would make a good substitute for the well-known Haydn D Concerto, Hob. XVIII/11. Charming early Viennese classic style. Editor has provided a most usable cadenza for the first movement. Int.

N

Nicholas Nabokoff (1903–   ) USA, born Russia
Concerto 1932 (Bo&H) 23 min.

Sulkan Ivanovich Nasidze (1927–   ) USSR
Concerto II 1955–56 (Musika 1964) 86pp. Three movements (FSF). M-D.

Yves Nat (1890–1956) France
Concerto 1953 (EMT 737) 32 min. Allegro molto quasi presto; Adagio (La Valse de la mort); Intermezzo—allegro molto moderato; Vif. Freely tonal. Effective pianism; exploits the instrument beautifully and incorporates a highly successful orchestral part. The two generally compliment each other. Modal; thematic ideas constantly evolve; Spanish influence. M-D.

Tadeusz Natanson (1927–   ) Poland
Concerto I 1956 (PWM) 25 min.
Symphonie Concertante 1961 (PWM) 24 min.

Sergiu Natra (1924–   ) Rumania
"Natra's music has been influenced by jazz, Stravinsky, Hindemith, and the twelve-tone music of Schönberg" (DCM, 507).
Variations 1966 (IMI).

Vaclav Nelhybel (1919–   ) USA, born Czechoslovakia
Concertino (Gen.) 7½ min.
Two movements (Gen). For piano and chamber orchestra. 8½ min.
Passacaglia 1965 (F. Colombo) 5 min. Neoclassic, thin textures, propulsive rhythms. Int. to M-D.
Cantus et Ludus (E. C. Kerby 1973). For piano, 17 wind instruments, string bass, and percussion. 16 min. Reproduced from composer's MS.

Peter Nero (1934–   ) USA
Fantasy and Improvisation "Blue Fantasy" (Chappell) 25 min. Shrewdly contrived to display a steely-fingered bravura technique. Pretentiously juxtaposes "blues" and Rachmaninoff-like materials. M-D.

Robert Nessler (1919–   ) Austria
Kammerkonzert 1962 (Modern 1503). For piano, clarinet, and strings. 20 min.

212

Günter Neubert (1936–) Germany

Concerto Ritmico 1978 (CFP) 23 min. Allegro marcato; Andante negligenti; Allegro risoluto: Expressionistic, strong rhythms, octotonic, flexible meters, glissandi, some experimental notation, clusters, cadenza for piano. Exploits many contemporary pianistic techniques and idioms. D.

Dika Newlin (1923–) USA

Chamber Concerto (ACA). For piano, oboe, cello, and orchestra. 28 min.

Concerto C (ACA) 10 min.

Louise Nguyen Van Ty (1915–) Vietnam

Fêtes du Têt (Lemoine 1954) 30pp. Joyeux Cortège; Offrande devant l'autel des ancêtres; Festin-Echange de Voeux—Année du Dragon; Chant d'Espérance. Colorful, MC, a few oriental sonorities. M-D.

Christoph Nichelmann (1717–1726) Germany

Nichelmann was associated with the musical activities surrounding the court of Frederick the Great and no doubt orchestrated his concertos under C. P. E. Bach's influence.

Clavier Concertos E, A 1758 (Lee—A-R Editions 1977). For keyboard and strings. 113pp. A helpful preface gives a brief biography of Nichelmann and discusses the music. Also includes notes on performance, description of editorial procedures, and critical notes. Concerto E: Allegrissimo; Andante; Vivace. Concerto A: Spirituoso; Adagio; Allegro. Numerous hand-crossings and repeated notes. Strong Baroque influence. The keyboard player is expected to fill a continuo function when not active as a soloist. Delightful writing. M-D.

Concerto A (Bittner—Nag 145 1938). For keyboard and strings. 30pp. Opening movement gives the right hand some fast passage work; the recapitulation opens with the tutti theme immediately taken up by the soloist. The slow movement is of Bachian nobility. Opening theme of Finale has repetitions of short phrases like the old *opera buffa* type of melody, in the style of Pergolesi and Telemann. Int. to M-D.

See: Douglas A. Lee, "Christoph Nichelmann and the Early Clavier Concerto in Berlin," MQ 57 (1971): 636–55.

Riccardo Nielsen (1908–) Italy

Capriccio (Bo&H) 8 min. Neoclassic. M-D.

Walter Niemann (1876–1953) Germany

Concerto C Op.153 (CFP 4477 1941) 19 min. Praeludium: energetic, perpetual motion, cantando second subject. Variationen über ein alt-Holländisches Wiegenlied: theme and six variations; cadenza; quiet closing. Alla Gagliarda: fugal, cadenza passages, short, effective. Int. to M-D.

Serge Nigg (1924–) France

"After an initial interest in twelve-tone techniques, [Nigg] reacted strongly against such abstraction and emphasis on process and turned to a kind of neoromanticism.

Since 1956 he has been experimenting with syntheses of romantic expression and contemporary techniques" (DCM, 512).

Concerto 1954 (Chant du Monde). Molto moderato–più mosso; Andante affetuoso–più lento; Vivo–Presto. Folk-song and Bartók influence; strong lyricism in a post-Bergian idiom pervades the entire work. M-D.

Concerto II (Billaudot) 22 min.

Scènes Concertantes (Jobert 1976). For piano and strings. 22 min. Eight short contrasting movements in an expressionistic style. Piano is used extensively in nos. 1 and 7. M-D to D.

Lazar Nikolav (1922–   ) Bulgaria

Nikolav teaches at the Sofia Conservatory.

Concertino 1964 (Naouka i Izkoustvo) 42pp. Allegretto; Andantino; Allegretto giocoso. Shostakovich influence; contains some clever spots; free use of twelve-tone techniques. M-D.

Tatyana Nikolayeva (1924–   ) USSR

Concerto Op.10 1951 (USSR). Allegro vivace: constant eighth notes, folk-song influence in thematic construction. Second movement: modal ambiguity, jazzlike. Third movement: Romantic gestures; "big" tunes; left hand is underworked; competent but uninspired writing. M-D.

Concerto II Op.32 (Soviet Composer 1976) 100pp. Andante. Moderato assai. Allegro molto. More freely tonal than *Concerto* I but still rather conservative. Colorful sonorities, effective closing. M-D to D.

Janko Nilovic (1941–   ) Yugoslavia

Concerto I 1978 (La Vie d'Artiste) (MS available from composer: 20 Avenue Victor Coupe, 94500 Coeuilly, France).

Bo Nilsson (1937–   ) Sweden

Traceable in Nilsson's music are influences of Stockhausen, Boulez, and Berio, but even when the details reveal influences from other composers his solutions to musical problems are highly personal.

Eurhytmical Voyage 1970 (CFP). For piano, brass, percussion, and tape. 11 min. Lazy and Beautiful; Cool; Die Away. Colorful; Impressionistic tendencies but more expressionistic. M-D.

Joaquìn Nin-Culmell (1908–   ) USA, born Germany

Concerto 1946 (ESC 6968 1958) 20 min. Allegro; Andante; Vivo. Freely tonal, strong melodies, interesting rhythmic usage. Vivo is based on popular children's tune. M-D.

Torsten Nilsson (1920–   ) Sweden

On the Threshold 1975 (ES) "Concerto for piano, wind instruments, and percussion." 25 min.

Marlos Nobre (1939–   ) Brazil

"Nobre's music was first influenced by the *Choros* of Villa-Lobos and by Milhaud.

After 1963 he began using serial techniques, but more in the 'Latin' tradition of Dallapiccola and Berio than in the 'Germanic' tradition of the Viennese School" (DCM, 514).

Concertino Op.1 1959 (Tonos). For piano and string orchestra. 11 min. Pouco animado; Calmo e saudoso; Animado.

Divertimento Op.14 1963 (Seesaw) 13 min. Alegremente; Moderado; Vivo.

Concerto Breve Op.33 1969 (Bo&H) 13 min. Intrada; 6 Variante; Coda.

Jón Nordal (1926–   ) Iceland
Concerto (Iceland Music Information Center).

Pehr Henrik Nordgren (1944–   ) Finland
Concerto Op.23 1975 (Finnish Music Information Center) 29 min. Strong melodies lend themselves to excellent polyphonic treatment; nonfunctional triads in congealed harmony with thick clusters are frequently encountered; tonal centers are present but not obvious. M-D.

Paul Nordoff (1909–1976) USA
Gothic Concerto 1959 (AME) 29 min. Allegro; Scherzo; Largo; Allegro.
Concerto (AME). For piano, violin, and orchestra. 22 min. The Children; The Lovers; The Dancers.

Per Nørgaard (1932–   ) Denmark
Concerto Op.21 (WH) 30 min. Contrapuntal textures, short tonal motives manipulated cleverly, serial influence. M-D.

Alex North (1910–   ) USA
Rhapsody 1939 revised 1956 (North & Son) 23 min. Three movements.

Spencer Norton (1909–   ) USA
Partita for Two Solo Pianos and Orchestra 1950 (AME) 22 min. Sinfonia; Corrente; Sarabande; Gavotte; Air; Toccata.

Ottokar Nováček (1866–1900) USA, born Hungary
Concerto Eroico c Op.8 (WH 1896) 45pp. In one movement with a number of divisions that are linked thematically. Dramatic and threatening opening, clangourous conclusion. Abstruse content. Technically difficult, requiring strong wrists, great finger dexterity, and the mental capacity to sustain an unusual mood through a closely woven score. M-D to D.

Jan Novák (1921–   ) Czechoslovakia
Concerto 1954 (CHF 5087). For two pianos and orchestra.
Concerto (Bo&H) 21 min.

Vítězslav Novák (1870–1949) Czechoslovakia
Concerto e (Melantrich 1949) 27 min. In one movement subdivided into three sections (FSF). Richly arpeggiated and solemnly cadenced in a characteristic virtuoso manner of Central European music. Advanced pianism required. M-D.

Lionel Nowak (1911–   ) USA

Concertino 1944 (CFE) 16 min. March–Interlude–Dance; Romance; Finale.

Chary Nurymov (1941–   ) USSR

Concerto (Muzyka 1977) 68pp. Allegro non troppo; Andante; Allegro con brio. Biting dissonance. Style a combination of Khachaturian and Prokofiev. The pyrotechniques would make this a good piece to observe! M-D to D.

Otmar Nussio (1902–   ) Switzerland, born Italy

Concerto Classico (Carisch 1959). For piano and strings. 16 min. Three movements. Tonal. M-D.

Concerto F (Carisch 1968) 22 min. Toccata; Elegia; Rondo. Freely tonal, neoclassic. Requires a big technique. M-D to D.

Gösta Nystroem (1890–1966) Sweden

Concerto Ricercante 1947 (NMS; Fl). For piano, string orchestra with harp, percussion, and celesta. 24 min. "Primary cells" in the melody and chords constantly return in new patterns; orchestral texture is strikingly tight. M-D.

O

Robert Oboussier (1900–1957) Switzerland
Konzert (Br 2474).

Jana Obrovská (1930–   ) Czechoslovakia
Concerto (Bo&H) 26 min.

John Ogdon (1937–   ) Great Britain
Ogdon is an outstanding pianist.
Concerto I "Concerto of Love" 1966–68 (Chappell) 27 min. Energico: SA,
    marchlike, cadenza for piano and trumpet. Moderato languido: slow; chro-
    matic 3/8 theme; romantic and chromatic; has a c key signature. Presto:
    brilliant and flamboyant toccata with cyclic overtones. The work is tonal,
    forceful, colorful, and eclectic, with fine ideas beautifully worked out. With
    the right performer it can be a dramatic and demonic crowd-pleaser. The
    style is not too far from Samuel Barber. D.

Maurice Ohana (1915–   ) France, born North Africa
Ohana has led French music in new directions. He has used the expanded pos-
sibilities of the percussion and various micro-intervals to particularly good effect.
Tombeau de Claude Debussy 1961 (Amphion). For piano, soprano, zither in 1/3
    tones, and chamber orchestra. 31 min. Hommage; Soleils; Ballade de la
    Grande Guerre; Autres Soleils; Miroir Endormi; Rose des Vents et de la
    Pluie; Envoi. Contains a few fragments from such works of Debussy as the
    Préludes, Etudes, En Blanc et Noir. The three solo parts are used to create
    both mood and color. Contains some unusual sonorities. M-D.

German G. Okunev (1931–1973) USSR
Concerto Op.38 1972 (Soviet Composer). For piano and chamber orchestra. An-
    dantino; Allegretto con moto; Moderato tranquillo. Shostakovitch influence
    combined with a highly refined taste. This work has musical and pianistic
    subtleties not found in many other Russian concertos. It is also rather short.
    M-D.

Arne Oldberg (1874–1962) USA
Symphonic Concerto g Op.17 (Wa Wan 1907; LC) 73pp. Moderato quasi maes-
    toso; Non troppo adagio; Tempo giusto e con brio. Rather Brahmsian but

scholarly; one of the most dignified large American works from this period. M-D.

Variations for Piano, Harp and Orchestra Op.40 (Fl).

Concerto II Op.43 1930 (Fl) 30 min.

Silvio Omizzolo (1906–   ) Italy
Concerto (Zanibon 4853).

Anne-Marie Ørbeck (1911–   ) Norway
Concertino 1938 (NK) 22 min. Four movements.

Leo Ornstein (1892–   ) USA, born Russia
This concerto was written when Ornstein was at the height of his fame as a brilliant young pianist and daring avant-garde composer.

Concerto 1925 (MS in Music Library, Yale University) 35 min. Moderato assai–Allegro con moto; Andante; Allegro. This giant relic is arranged from Ornstein's more conservative sonata for two pianos of 1921. Its modernity is expressed by the absence of key signature and the abundance of metrical shifts. The finale pursues its course in a rapid 5/8. Scored for gigantic orchestra; late-Romantic lushness has similarities to Busoni's 1904 Piano Concerto. Much of the piano writing shows the influence of Rachmaninoff. The primitive Indian music in the third movement seems out of place. D.

Juan Orrego-Salas (1919–   ) USA, born Chile
Concerto Op.28 1950 (PIC; IU) 22 min. Introducción—Allegretto: SA; double exposition is replaced by an imitative dialogue between piano and orchestra. Lento—Coral: ABA; cantabile; orchestral interlude leads directly to the Finale. Allegro Vivace—Fuga: four themes with transitions between various instruments. Neoclassic. M-D.

Concerto a Tre Op.52 1962 (PIC; IU). For piano, violin, cello, and orchestra. Moderato; Lento é libero; Vivo é rigoroso. Textures are kept thin enough for each instrument to play its role effectively in the ensemble. Strong neoclassic orientation. M-D.

Leon Orthel (1905–   ) The Netherlands
Scherzo Op.10 (Donemus) 7 min.

Concertino alla Burla Op.12 1930 (Donemus) 11 min.

Symphony IV Op.32 1949 (Donemus) 23 min.

Hans Osieck (1910–   ) The Netherlands
Concertino I 1937 (Donemus) 15 min.

Concertino II 1950 (Donemus) 17 min.

Concertino III 1971 (Donemus) 13 min.

Concerto 1954 (Donemus) 25 min.

Fantasie on "In een blauw geruiten kiel" 1936 (Donemus) 10 min.

Suite Concertante 1959 (Donemus). For piano, four-hands and orchestra.

Variations on "De bloempjes gingen slapen" 1942 (Donemus) 12 min.

Concerto 1942 (Donemus). For two pianos and orchestra. 15 min.

Slavko Osterc (1895–1941) Yugoslavia

Concerto 1935 (Gerig). For piano and winds. Three movements. Written in a modernistically (for 1935) percussive style, enlivened by asymmetric Balkan rhythms. M-D.

David Ottoson (1892–   ) Sweden

Konsert (STIM) 30 min.

P

Paul Pabst (1854–1879) Germany

Pabst was a pupil of Liszt. He settled in Moscow as a piano teacher at the Conservatory.

Concerto E♭ Op.82 (Senff; LC). Allegro maestoso; Andante cantabile; Allegro assai. A sizzling piano part (especially in the finale) gobbles up the keyboard. Every range of the instrument is brought into play, and a rip-roaring good time (á la Russe) is had by all. M-D to D.

Tadeusz Pachiorkiewicz (1916–   ) Poland
Concerto I 1952 (PWM) 25 min.
Concerto II 1954 (PWM) 27 min.

Henryk Pachulski (1859–1921) Poland
Fantaisie A Op.17 (Jurgenson 1901; IU) 60pp. In three parts: Andante; Scherzo; Finale. In nineteenth-century Romantic-virtuoso tradition. M-D.

Ignaz J. Paderewski (1860–1941) Poland
Concerto a Op.17 1888 (Bo&Bo 13437; Ashdown; Fl) 30 min. Allegro: cadenza based on folk-song influence that is a part of the concerto's initial theme. Romanza: attractive succession of solo passages for violin, cello, and flute, which accompany the piano. Allegro molto vivace: filled with personal melodic and orchestral ideas. M-D.
Fantaisie Polonaise Op.19 1893 (Bo&Bo 14132; GS; CF) 21 min. One movement divided into three large sections. Based on Polish folk songs. Technical demands on the pianist are more spectacular than the concerto. Includes double glissandi, complex textures, and brilliant figuration. D.

Giovanni Paisiello (1740–1816) Italy
Concerto I C (Brugnoli—Ric 1937; Laualdi—Carisch 1948; Fl) 21 min. Allegro; Larghetto; Allegro. This work and *Concerto* II F are light and cheerful and allow the soloist impressive figurations without being too demanding technically and interpretatively. The spirit of Mozart pervades *Concerto* I. Int.
Concerto II F 1770's (Tintore—Ric 130482) 23 min. Allegro; Largo; Allegretto. Filled with typical keyboard figuration of the day, which bounces along and sings in a captivating manner. Written for a Russian grand-duchess who was

an amateur clavichordist, so there is no virtuosity here. Would make an excellent substitute for the Haydn *Concertos* in D and F. Int. to M-D.

Concerto D (Brugnoli—Ric 1937). An excellent introduction to the classical piano concerto. Int. to M-D.

Concerto B♭ (Vitale—EC 1960). For keyboard and strings. 45pp. Text in Italian, French, and English.

Josef Páleniček (1914–   ) Czechoslovakia, born Yugolavia
Páleniček is well known in Europe as a concert pianist.
Concerto I (Artia) 25 min.
Concerto II (Artia) 31 min.
Concerto III (Artia).
All three works are composed in the style of Ravel–Prokofiev and are accessible and bright. They also fit the Soviet model as a virtuoso vehicle. M-D to D.

Selim Palmgren (1878–1951) Finland
Palmgren composed in the tradition of Grieg, Liszt, and Sibelius.
Concerto II Op.33 "The River" (Friedman—WH 1914) 23 min. In one movement. Gives a fine picture of rushing water and the gradual growth of the river during the course of the excellently worked-out program. M-D to D.
Metamorphoses Op.41 Concerto III (WH 1927) 18 min. M-D.
Concertos II and III are somewhat Impressionistic.
Concerto IV Op.85 "April" (GM 1935) 18½ min. M-D.
Concerto V Op.99 (Fazer W 11907-3) 25 min.

Konrad Palubicki (1910–   ) Poland
Concerto IV (AA) 25 min.

Joan Panetti (1941–   ) USA
Concerto (MS available from composer: % School of Music, Yale University) 15 min.

Guido Pannain (1891–   ) Italy
Concerto 1968 (EC 8844) 20 min. Allegro moderato; Assai sostenuto; Allegro molto mosso. Freely tonal; some gestures remind one of the Grieg *Concerto*; brilliant passage work in the last movement. M-D.

Raymond Pannell (1935–   ) Canada
Concerto 1967 (CMC) 20 min. Three movements. Expanded tonal idiom, flexible meters, octotonic, piano cadenza. Requires fluent octave technique. D.

Marcello Panni (1940–   ) Italy
Allegro Brillante 1975 (Studio da Concerto) (SZ) 5 min.

Andrzej Panufnik (1914–   ) Poland
Concerto 1964 recomposed 1972 (Bo&H) 20 min. Molto tranquillo; Molto agitato. First movement is 13 minutes long. Very personal style of atonal writing. Brilliant orchestral palette. Based mainly on major and minor seconds and uses a palindromic form. M-D.

Boris Papandopulo (1906–   ) Yugoslavia, born Germany
Concerto (Jugoslawenska Akademija 1959). For piano and strings. 101pp., full
    score. Allegro con brio; Andantino con moto; Allegretto vivace. Freely tonal,
    neoclassic, fast full chords, octotonic, strong asymetric rhythms, flexible
    meters in finale. M-D.

Jean Papineau-Couture (1916–   ) Canada
Papineau-Couture's style is a combination of the twelve-tone scale and major-
minor tonality.
Concerto Grosso 1943 revised 1955 (CMC) 22 min. Rhythm is an important aspect
    of this neoclassic work. First movement is in SA; second movement is in a
    modified da capo aria form; and the third is a rondo. M-D.
Pièce Concertante I "Repliement" (BMI Canada 1957). For piano and string
    orchestra. 13 min. This miniature concerto is serial with well-contrasted
    dissonant ideas. On p.14, line 4, second bar, the "repliement" (folding back)
    begins—a complete mirror inversion to the end with a few rhythmical
    changes. Material is strong and contrapuntally willed; textures are tight.
    Similar in treatment to the Hindemith *Ludus Tonalis* Praeludium and Post-
    ludium. M-D to D.
Concerto 1968 (MS available from composer: 657 Rockland Ave., Montreal P.Q.
    Canada) 20pp. Influences of Hindemith, Stravinsky, and Varèse (feeling for
    musical space). M-D to D.
Concerto (Berandol) 18 min.

Lajos Papp (1935–   ) Hungary
Dialogues for Piano and Orchestra 1965 (EMB) 12½ min. Expressionistic, un-
    usual sonorities, expanded tonality. M-D.

Pietro Domenico Paradies (1707–1791) Italy
About the middle of the eighteenth century Paradies was one of London's most
popular and sought-after keyboard teachers, and his *Sonate di gravicembalo*, published in 1754 and reprinted many times during the composer's lifetime and
thereafter, have kept his name alive to this day.
Concerto B♭ (Ruf-Schott 5368; Vitale—EC). For keyboard and strings. 12 min.
    Vivace e staccato; Allegro; Adagio; Allegretto. Charming and delightful
    throughout. Students will enjoy performing this work tremendously. Int.

Paul Paray (1886–1979) France
Fantasy 1909 (Jobert) 14 min. One movement. Similar in style to Faure *Ballade*.
    Freely tonal around A, pianistic. M-D.
Fantasy 1923 (Jobert). For piano, winds, and percussion. 13 min.

Gen Parchman (1929–   ) USA
Parchman is a member of the Cincinnati Symphony Orchestra string bass section.
Twelve Variations on an Original Theme 1960 revised 1963 (Seesaw 1971). For
    two pianos and orchestra. 17 min. Adagio molto theme in orchestra; each

variation is in a different tempo and mood; variation 12 is a Finale alla Fugue with cadenza for both pianos; brilliant coda. Octotonic, parallel chords. Freely expanded tonality, neoclassic. Large span required. D.

Concerto 1963 (Seesaw). For piano, four-hands and orchestra. 12½ min. Can also be performed as a concerto for two pianos and orchestra. Allegro con brio; Doppio più Lento: leads to Tempo I; cadenza for both pianists. Freely expanded tonal idiom. Requires expert ensemble experience. M-D.

Concerto III (MS available from composer: 1502 Clovernoll Drive, Cincinnati, Ohio 45231). Three movements. Contemporary-Romantic style. M-D.

Robert Parris (1924–   ) USA

Concerto 1954 (ACA). For piano and strings. 20 min. Allegro; Andante; Rondo. Varied repetition, colorful and sometimes flashy instrumentation, interesting rhythmic patterns. M-D.

Ian H. Parrott (1916–   ) Great Britain

Concerto (Novello) 30 min.

Merab A. Partskhaladze (1924–   ) USSR

Concerto Op.12 (USSR 1957) 29 min. Moderato e molto risoluto; Andante ma non troppo; Allegro vivo. Tonal; virtuosic in spots. M-D to D.

Claude Pascal (1921–   ) France

Concerto for Piano and Chamber Orchestra 1958 (Durand) 18 min. Un peu animé; Doux et calme; Presto. Expanded tonality, neoclassic. M-D to D.

Jean Pasquet (1896–   ) USA

Concertino g (JF 7814 1942) 15 min. Three contrasting movements, cadenza passages, tonal. Int.

Ernst Pauer (1826–1905) Austria

Concerto B♭ (K&S).

Gustaf Paulson (1898–1966) Sweden

Konsert Op.26 (STIM) 25 min.

Konsert II Op.115 (STIM) 20 min.

Emil Paur (1855–1932) Germany

Concerto b♭ 1896 (Fritzsch) 76pp.

Juan Carlos Paz (1901–1972) Argentina

Paz departed from the post-Romantic style of Debussy's time and followed polytonal and neoclassic trends for a while. Later he adopted the twelve-tone system of Schoenberg, and it is this style that his works have exhibited since 1930.

Musica para Piano y Orquesta 1963 (PAU) 15 min. Rondo-like; blurred movement divisions but three movements are suggested. Flexible meters, thin textures, cluster sonorities at conclusion, atonal. Complex textures, awkward intervals, very little virtuosity present. Paz relies heavily on intuition for his choice of musical materials. D.

See: David Henry Sargent, "Juan Carlos Paz, Self-Taught Twelve-Tonalist and Innovative Argentine Composer," DMA diss., University of Illinois, 1975.

Arrigo Pedrollo (1878–1964) Italy

I Castelli di Giulietta e Romeo (Zanibon 4363 1960) 20 min. Based on the tale of Luigi da Porto of Vicenza about the Castles of Montecchio. "This legend, written almost in the form of a Concerto, is purposely developed with great simplicity of expression, without any particular theoretical or formal aims, leaving free scope to sentiments and faithfully reproducing the world of phantasy from which it draws its inspiration" (from the score). Post-Romantic idiom, modal. M-D.

Flor Peeters (1903–   ) Belgium

Concerto Op.74 (MS available from composer: % CFP) 18½ min. Andante energico: brief introduction. Allegro ma non troppo: SA. Arioso: ABA; expressive; coda serves as introduction to the Allegro vivo e fermo: in perpetual motion style, exciting, MC. M-D.

Elis Pehkonen (1942–   ) Great Britain

"Pehkonen has been influenced by Mauricio Kagel, Krzysztof Penderecki, and the writings of R. Murray Schafer; he feels no affinity with serial methods" (DCM, 558).

Concerti with Orchestra 1968 (UE 15375). For piano, instrumental quintet (flute, clarinet, trumpet, violin, cello), percussion, and orchestra. 14 min. "For young players." "The word *concerti* refers to the practice of such composers as Vivaldi and Corelli of writing for alternating groups of soloists" (from score). Requires 50 performers in four separate groups: Group I, orchestra; II, quintet; III, solo piano; IV, percussion. Traditional notation combined with clusters; some improvisation required. Piano provides short, complex cadenzas, which contrast with the other groups. A fine introduction to contemporary techniques for young musicians who have a "feel" for this style. Int. to M-D.

Nikolai Peiko (1916–   ) USSR

Peiko studied with Miaskovsky. He has taught at the Moscow Conservatory since 1944.

Concerto B♮ 1954 (USSR 1967) 71pp. Molto sostenuto: tertian harmony, built on a Lydian variant of B♭ (only one flat in the key signature); freely tonal à la Prokofiev. Andante and Allegro movements are connected with an attacca. Strong materials, well crafted, effective. Piano and orchestra share in discourse. M-D to D.

Willem Pelemans (1901–   ) Belgium

Concerto I (CeBeDeM 1945) 28 min.

Concerto II (CeBeDeM 1950) 32 min.

Barbara Pentland (1912–   ) Canada
"Her music has been influenced by the works of Anton Webern and related developments in postwar Europe" (DCM, 560).
Colony Music 1947 (CMC). For piano and strings. 12 min. Overture; Chorale; Burlesque. Serial influence. M-D.
Concerto 1956 (BMI Canada). For piano and strings. 15 min. Three movements (FSF). Twelve-tone; transparent textures; finale most interesting. M-D.

Clermont Pépin (1926–   ) Canada
Concerto I 1946 (MS available from composer: 3450, rue Drummond, appt. 906, Montréal, Québec H3G 1Y2) 20 min. Three movements.
Concerto II g♯ (MS available from composer) 16 min. Four movements. Serial themes but still basically tonal writing. M-D.
Nombres 1962 (MS available from composer). For two pianos and orchestra. Serial.

Ernst Pepping (1901–   ) Germany
Konzert d 1950 (Br 2278) 22 min. Three movements (FSF). Expanded tonal idiom, strong neoclassic tendencies, jazz rhythms. M-D.

Mario Peragallo (1910–   ) Italy
Concerto 1952 (UE 12049) 25 min. Scorrevole: variation form; row appears at opening and is used in toto or partially in each variation; piano has fast repeated notes; chordal accompaniments; diatonic scales; some pointillistic usage; leads without break to Lento: rondo; slow; big orchestral arioso opening; mid-section builds to dramatic climax; well-developed pianistic elements; leads without break to the finale, Allegro: rondo; some tertian sonorities; delightful; dance influence. Dodecaphonic usage disappears in the second and third movements. Atonal; classically derived piano style. D.

Rudolf Perdeck (1925–   ) The Netherlands
Scherzo 1968 (Donemus) 12 min.

Moses Pergament (1893–1977) Sweden, born Finland
Pergament's music contains Jewish and Nordic characteristics: The former are seen in the long melodic arabesques. The latter are best displayed in a late Romantic style with Impressionistic features—a result of Pergament's stay in Paris in the 1920s.
Konsert Op.27 1952 (ES) 27 min.

Julia Perry (1927–   ) USA
Concerto II 1965 (PIC) 14 min. Two movements.

Vincent Persichetti (1915–   ) USA
Persichetti's music is mainly homophonic with a strong, freely tonal base. His style displays a vertical progression of harmonies rather than the interplay of contrapuntal line. Persichetti is an outstanding pianist and knows how to write effectively for the piano.

Concertino Op.16 1941 (EV) 9 min. One movement. Neoclassic, spiced with dissonant counterpoint, superb craft, brilliant conclusion. M-D.

Concerto Op.90 1962 (EV; Fl) 27 min. Allegro non troppo: SA; motto subject at opening contains the seeds for the harmonic and melodic material of entire work; cyclic idea with every note seemingly radiating from motto subject. Andante sostenuto: loosely organized variations built on a harmonic scheme. Allegro vivace: freely sectional. Expanded tonality; many embellishments and figurations; rhythmic shifts add interest; alternating hand figures. Cadenzas in the outer movements require the most virtuoso technique. D.

Pierre Petit (1922–   ) France
Concertino (Baron)
Concerto (Sal) 32 min.

Goffredo Petrassi (1904–   ) Italy
Concerto 1936 (Scarpini—Ric; SZ 4193) 25 min. Non molto mosso, ma energico; Arietta con variazioni; Rondo. Displays enormous vitality in its driving rhythms and strident dissonances, which alternate with consonant passages. Neoclassic; economy and concentration of ideas. M-D to D.
See: Olga Stone, "Goffredo Petrassi's Concerto for Pianoforte and Orchestra: A Study of Twentieth-Century Neo-Classic Style," MR 39 (August-November, 1978): 240–57.

Romano Pezzati (1939–   ) Italy
Dialoghi 1967 (SZ 6902). For piano, chamber orchestra, and percussion. 10 min. Expressionistic, pointillistic, atonal. M-D.

Johann Michael Pfeiffer (fl.1780) Germany
Concerto G (Steglich—Nag 79 1932). For keyboard and strings. 19pp. Allegro moderato; Adagio; Rondo. A delightful rococo work that most talented teenagers would enjoy. Int.

Hugo Pfister (1914–1969) Switzerland
Tre Pezzi Concertanti (Eulenburg 1972). For piano and chamber orchestra. 36pp. Octavo edition. Neoclassic. M-D.

Hans Pfitzner (1869–1949) Germany
Concerto E♭ Op.31 1922 (Bo&H; Schott) 40 min. Three movements (FSF). Freely tonal; Romantically oriented, with expansive lyricism and chromatic richness; unconventional rhythmic intricacies. Ideas are overworked. M-D.

Burrill Phillips (1907–   ) USA
Phillips "prefers 'hard edge' music, with clear harmonic content, clear lines, incisive rhythms" (DCM, 573).
Concerto 1938–42 (EV) 18 min. Moderato; Lento; Allegro molto.
Triple Concerto 1953 (Fl). For piano, clarinet, viola, and chamber orchestra.

Donald Phillips (1913–   ) Great Britain
Concerto in Jazz (Lawrence Wright 1957) 7½ min. In one movement with three

sections varied in style and rhythm. Requires a fine identity with both jazz and blues style; large span needed. M-D.

Robert Phillips (–   ) USA
Three Pieces (Seesaw 1978). For two pianos and orchestra. I. Poseidon: Andante moves to Allegro moderato; chordal; expanded tonal idiom; much arpeggiation; returns to Andante Tempo I; moving lines (melody) in one piano against triplets in other piano; "watery" figuration in upper register, ends in E♭. This is in reality a concerto for two pianos and orchestra. Second two movements are not (as of August 1980) ready. MC. M-D.

Silvano Picchi (1922–   ) Argentina, born Italy
Concierto 1965 (Angelicum S.C., Alsina 1601, 8° Piso, Buenos Aires, Argentina) 16 min. Two movements.

Giuseppe Piccioli (1905–1961) Italy
Burlesca (Carisch 1937) 8 min. Freely tonal around F, flexible meters, cadenza passages, clever. M-D.
Sinfonietta Concertante D 1947 (UE 11879) 14½ min. Allegro; Andante funebre; Presto. Neoclassic, expanded tonal idiom, octotonic. Requires large span. M-D.
Concerto 1950 (SZ 4660) 18 min. Vivace, alla Rossini; Andantino con semplicità; Rondeau Classique. Neoclassic, thin textures, MC. M-D.

Riccardo Pick-Mangiagalli (1882–1949) Italy
Sortilegi, Poema Sinfonico Op.39 1917 (Ric) 12 min. One large movement. Colorful; brilliant piano writing; requires a large orchestra. "The spirit of sortilege is illustrated by the lambent saltation of igneous instrumental colors" (MSNH, 292). M-D.
Concerto G 1930 (SZ 4264) 23 min. Vivace e con molto slancio; Moderatamente mosso; Rondo—Molto mosso e vivace. Octotonic; mainly uses a Romantic tonal vocabulary; strong rhythms. Well laid-out for the piano. M-D.

Gabriel Pierné (1863–1937) France
Fantaisie-Ballet Op.6 1887 (Leduc 7609) 15 min. Dated, but contains some charming moments; pleasant and entertaining. Int. to M-D.
Concerto c Op.12 1887 (Leduc) 20 min. Allegro; Scherzando; Final—Allegro un poco agitato. Three tuneful and cyclic movements cast in a large scale; broad melodies. The second movement, characterized by genuine Gallic piquancy, requires fleet fingers and a light touch. The outside movements are packed with exuberance and full sonorities. An expansively Romantic work. M-D to D.
Scherzo-Caprice Op.25 (Leduc) 12 min.

Willem Pijper (1894–1947) The Netherlands
Concerto 1927 (OUP; Donemus) 20 min. A one-movement work consisting of four symphonic pieces with piano obbligato separated by three unaccompanied piano solo sections. The opening germ-cell chord contains the basis

of the material used throughout this work. Shows influences of Debussy and Stravinsky mixed with dissonance and rhythmic sophistication. Orchestration includes a clarinet and saxophone in E♭ and a few unusual percussion instruments. M-D.

Vladimir A. Pikul (1937–   ) USSR
Concerto (Soviet Composer 1975) 65pp. Allegro animato; Adagio; Allegro assai. Freely tonal, glissandi, clusters, dramatic gestures. One of the more effective contemporary Russian piano concertos. M-D.

Mario Pilati (1903–1938) Italy
Suite (Ric 1927). For piano and strings. Introduzione; Sarabanda; Minuetto in Rondo; Finale. Written in a neoclassic "olden style." M-D.

Carlo Pinelli (1911–   ) Italy
Concerto (Ric). For piano, viola, and strings. 13 min.

Daniel Pinkham (1923–   ) USA
Concertino A 1950 (Ione) 18 min. Adagio; Intermezzo; Rondino alla burla. Classic form, Impressionistic mood, contemporary vocabulary. M-D.

Alois Piňos (1925–   ) Czechoslovakia
Concerto on BACH 1968 (CHF). For piano, cello, bass clarinet, percussion, and string orchestra.

Lubomir Pipkov (1904–   ) Bulgaria
Concerto Op.48 1954 (Naouka i Izkustvo) 92pp. Allegro molto; Largo; Allegro molto. Freely tonal, neoclassic tendencies mixed with nationalistic characteristics. M-D.

Aleksandr I. Pirumov (1930–   ) USSR
Concerto-Variations (Soviet Composer 1973) 47pp. Introduction and theme followed by 18 variations (var. 18 is the expanded coda). Freely tonal; brilliant and effective. M-D.

Walter Piston (1894–1976) USA
Concertino 1937 (AMP). For piano and chamber orchestra. 14 min. In one movement, three sections. A sparsely linear, harmonically astringent example of Piston's admirably consistent neoclassicism. The brilliant but substantial piano part dominates throughout. " 'An adventure of a musical idea,' as [Piston] characterized it in his introductory speech" (MSNH, 649).
Concerto for Two Pianos and Orchestra 1964 (AMP; Fl) 19 min. Allegro non troppo; Adagio; Con spirito. Displays a highly disciplined technique in harmony, counterpoint, and orchestration; musical ideas are cleverly manipulated and developed; freely dissonant; thin textures; much octotonic usage. M-D.

Thomas B. Pitfield (1903–   ) Great Britain
Concerto I (Hin) 24 min.
Concerto II "The Student" (Hin 715 1960) 12 min. Dance-Prologue: parallel

chords, octotonic, jestful. Interlude on White Keys: perpetual-motion style with an Andante teneramente e flessible mid-section; glissando ending. Air and Variations (The Oak and the Ash): three variations, chordal, effective. An MC, brilliant solo piano part but not especially difficult. A fine concerto for a talented high school student. Int.

Johann Peter Pixis (1788–1874) Germany
Pixis revels in Romantic orchestral sonorities in his early concertos, while his later ones (e.g., Op.100 C, written before 1830) display forceful pianistic virtuosity in passages and chordal work with strong Weber influence.
Grandes Variations sur un Thême favori de l'opéra du Barbiero de Seville de Rossini Op.36 (LC) 21pp.
Rondo Brillant Op.61 (LC) 24pp.
Introduction and Grand Rondeau Hongrois Op.64 (LC) 28pp.
Grandes Variations Militaires Op.66 (LC). For two pianos and orchestra. 13pp.
Concertino Op.68 (LC) 29pp. Allegro moderato; Adagio sostenuto con espressione. Rondo. M-D.
Grand Concerto C Op.100 (Haslinger 183?; NYPL; LC) 42pp. Allegro moderato; Adagio; Rondo. Displays good craftsmanship. Attractive melodies and fluent pianism. M-D.
Les Trois Clochettes, Rondo Brillant Op.120 (LC) 26pp.
Fantaisie Militaire Op.121 (LC) 21pp.

Ildebrando Pizzetti (1880–1968) Italy
Canti Della Stagione Alta (Concerto) 1930 (Ric 122911) 30 min. Mosso e fervente, ma largamente spaziato; Adagio; Rondo—Allegro. Post-Romantic harmonies and melodies; dramatic pianistic gestures. Fastidious craftsmanship. A few neoclassic characteristics are interspersed (thin textures, octotonic writing). M-D to D.

P. Plakidis (–   ) USSR
Music for Piano, Percussion and String Orchestra (Soviet Composer 1972) 39pp., miniature score. Opens with a piano cadenza that exploits lower register; flexible meters; chromatic; Piano has other cadenzalike sections, moves over keyboard, is treated as solo instrument throughout. M-D.
Concerto (USSR 1979).

Giovanni Platti (ca.1700–1762) Italy
Concerto I G (Torrefranca—Carisch; Fl). For keyboard and strings. 16 min. Three movements (FSF). *Galant* melodies, some counterpoint, conventional harmonies. A fine example of Italian concerto style from the first half of the Classical period. Int. to M-D.
Concerto II c (Carisch; Fl). For keyboard and strings. 16 min. Andantino molto mosso; Adagio; Allegro. Very expressive first two movements. Int. to M-D.

Ignace J. Pleyel (1757–1831) France
Symphonie Concertante II F (Oubradous—EMT 703 1972). For piano, violin, and

orchestra. Allegro; Allegro moderato (Tempo di Minuetto). The subjects are facile, constantly unfolding, and well calculated to display the solo instruments. M-D.

Petr Petrovich Podkovyrov (1910–   ) USSR
Concerto (USSR 1979).

František Xaver Pokorný (1729–1804) Czechoslovakia
Concerto F (Benker—Br&H 3866 1963) 13pp.

Valerie L. Poliakov (1913–1970) USSR
Concerto (USSR 1958) 115pp. Three movements (FSF). Tonal. M-D.

Manuel M. Ponce (1886–1948) Mexico
Balada Mexicana (PIC).
Concerto I (PIC) 20 min. Completed by Ruth Schoental.
Concerto II (Concierto Romantico) (PIC) 19 min.

Luctor Ponse (1914–   ) The Netherlands, born Switzerland
Divertissiment Op.13B 1946 (Donemus). For two pianos and orchestra. 18 min.
Concerto Op.17 1955 (Donemus) 31 min.
Concerto Op.33 1962 (Donemus). For two pianos and orchestra. 24 min.

Marcel Poot (1901–   ) Belgium
Poot's style is full of facile lyricism, naturalness, and spontaneity. His strong rhythmic usage is sometimes reminiscent of Prokofiev and Roussel.
Rondo (ESC 1928) 8 min. Tonal, parallel chords, neoclassic. M-D.
Musiquette (ESC 1930) 5 min. Tonal, neoclassic. M-D.
Légende Epique 1938 (ESC 5905) 12 min. One movement, sectional. Colorful; Impressionistic tendencies. M-D.
Concerto 1960 (ESC) 24 min. Allegro vivace con brio; Andante funerale; Allegro scherzando. Early twentieth-century techniques; effective piano writing. M-D.
Concerto Grosso 1969 (CeBeDeM). For piano quartet and orchestra.
Concerto II 1975 (H. Elkan).

Ennio Porrino (1910–1959) Italy
Sonata Drammatica d Op.35 1947 (SZ 4760) 18 min. One large movement, contrasting sections. Large cadenza; freely tonal; built on a post-Brahms idiom. M-D.

Quincy Porter (1897–1966) USA
Porter's musical language has strong elements of neoclassicism, with a preference for smaller performance groups. His writing exhibits a high degree of technical finish, coupled with a transparent harmonic and contrapuntal texture and expressive and lyrical musicality. His harmonic language tends to be diatonic or modal, yet retains its individuality.
Concerto Concertante for Two Pianos and Orchestra (ACA 1953) 19 min. A neoclassic one-movement work with the following tempo markings for the var-

ious sections: Lento; Poco allegro; Lento; Allegro; Lento; Allegro. A series of motives are used in various disguises throughout with alternations of lyrical and energetic sections. The two solo pianos are well integrated into the total orchestration. M-D.

Hans Poser (1917–1970) Germany

Concertino Op.19 (F. Colombo). For piano, trumpet, string orchestra, and percussion. 17 min.

Francis Poulenc (1899–1963) France

In his earlier writing, Poulenc indulged in a tongue-in-cheek style that was calculated to appeal to chic audiences wishing only to be amused. The irony and mockery were never completely abandoned, but by the 1930s Poulenc's work began to take on more serious aspects, and such characteristics as poetic and lyrical expressiveness, religious spirituality, and a sense of tragedy became evident in his writing. Poulenc was a member of the French group of composers known as "Les Six," and his writing, with its elegance, clarity, charm, and sincerity, may well prove to be the most lasting. Above all, Poulenc had the wisdom not to attempt anything beyond his reach.

Concert Champêtre D 1927–28 (Sal) 27 min. Dedicated to Wanda Landowska and originally written for harpsichord and orchestra. Poulenc also made this version for piano and orchestra. Allegro molto: brilliant and nimble. Andante (Mouvement de Sicilienne): melodic; gently rocking; old French Christmas carol quoted. Presto: requires Scarlattian agility and virtuosity. The spirit of Couperin and Rameau hovers over this piece, which is Poulenc's homage to the glory of aristocratic France in the countryside. Poulenc said he was thinking more of Poussin's landscapes than of Greuze's sheepfolds and that he intended the inscription *Champêtre* ("Rustic") in Diderot's and Rousseau's sense. M-D.

Aubade 1929 (Sal). Choreographic concerto for piano and eighteen instruments. 23pp. 1.Toccata; 2.Récitatif: Les compagnes de Diane; 3.Rondeau: Diane et compagnes; 4.Entrée de Diane; 5.Sortie de Diane; 6.Presto: Toilette de Diane; 7.Récitatif: Introduction à la Variation de Diane; 8.Andante: Variation de Diane; 9.Allegro feroce: Désespoir de Diane; 10.Conclusion: Adieux et départ de Diane. To be played without interruption. Poulenc uses the solo piano in an almost constant series of repartees with the chamber group, often creating a feeling of childlike naiveté through literal, immediate repetition of the work's numerous short motives. Sharp contrast between wit and brilliance in some sections and the Gallic melancholia of others. M-D.

See: Terpander, "Poulenc's Aubade," *The Gramophone* 1935, July, p.58; August, p.100.

Concerto for Two Pianos and Orchestra d 1932 (Sal) 19 min. Allegro ma non troppo; Larghetto; Allegro molto. This work has proved to be one of Poulenc's most durable and popular compositions, for it is written in his most witty and charming style, complete with engaging tunes using two-bar phrases, piquant dissonances, and amusing rhythmic effects. Allegro ma non troppo: two principal themes, the first a staccato four-note phrase introduced after an initial passage in the two pianos, and the second a music-hall type of theme introduced by the woodwinds and horn; some musically sentimental passages; quiet ending. Larghetto: a wistful nursery tune is announced by the first piano and taken up by the second; a climax is reached; ends with a restatement of the initial theme. Allegro molto: music-hall theme that resembles a march; much virtuosity in the solo instruments; ends with a flourish. Poulenc's understanding of the piano is reflected in the writing, for it is always idiomatic and effective, and usually lies easily under the hands. M-D.

Concerto 1949 (Sal) 21 min. Allegretto: SA; gay and brilliant in the tradition of Ravel; opens with the main theme given by the piano, followed by a more lyrical second theme heard in the English horn, accompanied by piano arpeggios. Andante con moto: ABA; principal theme, given in the strings against a salubrious marchlike accompaniment in the horns, opens and completes the movement; melancholy; peaceful. Rondeau à la française: presents the main theme in the piano; later uses the French song "Á la claire fontaine." Throughout, the writing for the piano is not from a virtuoso, soloistic standpoint, but rather as an integrated part of the orchestra; satiric and bright. M-D.

Henri Pousseur (1929–   ) Belgium
Pousseur has for a number of years held a monopoly of militant *avant-gardisme* in Belgium.

Concerto 1949 (Sal). Uses aleatory principles based on an extension of a type of transformation found in Webern's later works. D.

Les Ephemerides d'Icare II 1970 (MCA). For piano and chamber orchestra. 40 min.

Jan Pouwels (1898–   ) The Netherlands
Concerto 1967 (Donemus) 15 min. Three movements.

John Powell (1882–1963) USA
Rhapsodie Nègre 1919 (Hughes—GS; John Powell Foundation, Box 37711, Richmond, VA 23211) 14 min. Strong musical treatment of Negro tunes and rhythms. Brilliant piano writing throughout requires substantial technique. This work enjoyed great popularity during the 1920s and 30s, and, although it may sound a bit old-fashioned now, it is a real piece of Americana and still a dazzler. M-D.

Concerto b♭ Op.13 (John Powell Foundation).

Concerto E Op.23 (John Powell Foundation).

Ettore Pozzoli (1873–1957) Italy
Allegro di Concerto (Ric 129804 1932) 12 min. A one-movement work with

contrasting sections. Written in nineteenth-century style somewhat reminiscent of Saint-Saëns. Effective if somewhat dated. M-D.

Almeida Prado (1943–   ) Brazil

"Brazilian folk music, Villa-Lobos, and the serialism of Schönberg and Webern have been major influences on [Prado's] music" (DCM, 590). Since 1974 Prado has been professor of composition in the Music Department of the Arts Institute of the State University of Campinas, Brazil.

Variacoes sobre um tema do Rio Grande do Norte 1963–64 (Tonos) 20 min.

Exoflora 1974 (Tonos) 15 min.

Aurora 1975 (Tonos) 21 min.

Serge Prokofiev (1891–1953) USSR

The five piano concertos of Prokofiev represent a highly original and significant contribution to the development of the twentieth-century piano concerto. They reveal the essence of his piano style: percussive treatment of the instrument coupled with a great understanding of its lyric, melodic possibilities. Although dissonance is frequently present, the music is always tonal and displays a Classic orderliness. Though an important Soviet musical figure (Nicolas Slonimsky cited his music as "probably the greatest single influence in Soviet music"), Prokofiev was sometimes officially accused of the vices of Modernism and Formalism, notably in the Communist Party Central Committee's resolution of February 10, 1948. Only after his death—he died the same day as Stalin—was his work fully "reinstated" by the party during de-Stalinization in 1958. Both the second and third concertos have carved out a permanent place in the performance and popularity of twentieth-century piano concertos.

Concerto I Db Op.10 1911 (MCA; CFP; K; IMC; USSR) 16 min. This may be the most important single-movement concerto since Liszt's *Concerto* in A. There are numerous themes, but little development, and liberal sprinklings of brilliant and percussive writing for the piano. The work vividly represents Prokofiev's own distinctive piano style, combining the massive texture of chords and octaves with very difficult acrobatic leaps and pearly, etudelike runs. Piano and orchestra are equal partners. A mid-section Andante provides contrasting cantabile with piano decoration. The work concludes with a recapitulation in varied format of earlier material (three themes from the exposition). Most of the elements characteristic of Prokofiev's mature style are present in this early work. M-D to D.

See: M. Montagu-Nathan, "Prokofiev's First Piano Concerto," MT, January 1917, p.12.

Concerto II g Op.16 1913 revised 1923 (Bo&H; Br&H; K; IMC; USSR) 30 min. Andantino: ABA; stormy and Romantic; a large cadenza introduces the reprise; piano delivers theme in octaves; dense orchestration. Scherzo—Vivace: an exciting, furiously dynamic perpetuum mobile (toccata-like); sardonic flavored theme. Intermezzo—Allegro molto: tripartite, grotesque and barbaric march character, clever orchestration. Finale—Allegro tempestuoso: fast and frenzied; SA elements (sectional); Slavic folklike second subject; exaggerated expressiveness; glittering octaves; moves over keyboard with alternating hand technique, bitonal at spots, startling conclusion. The piano part completely dominates this work. D.

Concerto III C Op.26 1917–21 (Bo&H; MCA; IMC; K; USSR) 27 min. This work has won a permanent place in the repertoire of twentieth-century masterpieces. It is one of the most important piano concertos by a twentieth-century composer. Andante–Allegro: modified SA; six themes; piano enters with crashing unison octaves; toccata rhythm grows more violent; a thundering stretto closing; bravura texture is extremely varied, abounding in fine, smooth runs, ringing toccata-like passages, and complex chordal progressions. Tema e Variazioni: theme, five variations, and a coda; theme is naively melodic, graceful and in the spirit of some of the early dance pieces (Gavotte g, Op.12); variation treatment is strikingly imaginative and free; theme is transformed so as to be hardly recognized. Allegro ma non troppo: SA; ceaseless motion prevails; melodic element subordinated to a sharply accented dance rhythm; rhythm and brilliant virtuosity mount to the very end; generating an overwhelming, almost hypnotic, power. The Prokofiev recording of this work should be heard by all who wish to perform it. D.

Concerto IV B♭ Op.53 1931 (MCA; IMC; USSR). For left hand. Written for pianist Paul Wittgenstein, who did not like it and did not play it. It was not performed until September 5, 1956, in Berlin. Vivace: rondo in seven parts; abounds in virtuoso passages. Andante: rondo in five parts; beautiful Romantic lyricism. Moderato–Allegro molto: SA without recapitulation of the second theme; contains an intricate web of themes in the first part of the exposition. Vivace: displays virtuosic treatment throughout. D.

Concerto V G Op.55 1932 (Bo&H; MCA; IMC; USSR) 23 min. Allegro con brio: ternary design; five themes that employ the full length of the keyboard. Moderato ben accentuato: free design incorporating double variations; ironic character; bright and lyrical gavottelike theme. Toccata—Allegro con fuoco: contains two themes from the first movement; motoric; athletic quality of the early Toccata Op.11; full of wide leaps and daring hand-crossings; orchestral sonorities are like the metallic noise of a machine. Larghetto: ternary design; high point of the concerto; effective transitional sections; lullaby quality in main theme. Vivo: in two parts plus a coda, or could be thought of as a SA with the coda replacing the recapitulation; sheer piano acrobatics dominate; coda reminds one of Khachaturian or Tcherepnin. Orchestra and piano are well balanced throughout. D.

See: Fred Sahlmann, "The Piano Concertos of Serge Prokofiev: A Stylistic Study," diss., University of Rochester, Eastman School of Music, 1966.

Nicholas Slonimsky, "Prokofiev," The Book of Modern Composers, ed. David Ewen (New York: Alfred A. Knopf, 1942).

Toma Prošev (1931–   ) Yugoslavia
Concertino 1959 (Naklada Saveza Kompozitora Jugoslavije). For piano and strings. Full score, 48pp. Allegro moderato; Adagio; Allegro. Neoclassic, freely tonal, contemporary Alberti bass, octotonic, charming and attractive. M-D.

Stanislaw Prószyński (1926–   ) Poland
Concerto 1949 (PWM) 20 min.

Domenico Puccini (1771–1815) Italy
This Puccini was the grandfather of the composer of *La Boheme*, Giacomo Puccini.
Concerto B♭ (Abbado—Ric 1962; Fl). For piano and chamber orchestra. 19 min. This work is an example of the piano concerto written outside of Germany and Austria, in the period that followed the French Revolution—a period in which the spotlight tends to fall more usually on Mozart, recently dead, and on the young Beethoven. Allegretto; Adagio; Allegretto non presto. Traditional Classical figures, rhythms, and harmonies put together to make a delightful and charming work. Tasteful cadenza at conclusion of first movement added by the editor. Int. to M-D.

Raoul Pugno (1852–1914) France
Concertstück e (Heugel 1900) 57pp. Lento; Intermède; Finale. Franck-like opening, strong rhythms in last two movements, delightfully pianistic, nineteenth-century oriented. M-D.

Q

Felice Quaranta (1910–) Italy

Capriccio Concertante 1946 (EC 7324). For piano and strings. 12 min. One large movement, contrasting sections. Neoclassic, *ff* closing. M-D.

Concerto (EC 7325 1961). For piano and strings. 15 min. Toccata; Canzone; Capriccio. Neoclassic, freely tonal, interesting use of shifting rhythms, *pp* closing. M-D.

Marcel Quinet (1915–) Belgium

Starting from tonality, Quinet's musical language progressed toward plurimodality and developed into atonal chromaticism, which, however, is not serial. His forms are basically neoclassic. Quinet teaches at the Brussels Conservatory.

Concerto I 1955 (CeBeDeM) 14 min. Allegro moderato; Adagio; Vivo. Technically well crafted; freely atonal. Pianistic writing is only average. M-D.

Concerto II 1964 (CeBeDeM) 19 min. Allegro non troppo; Molto espressivo; Allegremente. More virtuosic pianistic writing than *Concerto* I. Dull compositional treatment. D.

Concerto III 1966 (CeBeDeM). For piano and strings. 13 min. In four short atonal movements. Quieto: long pedal points; fast repeated arpeggios; motives reminiscent of birdcalls; short cadenza leads to second movement: toccata-like; two attractive fast themes, one slower section; Prokofiev-inspired. Molto espressivo: polytonal arpeggios in a cantilena style. Finale: similar to second movement in rhythm, tempo, and mood; brilliant coda. M-D to D.

Concertino (CeBeDeM 1960). For piano and woodwinds.

Dialogues 1975 (CeBeDeM). For two pianos and orchestra. 9 min. Two large sections, atonal. Dialogue between pianos and orchestra and between pianos. M-D.

R

Sergei Rachmaninoff (1873–1943) USA, born Russia

The four piano concertos and *Rhapsody* of Rachmaninoff probably represent the most important body of works for this medium since Brahms. Their appeal continues to grow and *Concerto* c rivals the Tchaikowsky *Concerto* b♭ in popularity.

Concerto I f♯ Op.1 1891 revised 1917 (GS; Bo&H; K; IMC; USSR) 26 min. This work dates from the composer's student days in Moscow. Before leaving Russia in 1917 Rachmaninoff drastically revised the score. He did not add any new material but thoroughly modified structure and orchestration. The work is dedicated to Alexander Siloti, with whom he had studied piano at the Moscow Conservatory. Vivace; Andante; Allegro vivace. Long lyric lines and brilliant piano figuration make for an effective work. The very short Andante produces its main effect through emotional consistency. The large cadenza at the end of the first movement and other technical demands require a first-rate pianist to "bring off" this piece. D.

Concerto II c Op.18 1901 (Bo&H; GS; IMC; K; USSR; CF) 31½ min. This, the most popular of Rachmaninoff's concertos, was dedicated to a Dr. Nicholas Dahl, who treated the composer for melancholia between January and April 1900. A melancholic mood pervades most of this work until the ending, which is a strong affirmation of faith. Moderato; Adagio sostenuto; Allegro scherzando (rondo: ABABAB). Vivid use of Romantic orchestration adds color. Frequent important interludes. A highly effective fugato in the finale includes the piano. Simple rhythmic structure of the whole work helps one grasp its content quickly. Impeccable craftsmanship in every bar. M-D to D.

Concerto III d Op.30 1909 (Bo&H; GS; K; IMC; USSR; CF) 36 min. Dedicated to Josef Hofmann. This is the most complex, difficult, and interesting of the Rachmaninoff concertos. Allegro ma non tanto; Intermezzo—Adagio; Finale—Alla breve. More rhythmic and metric freedom than in *Concerto* II. Departures in form in the first movement from the stereotyped development and recapitulation and the accompanied cadenza add considerable interest. Development and rhythmic variations of material from the first movement appear in the finale. The well-developed orchestration is hardly able to keep pace with some of the dazzling material assigned to the soloist. Virtuosity required. D.

Concerto IV g Op.40 1927 revised 1941 (Schott; GS; USSR) 23 min. Rachmaninoff said of this work, "it's not a concert for piano, but a concerto for piano *and* orchestra," referring to the great amount of time the orchestra plays. Allegro vivace; Largo; Allegro vivace. Darkly Romantic, somewhat fragmentary, typically Rachmaninoff in spirit. Melodic invention is not as strong as in the other concertos. The piano writing continues to be brilliant and idiomatic with many effective features. D.

Rhapsody on a Theme by Paganini Op.43 1934 (Belwin-Mills; Schott; USSR) 22 min. The theme is that of the last of the *Twenty-four Caprices* by Paganini. Short introduction and 24 variations, divided into three groups, corresponding to the three movements of a conventional concerto. The *Dies Irae*, a section of the Catholic Requiem Mass for the Dead, is used in the seventh, tenth, and final variations. In the last one it is mingled with the original theme. After all the dazzling pyrotechniques, the piece ends quietly, tongue-in-cheek. Only for virtuosos. D.

See: W. R. Anderson, *Rachmaninoff's Concerti* (London: Hinrichsen, n.d.).

Richard Coolidge, "Architectonic Technique and Innovation in the Rakhmaninov Piano Concertos," MR 40/3 (August 1979):176–216.

Richard Larson, "The Four Rachmaninoff Piano Concerti," thesis, Catholic University, 1967.

Joachim Raff (1822–1882) Germany

Ode to Spring Op.76 1857 (Schott) 13 min. Larghetto; Presto. This concert piece does not contain a lot of substance but the piano shows off well, and there is some fine thematic material and interesting craftsmanship. M-D.

Concerto c Op.185 1870–73 (K&S) 27 min. Allegro; Andante, quasi larghetto; Allegro. Melody permeates this entire "glittery" work, especially the middle movement with its shades of Schubert leading to a lush climax. The finale contains some unusually piquant themes. Displays some outstanding contrapuntal craftsmanship. M-D.

Suite E♭ Op.200 1975 (K&S) 43 min. Introduction und Fuge; Menuett; Gavotte und Musette; Cavatine; Finale.

Väinö Raito (1891–1945) Finland

Concerto Op.6 1915 (Finnish Music Information Center) 21 min. Three movements (FSF). Romantic-Impressionistic, scintillating instrumental colors. M-D.

Stanojlo Rajicic (1910–   ) Yugoslavia

Concerto III 1950 (Nauchno Delo 1964) 25 min. Allegro; Andante; Presto. Tonal; conservative and restricted writing for the piano. M-D.

Nikolai Rakob (1908–   ) USSR

Concerto I G 1969 (USSR). For piano and strings. 20pp., miniature score.

Concerto II C 1969 published with *Concerto* I, 22pp., miniature score.

Two one-movement works, freely tonal, neoclassic tendencies, more like concertinos, MC. M-D.

Phillip Ramey (1939–   ) USA
Concert Suite 1962 (MS available from composer: 307 East 60th St., New York, NY 10022) 10 min. Six movements.
Concerto I 1969 (MS available from composer) 16 min. Andante con moto; Allegretto. "Extreme polytonality results in complex chord structures, tone clusters, and a tendency toward dissonant polyphony in separate choirs of the orchestra. The music, characterized by violent outbursts in the piano and orchestra, develops variationally from a few motives" (DCM, 603).

Gianni Ramous (1930–   ) Italy
Concerto (SZ 1963) 12 min. Allegro moderato; Lentamente; Allegro vivace. Twelve-tone; strong dissonance; triplets used extensively in opening movement; extensive cadenza in finale. Not the most grateful piano writing. M-D.

Shulamit Ran (1949–   ) USA, born Israel
Capriccio 1963 (CF) 9 min. Lento introduction leads to an Allegro vivace: flexible meters, freely tonal; Lento mid-section is for solo piano; tempo resumes; fluid octave section leads to closing. Excellent writing for a 14-year-old. M-D.
Symphonic Poem 1967 (CF) 20 min. Four movements.
Concert Piece 1970 (TP) 12 min. In one movement. Striking dramatic timbre and gesture; vivid coloristic resources; contains variety and strong determination. M-D.

Bernard Rands (1935–   ) Great Britain
Mésalliance 1971 (UE 15482) 15 min. Performance directions in English and German. Includes an organ in the instrumentation. Proportional rhythmic notation, controlled improvisation, some notation given in number of seconds, pointillistic, changing meters, long pedals, dynamic extremes, clusters. Pianist goes wild at the conclusion! Avant-garde. M-D.

Ture Rangström (1884–1947) Sweden
Ballad (STIM) 17 min.

György Rankin (1907–   ) Hungary
"1514" Fantasy 1962 (EMB) 21 min. After woodcut series by Gyula Derkovits, 1514. Five contrasting movements; expanded tonality. Virtuoso pianism required. D.

Sam Raphling (1910–   ) USA
Concerto I (Belwin-Mills 1946) 10 min. For young pianists. Lively; Somewhat fast; Fast. Int.
Concerto III 1960 (Mercury) 19 min. Expanded tonality, four movements, American idioms. M-D.
Concerto IV (Gen 1947) 16 min. Three movements.
Concerto (Gen 1960). For piano and string orchestra. 20 min. Allegro; Moderately

slow; Lively. Thin textures; expanded tonality; clever syncopations embedded in figurations. M-D.

Dance of Life (Rhapsody) (Gen 1960) 16 min.

Israel (Rhapsody) (Transcontinental 1957) 16 min. Four short contrasting movements. M-D.

Minstrel Rhapsody (Belwin-Mills 1962) 10 min. One movement, several sections.

Remembered Scene (Gen 1967) 8 min.

Kurt Rasch (1902–   ) Germany
Concertino Op.30 (Bo&Bo 1942).

Karol Rathaus (1895–1954) USA, born Poland
Concerto Op.45 1939 (Bo&H) 23½ min. Moderato; Andantino; Allegretto con moto. Highly chromatic in tradition of Austro-Germany post-Romanticism, sumptuous orchestral sonorities, tight textures, idiomatic. Brooding mysticism permeates much of the writing. M-D.

Aleksas-Rimvidas A. Ratsevichius (1935–   ) USSR
Concerto (Soviet Composer 1972). One movement. Freely tonal; cadenza passages. Shows flair for piano writing. M-D.

Einojuhani Rautavaara (1928–   ) Finland
Rautavaara's works reveal not only a discriminating control of technical resources but also the effects of a personal struggle for artistic expression, and in his solutions to the problems of form and in his intelligent organization of symbolistic devices. In spite of Rautavaara's conscious modernism, his output is also marked by adherence to conservative principles, which is reflected in his scores primarily by a cultivated taste.

Concerto Op.45 1969 (Br&H 6659) 20 min. Con grandezza: opens with a solo cadenza; clusters in right hand; continues with sweeping arpeggios as orchestra enters; much dissonance and bitonal writing; some melodic interest. Andante: chorale-inspired; slowly progressing chords; some chromatic glissandi; concluding solo cadenza interspersed with black and white clusters. Molto vivace: toccata-like; motoric; underlayed with a $3 + 2 + 3$ rhythm; percussive, exuberant, and spontaneous. Thoroughly contemporary writing. D.

Matti Rautio (1922–   ) Finland
Concerto 1971 (Finnish Music Information Center) 20 min. Introduzione alla marcia; Threnos: cadenza; Rondo giocoso. Freely tonal; neoclassic. Fluent instrumentation. M-D.

Maurice Ravel (1875–1937) France
The piano music of Ravel is characterized by precise attention to detail, sharp outlines, and clear forms. Ravel, a Classicist with Romantic leanings, extended the pianistic traditions of Franz Liszt. Ravel's influence on the piano writing of Claude Debussy was of major importance.

Concerto G 1931 (Durand; USSR) 21 min. Allegramente: SA. Adagio: ABA. Presto: SA. This work is witty, ironic, and glittering. The outer movements use a great deal of alternating hand technique, are characterized by strong rhythmic patterns, and are technically demanding for the soloist. The Adagio is lyric and melodic. This concerto is a kind of Gallic homage to the jazz spirit, if not to jazz itself. Except for the autumnal middle movement, it is streaked with non-European rhythms and syncopations and owes a great deal to ragtime. Beautifully displayed in this piece is Ravel's thriftiness—his ability to economize means, distill style, and, always, cut down extraneous matter. It is not a note too long. Added-note chords and modal twists add to the harmonic language. Ravel said: "The music of a concerto, in my opinion, should be light-hearted and brilliant, and not aim at profundity or at dramatic effects." The intent of this concerto was to please and amuse. It is no co-incidence that it opens with a whipcrack and ends at frantic speed. The piano writing is close to the refined style of *Le Tombeau de Couperin*. D.

See: Tedd Joselson, "Master Class—Ravel Concerto in G," CK, January 1979, p. 57.

A. Mendel, "Golden-haired Standard, New Ravel Piano Concerto," *Nation*, 28 December 1932, p. 652.

Concerto for the Left Hand D 1931 (Durand; USSR) 18 min. Written for Paul Wittgenstein. Consists of one large elaborate ternary movement with sections of contrasting tempo. Lento–Allegro–Lento. The Allegro section is also built in a ternary design, with a driving 6/8, and jazz influence. The Lento returns (this time in collaboration with the piano), and a cadenza based on the lyrical part of the main theme follows. A final piano and orchestra statement leads to a climax and brings this epic work to a close. One of Ravel's most powerful and dramatic works; contains a curious combination of Hispanic, jazz, and modernist (modal and polytonal) influences; a long way from the Impres-sionistic and neoclassic qualities so frequently associated with Ravel's style. The resources of the hand are greatly taxed. Power and technical dexterity are called for all over the keyboard. Careful balancing of tone (melody and accompaniment in one hand) is a *sine qua non*. D.

Alan Rawsthorne (1905–1971) Great Britain

The music of Rawsthorne is difficult to categorize. With a contemporary tonal instability that borders at times on atonality, it has deep roots in compositional forms of the Baroque, with continuous expansion techniques of the chaconne and concerto grosso structures. Moreover, Rawsthorne often expresses personal emo-tions in a way that could be termed Romantic. He possesses strong craftsmanship combined with a natural affinity for instrumental writing.

Concerto I 1943 (OUP) 19½ min. The writing is highly dissonant throughout. Capriccio: piano runs almost continually over the keyboard with highly ef-fective keyboard writing. Chaconne: a set of variations on an eight-bar theme, each statement being set a half-step higher. Tarantella: brilliant; rapidly shifting key centers; ends with a quiet reference to the opening of the movement. Highly dissonant throughout. Very demanding for the soloist. D.

Concerto II 1951 (OUP) 26 min. Allegro piacevole: modified SA; three main sections; main theme introduced immediately by a solo flute; second section consists of a light scherzando theme, which returns to a recapitulation of the opening section; coda follows. Scherzo—Allegro molto: driving rondo; followed without break by Adagio semplice–Poco allegro: Romantic; entire movement is derived from three phrases stated immediately in the solo bassoon, horn, and flute respectively. Allegro: energetic and lighthearted finale; episodic; built on a folk tune; concludes with a fugato passage that builds to a large climax. A significant work, which demands full maturity of musicality and technique of the performer. M-D to D.

Concerto 1968 (OUP). For two pianos and orchestra. 18 min. Allegro di bravura: opens with bravura passages for the soloist; a 6/8 section follows; a climax introduces another theme, very different in character; decorative passages of embroidery for the soloist follow; 6/8 is reintroduced by the orchestra; reprise of opening; slow, melancholy coda. Adagio: a slow interlude or intermezzo that bridges the way to the last movement, Theme and Variations: contrasting variations with the last one being quick and vigorous; energetic close. M-D.

Fausto Razzi (1932–   ) Italy
Movimento 1963 (SZ). Twelve-tone, pointillistic, dynamic extremes. M-D.

Gardner Read (1913–   ) USA
Music for Piano and Strings Op.45a 1946 (Fl) 21 min. In one movement.

Reginald Redman (1892–1972) Great Britain
Concerto (Hin). For piano and strings. 24 min.

Max Reger (1873–1916) Germany
Although Reger was one of those rare post-Romantic musicians who found polyphony and counterpoint a natural compositional expression, it would be a mistake to regard him as representative of the new Classicism. His "back to Bach" doctrine was strictly from a nineteenth-century viewpoint, with a consequent thickening of texture, a lyricism akin to Brahms, and a chromatic harmony derived from Wagner. He wrote in monumental structures equipped with complex harmony and counterpoint, fussy details, and a general overabundance of notes. Perhaps his best efforts took place when he wrote variations on other composers' themes, for here he could give free vent to all his compositional ingenuity in transforming a basic idea. His idol was J. S. Bach, and like Bach, Reger wrote an enormous quantity of music, much of it for keyboard. He cultivated such eighteenth-century forms as the prelude and fugue, chorale prelude, suite, and toccata. But unlike Bach, Reger wrote too much and was not able to discipline his imagination or cultivate self-criticism. His music speaks most directly to the German temperament.

Concerto f Op.114 1910 (Bo&Bo 17358) 45 min. Allegro moderato: large-scaled; wind instruments present the main theme in an orchestral tutti; the more lyrical second theme material is heard in the following Molto tranquillo section. Largo con gran espressione: piano presents the main thematic material; combines brilliance with poetry. Allegro con spirito: dancelike; develops several themes in fugato style; brilliant coda. Luxuriant Romantic style of high viscosity; involved and difficult writing. Should be attempted only by a pianist possessing strong intellect and technique. D.

Johann Friedrich Reichardt (1752–1814) Germany
Concerto G (Hoffmann—Mösler 1966). For keyboard, violin, and string orchestra. 39pp. Figured bass realized. Allegro e con spirito; Adagio; Allegretto con (3) variazioni. Keyboard and solo violin receive fluid treatment of ideas. Adagio is for solo keyboard and violin. "Tried and true" formulas and figurations continue to work for Reichardt. M-D.

Bernard Reichel (1901–   ) Switzerland
Concertino Op.68 (Br 3146) 19 min.

Aribert Reimann (1936–   ) Germany
Most Americans know Reimann as accompanist for singers such as Dietrich Fischer-Dieskau and Elizabeth Grummer, but he should also be considered one of today's most important composers.
Concerto I 1961 (Ars Viva) 28 min. Twelve contrasting sections that give the appearance of evolving variations; begins and concludes Largo. Twelve-tone influence; cadenza passages; many complex rhythmic ensemble problems. D.
Concerto for Piano and Nineteen Players (Chamber) 1972 (Ars Viva) 20 min. In three contrasting connected movements. Reimann says (in a note on the recording, Wergo WER 60072): "My idea was not to write a piano concerto in the traditional sense but chamber music in which the combination of the 19 instruments with the piano was to change continually." Skillfully structured form; imaginative juxtapositions of sonorities; pointillistic; clear textures. Epigrammatic statements are passed from one instrumental section to another with the piano participating heartily. M-D to D.

Carl Reinecke (1824–1910) Germany
Reinecke was one of Germany's leading musical conservatives in the latter half of the nineteenth century. Mendelssohn and Schumann were the major influences on his writing.
Konzertstück g Op.33 1848 (J. Schuberth 1890) 12 min. Three movements (FSF). M-D.
Concerto I f♯ Op.72 1860 (Br&H) 30 min. Allegro; Adagio; Allegro con brio. The first movement, in free SA design, is finely integrated between piano and orchestra. The glowing Adagio is the most impressive movement, perfect

in style and proportion. This pleasant enough work requires plenty of pianistic color, elegance, and Romantic rhetoric to make it come to life. M-D.

Concerto II e Op.120 1872 (K&S) 23 min. Allegro; Andantino; Allegro brillante. Strong Mendelssohn influence, simple and uncomplicated writing with pretty tunes and fluid piano writing, flavorful finale. A rather charming curiosity. M-D.

Concerto III C Op.144 1877 (K&S) 29 min. Allegro; Largo; Allegro vivace e grazioso.

Concerto IV b Op.254 1901 (Zimmermann) 19 min. Allegro; Adagio; Allegretto. Reinecke, who was a fine teacher, said that this work provided "a suitable introduction to the difficult concertos of recent times." M-D.

Hugo Reinhold (1845–1935) Germany

Suite Eb Op.7 (K&S 1878). For piano and strings. 24 min. Allegro ma non troppo; Tempo di Menuetto; Vivace; Largo; Allegro assai. Strong Liszt influence. M-D.

Franz Reizenstein (1911–1968) Great Britain, born Germany

Reizenstein studied with Hindemith and Vaughan Williams, and the influence of this unusual combination is apparent in his well-made, essentially academic work.

Concerto I G Op.16 1941 (Lengnick 3548) 27 min. Allegro moderato; Molto adagio; Allegro risoluto. Expanded tonality; interval of the fourth is important in the harmony and melodic line; effective pianistic patterns; movements show a Classical balance of design; based on thematic cells of a strongly rhythmic nature. M-D to D.

Concerto II F Op.37 (Lengnick 4108) 26 min. Allegro moderato; Andante tranquillo; Allegro ma non troppo. Uses an extended tonal vocabulary with the interval of the fourth still prominent. Strong pianistic writing; imitative techniques prevalent; virtuosic technique required. D.

Albon L. Repnikov (–   ) USSR

Concertino (USSR 1967) 59pp. Allegro; Moderato; Allegro. Freely tonal, neoclassic, attractive. M-D.

Ottorino Respighi (1879–1936) Italy

Concerto a 1902 (Ric 124792) 21 min. Moderato; Adagio molto; Presto. More virtuosic than the 1925 concerto; big cadenza at end of Presto. Flowing melodies, nineteenth-century harmonies, post-Brahms orientation. M-D to D.

Concerto in Modo Misolidio 1925 (Bo&Bo 19634) 30 min. Concerto in the Mixolydian Mode. A stylized neo-archaic work. Moderato: theme is derived from a Gregorian chant, "Omnes gentes." Lento: permeated with a medieval mysticism; followed immediately by Allegro energico: a passacaglia. M-D.

Toccata 1928 (Messina—Ric 121014) 18 min. Combines the virtuoso style of Liszt with the best of variation and contrapuntal technique. Contrasting moods and sections, cadenzalike passages for piano, imposing climax. M-D.

Rudolph Reti (1885–1957) USA, born Serbia
Concerto (AMP) 30 min.

Hermann Reutter (1900–   ) Germany
Concerto Op.19 1926 (Schott 3369). For piano and chamber orchestra. 22 min. The second movement (Improvisation) consists of a cello theme and variations.
Concerto g Op.62 (Schott) 28 min.
Concerto E♭ Op.63 1949 (Schott). For two pianos and orchestra. 17 min.
Concertino Op.69 (Schott). For piano and strings. 22 min.
Capriccio, Aria und Finale 1962 (Schott 5396) 22 min.

Roger Reynolds (1934–   ) USA
Reynolds is Director of the Center for Music Experiment and Related Research at the University of California, San Diego.
Only Now, and Again (CFP 66720). For piano, (3) percussion, and 20 winds. 11 min. To quote the composer, *"Only Now, And Again* is an expression of my continuing interest in questions of repetitions and identity. How does the 'meaning' of particular materials (of an experience) change when its context alters?" Performers experienced in contemporary techniques should find this work of varied timbres of moderate difficulty.

Josef Rheinberger (1839–1901) Germany
Concerto A♭ Op.94 1876 (Schott) 31 min. Moderato; Adagio patetico; Allegro energico. Masterfully constructed and very satisfying; not a virtuoso vehicle; strong Brahms influence. Requires broad pacing and rich tonal coloring for the most effective performance. Piano and orchestra are beautifully integrated. M-D.

Rhené-Baton (1879–1940) France
Variations sur un mode éolien Op.4 1902 (Durand) 36pp. Twenty contrasting variations; nineteenth-century style. M-D.

Eliane Richepin (–   ) France
Fantaisie (Sal) 12 min.

Franz Xaver Richter (1709–1789) Germany
Concerto e (Höchner—Vieweg 1933). For keyboard and strings. 51pp. Allegro; Pastorale cantabile; Allegro assai. Cadenzas to first and third movements by Hermann Heiss. Flowing figuration. Int.

Marga Richter (1926–   ) USA
Concerto (Belwin-Mills 1955). For piano, violas, cellos, and double basses. 20 min.
Landscapes of the Mind I (Concerto for piano and orchestra) 1973 (CF) 29½ min. One uninterrupted movement divided into two sections. Section 1: twelve subsections melt from one to another, often imperceptibly. Section 2: based on an Indian raga (Marwa). With a short opening statement from the piano,

the first section progresses on a precarious balance between tonality and atonality. After a climax constructed on frenetic Ivesian multilayered sonorities the music drifts peacefully into the second section. A piano cadenza leads to the final climax, which stops at the apex of the excitement. The whole work is a well-crafted blend of realism and transcendentalism, of East and West. It is unconventional but not eccentric, somewhat dissonant but never offensive. Accessible and emotionally appealing. M-D to D.

Hans Richter-Haaser (1912–   ) Germany

Concerto d Op.28 (Eulenberg 1935) 29 min. Gemessen; Schnell; Sehr langsam; Rondo. An extension of the Brahms–Reger tradition, octotonic. Big octave technique required. M-D to D.

Jaroslav Rídký (1897–1956) Czechoslovakia

Konzert Op.46 1953 (Ars Polona 290) 43 min. Moderato assai; Adagio non troppo; Allegro risoluto. Broadly conceived, freely tonal. D.

Wallingford Riegger (1885–1961) USA

Variations for Piano and Orchestra Op.54 (AMP 1954; Fl) 18 min. This work exists in three versions: Op.54 for piano and orchestra; Op.54a for two pianos; Op.54b for two pianos and orchestra. Its lines are etched with clarity and security. Handsome materials and their development in short, concise variations is imbued with a piquancy of musical intelligence and a sure sense of purpose and determination. Contains two cadenzas: a solo cadenza for performance with orchestra, and a double cadenza for performance by two pianos. D.

Duo Op.75 1960 (AMP) 10 min.

Ferdinand Ries (1784–1838) Germany

Ries composed nine piano concertos. He was a student and close friend of Beethoven.

Concerto Op.42 (LC). Allegro con brio; Larghetto; Air Russe—Rondo. M-D.

Concerto III c♯ Op.55 (Musica Obscura; CFP 1308) 30½ min. Composed in London and dedicated to Clementi. Allegro maestoso: well-contrasted ideas; materials manipulated fluidly. Larghetto: dreamy opening; evolves to more assertive passages. Allegretto: rondo; delightful piano subject; excursions away from the subject build in momentum and density; returns to it are always happy. M-D.

Concerto V Op.120 (NYPL; LC). Allegro; Andantino; Rondo. M-D.

Concerto VI Op.123 (LC). Allegro con spirito; Larghetto quasi andante; Introduzione—Adagio maestoso; Rondo. M-D.

Grand Concerto "Les Adieux Londres" Op.132 (LC). Grave–Allegro con moto; Larghetto con moto; Rondo. M-D.

Concerto VIII "Salut au Rhin" Op.151 (LC). Allegro con moto; Larghetto moto; Rondo. M-D.

Concerto IX Op.177 (LC). Allegro; Larghetto con moto; Rondo. M-D.

Carlos Riesco (1925–   ) Chile
Concerto 1961–63 (IEM; IU) 49pp., full score. Three movements (FSF). Freely
    atonal; suggests a kind of dissonant Impressionism. M-D.

Vittorio Rieti (1898–   ) Italy
Concerto I C 1926 (UE 8799) 15 min. Three movements (FSF). Neoclassic, freely
    tonal. M-D.
Concerto II (Gen) 25 min.
Concerto III (Ric 1958) 18 min. Three movements (FSF). Neoclassic, preference
    for secco sonorities. M-D.
Concerto for Two Pianos and Orchestra 1952 (Gen) 17 min. Allegro; Tema con
    Variazioni; Adagio; Finale.
Triple Concerto (Gen 1971). For piano, violin, viola, and orchestra.

Dennis Riley (1943–   ) USA
Concertino 1960–61 (CMP; LC) 7½ min. Prelude; Toccata. Tonal, neoclassic,
    could be handled by a good high school student. Int. to M-D.

Nicolas Rimsky-Korsakov (1844–1908) Russia
Rimsky-Korsakov was a member of the "Mighty Five," a group of nationalistic
Russian composers that included Cui, Balakirev, Borodin, and Mussorgsky. His
music is a bridge between the first generation of Russian musical nationalism and
composers of the early twentieth century. In his writing there is a strong interest
in Russian nationalism, as shown by the frequent use of folk materials and the
very melodic shape and harmonic coloring of the music itself. Rimsky wrote for
orchestra with a superb sense of color and imagination. He was a brilliant teacher,
and numbered among his pupils Stravinsky and Glazunof, but he was not a virtuoso pianist.
Concerto c♯ Op.30 1882 (Bo&H; IMC; Belaieff; USSR) 12 min. This work shows
    a definite Liszt influence both in the piano writing, with the heavy use of
    octaves, and in the use of thematic transformation in the compositional tech-
    nique. In one movement, with the main theme upon which most of the work
    is based stated at the very beginning in the orchestra. Many alternations of
    tempo throughout. The piano writing, aside from some demanding octave
    work, is not technically difficult. An effective work with a brilliant ending
    that would bear an occasional hearing. M-D.
See: Edward Garden, "Three Russian Piano Concertos," M&L 60 (April 1979):
    166–79.

Virgilio Ripa (1897–   ) Italy
Rapsodia Italica (SZ 1961). One large tonal movement. Not great but colorful
    writing; based on nineteenth-century pianistic idiom. M-D.

Milan Ristić (1908–   ) Yugoslavia
Concerto II 1973 (Academie Serbe des Sciences et des Arts) 23 min. Allegro
    assai; Sostenuto; Vivace. Freely tonal, octotonic, dynamic extremes, neo-

classic with nondogmatic applications of serial procedures. Large span required. M-D.

Jean Rivier (1896–   ) France

Concerto I C 1943 (Costallat) 53pp. Quasi marcia; Lento e funebre; Molto vivace. Neoclassic; humorous finale. M-D.

Concert Brève (Noël 6217 1954). For piano and strings. 11 min. Three contrasting movements. Attractive and accessible MC Gallic idiom; fondness for bitonal writing. M-D.

John Donald Robb (1892–   ) USA

Concerto 1951 (MS available from composer: 2819 Ridgecrest Drive, S.E., Albuquerque, NM 87108) 82pp. Fast; Slow; Fast. MC harmonies, clever rhythms, natural flowing flexible meters. Should be investigated. M-D.

George Rochberg (1919–   ) USA

Concert Piece for Two Pianos and Orchestra 1950 (MS available from composer: 285 Aronimink Drive, Newtown Square, PA 19073) 9 min.

Joaquìn Rodrigo (1902–   ) Spain

Concerto "Heroic" 1942 (UME 1957; Fl). Allegro con brio; Scherzo; Largo; Final. Tonal, many octaves and scales, subtle Spanish rhythms, soaring lines. M-D.

Robert Xavier Rodriguez (1946–   ) USA

Rodriguez is head of the Theory-Composition Department at the University of Texas at Dallas.

Concerto III 1973 (MS available from composer) 20 min. One movement. Rough divisions correspond to those of a Classical symphony (Allegro, Scherzo, Adagio, Finale), but lines of separation are disguised by a constant exchange of material between sections. Piano is used in a solo capacity as well as in combination with varying groups of instruments. Atonal, but frequent use is made of harmonies and melodic patterns based on minor seconds, thirds, and sixths—thus giving the feeling that the music lies on the verge of tonality. Twelve-tone influence, complex rhythms, flexible tempi, extensive use of rubato. M-D to D.

Marguerite Roesgen-Champion (1894–   ) France, born Switzerland

Acquarelles (Sal 1929). Prisme; Harmonies; Sérénade. Colorful, Impressionistic. M-D.

Roger-Roger (1911–   ) France

Jazz Concerto I (Sal) 8 min.

Jazz Concerto II "Concerto Romantique" (Sal 1947) 14 min. "Dressed up" or concert jazz, MC. M-D.

Jens Rohwer (1914–   ) Germany

Konzert 1963 (Möseler) 26 min. Lento; Vivo; Lento e vivo contempore. Freely tonal; complex rhythms. M-D to D.

Jean Rollin (1906–   ) France
Concerto 1951 (Sal). For piano and strings. 20 min.

José Rolon (1883–1945) Mexico
Rolon combined Impressionistic techniques with a nationalist esthetic, including use of folk and native Indian melodies.
Concerto Op.42 1935 (EMM 1967; Fl) 83pp. Allegro energico; Poco lento; Allegro con fuoco. Strong Romantic writing coupled with the above characteristics. The writing is novel enough to be exciting but not so unfamiliar in style as to be difficult to follow. Highly pianistic. M-D to D.

Julius Röntgen (1855–1932) The Netherlands
Concerto D Op.18 1880 (Br&H) 24 min. Allegro; Larghetto espressivo; Finale. Many third relationships, thin thematic material, post-Liszt idioms, Brahms influence. Contains some highly interesting piano and orchestra dialogues. M-D.

Robert de Roos (1907–1976) The Netherlands
Concerto 1944 (Donemus) 25 min.

Ned Rorem (1923–   ) USA
Concerto II 1950 (PIC 2106–89 1970; Fl) 18 min. Expanded tonal vocabulary. Somber and steady: free SA design; two contrapuntal subjects work together nicely; tertian sonorities of seventh, ninth, and eleventh chords; strong syncopations; fast octaves; quick double-note figuration in thirds, fourths, and sixths; cadenza begins freely and works into more polyphonic textures. Quiet and sad: extended ternary form; simple lines develop into more complex ones; decorative cadenza. Real fast!: free rondo form plus coda; jazz influence; widely spaced figuration; large span required. D.
Concerto in Six Movements (Bo&H 1969) 26 min. "Each of the six sections is based on the same material, the kernel planted by the soloist during the first two measures of the entire work. As to whether this material is developed serially, it may be, but I would be the last to declare it" (Ned Rorem, in the brochure "New Rorem," Bo&H, May 1978, p.5. 1. Strands: to be played by right hand alone; spun-out melodies move over entire keyboard; moves directly to 2. Fives: vicious; most of the solo material is grouped into quintuplets; semi-molto perpetuoso writing. 3. Whispers: Prestissimo; dashing figuration is interspersed with contrasting sonorities. 4. Sighs: slow; quiet beginning; pedal tone D holds mid-section together while piano partakes of ornamental flourishes. 5. Lava: stagnant; murky orchestral color provides contrast to brittle piano spurts; leads directly to 6. Sparks: Very fast; plenty of keyboard fireworks; dissonant chordal jabs; brief cadenzalike section; powerful conclusion. Orchestral part arranged for second piano is very difficult. In spite of a great deal of color in the work, it is mainly a lyrical piece. D.

Hilding Rosenberg (1892–1962) Sweden
Rosenberg's style is linear, as often reflected in long, arabesque-like cantilenas, in which Gregorian influence is unmistakable. The rhythmic intensity is striking, especially in his later works.
Five Pieces 1933–62 (ES) 12 min.
Concerto 1950 (NMS) 31 min. Three movements (FSF). Expanded tonality, twelve-tone influence. M-D.
Concerto II 1949 (GM) 27 min.

Albrecht Rosenstengel (1912–   ) Germany
Concertino 1958 (Br&H). For piano duet, percussion, and strings. 6 min. One movement. Neoclassic, tonal. Int.

Manuel Rosenthal (1904–   ) France
Concerto (Jobert) 27 min.

Norbert Rosseau (1907–   ) Belgium
Concertino Op.85 1963 (CeBeDeM). For piano and strings. 13 min. Serial influence, expressionistic, traditional forms. M-D to D.

Frederic van Rossum (1939–   ) Belgium
Symphonie Concertante Op.11 1967 (CeBeDeM). For piano, horn, percussion, and orchestra. 22 min. Allegro: somber; poignant yet enthusiastic and expressive; explosive sonorities. Adagio: restless; tense; sustained development. Vivace: dispels any melancholic feelings; displays an exuberant rush dominated by a zestful rhythm. Piano part is treated percussively throughout the entire work. M-D.
Concerto Op.30 1975 (CeBeDeM) 28 min.

Nino Rota (1911–1979) Italy
Fantasia Sopra 12 Note del "Don Giovanni" 1971 (Carisch 21872) 32pp. One movement, contrasting sections. The twelve note "theme" permeates all aspects of the work. MC, bitonal implications, *ppp* ending. M-D.

Martin Almar Röttgering (1926–   ) The Netherlands
Concerto (Donemus 1972) study score, 85pp. Freely tonal; no movement division. M-D.

Albert Roussel (1869–1937) France
Concerto C Op.36 1927 (Durand) 15 min. One of the piano's main roles is to define and highlight the rhythmic structure of the piece. Allegro molto: propulsive. Adagio: contemplatively somber, dirgelike. Allegro con spirito: a precipitate rondo with variations. The piano part is treated more like a piano obbligato, like a coloristic element rather than a solo instrument. M-D.

Howard Rovics (1936–   ) USA
Concerto 1960 (ACA) 25 min.

Poul Rovsing Olsen (1922–   ) Denmark
Concerto Op.31 1954 (Dan Fog 1970) 26 min. Maestoso; Larghetto; Allegro.
Freely tonal; melody is paramount, decorated and supported with biting
dissonance; fluid figurations; firm tonal C ending. M-D.

Albert Rozin (1906–   ) USA, born Russia
Little Concerto (Brodt) 17pp. Three contrasted movements of consonant charm
and just enough display. Cadenzalike arpeggiated figuration. Easy to Int.

Miklós Rózsa (1907–   ) USA, born Hungary
Spellbound Concerto 1945 (Chappell) 10 min. A well-made synthesis of the main
ingredients of a film score. M-D.
Konzert Op.31 1965–6 (Br&H 6530) 30 min. Three movements (FSF). Expanded
tonality; vibrant with colorful Lisztian pianism; sweeping, extravagant gestures; saturated with euphonious dissonance and vitalized by explosively
asymmetrical rhythms. The Vigoroso (Finale) contains a set of seven variations plus a brilliant coda. D.

Edmund Rubbra (1901–   ) Great Britain
Rubbra's music is imbued with serenity and strength; it is extremely listenable
and seldom reaches a high level of dissonance. Emphasis is on organic develop-
ment of the basic material in terms of textural variety and thematic growth.
Rubbra's procedures are basically polyphonic, and his themes are usually long
and supple.
Sinfonia Concertante Op.38 1936 revised 1943 (UE) 28 min. Fantasia; Saltarella;
Prelude and Fugue. Tonal; keeps the pianist busy; varied figurations. Large
span required. M-D.
Concerto G Op.85 1956 (Lengnick) 25 min. Corymbus; Dialogue; Danza alla
Rondo. Virtuoso writing throughout; freely tonal; carefully controlled Clas-
sical forms with new personalities; colorful. D.

Anton Rubinstein (1829–1894) Russia
Concerto I E Op.25 early 1850s (CFP; Fl) 39 min. Moderato: overly long (18½
min.); predictable ideas. Andante con moto: piano, horn, and strings exchange melancholy Chopinesque figurations. Con moto: virtuoso display
interspersed with some tuneful moments. Strong octave technique required.
M-D.
Concerto II F Op.35 (Cranz) 30 min. Allegro vivace assai; Adagio non troppo;
Moderato.
Concerto III G Op.45 1856 (Bo&Bo; CF) 35 min. Based on a program describing
a dream in which the instruments are assembled in a temple and subject the
piano to an examination. Discouraged, the latter grows arrogant, sets itself
up as an orchestra all by itself, and is duly thrown out of the temple. It is a
work of great virtuosity, tailor-made for the heaven-storming young (27-
year-old) composer. Moderato assai: begins with a melodic subject for vio-

lins; cadenza appears at measure five. Moderato: opens with a phrase for muted strings and woodwinds, with the piano entering upon a monologue in e. Allegro non troppo: in binary form; lively coda of sheer delight. M-D to D.

Concerto IV d Op.70 (GS; K; Sikorski; USSR; Simrock) 30½ min. Moderato assai; Andante; Allegro. One of the great "thriller" concertos of the nineteenth century; once a staple of the concerto repertoire. Thematic material, especially the two luscious inner themes of the first movement and most of the slow movement, has more character and individuality than Rubinstein's other piano concertos. Grateful and effective piano writing. Would make a good substitute for the Grieg *Concerto*. M-D.

Concerto V E♭ Op.94 (Rozsavölgyi; Leduc) 41 min. Allegro moderato; Andante; Allegro.·Josef Lhevinne made his American debut with this work in 1906. It glows with rich, warm melodies. Tchaikowsky studied with Rubinstein, and his *Concerto* in b♭ owes a great deal to the Rubinstein Op.94. In the finale a tune harmonized with perfect fifths (noted in the score as "Tarentella Napolitaine Populair") has the pianist galloping over the keys in chromatic flourishes while the orchestra sings away at a lyric theme. Large span required. D.

Konzertstück A♭ Op.113 (CF) 18 min. Resembles similar pieces by Mendelssohn, Schumann, and Weber. Attractive, soundly organized, effectively orchestrated. M-D.

Beryl Rubinstein (1898–1952) USA

Concerto C 1935 (K; Fl) 31 min. One of the strongest American concertos. Allegro: outstanding characteristics are the piquancy of the rhythmic patterns and the propulsive rhythmic vitality. Andante tranquillo: poetic with a mild Oriental atmosphere; wistful and reflective. Allegro con spirito: opens with a variant of the same pattern heard at the beginning of the first movement; rhythmic emphasis drives the movement inevitably to its brilliant climax. A beautifully crafted work. M-D.

Witold Rudziński (1913–   ) Poland

Concerto 1936 (PWM) 18 min.

Giovanni Marco Rutini (1723–1797) Italy

Concerto D (Illy—De Santis 1052 1966) For keyboard and strings. 48pp. Allegro; Andante; Allegro. In tutti passages only the first violin and bass parts are played with the solo keyboard part. The performer must decide, in accordance with the number of string parts participating, when and where full chords are preferable. The Andante requires the most interpretive decisions. Int. to M-D.

Peter Ruzicka (1948–   ) Germany

Emanazione 1972 (Sikorski).

Feliks Rybicki (1899–   ) Poland

Concerto Op.53 (PWM 1963) 18 min. Allegro moderato; Andantino semplice; Allegro non troppo. This concerto for "small hands" contains no harmonic intervals larger than a seventh. The middle movement is a set of seven variations on a popular Polish tune. A delightful work that sounds more difficult than it is but contains first-rate music throughout. Int. to M-D.

Azer Guseinovich Rzaev (1930–   ) USSR

Concerto (USSR 1965).

Concertino (USSR 1977) 43pp. Allegretto; Andante; Allegretto. Shostakovitch influence, thin textures, appealing. A fine work for an enterprising high school pianist. MC. Int.

S

Peter P. Sacco (1928–   ) USA
Concerto I (Ostara) 26 min.

Harald Saeverud (1897–   ) Norway
Concerto C Op.31 1950 (MH) 27 min. Allegro ma non troppo; Andante con moto; Allegro scherzando. Freely dissonant counterpoint, strong thematic and rhythmic material, brilliant piano writing. D.

Ketil Saeverud (1939–   ) Norway
Concertino 1964 (TONO) 8 min. One movement with varied tempi. Linear; octotonic; closes with an Allegro molto spiritoso. Neoclassic, MC. M-D.

Camille Saint-Saëns (1835–1921) France
"Saint-Saëns," wrote fellow countryman Romain Rolland in 1915, "had the rare honor of becoming a classic during his lifetime. He stood for the French classic spirit and was thought worthiest to represent us in music from the time of Berlioz until the appearance of the young school of César Franck. Saint-Saëns possessed, indeed, some of the best qualities of a French artist, and among them the most important quality of all—perfect cleanliness of conception. Compared with the restless and troubled art today, his music strikes us by its calm, its tranquil harmonies, its velvety modulation, its crystal clearness, its smooth and flowing style, and an elegance that cannot be put into words . . . and that is the secret of his personality and his value to us; he brings to our artistic unrest a little of the light and sweetness of other times. His compositions are like fragments of another world."
Concerto I D Op.17 1858 (Durand; CF) 27 min. Andante; Andante sostenuto quasi adagio; Allegro con fuoco. This work has youthful freshness and imaginative qualities. It contains a fine neo-Bach slow movement. Fluency is endowed with class and zest. M-D.
Concerto II g Op.22 1868 (Durand; GS; K; USSR) 22 min. This is the most popular and most frequently performed of the five concertos. Andante sostenuto: unusual mystical opening with a long Bach-like fantasia for solo piano; some electrifying virtuoso passages later on. Allegro scherzando: delightful light staccato chord playing à la Mendelssohn; brilliant finger technique; the rhythm of the timpani is used as a springboard for the vivacious scenario. Presto—Finale: full of virile energy and the whirling, leaping echos

of Italian folk dances; opens with a light tarantella theme; trills for alternating hands central episode; interlocking passages in the dazzling coda. This concerto opens like Bach and closes like Offenbach! M-D.

Concerto III E♭ Op.29 1869 (Durand; CF) 28½ min. Moderato assai; Andante; Allegro non troppo. The opening is loaded with piano arpeggios and the entire work displays plenty of solo virtuosity, almost excessively fluent. Saint-Saëns idolized the music of Liszt, and in this concerto may be seen the result of this affection. M-D to D.

Concerto IV c Op.44 1873 (Durand; GS) 24 min. Divided into two main sections: 1. Allegro moderato–Andante and 2. Allegro vivace–Andante–Allegro, each of which has two subdivisions. The opening theme is heard alternately in the orchestra and the piano and is followed by two variations. A transitional passage leads to the Andante, in which a choralelike theme, pianissimo, is heard. Some development follows, and the movement closes quietly. The early transition passage from the first movement now opens the second. A zestful version of the first subject of the concerto appears in the orchestra with brilliant accompanying figures in the piano. A crescendo leads to a new subject of strong rhythmic design. Some material is recapped, and a pianissimo closing on the dominant of c is arrived at. A clever orchestral fugato based on first movement material is continued by the piano, with a crescendo that leads to the final section. Material from the 4/4 chorale is now transformed into a lively 3/4, and the work concludes brilliantly. Treatment of materials is more imaginative than the materials themselves. M-D.

Allegro Appassionato Op.70 1884 (Durand; CF) 18pp. This graceful work also exists in a solo piano version. It opens Allegro with three chords vaguely reminiscent of Mussorgsky's *Pictures at an Exhibition*. There are rapid modulations, in turn to e, G (in which we hear a variant of the theme, dolce espressivo), and, in the following Andantino, to E. The concluding section, again Allegro, soon finds its way back to c♯. There are two chordal exclamation points at the end. M-D.

Rhapsodie d'Auvergne Op.73 (Durand 1884; CF) 23pp. This short and poetic piece, a charming setting of folk songs and a personal favorite of the composer, is effective and is hardly known. Three sections: an expressive Andante, a rhythmically graceful Allegretto, and a brilliant Allegro. The thematic material is very tuneful and attractive. The fast passage figuration of the Allegro presents the only technical problems. M-D.

Wedding Cake Op.76 1886 (Durand; CF). For piano and strings. 5½ min. A delightful little scherzo designed as a collection of mini-waltzes, written as a graceful wedding present for Saint-Saëns' friend Caroline Montigny Rémaury. M-D.

Fantasia—"Africa" Op.89 (Durand 1891; CF) 10 min. This clever tone-poem is somewhat more difficult than Op.73 and is much more brilliant and programmatic. Thematic materials are varied and unusually interesting. The dazzling piano writing is effective throughout. Firm, strong wrists are required for fast octaves and repeated thirds in the last section, with its frenetic conclusion. M-D to D.

Concerto V F Op.103 1895 (Durand; GS) 26 min. A highly skillful work demonstrating great technical knowledge. The most pictorial of all the concertos. The orchestration and sense of form are supreme. The first movement opens quietly in a broken rhythm. The middle movement provides strong rhythmic effects and unique color for the piano part. The brilliant finale is a kaleidoscope of virtuosic display and demands fingers of steel. The material for this movement also appears in Saint-Saëns' *Toccata* in the set of etudes, Op.111. D.

Carnaval des Animaux (Grande Fantaisie Zoölogique) (Durand). For two pianos and orchestra. An entertaining series of short pieces imitating various animals of a zoo. No special performance difficulties, humorous, supremely effective. M-D.

See: Paul Pollei, "Virtuoso Style in the Piano Concertos of Camille Saint-Saëns," DM diss., Florida State University, 1975.

Edward A. Rath, Jr., "An Analysis of the Second and Fourth Piano Concertos by Camille Saint-Saëns," DMA diss., Indiana University, 1975. Discusses some of the compositional techniques and constructive devices used in these concertos. Includes information for pianists preparing the works for performance.

Tat'iana Saliutrinskaya (–   ) USSR
Concerto (Soviet Composer 1958) 33pp. Three movements (SFS). Tonal. M-D.
Concerto (Soviet Composer 1963). One large movement. A little more venturesome tonally than the concerto listed above. M-D.

Aules Sallinen (1935–   ) Finland
Sallinen has taught at the Sibelius Academy in Helsinki since 1965.
Metamorphoses 1964 (Finnish Music Information Center). For piano and chamber orchestra. 20 min. Allegro; Passacaglia; Lento moderato; Rondo Interrotto. Freely tonal with some serial influence, excellent craft. M-D.

Vadim N. Salmanov (1912–   ) USSR
Sonata (USSR 1969). For piano and string orchestra. Three movements (SFS). Neoclassic, many syncopations, tonal. M-D.

Karel Salomon (1897–1974) Israel, born Germany
Concerto (IMP) 30 min.
Sinfonia Concertante, Piano Concerto 1947 (IMP 1950).

Giuseppe Sammartini (ca.1699–1770) Italy
Four Concertos Op.9/1-4 (NYPL) 74pp. For keyboard, two violins, and cello. Photostat of the Walsh, 1754 London edition.
Concerto A Op.9/1 (Illy—Br HM 196). For organ or harpsichord and strings. 40pp., 3 parts. Continuo is realized. Includes part for cello and bass. Andante spiritoso; Allegro assai; Andante; Allegro assai. Sammartini wrote out the

solo part completely, so there is no need for improvisation from the performer. Attractive, charming and spirited writing in the second and fourth movements. Int. to M-D.

Pierre Sancan (1916–   ) France

Sancan has won the Prix de Rome and teaches at the Paris Conservatory.

Concerto e 1955 (Durand) 28 min. Modéré: SA, freely tonal, arabesque lines, effective integration of orchestra and piano. Andante: one theme elaborated in various ways, chromatic, melancholy. Allegro vivo: light music-hall tunes, varied meters, brilliant cadenza, quiet close. Fluent and versatile pianism required throughout. Neoclassic. M-D to D.

Concertino (Durand 1967). For piano and chamber orchestra. 15 min. Vif; Andante; Presto. More tart and "secco" than the *Concerto;* attractive. M-D.

Pedro Sanjuan (1886–   ) USA, born Spain

Concerto G (ACA) 25 min.

Domingo Santa Cruz (1899–   ) Chile

Variaciones en tres movimientos Op.20 1942–3 (IEM; IU) 38 min. The first Chilean piano concerto of significance. A thick-textured piece of contrapuntal complexity. The function of the piano soloist is differentiated among the three movements. Muy lento–Movido (en forme de passacalle): piano treated as an orchestral instrument; contrasting variations. Tranquilo (en forme de canción): lyrical; piano is more important; alternating counterpoint between soloist and orchestra; ABA. Bastante movido (en forme de concierto): pianist is prominent; SA. There is a common thematic basis between the movements. M-D to D.

Claudio Santoro (1919–   ) Brazil

Santoro was the first Brazilian composer to adopt dodecaphonic technique. From 1948 to 1960 his works were influenced by the "national" school in Brazilian music, using elements of rhythm, melody, and timbre close to those of folk music without using actual folk themes. He later returned to serial technique, and in several of his works he introduced aleatory elements, always, however, subjected to defined and conscious control. He founded the Music Department of the University of Brasilia and was its first director.

Musica Concertante 1943–44 (Ediçao Savart) 12 min. Twelve-tone. M-D to D.

Concerto I 1951 (Ric Brazil; IU) 26 min. Lento e cantabile–Allegro: two contrasting themes, octotonic, driving syncopated cross-rhythms, strong syncopation. Lento: binary, flexible meters, quartal harmony, dramatic arpeggiated gestures, freely dissonant around e♭. Allegro: SA, fast chords in alternating hands, contrasting sections, fughetto textures, cadenza; large span required. A nationalistic work containing grateful pianistic writing. D.

Concerto II 1958–9 (Ediçao Savart) 22 min. Lento–allegro; Adagio; Allegro.

Concerto III 1960 (Ediçao Savart) 16 min. For youth. Allegro; Lento; Allegro. Int. to M-D.

Intermitências II 1967 (Jobert). For piano and chamber orchestra. 6½ min. Large
percussion sections, graphic notation, aleatory, clusters, avant-garde. Requires experience in the medium. M-D.
Intermitências III (Ediçao Savart) 10 min.

Jerzy Sapieyevski (1945–   ) Poland
Concerto 1977 (Mercury). For two pianos and orchestra. 18 min. Also available
in a one piano and orchestra version.

Jorge A. Sarmientos (1931–   ) Guatemala
Concerto I Op.10 (Direcion General de Bellas Artes 1957; LC). Three movements
(FSF). Freely tonal; many notes! M-D.

Emil Sauer (1862–1942) Germany
Concerto e (Schott 1900) 30 min. Allegro patetico; Scherzo; Cavatino; Rondo.
The opening movement recalls moments in the Tchaikowsky *Concerto* in b♭.
Colorful but somewhat dated. M-D.
Concerto II c 1903 (Schott; CF) 30 min. Moderato lamentoso–Vivacissimo; An-
dante; Allegro deciso, assai moderato. The movements are thematically re-
lated. M-D.

Henri Sauguet (1901–   ) France
Much of Sauguet's work shows that he is a strong inheritor of the Satie tradition.
Sauguet's style contains subtle ostinati, ambiguous harmonies, simplicity, and
the refined popular elements found in Satie.
Concerto I a 1933–34 (ESC) 52pp. Andante assai; Lento, quasi adagio; Allegro
moto. Freely tonal, melancholy lyricism, neoclassic. Requires fluent fingers.
M-D.
Concerto des Mondes Souterrains: Concerto III 1961–63 (Sal) 30 min. One ex-
pansive movement, contrasting sections, highly chromatic, almost atonal,
flexible meters. Advanced pianism required. D.

Domenico Savino (1882–   ) USA
Concerto (Robbins) 20 min.
Cuban Concerto (Robbins 1946) 7 min. One movement; contains a main theme
in 6/4 and a scintillating Allegro in guaracha rhythm. A sensuous creole
melody serves as an interlude between the two major themes. Int. to M-D.

Adnan Ahmed Saygun (1907–   ) Turkey
Concerto Op.34 1957 (PIC) 27 min.

Hans Schaeuble (1906–   ) Switzerland
Concerto Op.34 (SUISA) 19 min. In one movement.
Concerto Op.50 1967 (SUISA). For piano and string orchestra. Frank Martin
influence noted. First movement: built around Baroque devices, some antiphonal. Second movement: dominated by a haunting five-note figure. Third
movement: tends to ramble but contains some attractive moments. M-D.

Boguslav Schäffer (1929–   ) Poland
"Schäffer's music has been in the forefront of new developments in Poland"
(DCM, 653).
Quattro Movimenti 1957 (PWM) 16 min. A piano concerto in every way but name.
Andante; Allegro molto; Moderato animato; Presto. Beautifully written for
piano and orchestra. Flexible meters, unique sonorities, freely tonal. M-D.
Concerto per Sei e Tre 1960 (PWM). For a changing solo instrument and three
instrumental groups. 13 min. One movement. Six different solo instruments
perform in turn (clarinet, alto sax, violin, cello, percussion, piano). Each
soloist performs separately and has the task of introducing the next instrumental timbre. Experimental notation, avant-garde. M-D.
Azione a Due (Ahn & Simrock 1963). For piano and winds. 5 min. Avant-garde.
M-D.
Concerto for Three Pianos and Orchestra (AA 1972) 4½ to 9 min.

Karl Schäffer (1899–   ) Germany
Klavierkonzert Op.37 (Müller) 60pp. Three movements (FSF). Tonal; neoclassic,
almost "classic," style. M-D.

Christoph Schaffrath (1709–1763) Germany
Concerto Bb (Louwenaar—A-R Editions 1977). For keyboard and strings. 77pp.
The first modern edition of a concerto by Schaffrath, who was active in the
courts of Frederick the Great and Princess Anna Amalie in Berlin. Two
decorated versions of the middle movement survive, and both are printed in
an appendix to this edition. Outer movements combine Baroque ritornello
procedure with an essentially *galant* harmonic and melodic style. Includes
bibliographical references, preface, and notes. M-D.

Xaver Scharwenka (1850–1924) Poland
The four Scharwenka concertos were extremely popular until the concertos of
Rachmaninoff gradually replaced them. They deserve to be resurrected, for they
are in some respects more exciting and interesting than some of the concertos that
are considered standard today. They are of the same large scale as the concertos
of Tchaikowsky, Rachmaninoff, and Brahms and are extremely interesting, highly
melodic, and harmonic. The orchestral writing is brilliant, and the writing for the
piano "fits" the hands well. A formidable, Lisztian technique is needed. The
technical demands include large chords, octaves, scales, and double notes.
Concerto I bb Op.32 (Music Treasure; CF) 30 min. Allegro patetico–Adagio;
Allegro assai; Allegro non tanto. Von Bülow thought this work was "interesting and original, amiable throughout, perfect in form, and similar to
Chopin's concertos in its genuinely pianistic qualities, but superior to them
in its admirable instrumentation" (from the preface in the Music Treasure
edition). Ideas from the first movement are recapitulated and developed in
the finale to form a broad, archlike structure. M-D.
Concerto II c Op.56 (Br&H 1893) 30 min. Allegro; Adagio; Allegro non troppo.

Dramatic gestures, rich sonorities, reminiscent of Brahms in its broad sweeping style and in orchestral prominence, rolling basses. Many delightful tunes, especially in the Finale, which was frequently performed by itself. M-D.

Concerto III c♯ Op.80 (Br&H 1888) 30 min. Maestoso; Adagio; Allegro non troppo. Broad nineteenth-century gestures, weak thematic material. M-D.

Concerto IV f Op.82 1908 (Leuckart) 67pp. Allegro patetico; Intermezzo; Lento–Allegro con fuoco. Virtuosic pianism throughout. M-D to D.

Ernest Schelling (1876–1939) USA

Suite Fantastique Op.7 1905–6 (Rahter) 28 min. Really a concerto in four movements. Allegro marziale; Molto vivace; Intermezzo; Virginia Reel. Nineteenth-century oriented throughout, pianistically satisfying. M-D.

Symphonic Variations, "Impressions from an Artist's Life" 1913 (Leuckart) 36 min. Theme and eighteen variations. Post-Romantic idiom with strong Reger influence. Pays tribute to musicians like Paderewski and Mahler and contains a reminder of the "call to arms, August 1914," without having a great deal to say musically. M-D.

Armin Schibler (1920–   ) Switzerland

Concerto Op.76 1962–63 (Eulenburg 1251). For piano, percussion, and string orchestra. Miniature score, 148pp. Preface in German and English. Recitative; Le jeu des petites timbales; La magie du vibraphon; Le tambour; Le silence de la nuit; Variationen über ein Negro spiritual. Percussion instruments divided into five groups. Unusual and effective timbres. Piano part is not as difficult as the ensemble problems. I wonder how much the piano can be heard in the last movement where all the percussion are playing! M-D.

Peter Schickele (1935–   ) USA

Three Girls, Three Women (EV). For male singing pianist and orchestra. 20 min.

Poul Schierbeck (1888–1949) Denmark

Night-Symfonisk Scene Op.41 1935–36 (Samfundet Til Udgivelse af Dansk Musik 1958) 12 min. Originally a ballet. Sectional, MC. M-D.

Lalo Schifrin (1932–   ) USA, born Argentina

Concerto (MJQ) 23 min.

Karl Schiske (1916–1969) Austria

Concerto Op.11 1939 (Dob 1974) 20 min. Toccata; Passacaglia; Sonata. Cosmopolitan neoclassic idiom. M-D.

Franz Schmidt (1874–1939) Austria

The two works that follow were originally composed for the left-handed pianist Paul Wittgenstein, but were rewritten for two hands and orchestra by Friedrich Wührer.

Concertante Variationen über ein Thema von Beethoven 1923 (UE 12035; Fl) 26 min. Variations are based on a theme from the Scherzo of the *"Spring" Sonata* F Op.24 for piano and violin. M-D.

Concerto II Eb 1934 (UE 12032; Fl) 38 min. Allegro moderato un poco maestoso; Andante; Vivace. "In three movements, with the vivacious finale containing a virtuosistic sinistromanual cadenza" (MSNH, 601). M-D.

Camille Schmit (1908–   ) Belgium
Schmit teaches at the Conservatory in Liège.
Musique pour Piano et Orchestra 1949 (CeBeDeM 1965) 19 min. A concerto in most respects except its name. Allegro: rhapsodic; sections with tempo and meter changes; thin textures for the piano. Largo: piano enters only at climax; twelve-tone row emerges from the cellos. Allegretto vivo: dramatic gestures for both piano and orchestra. Atonal, one of the most original concertos to come out of twentieth-century Belgium. M-D to D.
Concerto 1955 (CeBeDeM) 20 min. Full sonorities. Atonal. D.

Florent Schmitt (1870–1958) France
J'entends dans le lointain Op.64/1 1917 (Durand) 8 min. From *Ombres*. Colorful, contrasting sections, dramatic, Impressionistic. M-D.
Symphonique Concertante g Op.82 (Durand 1933) 30 min. Assez animé; Lent; Animé. This large work shows the influence of Fauré, considerable structural power, richness of color, and impressive eloquence. M-D.

E. Robert Schmitz (1889–1949) USA
Concerto I (CF; Fl) 22 min. Lento; Adagio; Allegro giusto.

Alfred Schnittke (1934–   ) USSR
Music for Piano and Chamber Orchestra (UE) 14 min.

Johann Schobert (ca.1720–1767) Germany
Six Concerti 1767–1774. Two of these works, Op.19 G and Op.12/2 Eb, are found in the DDT, vol. 34. Mozart may have heard these pieces in Paris, for Schobert's piano style seems to have influenced him considerably, especially in triplet- and sixteenth-note passages and cross-hand activity. But the left-hand parts in the Schobert works are rather simple, somewhat closer to J. C. Bach's keyboard style. The concertos are mature in form, beautiful in sound, and brilliant in technique. Int. to M-D.
See: Stewart G. Graham, "The Keyboard Concertos of Johann Schobert," thesis, Yale University, 1967.

Arnold Schoenberg (1874–1951) Austria
Concerto Op.42 1942 (Steuermann-GS; Ph 462) 28 min. This innovative and reflective masterpiece is based on twelve-tone technique but the technique is free enough to allow octave doublings and, because of the row material, tertian chords for some accompanimental passages. It is a sympathetic work, gentle and tender, pastoral and lyric in feeling. The movements are connected by elision and common thematic material and therefore it is possibly inspired by Liszt. The first movement is a theme and five variations with a coda beginning with a BACH statement. A scherzo-type movement, Molto allegro, follows after a fermata at bar 176. It is in ternary design and closes with

a powerful coda. The slow movement, Adagio, begins at bar 264. The lead motive is the inverted BACH statement. Sections are not strongly contrasted; after an orchestral climax the piano dissolves through a transition to the finale, Giocoso (bar 329), a five-part rondo with coda. The stretta coda is based on the main concerto row with some reference to the BACH statement. A surprising final C chord completes the work. The most complex textures are difficult for the pianist but there is never any display of virtuosic pyro-techniques. D.

See: Dika Newlin, "Secret Tonality in Schönberg's Piano Concerto," PNM, Fall-Winter 1974, 137–39.

Ruth Schonthal (1929–   ) USA, born Germany
Concerto II 1977 (OUP). Allegro moderato; Adagio tranquillo e semplice; Allegro moderato. Thin textures, flexible meters, cadenza passages, clusters, octo-tonic, fluent writing, MC. M-D.

Kees Schoonenbeek (1947–   ) The Netherlands
Concerto 1975–76 (Donemus) 15 min. Three untitled movements. Piano is treated in a neoclassic manner with octotonic, alternating hand patterns. Expanded tonal idiom. M-D.

Herman Schroeder (1904–   ) Germany
Konzert B Op.35 (Gerig 1958) 18 min. Allegro; Lento espressivo; Allegro spir-ituoso. Neoclassic, freely tonal. Lento contains some of Schroeder's loveliest melodic writing. Large span required. M-D.
Concertino Op.42 (Gerig). For piano and brass; also available in a two-piano score. Atonal and dissonant, similar to Hindemith. M-D.

Johann Samuel Schröter (1750–1788) England, born Poland
Charles Burney said of Schröter: "He became one of the neatest and most ex-pressive players of his time, and his style of composition, highly polished, re-sembled that of Abel more than any other. It was graceful and in good taste, but so chaste as sometimes to seem deficient in fire and invention" (GD, Vol.VII, 534).
Konzert C Op.3/3 (Schultz—Schott 4974). For keyboard and strings. 26pp. Al-legro; Grazioso; Rondeau. Cadenzas by K. Schultz-Hauser. Int. to M-D.

Heinz Schubert (1908–   ) Germany
Abrosianisches Concert "Choral-Phantasie über 'Verleih' uns Frieden gnadiglich" (MWV) 32 min. Praeludium (Choral); Phantasie; Inventionen; Gigue; Can-zone. Based on a chorale melody by Martin Luther and "Dona nobis pacem" from the J. S. Bach b minor Mass. An extension of the Reger tradition, freely tonal. *Ppp* G conclusion. M-D.

Erwin Schulhoff (1894–1942) Czechoslovakia
Double Concerto 1927 (Panton). For piano, flute, and orchestra. 23 min. Preface in Czech, Russian, German, English, and French. Allegro moderato: ener-getic, rich polyphony and strong dissonance, extensive cadenzas for both

solo instruments. Andante: melancholy; on quiet side; concludes with the flute, which gradually fades away. Allegro con spirito: a capricious rondo the basic theme of which is like a simple and playful canzonet; intermezzo-like middle part in a blues tempo. M-D.

Gunther Schuller (1925–   ) USA

Concerto 1962 (Schott 10895) 20 min. Three movements in a highly organized serial idiom. First movement, quarter-note = 84: row is heard at opening; unfolds as a set of character variations. Scherzo: five-part; driving sections alternate with more calm floating sections. Moderato: sectional, pointillistic, recitatives, fast cadenza, richly textured sonorities. Bold orchestration, austere and clean lines for the piano, thin linear texture, varied and individual use of scales, arpeggios, trills, grace notes. "Third Stream" (jazz) influence is more noticeable in the corky syncopations and seventh chords. Third-stream music is referred to as the combination and collaboration of jazz and symphonic music. M-D to D.

Colloquy 1966 (AMP). For two pianos and orchestra. 20 min.

William Schuman (1910–   ) USA

Concerto 1937–42 (GS) 21 min. Based on a concerto composed in 1938 and now withdrawn. Both MMS are available for comparison at LC. First movement: SA treated freely. Second movement: grows in complexity from a few melodic and rhythmic ideas. Finale: effective use of a six-note ostinato and a four-voice fugue. Polytonal; ambiguous key centers; quartal harmony; parallelism; harmonic developments grow from melodic ideas; vigorous rhythms (boogie-woogie left hand patterns); brilliant octaves; fast figurations; crisply articulated staccato lines and chords; cadenza at end of Finale; prismatic orchestration. A fine example of "Art Deco" music; solidly crafted, clean lined, and uncomplicated! D

Clara Schumann (1819–1896) Germany

Concerto a Op.7 1833 (Heuwekemijer; Hofmeister) 20 min. Allegro maestoso; Romanza; Finale. Conventional harmonic progressions lack direction; undistinguished melodies; inept orchestration; a cloying treacle runs throughout this work. Mme. Schumann may have been a fine pianist but she was no composer, at least not at age 14. Only the lavish Romance with a cello solo shows much promise. M-D.

Georg A. Schumann (1866–1952) Germany

Fantasie-Scherzo Op.68/1 (Leuckart 1966) 25pp. Freely tonal, neoclassic, grandiose conclusion. Large span required. M-D.

Robert Schumann (1810–1856) Germany

As a critic, Schumann had many opportunities to hear a never-ending stream of contemporary concertos, and in a letter to Clara Wieck he said, "I cannot write a concerto for virtuosi; I must think of something else." And he succeeded in a magnificent manner by composing what is probably the most beautiful of all Romantic concertos.

Concerto a Op.54 (CFP; GS; K; WH; CF; JWC; EC; Eulenburg; Novello; Hug; Ph 424; Augener) 31 min. Allegro affettuoso; Intermezzo—Andantino grazioso; Allegro vivace. The first movement (originally called Phantasie) was written in 1841; the remainder of the work was finished in 1845. This flawless masterpiece is one of the most outstanding and Romantically inspired concertos in the repertoire. It is warmly lyrical, rich in its orchestration, and never overly virtuosic. The piano writing is idiomatic and effective. The Classical concerto form is not strictly preserved, but the general SA design is maintained in the outer movements. The cadenza at the end of the first movement offers the greatest challenge to the pianist's technique. The piano is most subtly woven together with the orchestra. The Andantino runs into the Finale—Rondo without a break and thereby provides a great sense of unity. M-D to D.

See: Malcolm Frager, "The Manuscript of the Schumann Piano Concerto," CM 15 (1973): 83–87. Errors from earlier editions are listed.

Concertstück G Op.92 1849 (Introduction and Allegro appassionato) (GS L1707; Eulenburg study score; Pauer—Schott; Augener). Short, grateful writing, not as difficult as *Concerto* Op.54. A brief Adagio, with the melody in the orchestra, is accompanied by piano arpeggi. It leads to a rhythmic Allegro with varied material. A double-note staccato passage requires firm rhythmic control. Contains more technical problems for the pianist than Op.134. M-D.

Introduction and Allegro d Op.134 1853 (GS; Busoni—Br&H; Pauer—Schott; Augener) 15 min. This late work is straightforward and serious but also brilliant in its conception and execution. Quiet introduction followed by the Concerto Allegro in SA design. Closes with surging chords, rushing scales, and a fortissimo finale by all forces. Both Op.92 and this work are near masterpieces; the music world is finally becoming aware of their existence. M-D.

Gerard Schurmann (1928–   ) Great Britain, born Indonesia

Concerto 1972–73 (Novello) 29 min. The composer states in program notes that "this concerto is an attempt to reconcile a contemporary idiom with a featured solo part of virtuosic proportions, avoiding meaningless pyrotechniques." It is based on the Liszt–Rachmaninoff tradition and is in two movements. The first, Allegro, is preceded with an arresting cadenza that provides some material used later in the movement. The second movement is tripartite in design, comprising an Adagio molto, Presto, and an Allegro vivace. Textural sameness in both movements. D.

Eduard Schütt (1856–1933) Germany, born Russia

Concerto g Op.7 (K&S 1897; Fl). Allegro energico; Moderato assai; Allegro grazioso. Grateful pianistically; contains some lovely tunes. M-D.

Concerto f Op.47 1896 (Simrock; K; Fl) 35pp. Allegro risoluto; Andante tranquillo; Allegro vivace. This technically brilliant concerto is worthy of being revived. The writing is not only pianistic but grateful both melodically and harmonically. Tunes in the slow movement remind one of Rachmaninoff, who had not at the time of this work begun to write his best compositions. My teacher, Olga Samaroff, played this work with the Philadelphia Orchestra in 1907. M-D.

Elliot Schwartz (1936–   ) USA

"Many [of Schwartz's] works, beginning with Dialogue (1966–7), exploit the spatial placement of sound sources, motion, and performer activity" (DCM, 666).

Magic Music 1967 (CF). For piano, orchestra, and other sounds. 13 min. Contains performance directions; uses four types of notation. A "theater piece" that must be seen as well as heard. The musicians leave their customary chairs to attack the piano, and the pianist doubles at the organ. The music is hummed and strummed, lashed and crashed, shouted at and stroked, all in dead seriousness. The score has definite form and contains many passages of interest and some brilliant percussive effects. A magnificently elaborate and ingenious spoof. M-D.

Janus 1976 (MS available from composer: % Music Department, Bowdoin College, Brunswick, ME 04011) 24 min. Three untitled movements. Mostly traditional notation; performance directions; clusters; some sections are "free in 15 beats"; cadenzas for piano and oboe; harmonics; avant-garde tendencies. M-D.

Chamber Concerto III 1977 (MS available from composer). For piano and chamber orchestra. 14½ min. No parts; all players read from copies of the full score. A single-movement work based on two principal ideas—suspensions and a rapidly repeated single note, which keeps appearing at various places on the keyboard and among various instruments and groups in the orchestra. Contrasting sections and tempos; piano part, largely percussive, uses all the glittering devices of the traditional virtuoso concerto, plus stroked and plucked piano strings. Effective; strong in ingenuity and skill. M-D.

Ludvig Schytte (1848–1909) Denmark

Concerto c♯ Op.28 (Hainauer 1894) 58pp. Allegro; Intermezzo; Finale. Virtuoso figures, large skips, outside movements brilliant; in Liszt tradition. M-D to D.

Valdo Sciammarella (1924–   ) Argentina

Variaciones Concertantes (Sociedad Argentina de Autores y Compositores de Musica Lavalle 1547. Buenos Aires, Argentina) 19 min.

Salvatore Sciarrino (1947–   ) Italy

Clair de Lune Op.25 (Ric).

Cyril Scott (1879–1970) Great Britain

Concerto I C 1913–14 (Schott) 25 min. Allegro maestoso; Adagio; Allegro poco moderato. Contains characteristics of Ravel, Delius, Scriabin, and a little Gershwin. Many nonresolving chordal patterns and frequent repetitions of short motivic filigrees. Warm, sumptuous, jadelike sonorities; hypnotic sequences; subtle instrumental contrasts. Piano's role is more functional than virtuosic. Scott said of this piece: "Not a deep work but an enlivening one." M-D.

Early One Morning. Poem for Piano and Orchestra (Bo&H 1931) 16 min. Variations based on the traditional song "Early One Morning." This tantalizing piece is extremely subtle and presents a fine example of Scott's understanding of the orchestra. First published for two pianos and orchestra in 1931, revised for piano and orchestra in 1962. M-D.

Concerto II (Schott 1950) 25 min. Not as effective as *Concerto* I. Con moto: modified SA. Tranquillo: Debussy and Delius influence. Energico: piano opening repeated by orchestra; question-and-answer section before a return to the main idea, tempo primo. M-D.

Concertino (PRS). For two pianos and orchestra. 18 min.

Alexander Scriabin (1872–1915) Russia

Concerto f♯ Op.20 1896 (Belaieff; Bo&H; MCA; K; BB study score; Eulenburg miniature score 1287) 27 min. The opening Allegro and the concluding Allegro moderato are in 3/4. The second movement (Andante) consists of a short theme and variations (an unusual form for Scriabin) in F♯, so all three movements maintain the same tonal center. The solo part is continuously employed and makes considerable demands. The orchestration owes much to Tchaikowsky, while the piano writing shows the influence of Anton Rubinstein. Many sections are very beautiful but they do not add up to a convincingly unified dramatic whole. D.

Humphrey Searle (1915–   ) Great Britain

Concerto d Op.5 1943–44 (Lengnick) 24 min. Allegro; Andante; Molto vivace. Written in a kind of atonal style partly influenced by Bartók. Large dramatic gestures, plenty of pianistic excitement. M-D to D.

Concertante Op.24 1954 (Schott AV 60). For piano, strings, and percussion. 6 min.

Concerto II Op.27 1955 (Schott 10397) 23 min. Three movements (FSF) but bridged together. Atonal, busy piano style. Bartók's influence is seen in the second movement, while the finale, Allegro scherzando, dances in a clean and crisp style. D.

Max Seeboth (1904–   ) Germany

Concerto C (Heinrichshofen 1940) 30 min. Polytonal, neoclassic. One large sectionalized movement. M-D.

Erich Sehlbach (1898–   ) Germany

Concerto 1953 (Möseler). Displays strong influences of Hindemith, Schoenberg, and Bartók. M-D.

Carlos Seixas (1704–1742) Portugal
Seixas was Portugal's most important composer for the keyboard in the eighteenth century. He wrote approximately 150 works for the keyboard.
Concerto em Lá Maior (Salzmann—Gulbenkian Foundation 1969). For keyboard and strings. 19pp. Allegro; Adagio; Giga—Allegro. Charming period writing that comes off well on the piano. Int. to M-D.

Tibor Serly (1900–1978) USA, born Hungary
Modus Lascivus is a system of composition Serly developed over a period of years.
Concerto for Two Pianos and Orchestra (PIC) 25 min. Moderato (1940): SA; first theme lends itself to Baroque contrapuntal dissonant treatment; second subject is almost jazzlike. Adagio (1955–58). Allegro (1955–58): Modus Lascivus techniques used with more abandon than in the second movement; sonata–rondo forms; three main themes; Vivace coda begins pianissimo, gains momentum, and ends *ff*. M-D to D.
Concertino Three Times Three (in Modus Lascivus) 1954–55 (PIC) 30 min. Allegro moderato; Sostenuto; Vivace. This work is two totally different compositions, one for orchestra and one for piano, making nine movements when combined. M-D.

Kazimierz Serocky (1922–   ) Poland
Forte e Piano. Music for Two Pianos and Orchestra 1967 (PWM) 12 min. Explanations in Polish, English, and German. Abbreviations and symbols; clusters; graphic and other types of notation; certain sections are notated in number of seconds. Intricately structured patterns, dynamic extremes, avant-garde. D.

Roger Sessions (1896–   ) USA
Concerto 1956 (EBM; Fl) 20 min. Based on Sessions's personal style of twelve-tone technique tempered with touches of neoclassicism. Three movements played without interruption. Tranquillo: SA. Adagio: ABA. Allegro: Rondo. A diagnostic and strong atonal work that inquires, probes, analyzes, and thoroughly reexamines a number of modern idioms, styles, systems, and forms but is organized according to traditional principles. Piano writing is sonorous and effective but is almost totally lacking in virtuosity. Eminent craftsmanship throughout. D.

Giovanni Sgambati (1841–1914) Italy
Concerto g Op.15 1885 (Schott) 20 min. Moderato maestoso; Romanza; Allegro animato. Darkly scored, large-scale, sonorous work. Modulation and chromaticism run the piece all over the tonal map. Long orchestral introduction. Cadenza is placed between the first and second themes in the recapitulation. Many poetic touches, glistening figurations for the piano, unexpected flights of fancy. D.

Harold Shapero (1920–   ) USA

Since 1952 Shapero has been on the faculty of Brandeis University.

Partita C 1960 (PIC) 17 min. In eight movements: Sinfonia; Ciaccona; Pastorale; Scherzo; Aria; Burlesca; Cadenza; Esercizio. Shapero says of this work: "My Partita is a neo-baroque piece in which I have combined tonal and serial elements. The same twelve-tone series appears in each movement metamorphosed in character and absorbed in the overall tonal texture. The final movement 'Esercizio' is entirely composed with the aid of this series, though it clearly ends in C. The Partita is not a Piano Concerto in a usual sense, but employs the soloist in the Baroque tradition, the piano blending constantly with other instruments and emerging for several solo passages and a cadenza. The small orchestra I have adopted is larger in sound than a chamber ensemble, though lighter than the full classical orchestra" (from record liner, Louisville Orchestra First Editions Records). M-D.

Adrian G. Shaposhinkov (1888–1967) USSR

Concerto (Soviet Composer 1967) 93pp. Moderato risoluto; Andante amabile; Allegro. Freely tonal, modal. M-D to D.

Rodion K. Shchedrin (1932–   ) USSR

Concerto I D 1954 (Soviet Composer 1975) full score, 152pp. Reorchestrated 1974. Maestoso con moto: SA; second theme is folkish; ostinato figures; first theme is second in the recapitulation. Scherzo—Toccata: polytonal arpeggi; mostly *pp*. Passacaglia: slow; the least interesting movement. Finale —Presto festoso: brilliant, clear structure, exciting pianistically, appealing. Contains characteristics of Khachaturian, Prokofiev, Rachmaninoff, Gershwin, and Stravinsky. Would make a good substitute for the Prokofiev *Piano Concerto* III. Exuberantly virtuosic and blazingly effective. M-D to D.

Concerto II 1966 (CFP 5720) 23 min. Dialogue: opens with solo piano cadenza, which returns twice before concluding the movement; alternation of ideas and materials between soloist and orchestra reinforces title of movement. Improvisation: "a toccata–scherzo, in which two dominant themes are freely copulated in versatile improvisatory manner." Contrasts: "wherein the piano plays single notes and chords as if tuning up the instrument, eliciting an antiphonal reaction from the orchestra" (MSNH, 1269).

Concerto III "Variations on a Theme" 1973 (Soviet Composer) 22 min. Tumultuous writing in the style of the 20s in the Western world. Little use is made of aleatory, polytonal, and twelve-tone techniques. Liszt and Sibelius influences present, exciting percussion effects, plus a few squealing electronic effects. Brilliant orchestration; unmistakable Russian character. Strong idiomatic pianistic writing. M-D to D.

Mordechai Sheinkman (1926–   ) Israel

Konzert Op.3 1955 (Bo&Bo) 19 min. Allegro; Adagio; Allegro. Expanded tonal idiom, strong rhythms, exhilarating closing. M-D.

Dmitri Shostakovitch (1906–1975) USSR
Concerto I C Op.35 1933 (USSR; MCA; K; IMC). For piano, trumpet, and string
orchestra. 21 min. Allegretto; Lento; Moderato. Shostakovitch pays homage
to the neoclassic spirit in this work. The style is lean and acerbic and has
some musical irony tinged with Slavic melancholy. A short interlude connects
the second and third movements. The trumpet forms an admirable foil to a
contrasted tone color, especially in the outer movements. In place of thematic
development similar new material keeps unfolding. The dry toccata-like
passages in the third movement show the composer's predilection for the
grotesque. This work always "sounds," and the effects are sure-fire. M-D.
Concerto II F Op.102 1957 (USSR; MCA; CFP; K; IMC; Fl) 16 min. This light-
hearted work was written for the composer's son Maxim. The piano part
suggests a "youth" concerto although it has the brilliance of velocity and
the orchestration is colorful. Allegro: SA; Poulencish; marchlike; much octotonic writing; toccata-like passage work; powerful octaves; cadenza. Andante: simple part form; arioso; melodic. Allegro: SA; driving rhythms;
effective use of 7/8; octotonic; a subordinate theme is based on a satirical
reference to one of Hanon's famous exercise patterns. M-D.
Both concertos are contained in vol. 12 of the *Complete Edition* (USSR); and a
two-piano reduction by the composer is in vol. 13.

Otto Siegl (1896–   ) Austria
Kammerkonzert (Dob 1962) 28 min. Three movements (FSF). Tonal, neoclassic.
M-D.

Elie Siegmeister (1909–   ) USA
Siegmeister is Professor of Music and Composer-in-Residence at Hofstra
University.
Concerto 1974 (CF) 25 min. In three movements. Harsh dissonances, much agi-
tato, aggressive syncopation, difficult cadenza in finale. Influences of Gersh-
win, jazz, and ragtime. D.

Paul J. Sifler (1911–   ) USA, born Yugoslavia
From Barn to Boogie (Fredonia Press). For piano and band. An American Dance
Rhapsody.

Thorkell Sigurbjörnsson (1938–   ) Iceland
Duttlungar (Caprice) (Iceland Music Information Center) 11 min.

Tomasz Sikorski (1939–   ) Poland
Concerto Breve 1965 (PWM). For piano, 24 winds, and four percussion players.
10 min. Facsimile of score. Twelve sections differing in color and type of
dynamics. Aleatory, many figures repeated by the instrumentalists greatly
enhance the spontaneity and dynamics of the music. A brilliant concertato
work. M-D.
Music in Twilight 1977–78 (PWM). Many repetitions and much static music.
M-D.

Nikolai I. Silvanski (1915–   ) USSR
Petit Piano Concerto (GS 7712) 22pp. For student and teacher. Int.
Concerto III d (Musica Ukraina 1967) 40pp. Freely tonal; some modality; no
    division of movements. Requires a big chord technique. M-D.
Pionerskyi Kontsert (Musica Ukraina 1969) 31pp. One movement, sectionalized.
    Contains some Kabalevsky "impetuosity"; appealing. Int.

Homer Simmons (1900–1971) USA
Phantasmania 1923–24 (GS) 17 min. Jazz influence; fluctuating tempi. A fun
    piece but not easy. M-D.

Nadezhda S. Simonian (1922–   ) USSR
Concerto (Soviet Composer 1963) 104pp. Three movements (FSF). Freely tonal.
    M-D.
Poem-Concerto 1968 (Soviet Composer) 74pp. One large sectionalized move-
    ment. Picturesque writing; modal; much chromatic usage. M-D.

Christian Sinding (1856–1941) Norway
Concerto D♭ Op.6 1887–88 (WH) 30 min. Allegro non troppo; Andante; Allegro
    non assai. Influences of Wagner, Schumann, Liszt, some folk music, and
    even Franck in its reliance on cyclic procedures, but there are moments of
    strong individuality. The aristocratically assertive opening motto-theme
    (quite Brahmsian) is given due weight throughout the work's elaborate and
    technically demanding musical argument. A hand-filling and ear-filling
    work. M-D to D.

Otto Singer (1863–1931) Germany
Concerto A Op.8 (Leuckart 1906; Fl) 69pp. In one movement. Strong nineteenth-
    century orientation; many chromatic figurations; good taste displayed
    throughout. M-D.
Rhapsodie C (John Church 1881; LC) 27pp. Strong Liszt influence. M-D.

José Siqueira (1907–   ) Brazil
Concertino 1973 (MS available from composer: % Uniaõ dos Musicos, Av. Rio
    Branco 185/701, Rio de Janeiro, Brazil). For piano and chamber orchestra.
    31pp. One large movement; sections flow into each other. Freely tonal, even
    borders on atonal; 4 with 3; chromatic figurations; tremolando chords be-
    tween hands. M-D.

Pavel Sivic (1908–   ) Yugoslavia
Concerto (Gerig) 16 min.

Nikos Skalkottas (1904–1949) Greece
Concerto I 1931 (SSF [Society of Skalkottas's Friends], Athens, Greece). Closely
    related to the style of Schoenberg, with whom the composer was studying
    at the time.
Concerto II 1937–38 (SSF).
Concertino 1935 (UE 14296 LW). For two pianos and orchestra. 14 min. Allegro;

Andante; Allegro giusto. Graceful dignity felt in the opening movement, tremendous emotional range covered by the terrifying darkness of the slow movement, and much wit in the last movement. Unique twelve-tone usage mixed with Greek background provides one of the most interesting works in the repertoire for this medium. M-D.

Concerto III 1939 (UE; SSF). For piano, ten winds, and percussion.

Andante Sostenuto (UE 1954). For piano, ten winds, and percussion. 18 min. Expressionistic, involved, flexible meters, quiet ending, much motivic dovetailing. D.

Concerto 1929–30 (SSF). For piano, violin, and orchestra.

Lucijan Skerjanc (1900–1973) Yugoslavia, born Austria

Concerto (SAZU 1954) 25 min. Three movements (FSF). Freely tonal. Pianistic expertise abounds. M-D.

Concertino (DSS 1963). For piano and string orchestra. 9 min. Three contrasting movements. Neoclassic; reminiscent of Jean Françaix *Concertino* style. M-D.

Concerto (SAZU 1967). For piano, left-hand and orchestra. 25 min. Lento; Calmo e sentito; Allegretto; Moderato rapsodico. Freely tonal, gives the left hand every conceivable type of workout. The second movement is especially beautiful. D.

Dane Skerl (1931–   ) Yugoslavia

Concertino I (Gerig) 12 min.

Concertino II 1958–59 (DSS). For piano and strings. 14 min. Three contrasted movements. Neoclassic; tonal with touches of chromaticism; big buildup, then subito *p* ending. M-D.

Karl Yngve Sköld (1899–   ) Sweden

Concerto I Op.7 (ES) 30 min.

Concerto II Op.46 (ES; Fl) 30 min.

Concerto III Op.67 1967 (ES) 30 min.

Fritz Skorzeny (1900–1965) Austria

Double Concerto (Dob). For piano, violin, and orchestra. 25 min.

Leo Smit (1921–   ) USA

Smit teaches at the State University of New York at Buffalo.

Concerto for Orchestra and Piano 1968 (CF) 15 min.

Leo Smit (1900–1945) The Netherlands

Concerto 1937 (Donemus). For piano and wind instruments. 16 min.

Hale Smith (1925–   ) USA

Concert Music 1972 (CFP) 14 min. In one movement. Serial influence, expressionistic, "freely introspectively" indications, cadenza. M-D.

Julia Smith (1911–   ) USA

Concerto e (Mowbray 1971) 18 min. Assai lento: opens with brooding octave theme; strong melodic writing with "Americanist" elements; freely tonal around e. Lento: lyrical; elegaic mood; works to large climax; harmonics prepare for finale. Andante e pesante: Cadenza-like passages lead to an Allegro ben ritmico; broad Romantic gestures; glissandi; surprising ending. Effective. M-D to D.

Russell Smith (1927–   ) USA
Concerto I 1952 (ACA) 20 min. One movement, an allegro following a brief, slower-paced introduction. Dance influence. Piano is treated both as a solo instrument and as a part of the general ensemble. M-D.
Concerto II 1956 (ACA) 25 min. Three movements (FSF) in a sinewy "modern classic" form. Effective piano figuration, trills, double-note passages, and first-movement cadenza but no overly virtuosic display. Unambiguously tonal in orientation and powerfully virile in expression. M-D.

Theodore Smith (fl.1778–1810) Great Britain
Six Concertos Op.13 (Longman & Broderip ca.1780). For keyboard and strings. 38pp. NYPL has a complete set.

Michael Smolanoff (–   ) USA
Concerto Op.29 (Seesaw 1973). For piano, four-hands with string orchestra and percussion. 12 min. One movement with contrasting sections. Strong twentieth-century flavor with numerous contemporary techniques. Requires versatile and experienced ensemble pianists. M-D to D.

Jerzy Sokorski (1916–   ) Poland
Concerto 1941 (PWM) 30 min.

Josep Soler (1935–   ) Spain
Concierto (PIC). For piano and chamber orchestra. 16 min.

Louis Somer (1901–1966) The Netherlands
Burlesque (Donemus).

Harry Somers (1925–   ) Canada
Somers frequently juxtaposes dodecaphonic and tonal materials à la Charles Ives. Most of his music uses twelve-tone procedures.
Concerto I 1947 (CMC). Eclectic, technically agile, effective instrumentation. M-D.
Concerto II 1956 (BMI) 43 min. Allegro vivace; Lento; Allegro. Individual serial usage infused with strong forms and some Impressionistic tendencies; MC. M-D.

Arthur Somervell (1863–1937) Great Britain
Normandy. Symphonic Variations (Augener 1912) 43pp. One sectional movement based on a French folk song. Freely tonal with Impressionistic touches. M-D.

Ahti Sonninen (1914–   ) Finland
Concerto Op.22 1945 (Finnish Music Center) 28 min. Bartók, Shostakovitch, and

folk-music influence; violent tonal eruptions. Allegro energico; Andante; Allegro con fuoco (cadenza, sweeping gestures). M-D to D.

Kaikhosru Sorabji (1895–   ) Great Britain
Concerto II 1920 (OUP 1923) 40 min. One large rhapsodic movement—has to be seen and heard to be believed! The inner logic and the natural drift of the music create its own form. Combines incredible contrapuntal skill with almost unparalleled control of kaleidoscopic sound. Scoring is rich and colorful and is filled with many novel and original instrumental schemes. Some places require four or five staves for a clear presentation to the eye. Combined rhythmic schemes are a real problem. D.

Enrico Soro (1884–1954) Chile
Concerto C Op.32 1919 (Ric) 25 min. Andante ma non troppo; Scherzando; Allegro ma non troppo. Dramatic virtuoso writing in a direct line with the great Romantic virtuosic concertos. M-D to D.

Konstantin S. Sorokin (1909–   ) USSR
Concerto Op.42 (USSR 1970) 72pp. Allegro festivo; Allegro barbaro. Freely tonal, virtuosic, colorful second movement. M-D to D.
Youth Concerto Op.50 (USSR 1972) 31pp. Three movements (FSF). Tonal, colorful. Requires facility for moving over keyboard quickly. Int. to M-D.

Boris A. Sosnovtsev (1921–   ) USSR
Concerto (Soviet Composer 1972) 60pp. Allegro molto; Adagio; Presto. Sounds like Kabalevsky but with a little less color. M-D.

João de Souza Lima (1898–   ) Brazil
Souza Lima is considered to be one of the most outstanding musicians of Brazil and is well known in the area of piano pedagogy.
Suite Mirim 1959 (MS available from composer: Rua Higienópolis, 360 - Ap.51 01238 São Paulo (SP) Brazil) 12 min. Five movements.
Concerto a 1965 (MS available from composer) 25 min.

Leo Sowerby (1895–1968) USA
Concerto I F 1917 revised 1919 (MS at LC). For piano and orchestra, with a soprano obbligato. 30 min. This concerto, "condensed and exuviated of its ectoplasmic soprano part was performed by Sowerby for the first time in the new version with the Chicago Symphony Orchestra on 5 March 1920" (MSNH, 277).
Ballad, King Estmere 1921 (Fl). For two pianos and orchestra. 16 min.
Concerto II E 1932 (location of MS unknown).

Leopold Spinner (1906–   ) Great Britain, born Poland
Concerto for Piano and Chamber Orchestra Op.4 1947 (Bo&H) 51pp. Moderato; Allegro poco moderato. Twelve-tone, proportional rhythmic relationships, flexible meters, pointillistic, thin textures. M-D.

Michal Spisak (1914–1965) Poland
Concerto 1947 (PWM) 20 min.

Alexander Spitzmueller (1896–1962) Austria
Concerto I (Bo&H) 16 min.
Concert dans L'Esprit Latin Op.37 (Bo&H 1952) 19 min. Sinfonia; Serenata del Corso; Permutazioni; Commedia. Strong rhythms in a neoclassic mold. Piano is treated as an equal ensemble partner. MC. M-D.

Edward Staempfli (1908–   ) Switzerland
Concertino (Müller 1954) 12 min. Allegro; Molto lento; Vivace. Thorny; highly chromatic; a tune peeks through from time to time in this twelve-tone work. M-D.
Concerto III (Bo&Bo) 26 min.

Alphonse Stallaert (1920–   ) The Netherlands
Concerto 1950 (Billaudot 1966) 30 min. Allegro agitato (cadenza); Andante; Presto giocoso. Freely tonal, strong rhythms in outer movements. M-D.

Patric Standford (1939–   ) Great Britain
Concertante (Novello). For piano and chamber orchestra. 22 min.

Karl Stamitz (1746–1801) Germany
Concerto F (Rhaw—Br&H 5955) 21½ min. Three movements (FSF). Contains many rapid broken octaves, smooth singing melodies, bright staccato themes, and arpeggiated rhythmically moving harmonies. Not especially memorable but a pleasure to perform and hear. Int. to M-D.

Charles Villiers Stanford (1852–1924) Great Britain
Concert Variations on "Down among the Deadmen" Op.71 (Bo&H 1898) 23 min. Introduction, theme, twelve variations. M-D.
Concerto II Op.126 c (S&B 1926; Fl). Allegro moderato; Adagio molto; Allegro molto. Strong melodic interest, especially in the second and third movements. Grateful piano writing, no undue demands but requires mature pianism. M-D.

John Stanley (1713–1786) Great Britain
These concertos are taken from a set of six for strings and continuo, which were also issued as concertos for harpsichord or organ with string accompaniment. Bo&H editions include both versions. All Int. to M-D.
Concerto I D (Finzi—Bo&H) 10 min.
Concerto II b (Finzi—Bo&H) 14 min.
Concerto III G (Finzi—Bo&H) 8 min.
Concerto IV d (Finzi—Bo&H) 9 min.
Concerto V A (Finzi—Bo&H; Fl) 8 min.
Concerto VI B♭ (Finzi—Bo&H) 8 min.

Robert Starer (1924–   ) USA, born Austria
Concerto I 1947 (MCA) 21 min. Allegro; Adagio con moto; Allegro risoluto.

Combines free tonality and a complex rhythmic and contrapuntal organization. Communicative writing, thematic forthrightness, structured clarity. M-D.

Concerto II 1955 (MCA) 16 min. Allegro giusto; Lento; Molto allegro. Atonal. Well laid out for the piano. Also available transcribed for band (winds and percussion), with piano part unchanged (MCA). M-D.

Concerto III 1974 (MCA) 24 min. Moderato maestoso: leads to an Allegro, alternately percussive and lyrical. Lento: strong rhythmic control necessary. Allegretto: changing meters; rhythmic irregularity; fast dynamic changes in closing section. Presto: spontaneous, vigorous, varied rhythmic usage. D.

Bernhard Stavenhagen (1862–1914) Germany

This German-born disciple of Liszt was widely known as a brilliant concert pianist and a far-sighted conductor at the turn of the century. He was an outstanding Liszt player.

Concerto b Op.4 1894 (R&E; Fl) 25½ min. An impassioned transposition of the spirit of the Liszt symphonic poem to the three-movement concerto format. The form is somewhat similar to that of Liszt's *Sonata* in b. The complex harmonic and structural scheme is cleverly carried out. Melodically the work is memorable, especially the lofty, widespread, almost Brahmsian main idea, which threads through the two outer movements. The lovely, somewhat liturgical Adagio comes after the first-movement development, and the finale is the recapitulation. Orchestral scoring is reminiscent of the two Brahms piano concertos. Sustained beauty and inspiration. M-D.

Peter Pindar Stearns (1931–   ) USA

Reminiscence 1959 (ACA). For piano and string orchestra. 7 min.

Jacques Stehman (1912–   ) Belgium

Escapades 1968 (CeBeDeM). For piano and strings. 12 min. Pleasant, inventive, and easily accessible. M-D.

Concerto A 1972 (CeBeDeM) 20 min. In four movements. Subtle dissonance and unusual chords. Light and choice instrumentation enhance this score with charm and color. M-D.

Daniel Steibelt (1765–1823) Germany

Steibelt had a sense of sound and frequently some Romantic inspiration. His works foreshadow the concertos of Kalkbrenner and Chopin, and his piano writing is often inventive.

Concerto III E Op.35 (Musica Obscura; Br&H) "The Storm." Allegro Brillante; Air Ecossais; Rondo Pastorale (Dans le quel on à introduit une tempête). This work was one of the models for Beethoven's *Pastoral Symphony*. The third movement has a storm scene with dramatic tremolos and runs. This work achieved some popularity during its day. M-D.

Concerto V E♭ (Br&H). The slow movement is supposed to be based on a theme composed by Mary Stuart, Queen of Scots, during her imprisonment! Steibelt's grandiloquent ideas were hardly ever equaled by his musical talent. His works often employ picturesque titles.

Concerto VI g "The Voyage to Mount St. Bernard" (CFP).

Gitta Steiner (1932–   ) USA, born Czechoslovakia

Concerto 1967 (Seesaw) 15 min. In one movement, quarter-note = ca.60. Proportional rhythmic relationships, glissandi, tremolo clusters, pointillistic, expressionistic, cadenzalike section for piano, improvised passages in orchestra. Solo piano concludes work by itself. Complex and thorny. D.

Eric-Paul Stekel (1898–   ) France, born Austria

Concerto f Op.12 (Paterson's 1966) 44 min. Four movements. Dramatic, nineteenth-century inspiration, but slightly contemporary sounding. M-D.

Wilhelm Stenhammar (1871–1927) Sweden

Concerto I b♭ Op.1 1893 (ES; Fl; Hainauer) 45 min. Molto moderato e maestoso. Vivacissimo. Andante. Allegro commodo. Leans toward Brahms in the symphonic layout, overblown but has some redeeming moments in the Andante. M-D.

Concerto II d Op.23 (1905–7 (WH; Fl) 30 min. In one movement. Nineteenth-century style; craft is more tightly controlled here. Virtuoso pianism required. M-D to D.

Josef Anton Štěpan (Steffan) (1726–1797) Bohemia

Concerto D (Belsky—Artia 1959) 34pp. MAB 39. Biographical and analytical notes in Czech, German, and English.

Concerto D (Picton—OUP 1976) 30 min. Preface and critical note in English and German. Adagio–Allegro; Andante; Allegro. A late work. The Andante has two written-out cadenzas, the second of which is quite exceptional. The finale, a large-scale sonata–rondo, vies with the first movement in importance. The first and the last movements are each built on three main subjects and share several stylistic points (such as the use of the key of the mediant minor in the central section), all favorite devices found in a number of other Štěpan concertos. M-D.

Johann Franz Xaver Sterkel (1750–1817) Germany

Concerto I Op.20 1784–85 (Scharnagl—Schott 5760) 20 min. Preface in German, French, and English. Cadenzas and keyboard reduction (in second piano score) by A. Kaul. Allegro con spirito; Andante; Rondeau. ". . . a revealing contribution to the development of the piano concerto in the end of the eighteenth century, a work with all the more significance since many of Sterkel's stylistic peculiarities did not pass without influence on the young Beethoven" (from the score). Int.

Ronald Stevenson (1928–   ) Great Britain

Concerto I "Faust Triptych" (Novello 1973) 30 min. Largo; Fugue; Fantasy. Influences of Ravel, Gershwin, Rachmaninoff, and Busoni. Originally this was a triptych on *Faust* scenes with quotations from Busoni. Another version, for solo piano, is entitled *Prelude, Fugue and Fantasy.* The concerto version closely parallels the solo version. D.

Heinrich Sthamer (1885–   ) Germany
Concerto B Op.9 (Schlesinger 1913; Fl) 78pp. In one movement.

Milan Stibilj (1929–   ) Yugoslavia
Congruences 1963 (DSS) 9 min. Expressionistic, flexible meters, sudden tempo changes, thin textures in piano part and orchestration, twelve-tone influence. M-D.

William Grant Still (1895–1975) USA
Kaintuck' (Kentucky) 1935 (Fl) 14 min. One movement. An Impressionistic tone poem, contrasting sections, banjo figuration in piano part, cadenza, *pp* ending. M-D. Copies also available from Mrs. Still at 1262 Victoria Ave., Los Angeles, CA 90019.
Dismal Swamp (NME 1937) 12 min. A colorful, somewhat Impressionistic tone poem. Piano partakes of the ensemble but also has some solo moments. Deserves hearing. M-D.

Wolfgang Stockmeier (1931–   ) Germany
Variationen für Klaviertrio und Orchestra (Möseler).

Albert Stoessel (1894–1943) USA
Concerto Grosso (JF 1935). For string orchestra and piano obbligato. 22 min. Allegro; Saraband; Pavan; Introduction and Gigue. Neoclassic, closely related in style and treatment to the Ernest Bloch *Concerto Grosso* for piano and chamber orchestra. Tonal; MC. Deserves hearing. M-D.

Siegmund Stojowski (1869–1946) USA, born Poland
Concerto I f♯ Op.3 (Schott 1893; Augener; Fl) 79pp. Andante poco mosso; Romanza—Andante sostenuto; Allegro con fuoco. Beautifully laid out for the piano; somewhat dated but contains some beautiful melodies; virtuosic in places. M-D.
Rapsodie Symphonique Op.23 1906 (CFP 9131). Sectionalized, colorful, strong pianistic writing, cadenza sections, frequently performed by Paderewski. M-D.
Concerto II A♭ Op.32 (Heugel 1912) 61pp. Prologue, Scherzo et Variations. 32 min. A large effusive work with many effective moments, Saint-Saëns influence, thematic rhythmic transformation. M-D.

Robert Stolz (1880–1975) Austria
Traume an der Donau Op.162 (Edition Rex 1955). For piano with salon orchestra. M-D.

Vesseline Stoyanov (1902–1969) Bulgaria
Concerto I a 1952 (Edition d'Etat Science et Arts).
Concerto II d 1955 (Edition d'Etat Science et Arts) 90pp. Allegro; Adagio; Moderato. Freely tonal; conservative piano writing. M-D.

Joep Straesser (1934–   ) The Netherlands
Canterbury Concerto 1978 (Donemus). For piano and chamber orchestra. 12 min.
"The Canterbury Concerto is not a 'normal' piano concerto. The piano starts
as an instrument of the orchestra—it accompanies the orchestra—and develops gradually as a solo instrument. In this respect it reaches its top in the
'cadenza.' After that it falls back in its subordinate position, except in the
last bars of the piece" (from the score). Uses many contemporary techniques,
such as clusters and a pointillistic approach. M-D.
Just a Moment Again 1978 (Donemus). For piano, percussion, and string orchestra.
11pp., photostat.

Willard Straight (1930–   ) USA
Concerto (Chappell) 26 min.

Herman Strategier (1912–   ) The Netherlands
Concerto 1948 (Donemus) 20 min.

Richard Strauss (1864–1949) Germany   .
Burleske d 1885–86 (EBM; IMC; Eulenburg; K; Steingräber) 18 min. This piece
is permeated with humor; at times the piano and orchestra seem to laugh at
each other. Opens with a dialogue between the timpani and the orchestra,
which is quickly interrupted by the merry piano. This theme, a combination
of rhythm and scales, gives way to a second theme that is also introduced by
the piano, and, in its lyrically long melodic line, is reminiscent of Brahms.
Contains waltz sections that strikingly anticipate the "Der Rosenkavalier"
waltzes of a quarter-century later. Closes with the timpani having a last quiet
word. Wide tonal range exploited. Strauss liked this piece so much that he
programmed it at his last concert in London in October 1947. Firm rhythmic
control necessary. M-D to D.
Parergon zur Sinfonia Domestica Op.73 1924–25 (Bo&H). For piano, left-hand
and orchestra. The thematic materials are by-products (parergon) of the
"Sinfonia Domestica" (mainly the "theme of the child" is developed). Fierce
intervallic leaps and other passages require virtuoso technique. D.
Panathenäenzug Op.74 1926–7 (Bo&H) Symphonic Etudes in the form of a Passacaglia. For piano, left-hand and orchestra. 22 min.

Igor Stravinsky (1882–1971) USA, born Russia
Concerto for Piano and Wind Instruments 1924 revised 1950 (Bo&H) 20 min.
Largo–Allegro; opens with a march for orchestra with the piano interrupting
with the principal subject; rhythmical chords and nonlegato figurations; a
recap gives the piano complete dominance, and the orchestra joins in to
conclude the movement. Larghissimo (Largo, rev. ed.): expressive cantabile
material with two interrupted cadenzas for the piano. Allegro: metrically
flexible; martellato conclusion; requires a brilliant nonlegato technique.
Freely tonal, continuous repetition of motives, ever-changing meters—all
characteristic of Stravinsky's "middle period." D.

Capriccio 1928–29 revised 1949 (Bo&H; IMC; K) 19 min. Presto; Andante rapsodico; Allegro capriccioso ma tempo giusto. A concerto in everything but
name. Neoclassicism and Baroque archaism are evident throughout the work.
Clear forms; piano texture is transparently linear throughout. Ingenious orchestration with division into soli and ripieno string groups. The piano part
is molded with the orchestra and the only extended solo is a short cadenza
that closes the slow movement. Clean finger work is essential for the pianist.
M-D.

Movements 1958–59 (Bo&H 18677) 10 min. Five movements connected by short
instrumental interludes, based on a twelve-tone row with many permutations
and combinations. Webern influence is seen in the pointillistic and fragmentary approach and the extreme economy of notes. Canonic treatment of the
row passes freely from one part to another. Rhythmical treatment is the most
difficult of any of the elements; polyrhythms exist in vertical layers and
frequent accelerations and ritardandos add to the difficulty. Dry instrumentation. D.

See: Thomas Moore, "An Analytical Study of Stravinsky's *Movements* for Piano
and Orchestra," thesis, University of Michigan, 1969.

Willis A. Stevens, "The Concerted Piano Music of Stravinsky," Ph.D. diss.,
University of Rochester, Eastman School of Music, 1961.

Folke Strømholm (1941–   ) Norway
Concertino Op.1 1964 (TONO) 14 min. In three movements. Neoclassic. M-D.
Concerto Op.12 1967 (TONO) 9 min. In one movement. Avant-garde. M-D.

Hans Studer (1911–   ) Switzerland
Chamber Concerto (Br 2020). For piano and chamber orchestra. 19 min.
Little Concerto 1951 (Br 1914). For piano, four-hands and chamber orchestra.
Reproduced from holograph. 10 min. Allegro moderato; Lento; Allegro.
Neoclassic, freely tonal. Piano part is closely integrated with the other in-
strumentation, octotonic. Int. to M-D.

Eugen Suchoň (1908–   ) Czechoslovakia
Suchoň's harmonic vocabulary is derived from the modality of Slovak folk music.
Rhapsodic Suite 1965 (Supraphon; USSR 1977) 75pp.

Robert Suderburg (1936–   ) USA
Concerto: Within the Mirror of Time 1974 (TP) 25 min. Lyric Reflection: piano
begins with main thematic germ, which has a rhythmic outline similar to that
of the main idea in "Scarbo" of Ravel's *Gaspard de la Nuit;* this idea is
worked through with much development, using numerous freely tonal dramatic gestures; arpeggi and large chordal sonorities add excitement; *ppp*
conclusion. Presto: after orchestral introduction piano enters with staccato
eighth-note figuration; short spurts of scalar treatment interlaced with trills
decorate the melodic line carried in orchestra; two cadenzas for piano, one
for orchestra; opening figuration returns and leads to a great climax before

orchestra ends the movement. Ritual Dance: lower register of piano exploited in opening section; freely chromatic figures with triplet accompaniment show off melodic material in the piano; a bell-like section quickly provides contrast; pointillistic writing interspersed with chordal sonorities; opening idea from first movement returns with added glittering arpeggi. Piano is treated in an unashamedly Romantic and old-fashioned virtuoso style, thus providing some dramatic and exciting writing. Brilliant, colorful, and exciting orchestration. M-D to D.

Dana Suesse (1911–   ) USA

Concerto e 1939 (DS Music). For two pianos and orchestra. In four movements.

Concerto in Three Rhythms (DS Music: Dana Suesse Music Co., P.O. Box 2088, Frederiksted, St. Croix, Virgin Islands).

Concerto Romantico 1946 (DS Music) 18½ min.

Concertino (E. H. Morris 1945) 10 min.

Rezsö Sugár (1919–   ) Hungary

Rondo (EMB 1955). For piano and junior string orchestra. 29pp. Adagio introduction leads to a cheerful Allegretto treated in rondo fashion. Neoclassic. Would make a delightful work for a high school orchestra and teen-age pianist. Int.

Carlos Surinach (1915–   ) USA, born Spain

Doppio Concertino (Rongwen 1956). For piano, violin, and chamber orchestra. 15 min.

Concertino 1957 (AMP; Fl). For piano, strings, and cymbals. 16 min. Chacona; Andante; Vivace.

Concerto 1974 (AMP 1976) 23 min. Allegro: piano used percussively. Second movement: meditative, dialogue between piano and orchestra. Third movement: lively, cadenzalike passages. Even though this work is based on an eight-note scale characteristic of flamenco music, very little Spanish influence has found its way into the piece. Contains plenty of emotion, vitality, fine tunes, and interesting harmonies but tends to ramble at places. Heavily scored, including a full percussion battery. Virtuoso technique required for the rapid chordal passages up and down the keyboard, hammered-out trills, octave runs, and full-keyboard glissandi. D.

Heinrich Sutermeister (1910–   ) Switzerland

The music of Honegger, Prokofiev, and Verdi have been the main influences on Sutermeister's development.

Concerto I 1943 (Schott 3669) 36 min. Allegro; Adagio; Presto marcato.

Concerto II 1953 (Schott 4548) 25 min. Marsch; Choral; Fanfaren und Hymne. Expanded tonality. M-D.

Concerto III 1961–62 (Schott 4819) 33 min. In modo patètico; In modo pastorale; In modo capriccioso; In modo marziale. Expanded tonality. M-D.

Orazione (Schott 1951).

Margaret Sutherland (1897–   ) Australia
Concertino 1940 (J. Albert).

Tomas Svoboda (1939–   ) USA, born France
Concerto Op.71 1974 (Strangeland). Contains an emotional directness and
rhythmic drive. The distinctive melodic flavor is due in part to the composer's
Czechoslovakian heritage. M-D.

Adam Swierzynski (1914–   ) Poland
Concerto 1950 (PWM) 30 min.

Richard Swift (1927–   ) USA
"[Swift] describes his music as influenced by the Viennese twelve-tone school;
by the work and thought of Stravinsky, Babbitt, Perle, and Sessions; and by the
analytical methods of Heinrich Schenker" (DCM, 723).
Concerto Op.26 1961 (University of California Press, Berkeley). For piano with
chamber ensemble. 30 min. Introduction; Sciolto; Spianato; Lesto; Flessible;
Cadenza; Finale. Scored for flute (piccolo), clarinet, bass clarinet, percussion, violin, viola, and two cellos. In the sixth movement, the cadenza is
arranged on the principle of a child's flip-flop face book. Serial influence,
expressionistic. M-D.

William Sydeman (1928–   ) USA
Concertino 1956 (Seesaw). For piano, oboe, and string orchestra. 10 min. Adagio
lamentoso; Allegro energico. Atonal, chromatic figuration, dramatic
rhythmic gestures, fondness for seconds, changing meters, octotonic, trills,
fast figures in alternating hands. M-D to D.
Concerto 1967 (Ione). For piano, four-hands with chamber orchestra. 17 min.
The composer has said of this work: "The Concerto is conceived as a huge
arch form in two large divisions. The climax of the work is the end of the
first movement. The second movement, which is divided in two parts, functions as a return to serenity after the cataclysms of the first. . . . Part one
sustains a sonority throughout, in which fragmented events by piano and
percussion occur—part two superimposes orchestral fragments over a consistent terribly high, terribly quiet, terribly omnipresent flow of piano notes.
The piece sort of floats away at the end" (from Desto record jacket DC-
7131). The work as a whole is brilliant and, in the best sense of the word,
entertaining. D.

Boleslaw Szabelski (1896–   ) Poland
Concertino 1955 (PWM) 18 min.
Verses 1961 (PWM) full score, 41pp. Four sections. Pointillistic, proportional
rhythmic relationships, dynamic extremes, remarkable polyphony, apho-
ristic, avant-garde. M-D.
Concerto 1978 (PWM). In one movement. Powerful and massive beginning, vigorous and vibrant, highly dissonant, contrasts of texture, pointillistic, horizontal and perpendicular atomization of ideas. D.

Endre Szekely (1912–   ) Hungary
Concerto for Piano, Percussion and Strings 1958 (EMB) 20 min. Three movements (FSF). Expanded tonality. M-D.
Sinfonia Concertante 1960–61 (EMB). For piano, violin, and orchestra. 14 min. Five contrasting movements. Expanded tonality, flexible meters, clusterlike chords, cadenza passages for the piano and violin. Piano and violin have the second movement (Intermezzo) to themselves, Hungarian flavor seeps in through modal usage. M-D.

István Szelényi (1904–1972) Hungary
Summa Vitae "Fantasy for Piano and Orchestra on a Motive of Franz Liszt" 1956 (EMB) 12 min. A one-movement concerto based on a motive written by Liszt a few weeks before he died. This motive looks forward to the twentieth century (Bartók and Schoenberg especially). "The title is intended to express the summing up of a life as if condensed into a revelation just before death" (from the score). MC. M-D.

Tadeusz Szeligowski (1896–1963) Poland
Concerto D 1946 (PWM) 64pp. Allegro con brio: piano part is very much in the foreground. Andante: nocturne-like and linked to the Allegro risoluto. Neoclassic, interesting rhythms. Humorous finale, in which the piano has dialogues with the orchestra in the rhythm of an oberek (native dance). M-D.

Sándor Szokolay (1931–   ) Hungary
Concerto 1958 (Zenmukiado) 19 min. Rapsodia; Ostinato; Capriccio. Asymmetric rhythms, modal, Bartók influence. M-D.

Erzsebet Szönyi (1924–   ) Hungary
Trio Concertino (EMB). For piano, violin, cello, and orchestra. Allegro moderato. Andante: a trio sonata for the soloists. Con moto, ma non troppo: theme and eight variations. Neoclassic. M-D.

Karol Szymanowski (1882–1937) Poland
Szymanowski is one of the most important creative figures to emerge from Poland since Chopin. Although influenced by other twentieth-century figures such as Richard Strauss, Debussy, and Stravinsky, Szymanowski does not belong to any of the more popular twentieth-century areas of influence. There is an intense rhythmic force in his writing, coupled with rich harmonic colors, and much of his work has an oriental sensuality that derives from Slavonic folk music. Szymanowski's piano compositions, especially the later ones, are highly personalized in musical content and pianistic layout, and are very complex and difficult.
Symphonie Concertante II Op.60 1932 (PWM 2262; ESC; USSR) 21½ min. Allegro moderato; Andante sostenuto; Allegro non troppo. This work was actually Szymanowski's fourth symphony, but the title indicates the equal importance of the orchestra and solo instrument. Thematic materials are derived from Polish songs and dances of the Tatra Mountains region. Brilliant rhapsodic outer movements enclose a beautifully lyrical second movement,

which is a lovely slow crescendo with a highly ornamented piano narrative throughout. There is a breathtaking climax to the whole work. Demands musicality and pianism of the very highest order. D.

Zbigniew Szymonowicz (1922–   ) Poland
Concerto 1956 (PWM) 23 min.

T

Ricardo Tacuchian (1939–   ) Brazil
Tacuchian teaches at the Music Department of the Federal University of Rio de Janeiro.
Concertino 1977 (SDM). For piano and strings. 15 min.

Gino Tagliapietra (1887–1954) Italy
Concertino a (Carisch 1930) 22 min. One movement, contrasting sections. Nineteenth-century style with a few MC devices, cadenza passages, attractive piano writing. M-D.

Germaine Tailleferre (1892–   ) France
Concerto D 1924 (Heugel 28.745) 12 min. Allegro; Adagio; Allegro non troppo. Written in a lively, neoclassic French style that uses contrapuntal opposition of tutti and solo. Delightful, graceful. Contains some musical moments and some thin, dissonant textures. MC. M-D.
Ballade (JWC 1925) 43pp. A ravishing work, beautifully scored, grateful pianistic writing. M-D.
Concerto 194? (MS at LC). For two pianos and orchestra. 33pp. Much doubling; lighthearted mood; clever cross-rhythms. M-D.

Jenö Takacs (1902–   ) USA, born Austria
Tarantella Op.39 (UE 1094 1939) 12 min. Bartók influence in polytonal spots, short, effective, brilliant, MC. M-D.

Toru Takemitsu (1930–   ) Japan
Takemitsu is one of the leading figures among Japan's ever-increasing number of contemporary composers.
Arc 1963 (Sal) 30 min. Pile: senza tempo. Solitude: contains a free piano cadenza. Your Love and the Crossing: spastic directed improvisation for four minutes. Avant-garde. M-D.
Asterism 1968 (CFP) 12 min. Contains a largely expanded percussion section that pursues some tortuous, disjunctive lines plus a great atomistic rush of sounds à la Xenakis. But somehow it all adds up to very communicative music. Piano is to have the cover removed. Avant-garde. D.

Shalva M. Taktakishvili (1900–   ) USSR
Concertino (USSR 1960) 87pp. Allegro cantabile; Andante; Vivace. Thin textures,

freely tonal, MC. A good high school student could handle this with aplomb. Int.

Otar V. Taktashvili (1924–   ) USSR
Taktashvili is perhaps the most famous of all the Georgian composers today.
Concerto c 1951 (State Music Publishers of the Georgian SSR) 33 min. Allegro
molto; Vivo e leggiero; Andante; Allegro molto.
Concerto II "Melodies of the Mountains" (USSR 1976) 66pp. Andante; Allegro
alla breve.
These two lush works are in a pan-Caucasian style not unreminiscent of Khachaturian. Romantically broad-gestured with cadenzas; ethnically melodic.
M-D to D.

Joseph Tal (1910–   ) Israel, born Poland
Concerto II 1953 (IMP) 22 min. "In one tripartite movement, based on a traditional modal cantillation of Jeremiah's lament, developing according to serial principles" (MSNH, 1119).
Concerto III 1956 (IMP; Fl). For piano and orchestra with tenor voice. 18 min.
In one movement.
Concerto V 1964 (IMI). For piano and orchestra with tape.

Louise Talma (1906–   ) USA
"All of Talma's works before 1953 are neoclassic in style; those after 1953, serial" (DCM, 730).
Dialogues 1963–64 (CF) 22 min. In five movements.

Tōru Tamura (1938–   ) Japan
Piano Concerto 1979 (MS available from composer: 3392–36 Shinyoshida-cho,
Kōhokuku Yokohamashi, Kanagawa-Ken, Japan F223). Adagio–Andante;
Grave; Allegro. Neoclassic, fondness for asymmetrical melodic and
rhythmic units, sophisticated orchestration, varied meters. M-D.

Sergei I. Taneyev (1856–1915) Russia
Concerto E♭ (Lamm—USSR 1953). Conceived in three movements but only the
first two parts (Allegro: cheerful and vigorous; Andante funebre: austere and
steady) were completed. The third part was only arranged for two pianos.
Tchaikowsky greatly appreciated this concerto. Displays a combination of
Russian melos and Germanic contrapuntal writing. M-D.

Alexandre Tansman (1897–   ) Poland
Concerto I 1925 (ESC 1615) 19 min. Allegro molto; Lento; Intermezzo; Finale.
Neoclassic, "with harmonies enhanced by pandiatonic quartal excrescences
and bitonal superimpositions on resonantly spaced triadic basses, and distinguished by authentically inflected Polish dance melorhythms" (MSNH,
433). M-D.
Concerto II 1927 (ESC 2165) 24 min. Allegro risoluto; Scherzo; Lento e Finale.
"In three movements, of which the last opens with a *Berceuse* set in nostalgic

Polish inflections and then erupts into a rhythmic finale" (MSNH, 465). M-D.

Suite 1928 (ESC 4458). For two pianos and orchestra. 25 min. Introduction et Allegro; Intermezzo; Perpetuum Mobile. Variations [5], double-fugue et Finale sur un thême slave. Neoclassic; instrumentation and ensemble writing are exceptionally fine; clever dissonant technique. M-D.

Concertino 1931 (ESC) 16 min. Toccata: opens with a piano cadenza; octotonic. Intermezzo Chopiniano: chordal and melodic. Allegro Risoluto: giocoso, rhythmic, brilliant, and frothy. M-D.

Fantaisie 1937 (ESC 5909) 16 min. Introduction et Scherzo: agitated, quartal and quintal harmonies, Presto perpetual motion section. Adagio e Finale: improvisatory opening, melody accompanied with repeated chords (Adagio cantabile), Allegro molto driving conclusion. M-D.

Béla Tardos (1910–1966) Hungary

Concerto 1954 (Belwin-Mills) 30 min.

Fantasia 1961 (EMB) 12 min. Freely tonal, mildly dissonant, large cadenza for piano, Romantic overtones, glissandi. M-D.

Svend Erik Tarp (1908–   ) Denmark

Concerto C Op.39 (Engstrøm 1944) 20 min. Molto vivace; Lento; Allegro con brio. Neoclassic; MC; much activity in outer movements. Large span required. M-D.

Antonio Tauriello (1931–   ) Argentina

Concerto (Barry 1968) 20 min. Subdivided into eleven structures with an optional synchronization between the soloist and orchestra. Aleatory techniques, experimental notation. M-D to D.

Gunther Tautenhahn (1938–   ) USA, born Lithuania

Numeric Serenade 1978 (Seesaw) 9 min. Seven contrasting sections. Proportional rhythmic notation, pointillistic, changing meters, expressionistic. Rhythmic and metric problems are especially difficult. D.

Hekel Tavares (1896–1970) Brazil

Concerto in Brazilian Forms Op.105/2 (Bo&H) 24 min. Modinha; Tempo di Batuque; Ponteio; Maracatu. A brilliant, evocative, richly colored, and full-blooded work. Conventional harmonic idiom; Romantic and warmly turned melodies; juxtaposition of elemental, sometimes barbaric, rhythms and long, expressive melodic lines. Folk idiom permeates the work but tunes are all original. M-D.

John Tavener (1944–   ) Great Britain

"Tavener's strength lies in his unerringly sure sense of architectural design and his ability to manipulate time through the use of ritual to construct large-scale forms" (Tim Alps, M&M 27 [May 1979]:62).

Palintropos 1978 (JWC) 25 min. Four continuous sections. The title refers to the work's structure, which returns at the close to its starting point: a simple and striking gesture carried through the strings. Evocative, Impressionistic. Orchestration is somewhat static. Solo piano part is continually busy with Messiaen-like, chattering figuration but never really occupies the foreground. Climax is reached in the fourth section, where the piano has a frenzied cadenza against choralelike chords in the brass instruments. An impressive work. M-D to D.

Alexander Tchaikowsky (1925–   ) USSR

Concerto (Soviet Composer 1977) 68pp. Toccata; Phantasy; March. Modal, colorful, strong rhythms, preference for seconds in chords, freely tonal. Virtuoso octave technique required. D.

André Tchaikowsky (1935–   ) Great Britain

Concerto Op.4 (Weinberger 1975) 28 min. Introduction leads immediately to Passacaglia; Capriccio; Finale. Freely tonal and at times atonal; involved rhythms; strongly linear; many rubatos requiring great control; textures generally thin; many changing meters. Mature musicianship and pianism required. D.

Peter I. Tchaikowsky (1840–1893) Russia

Concerto I b♭ Op.23 1874–75 (GS; CFP; Eulenburg; K; WH; EC; Zen-On; IMC) 28 min. Perhaps the most famous of all piano concertos, and for good reason: beautiful themes, flamboyant pianistic expertise, magnificent orchestration, and perfect interplay between piano and orchestra. Allegro non troppo e molto maestoso: highly original form, dramatic climaxes balanced with exquisite lyricism. Andante semplice: a nocturne; subtle varied treatment of the opening melody at every repetition; the whole movement is a mixture of the lyrical and the whimsically fantastic. Allegro con fuoco: a rondo whose first theme (played by the pianist) is a syncopated dance of Ukrainian origin; second theme becomes the climax of the large coda of the concerto, which ends, spectacularly, in a blaze of color in the major tonality of D♭. A wide range of tone and rhythmic vitality plus great power are requisites. D. See: James Friskin, "The Text of Tchaikowsky's B-flat minor Concerto," M&L, April 1969:246–51.

Edward Garden, "Three Russian Piano Concertos," M&L 60, April 1979; 166–79.

Concerto II G Op.44 1881 (Paragon; Alkor; CFP; Eulenburg; CF; Jurgenson; Rahter) 34 min. Wonderfully crafted, expressively direct, temperate in mood, not as emotional as but more difficult than *Concerto* I. All three movements contain excellent ideas. Allegro brillante e molto vivace: free SA design; orchestral introduction immediately followed by piano; a lovely lyrical section in E♭ follows, building gradually to a stunning climax and then receding for the return of an earlier cantabile theme in C; sweeping octaves recall the orchestra, and the rest of the movement is predictably effective. Andante non troppo: some concertante feeling shared with a solo violin and cello, but the piano is given the main emphasis. Allegro con fuoco: rondolike;

short; Russian folk-song influence but all melodies are original with the composer. Alexander Siloti (who edited the Jurgenson edition) did a simplified version of this concerto but it is no longer available. D.

Concerto III E Op.75 1895 (Sikorski; Jurgenson; K) 30 min. A single movement (Allegro brillante) in large SA design with three strong, distinct thematic ideas. The first, clearly symphonic, appears in the bassoons over a timpani pedal point with the piano echoing it in double octaves. The solo piano plays the second theme in G, Schumannesque in character, which later dominates the cadenza. The most notable thing about the third theme is its staccato usage. The clangorous excitement that unfolds requires the strongest whirlwind virtuoso technique. D.

Concert Fantasy G Op.56 1891 (K; Jurgenson; CF; Hinrichsen). This short and attractive work is less pretentious than the second concerto. The two main sections, Quasi rondo and Contrastes, contain brilliant piano writing, effective orchestration, and strong thematics. Virtuoso technique required. D.

Andante and Finale B♭ Op.79 1893 (Belaieff; Paragon; K) 19 min. Based on the same source as the one-movement *Concerto* III, Op.75. Orchestrated by Taneieff. The Andante is lyrical and appealing. M-D.

Alexander Tcherepnin (1899–1977) USA, born Russia

Concerto I F Op.12 1919–20 (Philipp—JWC) 18 min. In one movement.

Concerto II A Op.26 1923 (Heugel) 15 min. In one movement in a widely enlarged Classical sonata structure. Eclectic, natural writing that is appealing and exciting. Built around a complex nine-note scale; displays some remarkable polyphonic and rhythmic devices. Interplay between piano and orchestra provides a scintillating tension. A powerful lyricism permeates the entire work. M-D to D.

Concertino Op.47 1931 (UE 1053). For piano, violin, cello, and string orchestra.

Concerto III B♭ Op.48 1931–32 (Schott 3269) 20 min. Unusual two-movement form. Moderato: a kind of prelude to the Allegro: a complex fugue in "intrapuntal style." Complex rhythmic textures, forceful rhythms, percussive. Demanding solo part. M-D to D.

Suite Géorgienne Op.57 (ESC 1938) 23 min. Use of Georgian folk materials. This culture was absorbed by Tcherepnin during the three years he lived in Tbilisi. Tarantella-like conclusion to this four-movement work. Soloist plays continuously. M-D.

Fantaisie Op.78 (Concerto IV) 1947 (Hin) 27 min. A programmatic piece inspired by Chinese folklore. All three movements use major, minor, and pentatonic modes. Virtuosic. D.

Concerto V Op.96 1963 (Belaieff) 21 min. Allegro moderato: ABA, uses much chromaticism and borders on atonality. Andantino: rondo. Animato, ma poco rubato: rondo, brings back material from the first movement's B section. The piano writing is never thick but is always varied and effective. Employs Tcherepnin's own eight-note scale. M-D to D.

Concerto VI Op.99 1965 (Belaieff) 24 min. Allegro: toccata-like. Andantino: ABA. Animato: a large three-part form. D.

Compare the two-piano reductions with the miniature full scores when possible, especially in *Concertos* V and VI, as there are considerable differences.

See: Guy Wuellner, "The Piano Concertos of Alexander Tcherepnin," Part I, AMT 27 (June-July 1978):11–13; Part II, AMT 28 (September–October 1978): 18, 20–21.

Nikolai Tcherepnin (1873–1945) USSR

Concerto c♯ Op.30 1910 (Jurgenson) 26 min. In one large movement, contrasting sections. Dark colors; virtuosic pianism and orchestration. Tries to emulate Tchaikowsky. M-D to D.

Alexandre Tchesnokoff (–   ) Russia

Ballade Op.41 (LC) 19pp., photostat. Franck-like, nineteenth-century pianistic gestures, sectional, colorful. M-D.

Alec Templeton (1910–1963) USA, born Wales

Concertino Lirico 1942 (SP) 18 min. Adagio–Allegro moderato; Allegro vivace; Allegro moderato. Long lyric lines; basically Romantic in conception. M-D.

Gothic Concerto (SP 1954) 22 min. Allegro robusto: cadenza; Andantino tranquillo; Alla marcia. Tonal, Romantic, tuneful. M-D.

Rhapsodie Harmonique 1954 (SP) 11 min. Adagio: Introduction, strongly contrasted sections. Andante con moto: theme, variations, and cadenzas. Minuet. Andante: broad conclusion. More MC than the other works. M-D.

All three concertos would made excellent and effective movie music.

Flavio Testi (1923–   ) Italy

Musica da Concerto III 1961 (Ric) 17 min. Allegro; Canzonetta; Finale. Chromatic, brilliant writing, dramatic, MC. Percussive quality of piano emphasized in the outer movements. M-D.

Opus 23 (Ric 1973). For two pianos with two chamber orchestras. Reproduced from holograph, 15 min. A brilliant showpiece for everyone. Much complex rhythmic interplay between the groups. D.

Werner Thaerichen (1921–   ) Germany

Konzert Op.39 1960 (Bo&Bo) 24 min. Three movements (FSF). Expanded tonal vocabulary. M-D.

Konzert II Op.44 (Bo&Bo) 24 min.

Sigismond Thalberg (1812–1871) Germany, born Switzerland

As a pianist, Thalberg was a rival of Liszt and Chopin.

Concerto f Op.5 (NYPL; Fl) 20 min. Allegro maestoso; Adagio; Rondo. Admirable pianistic treatment but the work is full of pretentious hollowness. Contains vague echoes of Rossini, Weber, Chopin, and Field and is a concoction of playable pianistic confetti. M-D.

Ferdinand Thiériot (1838–1919) Germany
Concerto Op.77 (J.M. Rieter-Biedermann). For two pianos and orchestra.

Kurt Thomas (1904–1973) Germany
Concerto Op.30 (Br&H EB5537) 30 min. Breite Halbe; Sehr breit; Sehr lebhafte Viertel. Freely tonal, neoclassic. Much activity including glissandi and imitation. M-D.

Randall Thompson (1899–   ) USA
Jazz Poem 1927 for piano, 1928 with orchestra (Fl) 14 min.

Francis Thorne (1922–   ) USA
Thorne's "music is characterized by the strong influence of both modern jazz and twelve-tone serialism" (DCM, 762). A late bloomer, Thorne switched from business and jazz piano to serious composing at age 43.
Concerto 1973–74 (Joshua). For piano and chamber orchestra. 26 min. Complex, driving rhythms with many syncopations; disjunct melodies; overflows with tension and rhythmic compression. The first of the two movements progresses from loud and fast to soft and slow; the second reverses the process, quoting other composers toward the end. Virtuoso cadenzas, potent piano-orchestral interplay. M-D to D.
Rhapsodic Variations 1965 (AMC) 14 min. Interesting material, expert use of the jazz medium; properly unrestrained at spots. M-D.

Leif Thybo (1922–   ) Denmark
Concerto 1961–62 (Fog) 22 min. Largo pesante–Allegro; Elegia; Allegro. Expanded tonal idiom that verges on atonality; brilliant piano writing with Bartók influence but short on emotional variety. M-D.

Heinz Tiessen (1887–1971) Germany
Concertante Variations Op.60 1962 (R&E) 23 min. Introduction—Alla tirolese; Corrente; Elegia; Disputa; Romanza; Fantasia; Burletta; Interludio I; Notturno; Interludio II; Marcia; Cadenza; Galoppo. Chromatic; short contrasting movements; neoclassic; some effective moments. M-D.

Michael Tippett (1905–   ) Great Britain
Fantasy on a Theme by Handel 1942 (Schott 10122) 16 min. Theme from Handel's *Suites de pièces pour le clavecin* 1733. Short; five clever variations; robust; luxuriant tonal style; effective concluding fugue. M-D.
Concerto 1955 (Schott 10592) 32 min. Allegro non troppo: SA; closely related material; interlocking octaves at climax; quartal and quintal harmonies. Molto lento e tranquillo: Classical; rhapsodic; nocturne-like; Impressionistic; soaring arpeggi; finest movement of the work. Vivace: a fast toccata in an orchestral rondo; texturally imaginative pianistic conception. A work of real substance, the music flows with extraordinary naturalness. M-D to D.
See: Colin Mason, "Michael Tippett's Piano Concerto," *The Listener* 56, no.1439 (October 25, 1956):681.

————. "Tippett's Piano Concerto," *The Score* 16 (June 1965):62–63.
Wilfrid Mellars, "Tippett and His Piano Concerto," *The Listener* 61, no.1554 (January 8, 1959):80.

Boris Ivanovich Tishchenko (1939–   ) USSR
Tishchenko received diplomas from the Leningrad Conservatory in composition in 1962 and piano in 1963. He did postgraduate work with Shostakovitch. Tishchenko is a consummate pianist and one of the brightest young stars in the USSR compositional world. His music displays a strongly Slavic expressionism based on a solid musical heritage.

Concerto Op.21 1962 (USSR 1976) 83pp. Allegro moderato; Allegretto; Allegro vivo. Octotonic, jazz influence, dynamic rhythms, textural clarity, strongly juxtaposed timbres, burlesco finale. Fluid architecture that never goes where you expect it to; some similarities to Shostakovitch style. Advanced pianism required. D.

Concerto Op.54 1972 (USSR 1975). For piano, flute, and string orchestra. 63pp. Five contrasting movements. Freely tonal, jazz influence, rapid-fire clusters in third movement. Multi-divisi writing: sometimes every instrument is assigned a different line. Piano eliminated from first movement. The surface dazzle of this work tends to obscure its orderliness and workmanship. M-D.

Antoine Tisné (1932–   ) France
Tisné studied with Jean Rivier and Darius Milhaud at the Paris Conservatory. He won the Prix de Rome in 1962.

Concerto I 1958 (Billaudot).

Concerto II 1961 (Billaudot).

Concerto III 1963 (Billaudot) 23 min. First movement: SA. Second movement: tripartite with some SA characteristics. Third movement: sonata–rondo, two major themes, coda. Atonal throughout, bold dissonant chords, intense chromatic themes, somber character, dodecaphonic. D.

Gian Luca Tocchi (1901–   ) Italy
Concerto 1935 (Ric). For two pianos and orchestra. 28 min. Dolcemente mosso e volubile; Calmo e pensoso; Andantino vivace. Big dramatic writing with Impressionistic touches; much interplay between pianos and between pianos and orchestra; many tempo changes in the finale. M-D.

Ernst Toch (1887–1964) USA, born Austria
Concerto I Op.38 1925 (Schott 31647) 22 min. Molto pesante; Adagio; Rondo disturbato. Traditional form, polytonal harmony. "Set in a modernistic and richly rhythmical style in fluid tonality" (MSNH, 438). "Dynamic and transcendentally modernistic" (MSNH, 458). The third movement radiates with a boisterous humor. M-D to D.

Concerto II Op.61 1932 (Schott 3277) 26 min. Allegro; Lebhaft; Adagio; Cyclus variabilis. Imitation, driving rhythms, freely tonal, neoclassic, more dramatic than *Concerto* I. D.

Dmitrii A. Tolstoi (1923–   ) USSR
Concerto I Op.44 (USSR 1974) 1116pp. Allegro; Andantino; Allegro. Freely tonal, style is a mixture of Shostakovitch and Kabalevsky. Dramatic finale. M-D to D.

Václav Jan Tomášek (1774–1850) Bohemia
Tomášek's fame rests mainly with his piano works, which inaugurated Romantic instrumental lyricism and considerably influenced Schubert.
Concerto I C Op.18 1805 (Steiner; Haslinger) 26 min. Allegro con brio: careful confrontation between piano and orchestra; piano sails forth in full virtuosic flair. Lento: beautiful interaction between piano and orchestra. Allegro: built on a single and simple theme that is subjected to extensive modulation. This is Tomášek's only piano concerto. It resembles Mozart and Hummel with a few Romantic gestures appearing mainly in the episodes of the finale. Very competent writing; grandiose and promising exposition in the opening movement. M-D.

Evan Tonsing (–   ) USA
Concerto for a Young Pianist Op.40 (Accura 1968) 5 min. Much alternating hand figuration, meno mosso mid-section, short cadenza. Basically in e throughout with colorful chromaticism; MC; effective. Int.

Franz Tournier (1923–   ) France
Concerto (Editions Rideau Rouge 1968). Maestoso; Lento; Vivace assai. Extension of nineteenth-century pianistic techniques, cadenza at end of first movement, contemporary Alberti bass, MC. M-D.

Donald Francis Tovey (1875–1940) Great Britain
Concerto A Op.15 1903 (Schott; Fl) 30 min. Classic vocabulary set with dignity, beauty, and a fine formal craft. Anachronistic. M-D.

Roy Travis (1922–   ) USA
"Travis has drawn inspiration from Greek drama and African tribal music" (DCM, 766).
Concerto 1969 (OUP) 19 min. In three movements.

Ynge Jan Trede (1933–   ) Germany
Capriccio (CFP) 15 min.

Georg Trexler (1903–   ) Germany
Concerto (Tetra) 18 min.

Bogdan Iakovlevich Trotsyuk (1931–   ) USSR
Concerto-Suite (USSR 1976). For piano, orchestra, and jazz ensemble. Six contrasting movements. Symphonic jazz. M-D.

Richard Trythall (1939–   ) USA
Composition for Piano and Orchestra 1965 (MS available from composer: Via 4 November 96, Roma 00187, Italy) 10 min. In one movement.

Aleksandr N. Tsfasman (1906–1971) USSR

Concerto (USSR 1972). For piano and symphojazz. One large movement with contrasting sections, cadenza passages for pianist, effective instrumentation, MC. M-D.

Sulkhan Tsintsadze (1925–   ) USSR

Concerto "Kontrasti" (Musika 1970) 72pp. One large movement, strongly contrasting sections, freely tonal. M-D.

Vladimir I. Tsytovich (1931–   ) USSR

Tsytovich teaches composition at the Leningrad Conservatory.

Concerto (GS 7705) 31pp. For student and teacher. Int.

Concerto 1960 (Musika) 78pp. Lento; Allegro; Largo. Unusual tempi in order of movements, freely tonal, thin textures. M-D.

Eduard Tubin (1905–   ) Sweden, born Estonia

Tubin's works are based on the folk music of his native country.

Concertino 1947 (Körlings Förlag) 24 min. One large movement, contrasting sections, freely tonal around E♭, interesting rhythms. M-D.

Joaquín Turina (1882–1949) Spain

Rapsodia Sinfónica 1931 (UME; UE) 8½ min. Chordal, chromatic, colorful, parallel planing arpeggiation, sweeping gestures, syncopation, sensuous sonorities, Vivo closing. In two sections: a slow introduction in which several themes of warmly passionate nature are heard, and a longer, lively part in which two main contrasting subjects take the stage in turn. Effective piano writing without making any great technical demands on the player. M-D.

Concerto Op.88 1935 (UME).

Ferdinando Turini (1749–1812) Italy

Turini is best known as a composer of piano sonatas, in which he shows himself an ancestor of Dussek and Clementi.

Concerto g (Sartori—Zanibon 5416 1976). For keyboard and strings. Three movements (FSF). The editor has restricted herself to "elaboration, revision and cadenzas." Early Romantic flavor in many places, brought about by use of foreign tones in a traditional harmonic approach. A fine work that would serve as a substitute for one of the easier Mozart concertos (K. 37, 39, 40, 41) where full orchestra is not desired. Int. to M-D.

Robert Turner (1920–   ) Canada

Concerto 1971 (CMC). For two pianos and orchestra. 18 min. Scena; Rituale; Ballo. Neoclassic, generally thin textures. Pianos fit nicely into the total fabric but shine at certain spots; effective percussive usage. M-D.

Geirr Tveitt (1908–   ) Norway

Concerto I Op.5 1930 (TONO) 25 min. In three movements.

Concerto II Op.11 1933 (TONO) 18 min. In one movement.

Variations on a Folk Tune from Hardanger 1937 (TONO). For two pianos and orchestra. 25 min.

Concerto III "Homage to Brahms" 1947 (TONO) 30 min. In three movements.

Concerto IV "Northern Lights" 1947 (TONO) 35 min. In three movements.

Concerto V Op.156 1954 (TONO) 30 min. In three movements.

Concerto VI (TONO).

U

Marius Moaritz Ulfrstad (1890–1968) Norway
Concerto I 1935 (NK) 26 min.

Hermann Unger (1886–1958) Germany
Concerto I d Op.47 (Tischer & Jagenberg) 22 min.

Erich Urbanner (1936–   ) Austria
Dialogue 1965 (Dob) 15 min. No division of movements; twelve-tone. M-D.
Concerto "76" (Dob) 22 min.

Vladislav Uspenskii (1937–   ) USSR
Concerto (USSR 1966). For two pianos and orchestra. 76pp., full score. Moderato; Lento; Presto, con fuoco. Expanded tonality, much use of octotonic writing, cadenza passages for both pianos, glissandi, ideas carefully developed. M-D.

Vladimir Ussachevsky (1911–   ) USA
Intermezzo 1951 (ACA). For piano and chamber orchestra. 6 min.
Interlude 1952 (ACA) 5½ min. Formerly a movement from a piano concerto. Well proportioned, excellent formal structure, MC. M-D.

Galina Ustvolskaia (1919–   ) USSR
Ustvolskaia was a Shostakovitch pupil.
Concerto 1946 (USSR). Displays dangerously modern tendencies for its date but is only moderately effective. M-D.

V

Genrikh Matusovich Vagner (1922–   ) USSR
Concerto (Musika 1969) 71pp. Allegro ma non troppo; Andante amoroso; Allegro vivo. Freely tonal, much octotonic writing and many octaves. Large span required. M-D.

Stasys Vainiūnas (1909–   ) USSR
Koncertas I Op.15 1946 (Valstybine Grozines). Three movements (FSF). Tonal.
Concerto II Op.22 1952 (Musika) 109pp. Maestoso; Andante; Vivo. Tonal. M-D.
Concerto III Op.33 1965 (USSR) 75pp. No division of movements. Expanded tonality. M-D.
Concerto IV Op.40 (USSR 1977). For piano and chamber orchestra. 67pp. Andante; Vivo; Tranquillo (with cadenza); Allegro energico; Andante mosso. Exploits lower register of keyboard, quiet conclusion. M-D.

Jiři Válek (1923–   ) Czechoslovakia
Symphony X Barocco 1973 (Panton). Double concerto for piano, violin, and orchestra. 20 min. Preface in Czech and German. Five contrasting movements. Pointillistic, expressionistic, sudden tempo and mood changes, mixture of styles, cadenza-like passages. M-D.

Fartein Valen (1887–1952) Norway
Concerto Op.44 1951 (Lyche 583A) 12 min. Allegro moderato: SA; intervals of the minor second and perfect fourth are very important. Larghetto: ABA; the last A section is shortened and leads directly attacca to the Allegro ma non troppo: a mono-thematic rondo. Contains some beautiful and very sensitive writing. Valen's last work and one of his most significant compositions. The solo part is not difficult but the interpretation requires a skillful musician. M-D.

Sergei I. Valfenzon (–   ) USSR
Concerto (USSR 1964) 48pp. Allegro giusto; Andante; Allegro con brio. Tonal, thin textures. M-D.

Mary Jeanne Van Appledorn (1927–   ) USA
Van Appledorn teaches at Texas Tech University in Lubbock, Texas.
Concerto Brevis 1954 revised 1958 (CF 1977) 13 min. Allegro energico; Air;

Presto. Strong rhythmic passages in outer movements; ideas develop naturally; MC; effective. M-D.

David Van de Woestijne (1915–   ) Belgium
Ballade 1940 (CeBeDeM) 17 min.

Johann Baptist Vanhal (1739–1813) Bohemia
Many passages in Vanhal's melodic writing show a connection with Bohemian folk song. Despite certain ties with the *galant* style of the eighteenth century, Vanhal's music is always fresh and full of vitality.
Concerto F (Haselbäch–Dob DM562) 36pp. This work is listed for organ and strings but it is also delightful on the piano. The main emphasis is on the right hand while the left hand provides harmonic figuration. The instrumentation (two violins and bass) and the style of composition are reminiscent of Mozart's church sonatas. Careful and clean edition. Int. to M-D.

Marc Vaubourgoin (1907–   ) France
Concerto 1947 (Technisonor 1969) 26 min. Modéré–Allegro très rythmé; Modéré; Allant. Freely tonal, borders on atonality at places. Octotonic, generally thin textures. M-D.

Constant Vauclain (–   ) USA
Suite (PIC). For piano and strings.
Symphony (PIC). For piano and strings.

Ralph Vaughan Williams (1872–1958) Great Britain
Concerto for One or Two Pianos (OUP 1973) 25 min. Written in 1933 for one piano and orchestra; rewritten in 1946 with Joseph Cooper for two pianos and orchestra. This edition contains both versions; orchestra parts are the same. The solo-piano version is the more difficult. Toccata: brilliant, full textures, heavy writing. Romanza: neoromantic, poetic. Chromatic Fugue: Tedesca style, rondo, effective. Lighthearted; robustly humorous, sometimes skittish; occasionally pokes fun (in the Romanza). Definitely wears a Romantic heart on its sleeve. M-D to D.
See: Frank Howes, "Vaughan Williams' Pianoforte Concerto," MT, October 1933:883.
William Mann, "Vaughan Williams' Pianoforte Concerto," in *The Concerto* (London: Pelican Books, 1952), p.425.
Robert Threlfall, "The Final Problem, and Vaughan Williams' Piano Concerto," MO 98 (February 1975):237–38.
Fantasia (Quasi Variazione) on the 'Old 104th' Psalm Tune 1949 (OUP). For piano with mixed chorus and orchestra. 15 min. Based on a strong historic psalm tune taken from Ravenscroft's Psalter (1621). Piano has an introductory cadenza; opening statement of tune given to the piano with sonorous harmonization. Four contrasting variations are shared with the orchestra. Contains some brilliant pianistic writing. Requires a large span. M-D.

Renier van der Velden (1910–   ) Belgium
Van der Velden's style exhibits a personal kind of expressionism with strong influences of Hindemith and Stravinsky.
Concertino (CeBeDeM 1968). For two pianos and brasses.
Concerto 1971 (CeBeDeM) 15 min.

Sándor Veress (1907–   ) Switzerland, born Hungary
"Hommage à Paul Klee" 1951 (SZ). For two pianos and string orchestra. 27 min.
     Zeichen in Gelb (Allegro); Feuerwind (Allegro molto); Alter Klang (Andante con moto); Unten und Oben (Allegretto piacevole); Steinsammlung (Allegretto); Grün in Grün (Andante); Klein Blauteufel (Vivo). Inspired by pictures of Klee. Pictorial writing with characteristics similar to those of the concerto. The two pianos occupy most attention but the string orchestra does more than just accompany. Effective program work, deserves to be heard. M-D.
Concerto 1952 (SZ). For piano with strings and percussion. 27 min. Andante con moto; Andante; Allegro molto. Shows influences of Bartók and Stravinsky's neoclassic style. Dramatic gestures, flexible meters, octotonic, colorful, MC. M-D.

Antonio Veretti (1900–   ) Italy
Concerto 1949 (SZ 4631) 24 min. Lento, misterioso; Andante desolato; Allegretto estroso. No pause between last two movements. Neoclassic, glissandi, effective trills, thin textures. M-D.

John Verrall (1908–   ) USA
Concerto 1958–59 (ACA) 22 min. Allegro: based on two synthetic scales (listed in score). Adagio: based on the second scale used in the first movement. Allegro: based on another synthetic scale (listed); consists of five variations, an Intermezzo, and a Finale Allegro energico. Effective if a little contrived. M-D.

Georg Bayer Vetessy (1923–   ) Germany
Concerto (Edition Modern) 21 min.

Louis Vierne (1870–1937) France
Poème Op.50 (Lemoine 1926) 55pp. One large colorful movement, contrasting sections. Tonal, Impressionistic. M-D.

Anatol Vieru (1926–   ) Rumania
Jeux 1963 (Sal) 17 min.

Heitor Villa-Lobos (1887–1959) Brazil
This great Brazilian artist began composing in a post-Romantic style, moved to Impressionism and folklore, later experimented with Classicism, and finally synthesized all these elements.
Mômo Precoce 1929 (ESC 3063) (Precocious Momus, the King of the Carnival) 25 min. A brilliant polychromatic and lively work describing a typical Bra-

zilian festival, using some of the themes from the series *Children's Carnival*. It is a series of short tone pictures connected by ingenious cadenzas. The piano part, which is an obbligato to the orchestral episodes, has the most interest, plays an important role in the texture of timbres, and offers some unexpected and amusing sounds. The whole piece is an amalgam of naiveté in themes and rhythms with sophistication in harmony and scoring. D.

Bachianas Brasileiras III 1938 (Ric 1958) 24 min. Preludio: Ponteio. Fantasia. Aria: a touching modinhas. Toccata: labeled "Picapao," a reference to a bird with habits like those of the woodpecker; virtuosic; dancelike. Artfully combines Brazilian musical folkways with Baroque devices of Bachian polyphony. All four movements have large gestures and a highly colored vivacity. M-D.

The *Chôros* are among Villa-Lobos' masterpieces. He composed sixteen of them for various combinations. They are, in the words of the composer, constructed according to a technical form, based on the vibrant manifestations of the usage and customs of the native Brazilians.

Chôros VIII 1925 (ESC). For two pianos and orchestra. 20 min. A highly subjective recreation of various popular and primitive musical traditions. Strong rhythms, polytonal, some atonality. M-D.

Chôros XI 1928 (ESC) 35 min. Treats the piano virtuosically and it is predominant over the orchestra. D.

Concerto I 1945 (ESC) 25 min.

Concerto II 1948 (ESC) 20 min.

Concerto III 1952–57 (MS at Villa-Lobos Library in Rio de Janeiro) 22 min.

Concerto IV 1952 (ESC) 24 min.

Concerto V 1954 (ESC) 20 min.

Alberto Villapando (1935–   ) Bolivia

Música para piano e pequeña orquesta 1968 (IU) full score, 15pp. El Mundo del Amor; El Mundo del Miedo; El Mundo del Silencio. Performance directions in Spanish. Clusters, plucked strings, harmonics, dynamic extremes, avant-garde. M-D.

John Vincent (1902–   ) USA

Consort 1960 (Belwin-Mills; Curlew) 25 min. Allegro con brio; Andante; Allegro vivo. "In a neo-Elizabethan style in copulative antiphony with superimposed harmonic acridities and rhythmic asymmetries" (MSNH, 1134).

Imre Vincze (1926–1969) Hungary

Rapsodia Concertante 1966 (EMB) 13 min.

Jórunn Vioar (1918–   ) Iceland

Concerto (Iceland Music Information Center).

Giovanni Battista Viotti (1755–1824) Italy

Concerto g 1792–94 (Giazotto—Ric 130171; Fl). For piano and chamber orchestra. 38 min. Allegro maestoso; Adagio non troppo; Rondo. Attractive, lively, refreshing themes, charming. First movement (18 min.) tends to wander after a while. Requires much tonal variety and large doses of Romanticism at spots to make a successful performance. Cadenzas are by Viotti. M-D.

Giulio Viozzi (1912–   ) Italy
Concerto II (Casa musicale Sonzogno 1968) 24 min. Reproduced from holograph.

János Viski (1906–1961) Hungary
Concerto 1952 (EMB) 27 min. Three movements (FSF). Late Romantic writing, more inspired by Liszt than by Kodály (Viski's teacher). Overblown clichés detract from the effectiveness. An ethnic spirit permeates the finale. M-D to D.

Berthe di Vito-Delvaux (1915–   ) Belgium
Concerto Op.120 1969 (H. Elkan).

Roman Vlad (1919–   ) Italy, born Rumania
Variazioni Concertanti 1954–5 (SZ) 28 min. "Based on a succession of twelve different notes artfully extracted from a pseudo-dodecaphonic passage in Mozart's *Don Giovanni*" (MSNH, 999).

Pancho Vladigerov (1899–   ) Bulgaria
Concerto I Op.6 (UE 1926) 30 min. "Written in a romantic manner with injections of typical Bulgarian melorhythms" (MSNH, 338).
Concerto III Op.31 (Edition d'état, Science et Arts 1952; USSR) 75pp. Con moto—mosso; Andante; Allegro vivace. Freely tonal. M-D.
Concerto IV Op.48 (Musika 1977) 94pp.

Jan van Vlijmen (1935–   ) The Netherlands
Sonata per Piano e Tre Gruppi Strumentali 1966 (Donemus). For piano and chamber orchestra. 16 min.

Ernst Vogel (1926–   ) Austria
Klavierkonzert 1962 (Dob) 35 min. Sostenuto—affetuoso; Lento; Impetuoso. Freely tonal with much chromatic usage, cadenza passages, flexible meters, strong rhythms in finale. M-D.

Georg Joseph Vogler (1749–1814) Germany
Concerto C (Drath—PWM; Lenzewski—Vieweg). For keyboard and strings. Allegro moderato; Andante. This is the first of six concertos written "for amateurs in an indulgent mood." Int.
Variations on "Marlborough" 1791 (Schott 4161). Theme, eleven variations, and Finale (Capriccio, Fuga, Molto vivace, Larghetto, Allegro and Larghetto—Les Adieux). Most of the variations are given to the pianist. The theme is the French satirical marching song "Marlborough s'en va t'en Guerre," written after the battle of Marlplaquet (1709) and concerning the English General, the Duke of Marlborough. Brahms was especially fond of these variations and often played the solo version for his own pleasure. M-D.

Hans Vogt (1909–   ) Switzerland
Concertino (Alkor 134). For piano, nine winds, and percussion.
Concerto (Alkor 288) 29 min.

Robert Volkmann (1815–1883) Germany
Volkmann was an important link between Schumann and Brahms.
Concertstück C Op.42 (Schott 1862) 49pp. This engaging and expertly written
    work has a brooding opening and a vivacious finale. In between is an An-
    dantino con (4) Variazioni. Piano part blends with orchestra unusually well.
    M-D.

Alexander Voormolen (1895–1980) The Netherlands
Concerto 1950 (Donemus). For two pianos and string orchestra.

Klaas de Vries (1944–   ) The Netherlands
Refrains 1970 (Donemus). For two pianos and orchestra. 14 min.

Roger Vuataz (1898–   ) Switzerland
Concerto Op.112 1963–64 (Henn H952) 21 min. Animé; Très lent; Très animé.
    Freely tonal, neoclassic, octotonic, cadenza. Impressionistic sonorities in
    the middle movement. Finale contrasts toccata-like sections with chorale;
    clever coda captivates conclusion. M-D.

W

Georg Christoph Wagenseil (1715–1777) Austria

Konzert I A (Bemmann, Ruf—Mösler). For keyboard and strings. Allegro; Largo; Allegro. Outer movements contain many predictable but attractive figurations. The Largo, in a, is especially moving. Int. to M-D.

Konzert C (Upweyer—Vieweg). For keyboard and strings. Like a divertimento; finale is a light dance. The whole style thrives on sequence and contains Mozartian melodic influence. Int. to M-D.

Concerto D (Br&H 3912; Fl). For keyboard and strings. 16 min. Allegro; Andante moderato; Allegro. A delightful work that could give the Haydn *Concerto* D Hob. XVIII/11 a rest. Int.

Joseph Wagner (1900–1974) USA

Concertino g 1935 (Seesaw) 12 min. Three movements (FSF). A student concertino. Int.

Rhapsody 1925 revised 1940 (Bo&H). For piano, clarinet, and strings. 10 min.

A Fugal Triptych (Fl). For piano, percussion, and strings.

Thomas S. Wagner (1931–   ) USA

Concerto (Bo&H) 40 min. In three movements.

Rune Wahlberg (1910–   ) Sweden

Ballad (STIM) 14 min.

Karneval (STIM) 15 min.

Konsert (STIM) 22 min.

George Walker (1922–   ) USA

Walker teaches at Rutgers University.

Concerto 1975 (Gen) 21 min. First movement: nonmelodic; soloist and orchestra go their own way with very little collaboration. Second movement: elegiac, touching. Third movement: declamatory, nonlinear, stern gestures. Granitic sonorities; virtuosic and dramatic writing for soloist and orchestra. D.

Fried Walter (1907–   ) Germany

Concertino (Ahn & Simrock 1961) 16 min. Allegro; Andante; Allegro con spirito. Tonal. Int. to M-D.

Divertimento (Ahn & Simrock 1955) 16½ min. Bolero; Nocturno; Rondo. Tonal, attractive. M-D.

Kleine Barock-Musik (Ahn & Simrock 1958) 11 min. Toccata; Sarabande; Gigue. MC. Large span required. M-D.

William Walton (1902–   ) Great Britain

Sinfonia Concertante 1928 revised 1944 (OUP). For orchestra with piano obbligato. 19 min. Maestoso; Allegro spiritoso; A tempo allegretto: big chord splashes; fast octave and chord technique required. Andante comodo: slow contrapuntal weaving of lines. Allegro vivo sempre scherzando: upper register mainly exploited with octave chords and sixteenth-note figuration. The three movements contain similarities in their thematic material, and in place of recapitulation treatment the material of each movement is summed up in an epilogue at the end of the last movement. Piano is treated as an orchestral instrument, with few places for real solo playing, but this is one of the truly viable English piano concertos. M-D.

Robert Ward (1917–   ) USA

Concerto 1968 (Highgate Press 1970) 19 min. Adagio–Allegro: SA, double exposition, cadenza at end of recapitulation. Grave—doppio movimento: gives the impression of being two movements—a slow movement leads attacca to a fast one; ternary design concludes with a cadenza and coda. Expanded tonality, flamboyant piano writing "in the grand manner," parallelism, varied meters, dramatic cadenzas. D.

Bruno Wassil (1920–   ) Italy

Concerto II F 1942–43 (Cora) 30 min. Andantino con moto; Andante, quasi adagio; Vivace. Tonal, neoclassic, interesting melodic ideas. M-D.

Alain Weber (1930–   ) France

Concertino (Leduc 1969) 40pp., 14 min. Allegro; Lent; Allegro. Freely tonal with much chromatic usage, changing meters, fast-moving chords over keyboard, octotonic, cadenza in finale, some pungent dissonance. M-D.

Ben Weber (1916–1979) USA

Concerto Op.52 1961 (ACA) 20 min. Weber uses a personal adaptation of twelve-tone technique. Fantasia: orchestra exposes main material and piano then develops it; SA characteristics. Second movement ("In memoriam, Dmitri Mitropoulous"): opening section is a free fantasy, with subtle writing; second part is a passacaglia with five variations and a coda; this movement contains the most moving music in the entire work. Rondo with complications: much virtuosity; ends with a mysterious coda and a bang. D.

Carl Maria von Weber (1786–1826) Germany

Weber was a first-rate pianist who loved his instrument and who knew its possibilities. His imagination was first of all theatrical and it shows up best in the dramatic-coloristic situation. These pieces are "nonoperatic" only in that they are instrumental, for they are full of operatic accents. They provide a great deal of variety and musical entertainment for pianist and listener. The best writing in the two concertos is in the dark slow movements and the dashing finales.

Concerto I C Op.11 1810 (CFP; Steingräber 1892; Eulenburg; Fl) 18 min. Allegro; Adagio; Finale—Presto. Brilliance and fantasy poured into conventional forms but solved in an uncomplicated Romantic manner. Virtuoso technique required. M-D.

Concerto II E♭ Op.32 1812 (CFP; Br&H 1885; Heugel; Eulenburg; CF; Fl) 23 min. Allegro maestoso: cadenza at end leads back to second theme. Adagio: dreamy, poetic, heartfelt music. Presto: almost Chopinesque at times, with touches of Rossini; effective use of leaps—the performer must be seen as well as heard! Excellent and fluent pianistic writing. M-D.

Konzertstück f Op.79 1821 (CFP; GS; K; Br&H; IMC; CF; Augener; Durand; Hug; Eulenburg; USSR; Fl) 17 min. Weber's finest piano concerto, in which a program shapes the form of the music. A one-movement work (560 bars) divided into four sections by tempo, mood, and key changes and bridged by modulations. Contains plenty of color and has the vitality of Weber's best operatic music. The piano part displays virtuosic athletics consisting of extended passage work, octave glissandi, arpeggi, chromaticism, and many other idiomatic effects. The piece is programmatic and attempts a musical description of medieval knights, ladies, and crusaders. Still a very effective work and only M-D.

Svend F. Weber (1934–   ) Great Britain, born Denmark

Concerto Op.2 "Academic Essay" 1957 (PRS). For piano and chamber orchestra. 18 min.

August Martin Wegner III (1941–   ) USA

Ice-Nine 1975 (MS available from composer: CA 216, University of Wisconsin—Parkside, Kenosha, WI 53140) 32pp. For prepared piano and chamber orchestra. The piano must be amplified.

Karl Weigl (1881–1949) USA, born Austria

Concerto for the Left Hand 1924 (ACA) 18 min. Allegro (with cadenza); Adagio; Rondo.

Concerto f Op.21 (Simon—UE 1932) 30 min. Allegro moderato; Andante sostenuto; Allegro molto. Follows the Brahms–Reger tradition. Chromatic, large pianistic gestures, a few virtuoso passages. M-D.

Rhapsody c 1940 (Bo&H; AMC; Fl) 10 min.

László Weiner (1916–1944) Hungary

Concerto (Zenmükiado 1965). For piano, flute, viola, and string orchestra. 21 min. Allegro maestoso molto risoluto; Andante (tranquillo); Allegro ma non tanto. Neoclassic. Strong melodies reinforced with careful and musical voice leading; piano has cadenzas at end of first and second movements. M-D.

Leo Weiner (1885–1960) Hungary

Concertino e Op.15 1923 (UE 8335) 18 min. Allegro amabile, quasi allegretto; Vivace. Composed in a relatively conservative harmonic idiom but piquantly spiced with an accent essentially Magyar yet distinctly original. Ingenious orchestration. A provocatively rewarding work, immediately intelligible. Int. to M-D.

Louis Weingarden (1943–   ) USA
Weingarden studied with Miriam Gideon and Elliott Carter. He was winner of the Prix de Rome in 1968.
Concerto 1974 (AMC) 29 min. Heavily orchestrated atonalism with a strong solo piano part. Luxuriant sonorities are sprinkled with gamelan brushings and xylophone accents. D.

John Weinzweig (1913–   ) Canada
Concerto 1965–66 (CMC) 18 min. Slow; Fast. Twelve-tone; displays formal clarity and warm emotions (especially for dodecaphonic technique); orchestration is simultaneously lean and specific; mature craft. M-D.

Julius Weismann (1879–1950) Germany
Konzert Op.33 (Müller SM1215).
Suite Op.97 1927 (Müller SM460) 39pp. Praeludium; Divertimento, quasi Variazioni senza tema; Canon; Finale. Neoclassic, tonal. M-D.

Waldemar Welander (1899–   ) Sweden
Concerto da Camera (STIM; Fl). For piano and chamber orchestra. 22 min.

Egon Wellesz (1885–1974) Austria
Klavierkonzert Op.49 (UE 10 252 1935) 20 min. Lento; Adagio; Adagio–Allegro energico. Post-Brahms idiom, highly chromatic. M-D.

Martin Wendel (1925–   ) Switzerland
Concerto (Mannheimer). For violin, piano, and string orchestra. 16 min.
Drei Konzertante Skizzen (SUISA). For piano, flute, and string orchestra. 10 min.
Musik für Klavier und Orchestra (SUISA). 14 min.

Felix Werder (1922–   ) Australia, born Germany
Concerto (APRA) 25 min.

Lars Johan Werle (1926–   ) Sweden
Since 1977 Werle has been Composer-in-Residence with The Gothenburg Theater and Concert Company.
Summer Music Op.4 1965 (NMS). For piano and eleven strings. 7½ min. A Romantic study in sound. M-D.

Gregor Joseph Werner (1695–1766) Germany
Concertante Pieces (Vecsey—EMB 1964) 35pp. Figured bass realized. Introductory material in Hungarian, German, and English. These works were originally for harpsichord or organ and chamber orchestra but are surprisingly effective on the piano. Int. to M-D.

Jean-Jacques Werner (1935–   ) France
Concerto I 1960 (Billaudot) 26 min. Allegro vivace; Adagio quasi lento; Final—allegro. Mainly neoclassic with some expressionistic influence. M-D.

Concerto II (Billaudot 1963). For piano, winds, and percussion. 34pp.

Concerto 1962 (ESC). For piano, horn, percussion, and string orchestra. 22pp. Allegro; Adagio; Allegro giocoso. Neoclassic, freely tonal, broad dynamic range, MC. M-D.

Charles Wesley (1757–1834) Great Britain

Charles Wesley and his younger brother, Samuel (1766–1837), were as precocious as W. A. Mozart. As children they aroused great interest, both as composers and as outstanding performers. Charles's early works were his best, and *Six Concertos for the Organ or Harpsichord* Op.2 are the most remarkable of this period. This opus dates from around 1778 and is probably the culmination in England of what is now called the *galant* school.

Concerto IV C (Finzi—Hin 290a) 17 min. Allegro; Largo; Allegro moderato. Figured bass is included in the tuttis even though continuo playing was on the wane in Wesley's time. This does give the soloist the option of devising an independent continuo accompaniment. Editorial additions are in brackets. Mozart influence apparent. Int.

Gayneyl Wheeler (–   ) USA

Concerto (CF 1975) 32pp. Maestoso; Andantino; Vivace. A fine work. MC, preference for fourth and fifths, colorful writing. Int. to M-D.

Emerson Whithorne (1884–1958) USA

Poem Op.43 1926 (CF; Fl) 20 min. Tonal, sectional, Impressionistic in places. M-D.

Ernst Widmer (1927–   ) Brazil

Widmer is Dean of the School of Music and Performing Arts of the Federal University of Bahia.

Bahia-Concerto Op.17 1958 (MS available from composer: % Escola de Música e Artes Cênicas Universidade Federal da Bahia Parque Universitario Dr. Edgard Santos (Canela) 40 000 Salvador-Bahia, Brazil) 17 min.

Prismas Op.70 1971 (MS available from composer) 21 min.

ENTROncamentos SONoros Op.75 1972 (MS available from composer) 21 min.

Charles Marie Widor (1844–1937) France

Concerto I f Op.39 (Hamelle 1880). Allegro con fuoco; Andante religioso; Allegro. Bears the stamp of bygone pianistic fashions. M-D.

Fantaisie A♭ Op.62 (Durand 1892) 37pp. Freely rhapsodic, sectional, flowing lines and figures. Requires a good octave technique. M-D.

Concerto II C Op.77 (Heugel 1905). Allegro con moto: alive with a restrained brilliancy. Andante: contemplative; almost Franckian; striking cadenza leads directly into the Allegro: many effective scale passages. Tonal, presents a kind of glacial exterior. A successful performance requires the pianist's fingers to speak a very finished French! M-D.

Jean Wiéner (1896–   ) France

Wiéner, a talented jazz pianist, helped stimulate France's interest not only in that idiom but also in the works of diverse modern composers. Wiéner began very much in the line of the French *Les Six* but went on to write in an almost popular style. He has had much success with film scores.

Concertino I *Franco-American* 1924 (ESC 1481). For piano and strings. 20 min. Très sonore et très marqué; Très lent; Alla breve. Tonal; rhythmic finale with jazz influence. A good example of Wiéner's early style. M-D.

Cadences (Sal 1930) 16 min. Jazz; Java; Tango Argentin; Final (Paso Doble). Strong jazz and blues influence; clever, even if a little dated. M-D.

Concert (Éditions Françaises de Musique-Technisonor 1974) 70pp., full score. Outer movements are untitled, middle movement is Lento. Colorful sonorities with flexible meters, thin jazz textures, freely tonal. M-D.

Adam Wieniawski (1879–1950) Poland

Concertino (PWM). This work always strives for clarity of texture and form; would transmit many emotions to a responsive audience. M-D.

Joseph Wieniawski (1837–1912) Poland

Brother of Henri Wieniawski.

Concerto g Op.20 1873 (Cranz). Allegro moderato; Andante; Allegro molto vivace. Written in a Liszt–Franck idiom; melodies beautiful but not well developed. Turbulence in finale explodes from time to time. M-D.

Ingvar Wieslander (1917–1963) Sweden

Mutazioni (STIM). For two pianos and orchestra.

Frank Wigglesworth (1918–   ) USA

Concertino 1952 (ACA). For piano and string orchestra. 14 min. Lean, sinuous; with strong lines and lucid structures. M-D.

Adolf Wiklund (1879–1950) Sweden

Konsert I e Op.10 1906–35 (WH) 33 min. Restrained Romantic style. M-D.

Konsert II b Op.17 1916 (WH) 27 min.

Konsertstycke 1902 (STIM) 25 min.

Jacques Wildberger (1922–   ) Switzerland

Since 1959 Wildberger has taught at the Badischen Hochschule für Musik in Karlsruhe, Germany

Divertimento (Edition Modern 998) 7 min. One movement, three contrasting sections (FSF). Neoclassic, flexible meters, *p* conclusion. M-D.

Raymond Wilding-White (1922–   ) USA, born England

Wilding-White teaches at De Paul University in Chicago, where he directs the LOOP GROUP, a multimedia performing ensemble.

Concerto 1949 (AMC).

Wilhelmina, Consort of Frederick William, Margrave of Bayreuth (1709–1758) Germany

Konzert g (Spilling—Leuckart 1959) 14 min. Allegro; Cantabile; Gavottes. Wilhelmina was Frederick the Great's favorite sister, and this work shows her to have been as musically gifted and sensitive as her brother. Delightful and charming. Int.

Healy Willan (1880–1968) Canada

Concerto c 1960 (BMI Canada) 25 min. Allegro energico; Adagio; Allegro con spirito. Tonal, well written, contrasting ideas, strong melodies, brilliant finale. M-D.

David Russell Williams (1932–   ) USA

Concerto Op.39 1963–64 (Fl). For piano, four-hands and orchestra. 17 min. Buoyantly; Ponderously; Brightly.

Malcolm Williamson (1931–   ) Australia

Concerto I (Weinberger 1958) 19 min.

Concerto II (Chappell 1961). For piano and strings. 16 min. Busy, syncopated motor rhythms; frolicsome overall. Straight entertainment music. Int. to M-D.

Concerto III Eb 1961 (Weinberger) 28 min. Toccata; Allegro: busy and brilliant in 11/16. Molto largo e cantando: very effective. Ben Allegro. The most accessible and flavorsome of the concertos. M-D.

Sinfonia Concertante 1965 (Bo&H). For piano, three trumpets, and strings. Miniature score, 64pp. Quarter note = 76; Andante lento; Presto. Colorful and versatile writing. Piano is especially effective in the Presto, with its rhythmic punctuation, *pp* closing. M-D.

Concerto 1973 (Weinberger). For two pianos and string orchestra. 19 min. Suave and delectable, tightly organized, neoclassic, features some brilliant writing for the pianists. M-D.

Richard Willis (1929–   ) USA

Concertino 1969 (MS available from composer: % School of Music, Baylor University, Waco, TX 76703) 18 min. In one movement, three sections.

Olly Wilson (1937–   ) USA

Akwan 1972 (LC). For piano, electronic piano (Fender Rhodes), and orchestra. Full score, 72pp. Includes two sets of strings, one set amplified with contact microphones. Soloist moves back and forth between pianos. Flexible meters, clusters, "directed" improvisation, pointillistic, jazz influence, *ppp* closing, unusual sonorities. M-D.

Thomas B. Wilson (1927–   ) Great Britain, born USA

Concertino 1949 (PRS) 22 min.

Gerhard Wimberger (1923–   ) Austria

Wimberger teaches composition and conducting at the Mozarteum in Salzburg.

Concerto 1955 (Schott 1977) 20 min. Moderato; Lento; Allegro molto (seven variations). Expanded tonality, expansive sonorities, expressionistic, finale contrasts contrapuntal elements in the orchestra with more homophonic treatment in the piano part, athletic pianistic gestures, *pp* closing. M-D.

Dag Wirén (1905–   ) Sweden
Since 1944 Wirén has used a variation procedure he calls "metamorphosis technique." "The procedure involves the building of an entire work from a single musical cell or from a set of cells that are revealed as the piece unfolds" (DCM, 819).
Konsert Op.26 1950 (GM) 19 min. Three movements (FSF). Expanded tonality.
    M-D.

Thomas K. Wirtel (–   ) USA
Music for Winds, Percussion, and Prepared Piano (ACA) 10 min.

Carl Anton Wirth (1912–   ) USA
Rhapsody (Fl).

Peter Wishart (1921–   ) Great Britain
Concerto (Galaxy) 20 min.

Stanislaw Wislocki (1921–   ) Poland
Concerto 1948 (PWM) 25 min. Allegro scherzando: developed from opening
    theme heard in trumpet. Andante molto cantabile: subtle contrasts between
    coloristic planes. Andantino improvisando. Allegro giocoso: draws on the
    national style by its oberek-like accents. This concerto owes its brilliance to
    a virtuoso juggling of motives and to an ingenious use of rhythm and meter.
    M-D.

Pierre Wissmer (1915–   ) France
Concerto II 1947 (P. Noël) 26 min. Allegro deciso; Andante; Allegro vivace.
    Tonal with dashes of chromaticism; attractive. M-D.

Georges-Martin Witkowski (1867–1943) France
Mon Lac 1921 (Sal) 23 min. Prélude; Variations et Finale. Strongly Impressionistic. M-D.

Gerhard Wohlgemuth (1920–   ) Germany
Concertino 1948 (CFP) 15 min.

Winfried Wolf (1900–   ) Germany
Klavier-Konzert Op.13 1952 (Bo&H) 17 min. Toccata: fast-changing harmonies,
    motoric. Elegie: lyric, restful, free metric usage. Rondo: opens with cadenza;
    thin textures. Entire work is freely tonal. M-D to D.

Joseph Wölfl (1772–1812) Austria
Concerto II Op.26 (Br&H 179?).
Concerto III F. Op.32 (André ca.1808; LC). Allegro; Andante; Finale—Presto
    (six variations and a cadenza). Fluent writing. M-D.
Le Calme Op.36 (Br&H 1808; NYPL).
Le Coucou Op.49 (Br&H 1811; NYPL; LC). Allegro moderato. Andante: folk-
    like theme. Le Coucou—Allegro molto: gives the piece its name. Charming.
    M-D.

Concerto da Camera E♭ (André ca.1800; LC) Allegro moderata. Romanza. Finale: strong dance element, colorful harmonies in coda. M-D.

Stefan Wolpe (1902–1972) USA, born Germany
Wolpe was a powerful musician who influenced many American composers.
For Piano and Sixteen Players 1960–61 (McGinnis & Marx) 12 min.

Detlef Wolter (1933–   ) Germany
Ritornell 1962 (Kahnt) 12 min. Neoclassic. Flexible meters. Octotonic, humorous, one mood, continuous fast motion. M-D.

Haydn Wood (1882–1959) Great Britain
Concerto d 1908 (Bo&H 1937) 26 min. Maestoso; Andante; Finale—Vivace. Grand nineteenth-century gestures; brilliant; dashing and effective in an "old fashioned" kind of way. Sounds somewhat like early Dohnanyi. D.

Joseph Wood (1915–   ) USA
Double Concerto 1970 (ACA). For piano, viola, and orchestra. 15 min.
Divertimento 1958 (ACA). For piano and chamber orchestra. 13½ min.

William B. Wordsworth (1908–   ) Great Britain
Concerto in One Movement d 1946 (Lengnick) 25 min. Slightly expanded tonality. M-D.

Wladimir Woronoff (1903–   ) Belgium
Strophes Concertantes 1964 (CeBeDeM) 17 min.

Boleslaw Woytowicz (1899–   ) Poland
Symphony III, Piano Concertante 1963 (PWM) 15 min. Directions in Polish, French, and German. Intrada; Dramatis personae; Fuga I; Scherzo I; Canto I; Canto II; Scherzo II; Fuga II; Coda. Contains a variety of sonorities from Impressionistic to expressionistic, although the basic style is neoclassic. Has characteristics in common with the Szymanowski *Symphonie Concertante* II Op.60. M-D.

Gerhard J. Wuensch (1925–   ) Canada
Concerto Op.57 1971 (CMC). For piano and chamber orchestra. 23 min. Allegro con brio; Tema con (5) Variazioni; Vivace. Expanded tonality, neoclassic. M-D.

Hermann Wunsch (1884–1954) Germany
Chamber Concerto Op.22 1923 (Schott). For piano and chamber orchestra. 20 min. In one movement. Pleasant, Hindemith style, contrapuntal. M-D.

Charles Wuorinen (1939–   ) USA
Wuorinen is a recognized innovator. His works provide constantly fascinating experiences in sound, and he represents all that is avant-garde.
Concert Piece 1956 (ACA). For piano and string orchestra. 14 min.
Concerto I 1966 (CFP) 17½ min. In a totally serialized one-movement fantasy of

mosiacs, highly colored, much repetition of the mosiac-like parts, arch form. Percussion (requires nine players) is almost as important as the piano. Post-Webernesque style, highly pointillistic, three sections (FSF). Legato possibilities of the instrument are totally disregarded; every note of "splash" is separately calculated; 659 measures or points of reference. D.

Concerto II 1974 (CFP). For amplified piano and orchestra. 23 min. One movement, tightly knit. Uses various serial sets and emphasizes intervallic permutations (seconds and thirds and their compounds particularly). Entirely in 4/4. The piano dominates throughout by generating all the main ideas and controlling their development. Amplification heightens the percussive quality of the piano; a variety of antiphonal amplified effects required (speakers in the hall, on the stage, etc.). An extended rhapsodic passage for the piano near the end of the piece concludes on the opening note of the work (C). "Pedaling for the soloist (and other articulative and dynamic indications as well) is shown only in a general, partial way. The soloist's task is in part the completion of these indications" (from the score). D.

See: *Contemporary News Letter,* May-June 1975, for a complete analysis of this work.

Concertante IV (ACA). For piano, violin, and chamber orchestra. 20 min.

Concertpiece (ACA). For piano and strings. 14 min.

Klaus Wüsthoff (1922–   ) Germany

Concertino (Birnback 1731 1961) 15 min. Andante–Allegro: fugal and rhythmic. Allegretto: contrasting sections and moods. Moderato: contemporary Alberti bass, cadenza. Neoclassic. M-D.

Drei Russische Fantasien 1964 (Birnback 1773) 12 min. Wolga Rhapsodie; Wiegenlied; Gopak. Modal, colorful, clever. M-D.

Yehudi Wyner (1929–   ) USA, born Canada

"All of [Wyner's] music shows a vivid consciousness of immediate effect, as befits one who has had an active career as a performer" (DCM, 824).

Concerto da Camera 1967 Part I (MS available from composer: % School of Music, Yale University, New Haven, CT 06520) 6 min. "*Da Camera* often deals with extreme contrast, with oppositions (often counterposed without transition) of fast and slow, violence and gentleness, disordered spasm and concentrated stillness. But it is also a display piece for piano offering the soloist the chance to exhibit fantastic figuration, athletic vigor as well as lyrical largesse. Within the title lurks a pun, pointing to the cinematic origin of the composition. The title also suggests a work of chamber music attitude, allowing individuals certain freedom and interplay within prescribed limits" (from program notes by the composer). This is the opening movement of a projected larger work in several parts. M-D.

David Wynne (1900–   ) Great Britain, born Wales

Concerto (PRS). For two pianos (three hands) and orchestra. 18 min.

Jürg Wyttenbach (1935–   ) Switzerland
Concerto 1964, revised 1966 (Schott) 15 min.
Divisions 1964 (Ars Viva). For piano and nine strings. 10 min. In four movements.
Follows Baroque forms with improvised permutations of principal themes in
free cadenzas. M-D to D.

X

Iannis Xenakis (1922–   ) France, born Rumania

Xenakis is one of the truly innovative intelligences in today's musical world. He has incorporated computer-determined probabilities and transferred certain architectural structures into his music.

Synaphai (Connexities) 1969 (Sal). Directions in English. *Connexity* is used in the sense of legato. "The pianist plays all the lines if he can" (from the score). Contains some loud, volatile, pulverizing, and incredibly dense, ear-splitting sonorities. Avant-garde. D.

Erikhthon (Concerto for piano and orchestra) 1974 (Sal) 15 min. A grand, massive sonic architecture. Communicates eloquently by reaching out and seizing the listener's ear, sometimes by a lot of primitive banging on the pianist's part. Avant-garde. D.

Y

Richard Yardumian (1917–   ) USA

Passacaglia, Recitatives and Fugue 1957 (EV) 18 min. Passacaglia: 20 variations, inspired by Bach's *Passacaglia and Fugue* c; piano writing is molded along Lisztian lines; based on an eight-bar period in triple meter. Recitatives: poetic, introspective, dialogue between piano and various instruments. Fugue: a glowing regal march; various canons and inversions are cleverly treated; the piano goes great guns throughout. The harmonic tension is somewhat comparable to that of William Walton. Fluently written. M-D.

Akio Yashiro (1929–   ) Japan

Yashiro teaches at Tokyo University and is a lecturer at the Tôhô Conservatory of Music.

Concerto 1964–67 (Ongaka No Tomo Sha) 27 min. Allegro animato; Adagio misterioso; Allegro. Expanded tonality, flexible meters, fluent handling of piano writing and orchestration, solid constructions. D.

Yellow River Concerto (People's Republic of China 1972; Fl; T. Front) 19 min. Prelude: The Song of the Yellow River Boatmen; Ode to the Yellow River; The Yellow River in Wrath; Defend the Yellow River. A Chinese popular song, "East Is Red," appears in the last movement. Adapted by a committee from the *Yellow River Cantata* composed by Hsien Hsing-hai in 1939. The solo piano part was possibly composed by Yin Cheng-chung. Chromatic coloration, glissandi, nineteenth-century pianistic idioms, cadenza passages, theatrical in places. Sounds like a mixture of Liszt, Mahler, and Rachmaninoff and in some ways is a first cousin to the *Warsaw Concerto*.

Yip Wai Hong (1930–   ) China

Yip studied at Yen-Ching University and the Peking Central Conservatory. He is head of the Music and Fine Arts Department of Hong Kong Baptist College and director of the Hong Kong Children's Choir.

Temptation 1978 (score available from composer: % Hong Kong Baptist College, 224 Waterloo Road, Kowloon, Hong Kong) 25 min. The development of material from the old tune "Jesus Loves Me" forms a large part of this composition. The three temptations of Jesus described in Matthew 4:1-11 provide the background for this work. Desert: the struggle between Jesus and Satan is portrayed in SA design, with the figure of Jesus represented by the first theme and that of Satan by the second. Temptations: rondo; depicts the three temptations, each represented by a contrasting theme. Victory: concludes with a fugal section. Traditional techniques mixed with Eastern sonorities. M-D.

Percy M. Young (1912–   ) Great Britain

Fugal Concerto g (Hin 205 1954). For piano and strings. 16 min. Built along traditional lines, fine craft. M-D.

Théo Ysaÿe (1865–1918) Belgium

Brother of Eugène Ysaÿe.

Concerto Op.9 (GS 1907) 77pp. Four movements. Tonal around E♭, Franck influence. M-D.

Z

Harold Zabrack (1919–   ) USA

Zabrack is an outstanding pianist and writes beautifully fashioned piano works. They constantly "fit" the pianist and "sound" well at all times.

Concerto I 1964 (MS available from composer: % Music Department, Westminster Choir College, Princeton, NJ 08540) 13 min. In one movement, contrasting sections. Piano cadenzas, highly pianistic, solidly integrated, rhythmically strong, expressive melodic content. M-D to D.

Symphonic Variations (Concerto II for Piano and Orchestra) 1971 (MS available from composer) 17 min. Virtuoso keyboard style set off by richly orchestrated passages of striding majesty. This conservatively Romantic piece evolves through flourish and splendor. Highly effective writing throughout. D.

Jan (Johann) Zach (1699–1773) Bohemia

Zach prepared the way for the new Classical style in southwestern German towns like Mainz, where he worked, and Mannheim.

Konzert c (Gottron—Nag 165 1947). For keyboard and strings. 23pp. Allegro spiritoso; Andante; Tempo di Minuetto. An attractive work in pre-classic style permeated with the spirit of Bohemian folk music. Int. to M-D.

Mario Zafred (1922–   ) Italy

Concerto 1957 (Ric 129923) 26 min. Allegro; Lento; Allegro giusto. Conservative expanded tonal style, solid thematic material, effective pianistic treatment. Much octotonic writing in the first movement. M-D.

Concerto 1960 (Ric). For two pianos and orchestra. 20 min. Lento; Mosso; Adagio–Allegro marcato. The two pianos complement each other as well as the orchestra. Ideas develop naturally. Neoclassic style with plenty of dissonance that arises from the flow of the material. M-D.

Variazioni Concertante su l'Introduction dell' Op.111 de Beethoven 1964 (Ric) 20 min. Sostenuto–Allegro moderato; Tempo di scherzo; Lento–Allegro misurato. The rhythmic part of the Beethoven Introduction is exploited. It leads to many unexpected consequences! M-D.

Metamorfosi 1964 (Ric 130699) 20 min. Sostenuto–Allegro giusto; Largo e disteso; Lento–Allegro vivo. Pointillistic, atonal, expressionistic, clever thematic evolution. M-D to D.

Concerto for Trio and Orchestra (Ric). For piano, violin, cello, and orchestra. 30
    min.

Henri Zagwijn (1878–1954) The Netherlands
Concertino I 1939 (Donemus) 13 min.
Concertino II 1946 (Donemus) 18 min.

Judith Lang Zaimont (1945–   ) USA
Concerto 1972 (AMC).

Danièle Zanettovich (1950–   ) Italy
Invenzione sopra un Tritono (EC 1976) 20 min. Invocation; Hymn; Circus March.
    Instructions in Italian. Clusters, glissandi on strings, proportional rhythmic
    relationships, avant-garde. D.

Margeris Zarins (1910–   ) USSR
Grecheshie Vazy 1962 (USSR) full score, 135pp. Five movements, Armenian folk
    influence, strongly modal, similar to Khachaturian style. M-D.

Aleksander Zarzycki (1834–1895) Poland
Concerto A♭ Op.17 (PWM; Bo&Bo). Dedicated to Zarzycki's teacher, Nicolas
    Rubinstein. Andante; Allegro non troppo. A mixture of styles reminiscent
    of Brahms and Tchaikowsky. Fluent pianism required. M-D.

Julien-François Zbinden (1917–   ) Switzerland
Concerto da Camera Op.16 1950–51 (Br&H 5995). For piano and strings, 16
    min. Allegramente; Adagio; Allegro giocoso. Neoclassic, mildly dissonant,
    flexible meters, expanded tonality. Last movement is fugal. M-D.

Demetrij Zebrè (1912–1970) Yugoslavia
Concertino (DSS) 22 min. Well written; some fine passages, but adds nothing
    essential to the composer's image. M-D.

Ruth Zechlin (1926–   ) Germany
Klavierkonzert 1974 (CFP) 19 min. Andante–Dolce e animato e tranquillo; Al-
    legro molto; Con fuoco e con spirito. Performance directions in German.
    Mixture of traditional and experimental notation. Great variety of sonorities
    from the most wispy to the most bombastic, large skips, cluster tremolos,
    strummed strings, avant-garde. M-D.
Thoughts on a Piano Piece of Prokofiev (Tetra). For piano and ten instruments. 10
    min.

Ladislav Zelenski (1837–1921) Poland
Concerto E♭ Op.60 (Litolff 1911).

Geza Graf Zichy (1849–1924) Hungary
Concerto E♭ (UE 1902). For piano, left-hand and orchestra.

Hermann Zilcher (1881–1948) Germany
Concerto b Op.20 1918 (Stradal—Br&H; Fl) 28 min. Ziemlich bewegt; Langsam,
    ausdrucksvoll. The finale has too many sections and mood changes to have

much effect. Continues the Brahms–Reger tradition but without a strong craft. M-D.

Nacht und Morgen Op.24 1917 (Br&H; Fl). Two pianos and orchestra. 18 min.

Efrem Zimbalist (1889–   ) USA, born Russia

Concerto E♭ (EV 1960; Fl) 23 min. Originally composed for William Kapell, but the music was lost in the airplane accident in 1953 in which the pianist died. Reconstructed by the composer. Allegro ma non troppo: pompous opening contrasts with lyric second idea. Canzone: orchestral melodic lines decorated with piano arpeggios. Finale: rondo, cheerful, humorous first theme, cadenza. M-D.

Jan Zimmer (1926–   ) Czechoslovakia

Concertino Op.19 (Artia 2538). For piano and strings.

Bernd Alois Zimmermann (1918–1970) Germany

Dialogue, Konzert für 2 Klaviere und Grosses Orchestra, "Hommage à Claude Debussy" (Schott 1960) 17 min. Seven sections; uses collage techniques and fragments from earlier music, particularly *Jeux* of Debussy; fragmentation; extreme ecleticism. M-D to D.

Walter Zimmermann (1949–   ) Germany

Akkord-Arbeit 1971 (Moeck 5131). For piano, orchestra, and three loudspeakers. Directions in German. Based on *Paganini Etude* I of Franz Liszt, although the listener is hardly ever aware of it (perhaps at bar 238, "Liszt plus Paganini")! Requires some virtuosic acrobatics on the part of all performers. Avant-garde. M-D.

Friedrich Otto Zipp (1914–   ) Germany

Festliche Musik Op.11A (Möseler 1974). For piano and strings.

Kammerkonzert Op.15 (Gerig 1964). For piano, clarinet, cello, and chamber orchestra. 20 min. Allegro energico; Andante sostenuto; Allegro giocoso. Neoclassic, melodic, thin textures, octotonic. M-D.

Iurii Znatakov (–   ) USSR

Concerto Op.9 (USSR 1955) 57pp. Allegro non troppo; Andante cantabile; Allegro con brio. Tonal. M-D.

Annotated Bibliography

This section, an extension of the entries following individual composers and single compositions, concentrates on English-language books, periodicals, and, particularly, dissertations. These sources are most helpful when used in conjunction with the musical scores.

Anson, George. "The Piano Concertos of Mozart." AMT 5 (March-April 1956).
————. The Student Piano Concerto." *Instrumentalist* 13 (August 1959):83–86.
ASCAP Symphonic Catalogue, 3d ed. New York: American Society of Composers, Authors and Publishers, 1977.
Baker, Theodore. *Biographical Dictionary of Musicians*, 6th ed. Edited by Nicolas Slonimsky. New York: G. Schirmer, 1978.
Bellamann, Henry. "Of Notable Piano Concertos, Neglected and Otherwise." MQ 7 (1921):399–407.
BMI Symphonic Catalogue. New York: Broadcast Music, Inc., 1971.
Boyden, David. "When Is a Concerto Not a Concerto?" MQ 43 (1957):220–32.
Brofsky, Howard. "Notes on the Early French Concerto." JAMS 19 (Spring 1966): 37–58.
Bull, Storm. *Index to Biographies of Contemporary Composers*. Metuchen, NJ: The Scarecrow Press, 1974.
I Classici musicali italiani. 15 vols. Milan: Fondazione Eugenio Brevi, 1941–43.
Culshaw, John. *The Concerto*. London: Max Parrish, 1949.
Dawes, Frank. "Cadenzas for Mozart," MT 107, no. 4 (1966):237.
Dennison, Sam, ed. *The Edwin A. Fleisher Music Collection*. Philadelphia: Free Library of Philadelphia, 1978.
Devereux, Sister Mary Sheila. "Bibliography of the Solo Concerto Instruments of the Orchestra." Thesis, Catholic University of America, 1969.
Downes, Edward. "Concerto Pioneers," *New York Times* November 17, 1957, Section 11, p.3.
Drummond, Pippa. *The German Concerto*. New York: Oxford University Press, 1979.
Engel, Hans. *The Solo Concerto*. Translated by Robert Kolben. Cologne: Arno Volk Verlag, 1964.
Erlebach, Rupert. "Style in Pianoforte Concerto Writing." M&L 17 (April 1936):131–39.
Friskin, James and Irwin Freundlich. *Music for the Piano*. New York: Rinehart, 1954; Dover, 1973.
Ganz, Rudolph. *Rudolph Ganz Evaluates Modern Piano Music*. Evanston, IL: The Instrumentalist Co., 1968.

Garst, Marilyn. *The Early Twentieth Century Piano Concerto as Formulated by Stravinsky and Schönberg*. Ann Arbor: University Microfilms, 1973.

Garvin, Florence Hollister. *The Beginnings of the Romantic Piano Concerto*. New York: Vantage Press, 1952.

Gerschefski, Edwin. *Cadenzas from Famous Piano Concertos* (CFE) 31pp. Contains the composer's cadenzas for: J. S. Bach, Concerto d; Beethoven, Concertos C Op.15 and E♭ Op.73; Brahms, Concerto d Op.15; Chopin, Concerto e Op.11; Mendelssohn, Concerto g Op.25; W. A. Mozart, Concerto A K.488; Anton Rubinstein, Concerto d Op.70; Schumann, Concerto a Op.54; Tchaikowsky, Concerto b♭ Op.23. Tastefully edited by Gerschefski.

Glennon, James. *Making Friends with the Concerto*. Adelaide, Australia: Rigby, 1964.

Grave, Floyd K. "On Punctuation and Continuity in Mozart's Piano Concertos." PQ 95 (Fall 1976):20–25.

Grove, Sir George. *Grove's Dictionary of Music and Musicians,* 5th ed. Edited by Eric Blom. London: Macmillan, 1954; supplement 1961.

Hanson, John. "Macroform in Selected Twentieth Century Piano Concertos." Diss., University of Rochester, 1969.

Hertelendy, Paul. "Which Cadenza Does Rubinstein Play?" *High-Fidelity* 22 (May 1972):63–66.

Hess, Willy. "Die Originalkadenzen zu Beethovens Klavierkonzerten," *RM Suisse* 112 no.5 (September-October 1972):270–75. "Beethoven's cadenzas developed from free improvisation to the written-out cadenza that was an integral part of the movement. Unfortunately, knowledge of the sources is incomplete. Sketches exist for otherwise unknown cadenzas for the first 3 concertos, and additional cadenzas for the C-major concerto are known to have existed. Extant are 3 cadenzas for the C-major concerto, one each for the B-flat major and C-minor concertos, and 6 cadenzas for the concerto in G major. In addition, there are 4 cadenzas for the piano version of the violin concerto."

Hill, Ralph. *The Concerto*. London, Baltimore: Penguin Books, 1952.

Hopkins, Anthony. *Talking About Concertos*. Belmont, CA: Wadsworth Publishing Co., 1964.

Howe, Richard E. "The Cadenza in the Piano Concerto." Ph.D. diss, University of Rochester, 1956.

Hutchings, Arthur. *The Baroque Concerto*. New York: W.W. Norton, 1961.

Johnson, Thomas Arnold. "Concerning Piano Concertos." *Musical Opinion,* October 1948:6–8.

Jones, P. Ward. "The Concerto at Mannheim, c.1740–1780." *Royal Music Association Proceedings* 96 (1969–70):129–36.

Krick, Charlotte Virginia. "The Piano Concerto; an Analytical Survey of Its Principal Forms." Thesis, University of Rochester, 1941.

Lendvai, Ernö. *Béla Bartók, An Analysis of His Music*. London: Kahn and Averill, 1971.

Lewis, R. "The Piano Concerto—Romantic Vintage." *Listen* 12 (2 January 1949).

McVeagh, Diana. "The Concerto: Contest or Cooperation?" M&L 27 (April 1947):115–20.

Meyer, John Alfred. "The Piano Concerto in the Twentieth Century." Diss., University of Western Australia, 1973.

Mies, Paul. *Das Konzert im 19. Jahrhundert. Studien zu Formen und Kadenzen.* Bonn: Abhandlungen zur Kunst, Musik und Literaturwissenschaft, Bouvier, 1972. Traces the development of the concerto cadenza in the nineteenth century, including a comparison of Brahms's cadenzas with those of Beethoven. Also discusses conventions of the nineteenth-century concerto, the recitative, the orchestral accompaniment, the relationship between the movements, and the development of the "symphonic" concerto. Draws on two earlier works, *Das instrumentale Rezitative* (The Instrumental Recitative), 1968, and *Die Krise des Konzerts bei Beethoven* (The Crisis of Beethoven's Concertos), 1970.

Milligan, T. B. "Concerto Accompaniments on the Second Piano." *Clavier* 7 (January 1968):44–46.

Mishkin, Henry G. "Incomplete Notation in Mozart's Piano Concertos," MQ 61 (1975):345–59. "A consideration of the *col basso* convention for piano participation in the tutti sections and the various instances of notational shorthand in K.491."

Montgomery, Patricia. "The Latin American Piano Concerto in the Twentieth Century." DM paper, Indiana University, 1970.

Nelson, Wendell. *The Concerto.* Dubuque: W. C. Brown, 1969.

Nicolosi, Robert J. "The Tempo di Menuetto as Finale in Mozart's Early Piano Concerti." PQ 95 (Fall 1976):40–43.

Owen, Stephanie Olive. "The Piano Concerto in Canada since 1955." Diss., Washington University, 1969.

Parkinson, Del R. "Selected Works for Piano and Orchestra in One Movement, 1821–1853." DM diss., Indiana University, 1974. Discusses twelve works by Weber, Mendelssohn, Chopin, Schumann, and Liszt. These five pianist–composers established the one-movement concerto form in the early part of the nineteenth century.

Phemister, William. "The American Piano Concerto." Part One: Published Piano Concertos by Native-Born American Composers. Part Two: A Bibliography of Published and Unpublished Compositions for Piano and Orchestra by American Composers. Ph.D. diss, Peabody Conservatory, 1973.

Reif, Frances Marie. "A Compendium of Piano Concertos for the Preparatory Student." Thesis, Catholic University, 1973.

Reimers, L. "The Solo Concerto in Twentieth-Century Sweden." MR 15 (1960):20–22.

Rezits, Joseph and Gerald Deatsman. *The Pianist's Resource Guide: Piano Music in Print and Literature on the Pianistic Art.* Park Ridge, IL: Pallma Music Corp. (Neil A. Kjos), 1974; rev. ed. 1978–79.

Rogers, N. "Correspondence: Forgotten Piano Concertos (19th Century)." *Gramophone* 50 (June 1952):140.

Schonberg, Harold C. "The Concerto: Virtuoso Music." *New York Times,* November 17, 1957, Section 11, p.2.

Simon, Edwin J. "The Double Exposition in the Classic Concerto." JAMS 10 (Summer 1957): 111–18.

Slonimsky, Nicolas. *Music since Nineteen Hundred,* 4th ed., rev. and enlarged. New York; Charles Scribner's Sons, 1971.

Smith, Steven Herbert. "The Piano Concerto after Bartók: A Survey for Performers of the Piano Concerto Literature with Emphasis on the Postwar Era, 1945–1970." Diss., University of Rochester, Eastman School of Music, 1978.

Sorabji, Kaikhosru. "The Modern Piano Concerto." In *Mi Contra Fa.* London: The Porcupine Press, 1947.

Talbot, Michael. "The Concerto Allegro in the Early Eighteenth Century." M&L 52 no.1 (1971):8–18.

Tovey, Donald F. *Essays in Musical Analysis,* vol. III: *Concertos.* London: Oxford University Press, 1935–44.

Upper, Henry A., Jr. "An Historical and Analytical Study of Selected Works for Piano Obbligato with Orchestra." DM diss., Indiana University, 1971. Discusses works by Falla, Fauré, Franck, and d'Indy.

Veinus, Abraham. *The Concerto,* rev. ed. New York: Dover Publications, 1964.

Vinton, John, ed. *Dictionary of Contemporary Music.* New York: E. P. Dutton, 1974.

Wallingford, Frances. "Concertos for the Novice." *Clavier* 1 (November-December 1962): 29–31.

Wiebusch, Janice. "The Piano Concerto since 1950." Thesis, University of Nebraska, 1969.

Young, Percy M. *Concerto.* Boston: Crescendo Publishers, 1968.

Indexes

Works for Two Pianos and Orchestra

Works for Three or More Pianos and Orchestra

Works for Piano One-hand, Three-hands, or Four-hands and Orchestra

Works for Piano One-hand, Three-hands, or Four-hands and Orchestra (cont.)

Works for Piano(s) and Band

Works for Piano and Strings

Works for Piano and Strings (cont.)

Works for Piano(s),
Other Instrument(s), and Orchestra

Works for Piano(s),
Other Instrument(s), and Orchestra (cont.)

Works for Piano(s) and Chamber Orchestra(s)

Works for Piano, Orchestra, and Voice(s)

Works for Piano, Orchestra, and Tape

Works for Prepared Piano and Orchestra

Intermediate to Moderately Difficult Works